W9-BIM-456

solutions@syngress.com

With more than 1,500,000 copies of our MCSE, MCSD, CompTIA, and Cisco study guides in print, we continue to look for ways we can better serve the information needs of our readers. One way we do that is by listening.

Readers like yourself have been telling us they want an Internet-based service that would extend and enhance the value of our books. Based on reader feedback and our own strategic plan, we have created a Web site that we hope will exceed your expectations.

Solutions@syngress.com is an interactive treasure trove of useful information focusing on our book topics and related technologies. The site offers the following features:

- One-year warranty against content obsolescence due to vendor product upgrades. You can access online updates for any affected chapters.

- "Ask the Author" customer query forms that enable you to post questions to our authors and editors.

- Exclusive monthly mailings in which our experts provide answers to reader queries and clear explanations of complex material.

- Regularly updated links to sites specially selected by our editors for readers desiring additional reliable information on key topics.

Best of all, the book you're now holding is your key to this amazing site. Just go to www.syngress.com/solutions, and keep this book handy when you register to verify your purchase.

Thank you for giving us the opportunity to serve your needs. And be sure to let us know if there's anything else we can do to help you get the maximum value from your investment. We're listening.

www.syngress.com/solutions

SYNGRESS®

1 YEAR UPGRADE
BUYER PROTECTION PLAN

CONFIGURING CISCO
Voice Over IP

Second Edition

Paul J. Fong

Eric Knipp

David Gray

Scott M. Harris

Larry Keefer, Jr.

Charles Riley

Stuart Ruwet

Robert Thorstensen

Vincent Tillirson

Michael E. Flannagan Technical Reveiwer

Jason Sinclair Technical Editor

KEY	SERIAL NUMBER
001	8TPK9H7GYV
002	H8UN7W6CVF
003	439HF5TS3A
004	Z2B76Z2N9Y
005	UT5R39SC4E
006	X6BUMP7NS6
007	4EPQ2AKG6R
008	9BKG8DM5D7
009	SW4KFAUPFH
010	5BVM39ZCV6

PUBLISHED BY
Syngress Publishing, Inc.
800 Hingham Street
Rockland, MA 02370

Configuring Cisco Voice Over IP, Second Edition

Printed in the United States of America

1 2 3 4 5 6 7 8 9 0

ISBN: 1-931836-64-7

Technical Editor: Jason Sinclair
Technical Reviewer: Michael E. Flannagan
Acquisitions Editor: Catherine B. Nolan
Developmental Editor: Jonathan Babcock

Cover Designer: Michael Kavish
Page Layout and Art by: Shannon Tozier
Copy Editor: Darlene Bordwell
Indexer: Nara Wood

Distributed by Publishers Group West in the United States and Jaguar Book Group in Canada.

Acknowledgments

We would like to acknowledge the following people for their kindness and support in making this book possible.

Ralph Troupe, Rhonda St. John, Emlyn Rhodes, and the team at Callisma for their invaluable insight into the challenges of designing, deploying and supporting world-class enterprise networks.

Karen Cross, Lance Tilford, Meaghan Cunningham, Kim Wylie, Harry Kirchner, Kevin Votel, Kent Anderson, Frida Yara, Jon Mayes, John Mesjak, Peg O'Donnell, Sandra Patterson, Betty Redmond, Roy Remer, Ron Shapiro, Patricia Kelly, Andrea Tetrick, Jennifer Pascal, Doug Reil, David Dahl, Janis Carpenter, and Susan Fryer of Publishers Group West for sharing their incredible marketing experience and expertise.

Jacquie Shanahan, AnnHelen Lindeholm, David Burton, Febea Marinetti, and Rosie Moss of Elsevier Science for making certain that our vision remains worldwide in scope.

David Buckland, Wendi Wong, Marie Chieng, Lucy Chong, Leslie Lim, Audrey Gan, and Joseph Chan of Transquest Publishers for the enthusiasm with which they receive our books.

Kwon Sung June at Acorn Publishing for his support.

Jackie Gross, Gayle Voycey, Alexia Penny, Anik Robitaille, Craig Siddall, Darlene Morrow, Iolanda Miller, Jane Mackay, and Marie Skelly at Jackie Gross & Associates for all their help and enthusiasm representing our product in Canada.

Lois Fraser, Connie McMenemy, Shannon Russell, and the rest of the great folks at Jaguar Book Group for their help with distribution of Syngress books in Canada.

A special welcome to the folks at Woodslane in Australia! Thank you to David Scott and everyone there as we start selling Syngress titles through Woodslane in Australia, New Zealand, Papua New Guinea, Fiji Tonga, Solomon Islands, and the Cook Islands.

Contributors

Sam Cushway is a Senior Consultant with Callisma where he designs and implements routing and switching solutions for several of Callisma's clients. His specialties include Cisco hardware, strategic network planning, network architecture and design, and network troubleshooting and optimization. Sam has 12 years of experience in data communications and his background includes positions as a Senior Network Engineer at TCI Cable and WorldCom. Sam is a CCIE candidate with a focus on internetworking and convergence.

Paul J. Fong (CCNP, CCDP) holds a bachelor's and master's degree from Stanford University. While pursuing his studies, Paul developed speech recognition software at the Xerox Palo Alto Research Center and published his work in *IEEE Transactions on Systems, Man and Cybernetics*. His background includes positions as an Advisory Systems Analyst at IBM where he developed a network monitoring system for NASA Space Shuttle telemetry, and as a Senior Member of the Technical Staff at MCI where he played a key role in the development of the SRDF-over-IP protocol. He is also a contributor to *Configuring IPv6 for Cisco IOS* (Syngress Publishing, ISBN: 1-928994-84-9). Paul is a member of the Colorado Springs Cisco Users Group and lives in Monument, CO with his wife, Sharon, and their daughter, Shana.

David Gray (CCNA, CCDA, CCNA-WAN Switching, MCSE, ASE, Brocade Fabric Professional) is a Consultant with Callisma. David specializes in IP telephony and convergence, Active Directory design and implementation, storage area networking, service provider networks to include optical design and implementation. David's background includes positions as a Senior Project Engineer for WorldCom, an engineer for Digital Equipment Corporation/Compaq, and as an analyst for a variety of other firms.

Scott M. Harris (CCDP, CCNP, MCNE) is a Senior Consultant with Callisma with a focus on internetworking and data/voice/video integration. His background includes 14 years of network experience in small, medium, and large network infrastructures. He currently provides business consultation on the planning, design, implementation, and Day Two support of Cisco AVVID. He has worked with a variety of public and private sector businesses and government institutions on switched LAN and WAN design, implementation, support, and training.

Larry Keefer, Jr. (CCNP, CCDP, MCSE, MCP+I, MCNE, CNE-3, CNE-4, CNE-5, CNE-GW, BCFP, BCSD) is a Senior Consultant with Callisma in Atlanta, GA. He currently provides senior-level strategic and technical consulting to Callisma clients throughout the United States. His specialties include Cisco routers and LAN switches, Microsoft Windows NT/2000, Novell NDS, IP telephony, storage area network (SAN) planning, design, implementation, and support for large enterprise organizations. Larry is a contributing author for Syngress Publishing's *Cisco AVVID & IP Telephony Design and Implementation* (ISBN: 1-928994-83-0). Larry's background includes a position as a Senior Network Engineer/ Team Leader at Rush Creek Solutions (formerly BPI) for enterprise and government organizations in the Rocky Mountain region. Larry holds a bachelor's of Science degree from Illinois Status University and has completed coursework towards a master's degree in Information Systems from the University of Phoenix. Larry currently resides in Woodstock, GA with his family, Carol, Kayla, and Kristin.

Eric Knipp (CCNP, CCDP, CCNA, CCDA, CIPT, CUSE, MCSE-2000, MCSE, MCP+I) is a Consultant with Callisma. Eric specializes in IP telephony and convergence, Cisco routers, LAN switches, Active Directory design and implementation, and network design and implementation. He has passed both the CCIE Routing and Switching written exam as well as the CCIE Communications and Services Optical qualification exam. Eric is currently preparing to take the CCIE lab later this year. Eric's background includes positions as a Project Manager for a major international law firm and as a Project Manager for Nortel. Eric is also a contributing author to *Cisco AVVID & IP Telephony Design and Implementation*

(Syngress Publishing, ISBN: 1-928994-83-0), *Managing Cisco Network Security, Second Edition* (Syngress Publishing, ISBN: 1-931836-56-6), and *Configuring IPv6 for Cisco IOS* (Syngress Publishing, ISBN: 1-928994-84-9).

Estevan Macias (CCIE#5236, CCNA, CCDA, CCNP, CCDP, CIPT, CSS1, CCIE WAN Switching, MCSE, MCP+I) is a Senior Consultant with Callisma. He currently provides senior-level strategic and technical consulting to all Callisma clients in the western region of the United States. His specialties include Cisco routers and LAN switches, ATM WAN switches, security, design and implementation, strategic network planning, network architecture and design, and network troubleshooting and optimization. Estevan's background includes positions as a Senior Engineer at Timebridge Technologies, and as a Network Engineer at Convergent Communications in the professional services division. Estevan holds a master's of Science in Telecommunications from the University of Denver, and a bachelor's of Science in Computer Networking from Regis University.

Charles Riley (CCNP, CSS1, CISSP, CCSA, MCSE, CNE-3) is a Network Engineer with a long tenure in the networking and security fields. Charles is the author of the *CCNP Routing Study Guide* (Osborne McGraw Hill). He has designed and implemented robust networking solutions for several Fortune 500 companies. He started with the U.S. Army at Fort Huachuca, AZ, eventually finishing his Army stretch as the Network Manager of the Seventh Army Training Command in Grafenwoehr, Germany. As a consultant for Sprint in Kansas, Charles developed and managed solutions involving data center design, network migration, storage technologies, and numerous IP routing and transport enterprises for many different customers. Charles holds a bachelor's degree from the University of Central Florida. He is fortunate to have the love and encouragement of his wife, René, and his daughter, Tess, who make life so wonderful.

Stuart Ruwet (CCNP–WAN Switching, HPOV Certified Consultant, SNIA Level 1) is a Consultant with Callisma. Stuart is a Cisco/StrataCom WAN specialist with broad experience in the telecommunications industry. He has worked with a wide variety of networking technologies and platforms including multiple transmission protocols, and network management systems with an emphasis in ATM and IP. Prior to working with Callisma, Stuart served as a Senior Network Engineer and Manager of Network Engineering for Convergent Communications, where he was responsible for designing and building a nation-wide ATM network. Stuart holds a bachelor's degree in International Business from the University of Denver. He currently lives in Castle Rock, CO with his wife, Meghan, and daughter, Kyla.

Robert Thorstensen (CCNA, CCNA–WAN, CCDA, CCNP, CCDP, CCIP, CSS1, CIPT, BCFP) is a Consultant with Callisma in Denver, CO and has five years experience in the networking industry. Robert has extensive experience with a wide variety of internetworking and optical technologies, protocols, and hardware platforms, with an emphasis on IP telephony, routing, switching, security, and optical networking. Robert's background includes positions as a second tier NOC Engineer at Rhythms NetConnections, and as a Network Engineer at Internet Communications Corporation. Robert would like to thank his wife, Lisa, and his three daughters, Brittany, Alyssa, and Aimee, for their patience and understanding on the numerous nights and weekends they would rather have been outside at the park instead of "tip-toeing" around the house.

Vincent Brian Tillirson is a Consultant with Callisma. Vincent is currently providing technical consulting to a large enterprise banking company in Atlanta, GA. His specialties are in WAN/LAN design, implementation and voice deployments. Vincent has participated in the design and implementation of voice and data networks across the United States, Europe and South America. Vincent holds a bachelor's of Science degree in Computer Science from North Georgia College and University.

Technical Editor

Jason Sinclair (CCIE #9100, CCNP, CCNA) is the Manager of the Network Control Center at PowerTel Ltd., which is Australia's third largest telecommunications carrier. Jason is responsible for all operational aspects of the PowerTel voice, data and IP networks. Jason's technical background is predominantly in large scale IP, Internet, VoIP and DLSW networking. He has also designed and deployed several large-scale networks that have made extensive use of BGP and MPLS technology. Previously Jason has worked for a number of ISP's and carriers in the Asia Pacific Region. Jason specializes in IP and IPX routing protocols, with particular focus on BGP, OSPF and ISIS. He is also an expert in IBM networking, ATM, Frame Relay, ISDN, Token Ring, and Ethernet. Jason has published an article for *Certification Zone*, which is a CCIE level discussion of the theory and configuration of EIGRP. He is also working on articles covering networking case studies, large-scale carrier networks and IBM Networking. Jason lives in Sydney, Australia with his wife, Michelle, and son, Andy.

Technical Reviewer

Michael E. Flannagan (CCIE #7651, CCDP, CSA, NNCAS) is a Network Consulting Engineer and Team Lead in the Advanced Services Group at Cisco Systems. Mike's experience includes extensive work with IP routing protocols and Quality of Service. Prior to joining Cisco Systems, he held positions as a Global Network Manager for an international corporation, and as a consultant specializing in Quality of Service. Other books from Syngress Publishing to which Mike has contributed include *Administering Cisco QoS in IP Networks* (ISBN: 1-928994-21-0), and *Cisco AVVID & IP Telephony Design and Implementation* (ISBN: 1-928994-83-0).

Contents

Chapter 2 Traditional Voice Telephony Principles

Chapter 9 Intra- and Interoffice VoIP Scenarios

Foreword

Internet Protocol (IP) telephony has progressed beyond a technological interest to a stable and cost-effective mechanism to transit and receive voice communications. Ease in performing moves, adds, and changes (MACs), infrastructure consolidation of otherwise redundant data and voice networks, reduced international long distance charges, and staff efficiencies are all valid economic reasons to adopt IP telephony. Perhaps more important, however, are the many ways that IP telephony can increase end-user productivity. The IP phone is a potent multimedia-computing platform supporting instantly available Extensible Markup Language (XML) capabilities as well as a traditional acoustical telephone interface. In particular, IP telephony is well positioned to truly converge voice and data, with the prominent example being unified messaging.

IP telephony now approximates traditional telephony in terms of voice quality and reliability, but the inherent complexities of melding voice and data disciplines into a convergenced infrastructure require attention to detail. A thorough understanding of traditional and IP telephony transport and signaling protocols as well as the ability to tune packet networks for simultaneous multiplexing of voice and data are required to successfully implement IP telephony. Configuring, testing, and troubleshooting are also critical project requirements. Most important, however, is experience in implementing IP telephony, with which the various case studies can help you.

About This Book

In addition to providing a general understanding of voice over IP (VoIP) networking, this book offers detailed and practical information on how to use Cisco's suite of VoIP products. Callisma's contributing authors are industry experts with real-world implementation experience who can help you understand the intricacies of packet voice. In reading this book, you will obtain a firm understanding of the complexities of converging your voice and data networks.

—*Ralph Troupe,*
President and CEO, Callisma

Introduction

Configuring Cisco Voice Over IP, Second Edition, follows some two years after the successful release of its predecessor. On its release, the first edition was at the very leading edge of voice over IP (VoIP) technology and was one of the first texts to be published on this subject. In the short time since the first edition, many aspects of this exciting and expanding technology have changed, and many new protocols and techniques have emerged. This second edition has been fully expanded to include information relating to all these new technologies, with coverage of topics such as Session Initiation Protocol (SIP) and Media Gateway Control Protocol (MGCP). Whether you are a relative newcomer to VoIP networking or currently maintain large-scale VoIP networks, this book will prove to be an invaluable addition to your current VoIP information library.

Since the time that the first edition of this book was released, VoIP support has increased exponentially and is now more widely deployed in many enterprises around the world. This second edition is intended to serve as a guide to VoIP technology, protocols, and theory. This book is not only a theoretical text, however; it also covers all areas of configuring VoIP with Cisco devices and addresses some of the nontechnical issues relating to VoIP. These include tasks such as preparing business justifications for deploying VoIP networks and preparing a return on investment (ROI) calculation to support your justification. The ability to perform an ROI calculation is a necessary skill in cost justifying a VoIP network.

In the early chapters of this book, we look at traditional or legacy voice networks and then analyze in detail the protocols and components that are used in these traditional models. Understanding traditional voice technology is an important and very pertinent aspect to cover, but it is most often overlooked in VoIP texts. Without a solid understanding of the basics of traditional voice networking, it is arguably almost impossible to understand VoIP. Even if VoIP is understood without this base-level knowledge of traditional voice networking, it is quite likely that certain fundamental aspects of your VoIP deployment will be less than optimal. Many VoIP networks are required to interconnect in some manner with a traditional voice network, such as to the public switched telephone network. An understanding of traditional voice-networking technology is also invaluable because the historic aspects of voice networking provide an insight into why certain VoIP protocols are designed and operate the way they do. After all, there would be no VoIP without traditional voice!

After presenting this solid foundation of traditional voice-networking theory, the book introduces an in-depth discussion of VoIP theory. Particular attention is paid to the various protocols that are the cornerstones of any VoIP implementation. The VoIP protocol suites are one of the most complicated aspects of truly understanding VoIP networking. Many network administrators admit that they have only a very basic knowledge of the ways the varying VoIP protocols operate, and often their understanding of such protocols is flawed in some manner. This book intends to dispel some of the myths and mysteries behind VoIP protocols and provide the theory and concepts that underlie these protocols in a clear and concise manner. Naturally, once you develop a sound understanding of VoIP principles, the logical next question is, "What equipment will I require to deploy a VoIP network?" This question is answered in depth in Chapter 4.

Cisco has been developing network equipment specifically for VoIP networks for several years, and it will surprise many readers to learn that several of Cisco's smaller router offerings have been extended to support VoIP networks. Many believe that VoIP requires specialized, expensive hardware and software; this is definitely not the case, and Chapter 4 contains information relating to this misapprehension as well as a detailed overview of current Cisco VoIP-capable devices. We then continue by looking at how these various pieces of hardware can all be configured using the Cisco IOS and the ways that each required configuration is the same, regardless of the hardware platform deployed. Whether you are configuring an analog telephone to connect to a 1700 series router or a 3600 series router, the required configuration commands are the same. This consistent approach to configuring Cisco devices is definitely one of the strengths of using Cisco devices to deploy VoIP.

Traditionally, voice network proponents tended to (and sometimes still do) view VoIP technology with some disdain and skepticism; in fact, many believed that VoIP would not be embraced at all. This attitude was mainly due to the fact that early development and deployment of VoIP technology resulted in voice calls that were of very poor quality and highly unreliable at the best of times. Several factors and developments have arisen that have altered this situation. These factors range from the fact that the fundamental VoIP protocols, such as H.323, have improved markedly, to another important factor that has lead to the improved quality of VoIP networks: quality of service (QoS) mechanisms that are now available. These mechanisms are numerous and are all supported on Cisco devices.

QoS is an often misunderstood and complicated subject; several books have been written on this subject alone. QoS is so crucial to VoIP networks that many networks that have been deployed without any QoS configuration have subsequently been removed and reverted to traditional voice network technology. This book not only offers a review of the available QoS techniques, it also provides actual configurations of ways to implement several techniques to maintain and improve voice quality.

In Chapter 6 we investigate what happens when a voice network fails. Traditionally, VoIP itself was blamed for failed calls in early deployments. VoIP, however, was not generally the cause of poor or failed calls. Underlying network failures tended to be one of the greatest issues regarding VoIP networks. We review some common troubleshooting techniques and then look at a specific technique for troubleshooting network topologies, with particular emphasis on how to troubleshoot VoIP issues.

The final two chapters in this book culminate in introducing you to common VoIP case studies. The information in these chapters will provide the answers and configurations to most, if not all, your VoIP requirements. These case studies cover a wide range of VoIP network configuration tasks, ranging from installing a simple analog handset in a router and replacing legacy tie-line connections between PBXs to designing and deploying complex dial plans and wide-scale VoIP solutions. These case studies provide situations in which most of the common VoIP commands are discussed and applied.

When you have completed reading this book, you will have a solid foundation of knowledge regarding VoIP networking, with particular emphasis on using Cisco devices. You will understand the protocols that are the essence of VoIP, and you will have as a reference some less commonly documented information regarding financial considerations and how to justify new VoIP deployments. This book provides, in a single reference, all the information you will require to understand, design, deploy, and maintain VoIP networks. This book will become an often-used tool in your collection of network resources.

—*Jason Sinclair, CCIE #9100*

Chapter 1

Introduction to Voice Over IP and Business Justifications

Solutions in this chapter:

- Introduction to Voice Over IP
- Common VoIP Implementation Scenarios
- Basic Toll-Bypass Designs
- Advanced Features and Integration Possibilities

- ☑ Summary
- ☑ Solutions Fast Track
- ☑ Frequently Asked Questions

Introduction

One of the main driving factors for deploying Voice over IP (VoIP) networks is the cost benefit associated with doing so. This chapter introduces the reader to this concept and the Cisco IP Telephony solution. The chapter presents examples of cost justification and some return on investment (ROI) scenarios.

In this chapter you will also be introduced to some exciting advanced VoIP features such as Web integration, multimedia integration, and telephony application programming interfaces (TAPI).

Introduction to Voice Over IP

Welcome to the new world of packetized voice! Although the idea of packetized voice might not be new, we now have the integrated solutions to make it happen. This text provides you with a thorough understanding of Cisco's current voice solutions, with an emphasis on *current*! The VoIP industry is a rapidly evolving one, perhaps changing even faster than the Internet. Keep this guide as a reference for voice integration possibilities, but always keep abreast of the latest technologies. What is hot today will be commonplace tomorrow.

The objectives for this chapter are to:

- Establish the basic differences between circuit-switched and packet-switched networks.

- Build a needs and cost justification for toll-bypass solutions.

- Explore the opportunities for replacing the traditional private branch exchange (PBX) with the Cisco IP Telephony system.

- Review software integration possibilities such as TAPI integration.

- Understand the link layer VoIP technologies such as voice over Frame Relay (VoFR) and voice over asynchronous transfer mode (VoATM).

Scattered throughout this chapter are several diagrams of network design concepts. Later in this book we delve into much greater detail regarding specific equipment and configuration issues. This first chapter focuses on the opportunities that arise from moving to a packetized voice architecture. Along with management and maintenance enhancements, we look at the all-important dollar.

Most companies have spent exorbitant amounts of money to install and maintain their PBXs. Packetizing voice allows for tremendous cost savings now and in the future. As more standards are ratified, the cost of setting up a VoIP network continues to drop. This is quite a different model from the traditional PBX cost trends of the last few decades. This chapter explores how to go about building an ROI proposal that in most cases will justify a conversion to packetized voice. We specifically discuss Cisco's VoIP solution, known as *Cisco IP Telephony (CIPT)*. We explore link layer VoIP technologies such as VoFR and VoATM. These are just the tip of the iceberg. As VoIP becomes more widespread and ubiquitous, we will begin to see applications that we can't even imagine yet. Moving voice from a closed proprietary system to an open standards-based architecture will revolutionize the phone industry and the world as much as the Internet has in terms of communication and the way business is transacted.

General Overview of Voice Technologies

There is a difference between implementing something piecemeal and actually installing a complete, integrated solution. The difference is in the functionality, the support required, and the life-cycle costs. The marketplace contains many VoIP offerings. Each caters to different needs, including toll bypass, IP transport of voice, public switched telephone network (PSTN) backup, click-to-dial technology, and yellow pages phone number lookup. Implemented separately, these various technologies conform to different standards, each requiring its own special brand of support.

We start by looking at the traditional PSTN and common VoIP implementations. Then we examine IP telephony solutions that offer integrated functionality, standardized support policies, lower life-cycle costs, and software expandability.

Today's VoIP Possibilities

Imagine a sunny day somewhere in corporate America. In the break room, you pour yourself a cup of coffee and stroll back into your office. While you sit there sipping your coffee, you see that the Messages icon on your Internet terminal is blinking, so you reach over and tap it. Up pops a list of all of your e-mails, voice-mails, and daily news information.

You see at the top of the list a voice-mail from your mom, who happens to live on the other side of the world. It looks as though the message came in around 1:00 A.M. your time. You tap on her message and hear her carry on for several minutes about the weather as you silently curse the day "long distance" calls became a thing of the past. But that's okay, because you want to talk to her about visiting anyway. So you tap **Reply** and you immediately hear a ringing tone from your terminal. Mom picks up on the other end and gives you a hard time about interrupting dinner. You talk to her while her dinner gets cold. You're not concerned, though, because there's no extra charge on your network bill, no matter how long you talk. Mom keeps talking but now all your business calls are being forwarded to you instead of going into your voice-mail. You hear a chime and see that your boss is calling, so you need to answer him. You tell mom to hang on a second and pick up your boss's call. He just wanted to remind you of the 9:00 A.M. meeting. While your Mom is on hold, she hears soothing music. You wrap up with mom. At 9:00 A.M., you host an ad hoc conference call by looking up the participants on your PC and calling them using a simple operation with your mouse. For the rest of the day, as you move about, your mobile phone and your PC phone trade roles as you deflect your calls from one to the other.

This is just the tip of the iceberg when it comes to the possibilities that VoIP presents, combined with other transport and service options. As wireless technology becomes cheaper, these ideas are becoming mainstream. By studying VoIP now and understanding the concepts, you place yourself in an ideal position to benefit from the next huge shift of the information age. VoIP might not appear as exciting as the Internet is to the public, but it will be the driving force behind more technology jobs than even the Internet has provided. This might seem like a bold statement, but think about how many people are on the Internet compared to how many people have phones. Virtually everyone has a phone!

The PBX Reality

Hopefully you're excited about these new possibilities, but let's take a step back and look at what makes this better than the current voice network and why it is easy to implement these new ideas. We start by looking at how the current circuit-switched voice network operates.

When you place a call, the circuit-switched network essentially dedicates a 64Kbps circuit for the duration of your call. This means that if you are calling from New York to Los Angeles, a dedicated circuit is set up from one end of the line to the other (see Figure 1.1). When you talk, 64Kbps of bandwidth is utilized, and when you are silent, you still consume 64Kbps. No matter what you do, you are tying up 64Kbps as long as you're on the line. If a switch goes down or someone cuts a fiber, your call ends.

The phone companies have gone a long way toward providing services such as call waiting, callback, and voicemail systems. But if you ask how to integrate those services into your home or business network, you can't. Those services are stuck on the phone companies' switches.

Figure 1.1 A Simple Circuit-Switched Call

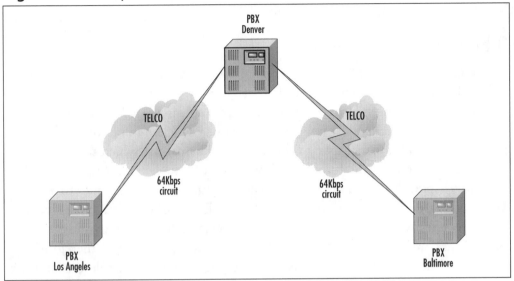

Here's where VoIP comes in. VoIP provides open standards. If you wanted to, you could write your own application for handling voice calls in a particular way. This would not be possible on your home phone or on a PBX at work. The traditional phone systems are closed systems that do not allow easy programming of third-party applications.

Open standards reduce costs. Ask any CFO what his or her company spends on its PBX and be prepared to hear groaning. PBXs are the gifts that keep taking with high-maintenance fees, lack of interoperability, expensive adds and moves, and closed application programming interfaces (APIs). Do you have a great idea for an application that you would like to see in a call center? With VoIP, it is easier and cheaper. You have access to documentation on open standards, so you can write code safely. On a PBX, you're looking at steep fees for becoming an application partner as well as having to code to their proprietary APIs. (In other words, there's no portability for your application—you're stuck with that PBX.) Do you want to move the accounting department to a new floor? How about a new building? A new city? With VoIP, you simply move the phones and watch as they join the network and register with the call management server. All the voice-mail services as well as phone templates stay in a central location, resulting in moves requiring zero effort. The same activities with a PBX would result in a substantial amount of time removing users and then adding users to the new location. Voice-mail service would also have to be migrated. Once again, with VoIP, moves are completely transparent.

The VoIP Bandwagon

You're probably thinking, "This is incredible! Where do I buy this?" The CIPT solution makes it possible to replace your PBX right now. In fact, Cisco has switched almost all of its locations to multiservice networks utilizing CIPT components, such as Cisco Call Manager and IP phones. Right now, a sizable number of CIPT components are installed in a corporate environment. The pace at which that this technology is moving rivals the Internet industry! You can implement it right now.

This chapter discusses how toll bypass initially motivated companies to adopt VoIP. Later in this chapter we look at the basic toll-bypass setup and discuss how it can be an effective introduction to VoIP and how attractive it is from an ROI standpoint. Unfortunately, toll bypass solutions are not globally legal; therefore readers outside of the U.S. should verify the legality of toll bypass solutions in their country. Ultimately, though, toll bypass is a foot in the door. The real excitement is in replacing the PBX. We will see how CIPT can enable this replacement and how the Cisco Unity unified messaging system can enhance a voice-mail system.

Common VoIP Implementation Services

Today's PSTN is based on the transmission of analog signals over switched circuits. In contrast, VoIP networks send digitized voice over a packet-based network. As we shall see, VoIP networks can offer telephony services at compelling prices.

Toll Bypass

Relative to the Internet, the PSTN offers voice services with expensive charges, or *tolls*. *Toll bypass* is the avoidance of PSTN charges by using data networks, such as the Internet, to carry voice conversations. Figure 1.2 shows a simple example of toll bypass using gateways that are capable of providing an interface between an IP network and a traditional PBX.

VoFR

Voice over frame relay (VoFR) is the use of a Frame Relay network to carry IP packets containing digitized voice packets. IP phones and voice-capable switches or routers may be hooked up to this Frame Relay network to digitize voice signals and place them into IP packets. The IP packets are carried to their destinations via the Frame Relay network.

Figure 1.2 Toll Bypass with Gateway Routers

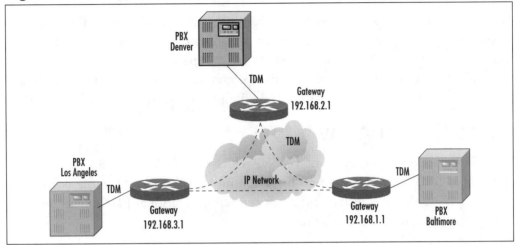

Building a private IP network to carry voice and data might not be financially feasible for many companies. A company can choose to lease Frame Relay services instead of building its own private network. A service provider offering this service will provide leased lines to a company's office locations. The lines are linked to Frame Relay switches to provide relatively inexpensive network services.

VoATM

Voice over asynchronous transfer mode (VoATM) is the use of an ATM network to carry digitized voice packets. Instead of carrying variable-length frames, an ATM network carries small fixed-length frames called *cells*. Each cell is 53 bytes long and contains a 5-byte header and a 48-byte payload. In an ATM network, the VoIP packet is segmented and placed inside these cells. The small fixed ATM cell size offers many advantages. Its small size means that the latency or delay as the cell passes through an ATM switch is very short. In contrast, the store-and-forward delay of an IP packet through a router is much longer because the last bit of the packet must be received before the first bit can be transmitted.

ATM switches are extremely fast, and the quality of service offered by ATM networks can be very high. In addition, ATM offers various class of service (CoS) options such as constant bit rate (CBR) that was designed specifically for transporting voice and other real-time protocols. CBR provides a better quality of service by minimizing time variations in the transmission of voice cells, a phenomenon known as *jitter*.

Point-to-Point Links

The use of point-to-point links to interconnect a company's offices allows a company to build and administer its own private network. Using VoIP over point-to-point links allows a common IP staff to operate both voice and data transmission services. Common link layer protocols used on point-to-point links are High-Level Data Link Control (HDLC) and Point-to-Point Protocol (PPP).

Cisco IP Telephony

The VoIP portion of the evolving Cisco Architecture for Voice, Video, and Integrated Data (AVVID) is Cisco IP Telephony, or CIPT. CIPT is the cornerstone of Cisco's VoIP solution and is fast replacing traditional PBXs. Let's discuss CIPT's major components (Figure 1.3).

Figure 1.3 Cisco IP Telephony

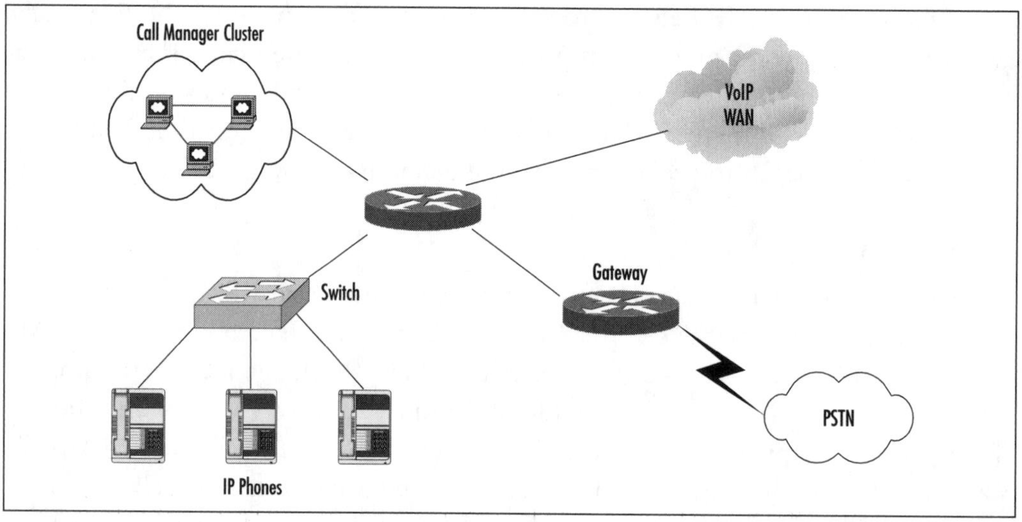

Cisco IP Telephony Clients

Telephones capable of digitizing voice signals are known as *IP telephony clients* or simply *IP phones*. They contain digital signal processors (DSPs) to perform this function. Cisco offers a variety of such IP telephony clients. In particular, the Cisco IP Phone 7960 and IP Phone 7940 are feature-rich and include small liquid crystal display (LCD) displays, control buttons, and multiline capabilities. The Cisco IP Conference Station 7935 is an IP conference phone.

IP Softphones

The Cisco IP SoftPhone is a virtual telephone that runs in a Windows desktop PC or laptop. *IP softphones* are personal computers that contain software to allow them to operate as IP telephony clients. The PCs contain speakers and microphones that can operate similarly to a telephone handset. In addition, the IP telephony software digitizes the voice signals and sends the voice packets across the IP network. Softphones provide a rich environment for development of TAPI applications, such as Web click-to-talk.

Cisco Call Manager

The Cisco Call Manager (CCM) is a software call-processing application that runs on a Cisco Media Convergence Server (MCS). The CCM takes the place of a PBX and performs several key functions:

- Registering IP telephony devices
- Call processing
- Administering dial plans and route plans
- Managing resources

A group or pair of redundant call managers can support up to 2500 users. A cluster of redundant call manager groups can support up to 10,000 telephony users.

In the Cisco IP telephony schema, call managers perform the functions traditionally performed by PBXs. As we shall see, being software-based, the CCM can be continually enhanced to provide features beyond those traditionally provided by PBXs.

Gateways

Cisco offers *gateways* to provide an interface between the IP telephony network and the PSTN. Gateways are needed to allow calls between the VoIP locations and off-net or PSTN locations. Calls made from your office IP phone to a traditional analog phone and vice versa pass through a gateway.

Gateways also provide redundancy. When the VoIP network is congested or when the wide area network (WAN) carrying VoIP traffic is down, the gateway diverts your outgoing call from the WAN to the PSTN. Gateways at each VoIP office location allow the offices to communicate with each other through the PSTN when the WAN is down or congested. The caller's gateway converts the digital voice packets into a traditional time-division multiplexed (TDM) voice stream and transmits the call through the PSTN. The destination gateway converts the incoming TDM voice stream into digital packets for processing by the destination IP phone.

Switches

Cisco offers switches that provide a high-performance support environment for IP phones. Switches have many advantages over traditional Ethernet hubs. First, the switches allow Fast Ethernet transmission speeds. Second, transmissions from one IP phone are not broadcast to other IP phones on the same switch. This eliminates frame collisions between IP phones. Third, many of Cisco's switches can supply inline power to the IP phones via the Ethernet cable. This eliminates the need to provide separate power to the IP phones.

Corporate Multimedia

Corporations today are demanding multimedia applications to deliver faxing and videoconferencing to the desktop. Let's discuss how that is possible.

Fax

Faxing can experience the benefits of packet telephony in a number of different ways, such as integration with e-mail. The Cisco Unity unified messaging system can provide a conduit for an incoming fax to be placed into an e-mailbox, enabling the fax to be transported anywhere e-mail travels as a Tagged Image File Format (TIFF) file. With this type of technology, there is no need to be at the fax machine in order to receive a fax. Typical paper faxes also degrade in quality after getting faxed multiple times. Once a fax is in e-mail, it can be forwarded to as many people as you like as many times as is necessary, with no degradation.

The other faxing benefit is from store-and-forward faxing capabilities. This feature can be enabled on the Cisco AS5300. It allows incoming faxes to be converted to e-mail and sent to a Simple Mail Transfer Protocol (SMTP) server for redistribution. It can also work in the opposite direction. An e-mail can be sent directly to the AS5300 with a TIFF file attachment. This feature conforms to the RFC 2305 standard established by the Internet Engineering Task Force (IETF). In a simple configuration, this can be used for sending faxes to a remote site over a private network.

Video

Video and audio conferencing applications allow users to communicate in pairs or in groups across the Internet or an intranet. Both Microsoft and Cisco offer corporate video applications.

Microsoft NetMeeting, widely used for conferencing, includes built-in audio, video, whiteboard, chat, file transfer, program-sharing, and collaboration functions. NetMeeting runs on Windows-based personal computers. Its transmissions are based on Transmission Control Protocol/Internet Protocol (TCP/IP) that makes it compatible with VoIP network infrastructures because it uses the same underlying protocol. In collaboration with Cisco, the NetMeeting application suite operates over Cisco's networking architecture.

Cisco IP/TV and IP/Videoconferencing (IP/VC) are components of the Cisco Advanced Voice, Video, and Integrated Data (AVVID) suite. The Cisco IP/TV product family streams high-quality video programs to PC users over IP networks. The Cisco IP/VC product family provides an IP-based network videoconferencing solution.

The Emerging Carrier and Intercarrier VoIP

Carrier and intercarrier VoIP solutions are now emerging as the latest application for VoIP. Two important implementations of VoIP in the carrier space are wholesale dial and IP transport.

Wholesale Termination

Many service providers are offering wholesale termination services to interconnect PBXs. The service provider IP network provides the transport for IP voice packets between PBX locations. Wholesale dial is ideal for companies that want to retain their existing PBX infrastructures. Figure 1.4 shows a wholesale termination network comprising two types of PBXs. A traditional PBX is mated with a gateway capable of interfacing with the PBX. Note that the IP-enabled PBX, or IPBX, in Baltimore can interface directly with the IP network, without a gateway.

IP Transport

Does VoIP offer anything to service providers? You bet it does! Unless forbidden by foreign governments or by point of interconnection (POI) agreements between carriers, IP transport of voice packets is generally permitted. The legal obstacles faced by VoIP are in foreign countries where government-sanctioned monopolies control the telephony network. These monopolies see toll bypass solutions associated with VoIP as a way of undercutting their toll charges.

Figure 1.4 Wholesale Termination

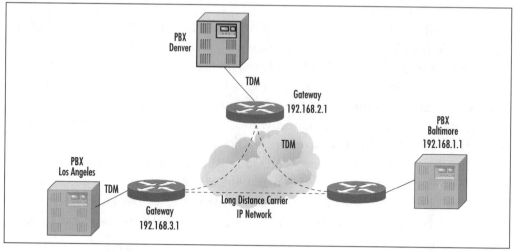

Many service providers and interexchange carriers (IXCs) are replacing their TDM circuit infrastructures with IP circuits (Figure 1.5). TDM allows a circuit to be "time sliced" to support different conversations. The switches and equipment to support TDM circuits are complex and expensive. In contrast, IP packet-switching equipment is not dependent on TDM and is relatively cheap and simple.

Figure 1.5 IP Transport

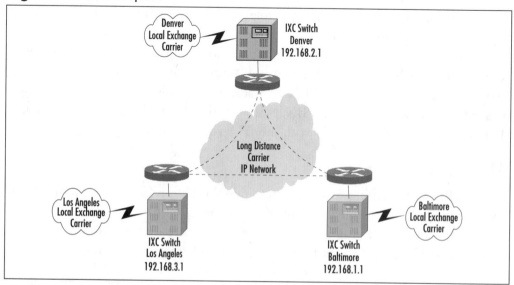

Service providers are replacing their traditional telephony switches with switches capable of digitizing voice into VoIP packets. Instead of supporting these IP-capable switches with a multitude of traditional TDM circuits, a few fast optical fiber circuits are used. This technology significantly reduces the number of circuits per switch and the related costs.

Basic Toll-Bypass Designs

One of the most attractive ways to get into a packetized voice solution is by lowering long distance phone costs. Let's explore the various methods of doing this.

Tie-Line Replacement

Many multisite businesses have a PBX at each office. Quite often, these PBXs are connected in order to allow people in both locations to use intercom dialing. These *tie lines* require dedicated connections that must always be available. Even though there might be no one speaking, the lines are still unavailable for any other use. This situation presents an opportunity for packetizing voice, because VoIP and data applications can share the same IP network at the same time.

Where the Money Is

Until now companies have had two choices for linking voice calls among offices. The first option was to simply call long distance. Discounted calling plans from the long distance carriers can reduce this cost. Regardless, it can still be a high expense if there is any substantial amount of traffic between offices. Not only does the business incur an expense for every long distance call, but the business also is charged for every call that goes to the PSTN. Unlike home phone users, in most large cities, businesses must pay for every call they make. Obviously, these charges can add up quickly if the call volume increases. Later in this section we look at some sample ROI cases.

The other option was to set up a dedicated connection among PBX sites. This is typically done with a tie line. A tie line is used for signaling among PBXs as well as transferring calls between them. Many companies already use this method. Tie lines are a fairly simple method for avoiding the per-call charges you run into when using the PSTN or long distance carriers. These lines allow you to make as many calls as you like, provided the capacity is available on the tie line, without incurring any added expenses. Tie lines are typically implemented over T1s. If the T1 is local, the cost is probably fairly reasonable. If the T1 has to go through a long distance carrier or IXC, the costs can be quite high. In addition, every two offices that you want to have connected must have a tie line running between them. There might be ways around this requirement if you have PBXs that are capable of handling advanced dialing plans. In Figure 1.6 you can see that calls between Baltimore and Los Angeles could pass through Denver, but you would be tying up two circuits for every coast-to-coast call. The alternative is to run a dedicated tie line between Baltimore and Los Angeles.

Figure 1.6 Tie-Lines Between Multiple Offices

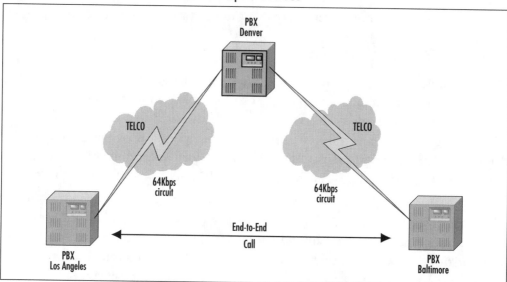

The Merging of Voice and Data Networks

Today many companies deploy separate networks for voice and data. Imagine merging these separate networks into one single network infrastructure that can carry both voice and data.

What About Data?

At some point you might hear the phrase "Voice rides for free." Well, nothing rides for free, but it sure can ride cheap. When someone says this, they are referring to the fact that many companies already have data lines running in parallel to the voice lines. As shown in Figure 1.7, this national network also has T1s supporting data running between them. Now we are paying for *two* very expensive networks.

Figure 1.7 National Network with Separate Voice and Data Networks Running Between All Offices

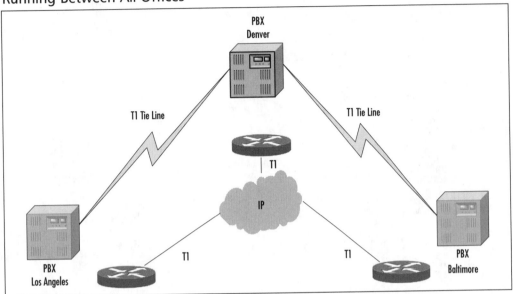

The data network can support many functions such as e-mail, Internet, and file sharing. With proper monitoring, any network administrator should know what the load is on these data circuits. Depending on the applications, there is a good chance that there is room to spare. This isn't always the case, so good monitoring and tracking tools will help make the case for packetized voice.

Convergence

Imagine the cost savings from turning off the tie lines. Even if data circuits need to be increased, the incremental cost of the bandwidth increase is going to be less than installing an entirely separate circuit. This would also allow calls to be made directly from Baltimore to Los Angeles through Denver (Figure 1.8). After all, at this point we are only dealing with data. Let's look at some of the different ways we can do this.

Figure 1.8 A Converged Network

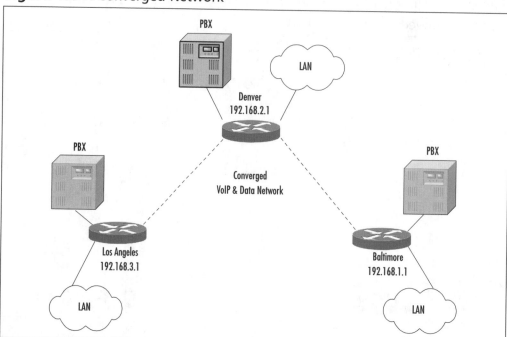

Configuring & Implementing…

H.323

H.323 is a standard that defines how voice and video devices can communicate. It specifies both signaling characteristics and host-to-host communication protocols. H.323 has rapidly become the protocol of choice for call setup on voice communications. Several Cisco products implement H.323 gateways for connecting to the PSTN as well as other features, such as their IP phones. Microsoft's NetMeeting is an H.323-compliant program that uses not only voice but video as well.

The PSTN as a Backup

To provide redundancy in VoIP networks, companies often use the PSTN as a backup. Gateways can provide this redundancy. When the VoIP network senses that the WAN carrying VoIP traffic is down, the gateway converts the digital voice packets into a traditional analog voice stream and transmits the call through the PSTN. The gateway also converts the incoming voice stream into digital packets for processing by the local VoIP devices.

Using Frame Relay for Toll Bypass

VoIP packets can be transmitted over a link using several link layer technologies, such as Frame Relay, ATM, or point-to-point circuits. VoFR has been around for several years, so the standards are more mature and the interoperability is a little more stable. For simple toll-bypass networks, VoFR can be a very attractive alternative. VoFR allows voice to be compressed and transferred across a Frame Relay permanent virtual circuit (PVC). Take a look at our example network in Figure 1.8. For the traffic between Baltimore and Denver, we have a 768Kbps committed information rate (CIR) Frame Relay circuit.

At each site, you have a data network as well as a PBX that already has a digital T1 port for implementing the tie line. In our example, we might use a Cisco 2600 or 3600 series gateway router at each location. All these routers support VoFR and can interoperate with each other. A gateway router has the capability of interfacing directly with the PBX via the digital T1 card that is available for it.

The gateway router can also connect directly to the frame circuit through either the multiflex trunk (MFT) or through a digital service unit (DSU) attached to its serial interface. At this point, a number of options are available. With our example network, you will most likely forward calls to the far-side PBX. In this situation, you will have the PBXs manage call routing while the routers compress and transfer the calls. Using the compression algorithm G.729a, you can squeeze voice calls down to about 8Kbps. With overhead, they end up taking up about 10.8Kbps. Although this is not a lot of bandwidth, it can add up if you have multiple calls active at the same time. Furthermore, with the 768Kbps circuit and G.729a encoding, you could theoretically support 70 concurrent calls. There are a few problems with that number. First, the 2600 or 3600 series router can support encoding on a maximum of 24 calls at any one time. This is because each compressed call utilizes half a DSP. In addition, if you are connecting the router to a PBX, it is likely that the connection will be with a digital T1, thereby limiting you to 24 channels. The realistic number of calls that could potentially be supported is 24. This is just as well, because the typical deployment requires saving some bandwidth for data.

Most typical installations require that data run over the same PVC as voice traffic. If the maximum number of voice calls is reached, they will take up 24 times 10.8Kbps, or approximately 260Kbps. On our example network, we have a

PVC that supports a CIR of 768Kbps. Frame relay works on the principle of having a CIR that is guaranteed and a port speed that you can burst to. Frame relay providers differ when it comes to the relationship between the CIR and port speed. The important thing to remember is that any frames that stray into the burst area are tagged and could be dropped. That leaves 508Kbps of bandwidth before we exceed the committed rate. What happens if the data traffic starts pushing the bandwidth into the burst area? The voice traffic will mix in with the data traffic, and it could be tagged for discard. Imagine how a conversation might sound if every other second was dropped. Quality of Service (QoS) issues are critically important when it comes to packetizing voice. In Chapter 6 we cover all the options for configuring QoS for voice networks. If configuration of QoS is not done correctly, you could end up with a very expensive project as everyone starts calling long distance just to have a coherent conversation.

Frame relay, at least in the eastern part of the United States, is becoming a very commonplace circuit. This makes it a good candidate for replacing traditional voice circuits.

Where to Use VoFR

Earlier in this chapter we looked at the advantages of implementing a toll bypass solution. VoFR is probably the least expensive way to implement this simple task. Frame relay networks are growing at an increasing rate, and Frame Relay is the circuit of choice for many interoffice connections. As was shown earlier, the cost of long distance frame circuits continues to drop, and unlike VoIP, standards for VoFR have been in place for several years. As always, open standards allow for vendor interoperability and, usually, a better-tested product. Chapter 8 discusses this option in detail and provides configuration information on how to achieve it.

The Growth Curve of Frame Relay

Frame relay has been growing at an incredible rate. If we look at the benefits, it is easy to see why:

- Costs related to frame relay are relatively low compared with the cost of other types of circuits.

- Once a port is purchased, adding PVCs, or the virtual connection between two Frame Relay ports, is simple and usually inexpensive.

- Frame relay can be oversubscribed. This allows more bandwidth to be mapped to a port than the port would theoretically allow. The principle is that the remote sites would not all be sending at the same time. Although this is a great feature for data traffic, it can have a severe impact on voice traffic.

- It is available just about everywhere.
- It can support a wide range of bandwidth.

There is no question that frame relay is the circuit of choice for WANs, at least for the foreseeable future. This makes it an excellent transport for voice applications.

When Does Frame Relay Make More Sense?

The single most useful aspect of VoFR lies in taking advantage of existing or low-cost circuits to provide tie-line functionality between PBXs. Where it excels is in minimizing bandwidth usage on the WAN connections. The header for frame relay takes up only a little more bandwidth. A call that has been compressed using G.729a uses about 8Kbps. Frame relay's overhead bumps that to about 10.8Kbps.

With a typical tie-line replacement, this level of compression and bandwidth savings provide much more room for data to travel over the same circuit (Figure 1.9).

Figure 1.9 Bandwidth Savings with VoFR

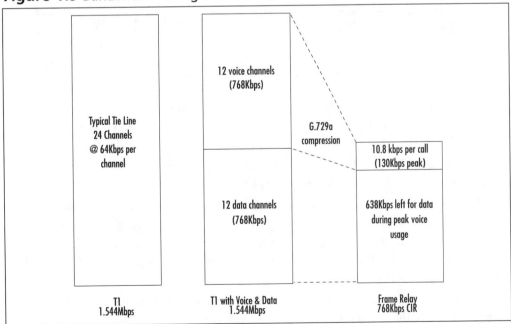

One of the most important things to avoid when packetizing voice is compressing and decompressing a call multiple times. Every time the call goes through a codec, there is a delay as the call is encoded or decoded. Multiple conversions can result in a degradation of quality. If we look at our example network again, we can see how this fact affects where VoFR can be used. In this sample configuration, Denver is the headquarters. Using frame relay to connect Denver to Baltimore and Los Angeles is a cost-effective solution for providing data and voice. For example, let's say that Donna picks up the phone in Denver and wants to call Bob in Baltimore. As her call is placed across the frame network, it goes through several processes. The first process is the receiving and then passing of any digits. The second process is encoding. Donna's voice is broken down from an analog waveform into bits (1s and 0s). This is the coding or compression process. These can include the algorithms for G.711, G.729a, or G.723.1. Each algorithm processes the waveform differently, but they all convert into bits. Once the call is in a packetized form, it is sent across the frame relay circuit. In Baltimore, the router receives the bits and processes them through its decoder. It is important to note that the codec used at each end must match. Once the router has converted the bits into an analog waveform, it sends the call out of the appropriate phone port (Figure 1.10).

Figure 1.10 Encoding and Decoding a Voice Call

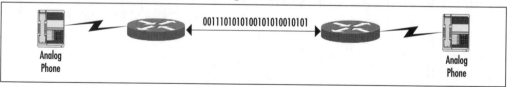

This is great news for a CFO because of the savings earned from avoiding long distance calls. Because Denver is the central site, the same scenario can be illustrated between Donna in Denver and Lewis in Los Angeles. Hopefully, most of the calls are between the remote sites and the central office. But what happens when there are calls between remote sites?

Let's say Bob in Baltimore wants to call Lewis in Los Angeles. Although it may be possible to configure the router in Denver to forward the calls back to Los Angeles, there are still several problems that would make this plan unfeasible, and this is where VoFR starts to fall apart. To begin with, you would be encoding and decoding the calls twice.

As the call leaves Baltimore it gets encoded, and when it arrives in Denver it gets decoded. Once again, the call gets encoded as it leaves Denver and is decoded as it enters Los Angeles (Figure 1.11). This pattern introduces all sorts of problems as far as quality and delay are concerned. The call would also occupy two codecs on the Denver router. That alone is an inefficient usage of hardware. The exception would be if you were using Cisco Switched VoFR, which would allow the call to be passed through without multiple encodings. FRF.11 would require multiple encodings.

Figure 1.11 Encoding and Decoding a Call Between Baltimore and Los Angeles

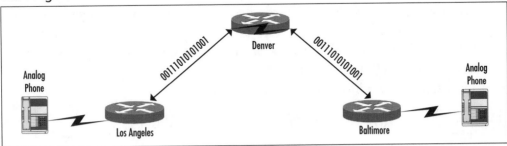

When end-to-end calls are needed across multiple locations, it becomes a better opportunity for other link layer solutions such as ATM or point-to-point circuits. VoFR has the edge from an ease-of-implementation and management standpoint as well as for long-term cost savings.

Using Asynchronous Transfer Mode for Toll Bypass

ATM has the unique ability to provide multiple levels of QoS. While the engineers work frantically trying to implement some QoS measures in IP, ATM has had these features all along. One of the big drawbacks to ATM is that it is not available at all locations. Nevertheless, we will see that ATM has compelling advantages in its delivery of QoS.

Where to Use It

Although ATM has had great success in penetrating the large WAN backbone market, it still has difficulty moving beyond that space. As Gigabit Ethernet begins to grow in popularity, ATM will have a more difficult time justifying itself in the corporate backbone. However, ATM can still provide true QoS measures for applications that need it, such as voice and video. These inherent QoS capabilities will allow ATM to outperform IP solutions in many bandwidth-intensive, time-sensitive applications such as voice and video. ATM will always have a speed advantage over Ethernet and Fast Ethernet.

The obvious place to use VoATM is where you have ATM networks already installed. If you are lucky enough to have ATM to the closet, VoATM becomes an excellent means of transporting voice. Or perhaps you are carrying ATM service to a remote office. To transport voice to the desktop, it helps to have the ATM network as close to the desktop as possible. A prime example of a situation in which it doesn't work is where ATM is used only in a backbone in a headquarters. If ATM is not extended to the remote offices in this situation, it cannot carry the voice to them.

Let's look at our example network again. With a Cisco 3810 in each office, we can terminate ATM circuits as well as peel off voice calls. Using ATM also has the advantage of providing end-to-end calls (Figure 1.12).

Figure 1.12 An ATM Network Providing End-to-End Calls

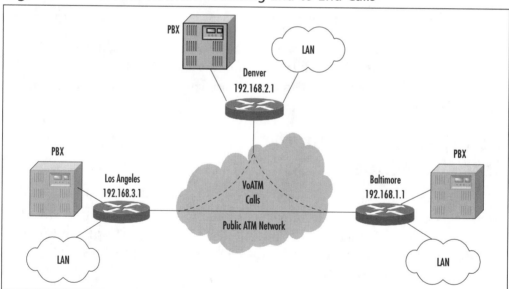

Now that the network is end-to-end ATM, calls can originate in Baltimore, pass through Denver, and end in Los Angeles without having to encode or decode the call multiple times. Due to ATM's ability to perform QoS, the voice calls can be placed into their own QoS queues. The result is that calls can be sent coast to coast without any degradation in quality while their timely arrival is still ensured. The various classes of service are discussed in more detail later in this book. In essence, data and voice are placed in queues that are treated differently throughout the ATM network.

Figure 1.13 illustrates how priority can be given to voice traffic over data traffic. In this example, a CBR is specified for voice traffic. A fixed bit rate is assigned to the voice traffic to minimize jitter. The data traffic is relegated to an available bit rate (ABR) queue. The data traffic on the ABR queue does not have a guaranteed bandwidth, but it can be allocated more bandwidth than the voice traffic when bandwidth is available. This type of queuing scheme can satisfy both voice and data traffic within the same network.

Figure 1.13 QoS Queuing with Voice and Data Traffic

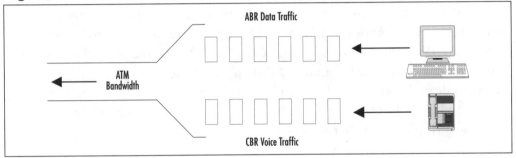

Many IP QoS measures that are currently being implemented are router specific. This is one of the major hurdles that IP engineers face. The current IP packet does not include detailed information about QoS other than the IP Precedence bits. Some headway is being made with enhancing these QoS tags, but this is still one of the major drawbacks to using VoIP in congested networks.

When ATM's QoS measures are used, the tagging information is carried for the life of the cell. A cell is ATM's equivalent of a frame. We will discuss the advantages and disadvantages of using ATM's QoS measures in a moment. As long as the voice call is carried through the ATM network, it can keep the higher QoS tag. This is also true for video because video's needs on a network are very similar to those of voice, the significant difference being the bandwidth needed. The bandwidth requirements for video are significantly higher. However, managing the efficient transport of video by using QoS measures is very similar to that of voice.

ATM is a completely different method of handling data flow. One of the major differences between ATM and other frame-based networks is that ATM breaks data into cells. A cell is 53 bytes long and contains a 5-byte header. This header contains all the ATM-specific information regarding source and destination address. This is one way that ATM can potentially gain a speed advantage.

In a frame-based network such as Ethernet, the frame size can vary. This variance causes the switches to have to either wait for the entire frame (also called *store and forward*) or take a chance and start sending the frame out the destination port as soon as it is received. Because ATM cells are always 53 bytes, the ATM switches know when the end of the cell has been received without an end-of-frame identifier or delimiter. This knowledge allows ATM switches to switch cells very rapidly. A problem arises with the fixed length of cells. Frames have the ability to match their size to the particular data that is being sent. ATM places as much data as possible in a cell, and if there is any space left over, it pads the cell. *Padding* is adding blank space to a cell in order to reach the 48-byte payload requirement. Imagine how much space this padding potentially wastes. The same voice call that was discussed in the VoFR section using G.729 for compression now takes up 14.13Kbps of bandwidth. Using G729 results in voice being segmented into 30-byte payloads. This results in 23 bytes of overhead, almost as much as the payload itself (Figure 1.14). This overhead can chew up a lot of bandwidth on slower connections, so it is important to understand the ramifications of using ATM on anything under T1 speeds. We go into much more detail on configuring VoATM later in this book.

Figure 1.14 ATM Cell and Potential Overhead

ATM Header 5 bytes	G.729a Payload 30 bytes	Unused Overhead 18 bytes
	53-byte ATM Cell	

Continuous Bit Rate

ATM provides a CBR service for the benefit of real-time information such as voice. Configuring an ATM link for CBR minimizes variations in time delay or jitter between successive voice cells, providing a high QoS to the end user.

CBR service provides a specific bit rate for voice traffic. This specificity minimizes timing variations in the delivery of voice packets, known as jitter. There is an unavoidable delay between the transmission and delivery of a voice packet. Although it is important to minimize that delay, it is also important to minimize the variations in the time delay between successive voice packets. Ideally, each voice packet must arrive on cue, not late and not too early.

QoS versus Availability

As we've discussed, the main advantage to using ATM is its built-in QoS measures. The ability to classify a voice call from end to end is a great advantage. In a campus wide environment, using ATM is as simple as running fiber between buildings. This scenario allows ATM to be extended as close to the desktop as the budget allows and would be an ideal solution for a school that has buildings spread over a large campus area. A single set of fibers can connect each building in order to enable data and voice across an ATM network (Figure 1.15). This setup allows for growth in data speeds and the ability to provide a level of QoS to voice traffic.

Figure 1.15 A Campus ATM Network Utilizing Voice and Data

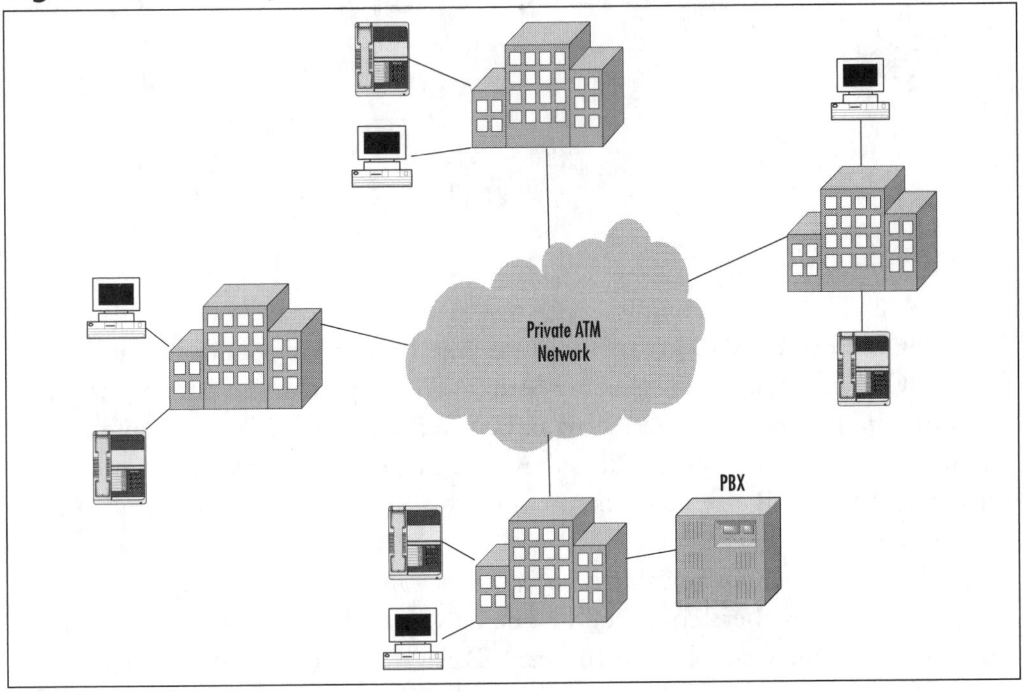

If we look at our example network again, we see that in some locales, finding an ATM network provider presents a potential problem. In the cities we have talked about so far, it is likely that some company provides ATM service. However, what if there is a remote office in Billings, Montana, that needs to be connected as well (Figure 1.16)? Although it is possible that ATM service is available in Billings, it is much more likely that Frame Relay would be the only circuit of choice. As we travel down the road of technology growth, this argument could disappear.

Figure 1.16 Adding a Remote Site Can Be a Problem with ATM

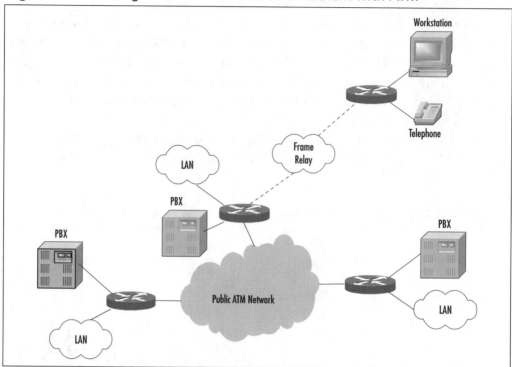

Using Frame Relay to get to a location like Billings might not be so far-fetched. One of the nice things about using ATM in part of the network is that it has some similarities to Frame Relay, and converting from ATM to Frame Relay and back again is not too complicated. Although QoS tagging would not carry through the Frame Relay network, it could be a means of extending voice to those remote sites.

ATM might become available everywhere at some point in the near future. When this happens, there could still be one drawback. The costs associated with ATM are still somewhat higher than Frame Relay. Equipment costs have come down quite a bit, and in a campus environment, ATM can be a very attractive solution. However, ATM service provider circuits are typically more expensive than Frame Relay circuits. This could make it difficult to justify ATM as opposed to Frame Relay. Keep in mind the following advantages that VoATM has over VoFR:

■ Complete and detailed QoS measures

■ End-to-end call routing without multiple encoding and decoding

- ATM popularity is still growing and services will be available every-where in the near future

- ATM in the backbone as well as the WAN means a homogenous topology throughout

Using Point-to-Point Leased Lines for Toll Bypass

If the implementation calls for using a point-to-point T1, there are two choices. The first option is to use voice over HDLC (VoHDLC). HDLC is a Layer 2 pro-tocol typically used for point-to-point T1s. VoHDLC is similar to VoFR in that it allows multiple calls to be placed over the T1 using compression. In the instance of tie-line replacement using T1s and Cisco equipment, VoHDLC can be an attractive alternative. One of the major drawbacks to VoHDLC is that it has very limited scalability. It was originally designed for point-to-point connections between Cisco routers (Figure 1.17).

Figure 1.17 A VoHDLC Configuration

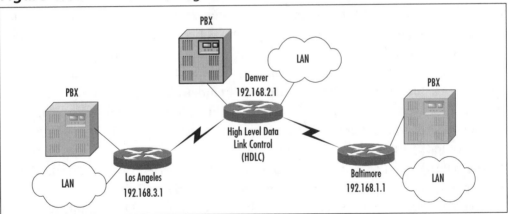

The second option is to use VoIP, because where VoHDLC and VoFR fail is in their scalability, resulting in encoding and then decoding voice calls multiple times. VoIP can scale with the network; anywhere IP can reach is a possible desti-nation for a voice call. Obviously, there are serious QoS issues. In theory and in practice VoIP will work across the Internet; however at best it will sound like you are talking on a CB radio. In the private network where QoS can be closely monitored and controlled, VoIP can have a far-reaching impact. In our simple example network (refer back to Figure 1.1), let's start by looking at the connec-tion between Baltimore and Denver. If the connection is a point-to-point T1,

Cisco's AS5300 could be used at either end for providing a digital T1 trunk to the PBXs. However, if only a few calls will be active at any time, it might be prudent to look at a 2600 or 3600 series router. A simple 2600 series router can support up to two voice slots. Moving up to the 3640 and 3660 allows for much greater growth and expandability. The 3640 can support up to 12 analog voice calls; the 3660 can support up to five T1s for digital connectivity to a PBX. Each slot can hold two FXO, FXS, or E&M ports. Each port can support a call. Specific details about what these ports are used for are addressed in Chapter 4.

A 2600 can support four analog voice calls at a time, which might be enough for a remote office. Keep in mind that the number of users in the remote office might be more than four. The question is, how many concurrent calls will they make to the central office? Predicting call volumes is a magical art and is done using something known as *Erlang's calculations*. An *Erlang* is simply a representation of a continuous one-hour voice call. Hardly anyone makes a one-hour call; it is just a method for estimating the appropriate number of ports to have available. For a software-based Erlang calculator, visit www.erlang.com.

For the Baltimore-to-Denver connection, using VoIP from the outset could make it easier to expand the voice network later. When Los Angeles is included in the network, the benefit becomes apparent. When users in Baltimore want to make a call to Los Angeles, it is ideal for the packetized voice to travel from one location to another along the most direct path possible. The traditional method is to have a tie line between the two cities or a tandem PBX performing the call switching in Denver. As was discussed earlier, this solution would lead to multiple encodes and decodes, thereby degrading call quality.

If we look at the data network, though, it can travel through Denver first before being routed to Los Angeles. Because VoIP is carried over IP, it follows the same path as any other data going between two locations. Calls can be placed between Baltimore and Los Angeles and be routed through Denver, just like any other data (Figure 1.18). The call is encoded and decoded only once, and QoS measures can be managed easily because of the internal network. This solution eliminates the need for the tie line between the two cities. It also allows for future expansion into other cities. As you will see later in this chapter, VoIP can also be used for expanded functionality. Combined with the signaling protocol H.323, VoIP can assist in building a solution to replace the traditional PBX.

Figure 1.18 VoIP Call Routing Between Baltimore and Los Angeles

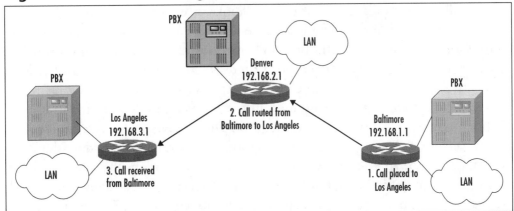

Return on Investment

Nothing can help sell a solution more than a good ROI. Creating an ROI can also help you make sure that you have covered all of the possible issues that could arise with use of the solution.

Reviewing Current Telephony Costs

Building an ROI model is the best place to start when you're trying to decide if packetized voice makes financial sense for your organization. One of the best things about packetized voice is that it sells itself with a rapid ROI. No matter who you are, you will most likely be trying to sell this solution to someone else. If that other person is the CEO or CFO of your company or a manager of a customer company, he or she will want to see how this solution is going to save them money. In some rare cases, most of which involve call centers, packetized voice can offer a different and more effective means of doing business. In most cases, the decision makers will be more interested in the bottom line. In that situation, an ROI will be the best way of selling the idea. Showing the manager how quickly the solution pays for itself in raw numbers as opposed to talking about features will allow you to make use of the rest of this book.

When you're building an ROI, the first thing to look at are the current phone bills, shown in Table 1.1. Most phone bills contain a wealth of information, but they can be quite long and will take a fair amount of time to get through. This section primarily covers justifying tie-line replacement. (Building an ROI for other services such as PBX replacement is dealt with later in the chapter.) Some of the things to look for on the phone bills are calls that are placed between offices. This might seem obvious, but it is important to make sure you get all of these calls. The next thing to look for is calls that are placed to locations that are local to the remote office. Taking our example network again, we will look at calls from Baltimore to Denver (Figure 1.19). Although many calls may be placed to the Denver office, there could be a high number of calls placed to the Denver area. In our example network, we can see that the Denver office is making local calls to customers in the Denver area. At a later time, the Baltimore office called the same customers in Denver over long distance circuits. These calls are expensive and are very important to consider in building the ROI report. Check to see if there are any 800-service lines. Perhaps the customers in Denver are calling the Baltimore office through an 800 number in order to avoid paying long distance charges. Having these calls placed through Denver and then routed to Baltimore could allow for significant reductions in the number of calls to the 800 lines. These are all important items to take into account when you're building an ROI for tie-line replacement.

Table 1.1 Analyzing Current Phone Costs for Calls from Baltimore

	Dollars	Minutes
Calls to Denver	$713	10,182 @ $0.07/minute
Calls to Local Denver Area	$1691	15,376 @ $0.11/minute
Calls to 800 line from Local Denver Area	$1963	12,268 @ $0.16/minute
Total Per-Month Cost of Replaceable Calls	$4367	N/A

Designing & Planning…

Key Points on Phone Bills

The following are some key points to keep in mind as you review phone bills:

- Get organized first.
- Separate calls going to:
  1. Remote offices.
  2. Local calling areas around remote offices.

Continued

3. 800 service line.

4. Random and disbursed.

- Understand the business model.
- Quantify the impact of losing discounts for bulk calling plans.

There are a few things to be careful of when you're looking over the phone bill. First, don't get overwhelmed. Try to arrange the bill into a simpler format by sorting different parts of the bill into separate sections. Incidentally, this is another selling point to keep in mind: Wouldn't it be nice to have a short, understandable phone bill? Random dispersed calls are items to quickly scan. There will always be a number of long distance calls that go to uncommon areas. By uncommon, we simply mean uncommon to the particular business. There is not much that can be done with those calls at this time. It is important to understand what those calls are for, however. If the business model is that all calls are geographically uncommon, building an ROI will be more difficult but not impossible. There could be a way to change the business model in order to lower costs. As packetized voice becomes more pervasive, there will be no uncommon geography. However, for now it is difficult to find a method for lowering those costs.

Depending on the total number of long distance calls, the customer may be taking advantage of a bulk discount pricing plan. As we will see later, it can affect the ROI significantly if the remaining long distance calls are priced much higher due to the loss of the discount. Typically, this amount will not be significant enough to overturn the justification for packetizing voice, but it could have enough of an impact to extend the ROI quite a bit. Figure 1.19 presents the current long distance calling patterns.

Figure 1.19 Long Distance Calling Patterns

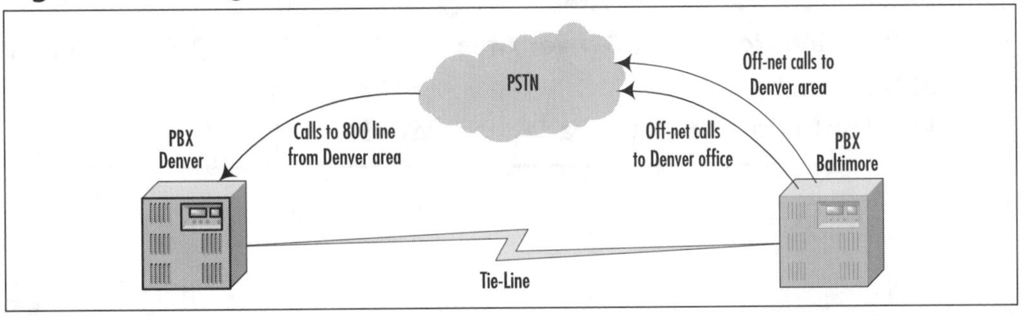

Designing the New Solution

Understanding the current calling patterns and bills will help you build an effective solution. Since we are only looking at tie-line replacement at this point, the configuration would probably be relatively simple—perhaps a 2600 series router with a digital T1 card to interface with the PBX. Whether you're using VoFR, VoHDLC, or VoIP between routers, it is still a simplistic configuration. Later chapters delve into much greater detail regarding planning of capacity and equipment issues. The key issue now is determining the bandwidth needed to support the predicted call volume. Although up-front costs for equipment might be high, the long-term impact of circuit costs is what will matter the most. Accurately predicting bandwidth can be the key in making sure the recurring costs are low enough to pay for the new equipment in a short period of time. There are many tools for predicting call volumes and the necessary number of phone lines or trunks to support them. A popular tool is an Erlang table, discussed earlier. Entire books have been written on this topic, and the phone industry has perfected the process over the decades. For more detailed information as well as software-based Erlang calculators, refer to www.erlang.com.

The important thing is to determine how much equipment will be needed to support the predicted call volumes. It is also the key in deciding what type of circuit to price. Particularly when dealing with Frame Relay, you'll find that a fair amount of customizing can be done in regard to the speed of the circuit. In order to build an effective ROI, you must include real-world pricing for circuits (Table 1.2). Notice how the pricing on the 800 line has increased. This is due to losing the discount from the greater number of calls.

Table 1.2 New Solution Pricing for Calls from Baltimore

	Dollars	Minutes
Off-Net Calls to Denver	$0	0
Off-Net Calls to Local Denver Area	$0	0
Calls to 800 Line from Local Denver Area	$226	1256 @ $0.18/minute
Cost of New Frame Circuit	$1637	N/A
Total Per-Month Cost After Upgrade	$1863	N/A

Building the ROI and Payback Period

There are three steps to building the ROI and payback period. The first step is to review current expenses. The second step is to detail the costs involved in a new solution, including the new circuit costs. The third step is to combine the two and show the time frame for the payback period. In your justification, always include business reasons as well as the numbers. Usually the numbers speak for themselves, but it doesn't hurt to throw in some good ideas about how packetized voice can help move the organization forward. Don't forget to include hardware costs (Table 1.3).

Table 1.3 Building the Complete ROI

Item	Cost	Total Cost
Current monthly phone calls	$4367	N/A
Recurring costs after upgrade	$1863	N/A
Total monthly savings	N/A	$2504
Cost of two new 2610s w/voice	$22,390	N/A
Labor for installation	$1200	N/A
Installation costs for frame circuit	$1000	N/A
Total upgrade costs	N/A	$24,590
Payback period	N/A	9.82 months

In the example, the payback period is only 9.82 months. The ROI calculated from the payback value (the period of operation, 12 months, divided by the payback period, 9.82 months) gives the percentage of the initial outlay that is recovered in the first year, which in this case is 122 percent.

Of course, every network is different, but this is a good example of what makes packetized voice so attractive. In nearly all situations in which there is a high volume of calls to a single office or area, a short payback period will be common. Keep in mind that geographic proximity makes a difference. This model quickly falls apart when the calls are widely disbursed. What makes this model work is the ability to eliminate a large number of public calls and place them on the private network.

Case Study: PBX Replacement with IP Telephony

As the world moves toward packetized voice, more companies will want to convert. Much like the adoption of the Internet in the business world, common use in the market place will start driving more companies toward packetized voice. In the meantime, there is still one key area where opportunity exists.

Many lower-end PBXs are supplied with a fixed number of ports. This is especially true for small offices that are just getting started. They could purchase a 48-port PBX and outgrow it. Nearly all these systems have fixed port sizes. When the company expands to the 49th person, it has a problem. The company can either not give that person a phone, which is unlikely, or it can do a forklift upgrade. In a *forklift upgrade,* the old PBX comes out and a new one goes in. Although many PBX vendors have trade-up programs, this can still be very expensive. What is worse is that they might need just a few more ports. The next-size PBX might have 250 ports as a minimum. The cost would be outrageous for the benefit of getting phones for a few more people. Another large source of cost is the maintenance fees. PBX vendors typically charge hefty maintenance fees that are proportional to the size of the PBX. Now a company that simply wanted to add a few more people is paying maintenance fees on a PBX that has far more capacity than it will use.

This is a prime opportunity to replace the system with an IP telephony system. The advantage is that the company can keep the existing system and gradually migrate to an IP-based unified messaging system. This solution solves the short-term concerns of getting phone service to the few extra employees and allows the company to start growing toward the future.

Within a few months, the company can have everyone on the new system and it can get rid of the old PBX. This is one of the great advantages of IP telephony systems. Moves, adds, and changes are inexpensive. Using truly IP-based phones, the user simply takes his or her phone when the user changes offices. Configuration is done through a central configuration point for new users, and users can facilitate administration of their own phones through a Web interface. This user administration will be much simpler than trying to read through the thick manuals provided by traditional PBX vendors.

Table 1.4 provides a sample cost comparison between a traditional PBX system and a high-end IP telephony system for a site of 450 users. The IP telephony system uses the same Category 5 cabling plant as the data network and comprises the following components and functions:

- Four hundred fifty full-featured IP phones with digital signal processors
- Twenty-five IP conference stations

- Three Call Manager servers for redundancy
- Multiple voice gateways for PSTN connectivity
- Conferencing, call transfer, and hold-and-forwarding features
- Voicemail and fax-e-mail

Table 1.4 Sample Savings Analysis for IP Telephony

Item	Traditional PBx	IP Telephony	Annual Savings
Maintenance and support	$50,000	$35,000	$15,000
Moves, adds, changes	$22,500	$11,250	$11,250
Conference calls	$45,000	$0	$45,000
Annual recurring costs	$117,500	$46,250	$71,250

Even assuming that the initial outlays between the two systems are similar, the functionality and cost savings of the full-featured IP telephony system provide the better investment. Let's look at some of the cost savings in depth.

Maintenance and Support

Since the new IP telephony system uses the same technologies as the data network, staff efficiencies can be achieved. Through simplified network management, network support staff productivity can be improved. Some IP telephony customers are seeing productivity improvements in the range of 30 percent.

Moves, Adds, and Changes

In an IP telephony system, DHCP services, autoregistration, and Web-based configuration services can facilitate the inevitable modifications to a telephony system. Move, add, and change (MAC) savings were calculated as follows:

An average cost of $25 per move, add, or change is assumed (based on industry standards). Based on published analyses, it is assumed that IP telephony can save approximately 50 percent on MACs, bringing the cost down to about $12.50 per move. This estimate is based on saving 100 percent on intrabuilding moves and significant amounts on adds and interbuilding moves. Assuming each of the 450 employees will require two MACs during a year, the yearly cost savings can be calculated as follows:

$12.50/MAC x 2 MACs/person/year x 450 people = $11,250

Conference Call Savings

If the current PBX does not support conferencing, IP telephony can perform this function free of additional tolls. Enormous cost savings can be realized by eliminating this dependence upon service providers. Conference call savings were calculated as follows:

Each conference call was assumed to cost $0.15 per minute for each port used, last an average of 60 minutes, and have an average of four participants. Furthermore, we assumed that 450 business users would have five conference calls per day. The yearly cost savings can then be calculated as follows:

$0.15/min/port x 4 ports x 60 minutes/call x 5 calls/day x 250 days/year = $45,000

Future Cost Savings

In addition to the benefits mentioned, additional savings would be accrued in the future if an IP telephony solution were eventually deployed throughout the enterprise network. The following are some of the benefits that would be achieved if an enterprisewide IP telephony solution were implemented:

- Long distance savings would be achieved by diverting calls over the private data network (toll bypass). It should be noted that additional bandwidth might be required on the private data network to accommodate voice as well as data. However, in most cases there would be an overall cost savings due to the reduction in total number of circuits required throughout the network.

- Lower administration costs would accrue by consolidating voice/IT staff requirements. Reduction in workload is possible, and smaller sites don't need two distinct technicians for separate voice and data.

- Lower administration costs would be achieved by consolidating infrastructure components.

- Voice connectivity over data applications would be achieved (i.e., unified messaging).

- The number of network service providers would be reduced.

- Application offerings would be increased, leading to increased efficiency.

The last thing that sets IP PBXs apart from traditional PBXs is open standards. As IP telephony becomes more prevalent, the costs associated with equipment and software will continue to drop. This is completely opposite from the traditional solution. PBX prices have hardly dropped at all over the last decade. With open standards, anyone can go down to a local computer store and purchase a $100 universal serial bus (USB) camera; then not only can they talk across the Internet, they can videoconference. The video quality across the Internet can vary, but performing this task across a private network is not a problem. For example, we had a videoconference with a man in the United Arab Emirates; the speech and video were a little stuttered, but it was nothing less than we would have expected from a satellite phone. The best part was that it was free, using a low-end eyeball-type camera and the sound card in a laptop. This rapid level of growth is sure to make packetized voice incredibly inexpensive over the coming years.

Advanced Features and Integration Possibilities

What makes the transition to packetized voice so revolutionary is its openness. With the growth and adoption of open standards, new possibilities arise. Instead of paying exorbitant fees to a single PBX manufacturer in order to create a value-added service, programmers can create applications based on these open standards with confidence that their programs will work with many different systems. This simple concept will open the floodgates to applications and services that haven't even been considered yet. It will also make higher-end features more affordable to small businesses.

Replacing the Traditional PBX

Tie-line replacement is often a good way to begin introducing packetized voice into an organization. The ultimate goal, however, is to replace the traditional PBX altogether. The comforting thing about tie-line replacement is that it is fairly straightforward.

When you're looking to replace the PBX, you must consider many more factors. Instead of calls passing across a single WAN link, they might travel all over the network. This can have an impact on bandwidth, although it would probably be a minor problem on a LAN. However, several other issues can have an impact on the design. For instance, is the current IP allocation clean? Are there available IP ranges? Every new phone, unless it is a PC-based phone, requires its own IP address. That would probably mean the need for twice as many IPs available to a network. That could be a problem for a large organization. Where should the Call Manager servers be placed in order to perform the best? Where will PSTN connections be made for outbound calls? What third-party services will be implemented on the phone system? As you can see, many questions can arise when you're replacing the PBX.

Call Routing

When you begin talking about placing the PBX on the network, you need to look at how calls will travel across the network. The calls will move from one IP host to another, so it is critical that the routing on the network is stable. It is also important to make sure that a sufficient number of IP addresses are available. In this situation, Network Address Translation (NAT) might not help for adding IP addresses later. Currently, NAT is supported in H.323, but the implementation requires use of a proxy and a gatekeeper. It is functional but can be difficult to set up. However, NAT is not supported when Cisco's Skinny protocol is used. The Skinny protocol is used by Cisco's IP phones.

There might not be a problem with using a separate private range of IP addresses for the VoIP system as long as the entire range is in the same IP range. This solution could cause a problem if you decide to use PC-based virtual phones, however. The virtual phone resides on the PC and inherits the IP address of that PC. If the PC is on a real Internet IP and the rest of the phone system is on private IPs, you might think about using NAT. Once again, this can work, but it complicates the design (Figure 1.20). It is important to note, once again, that the Cisco IP phones use the Skinny protocol and do not support NAT implementations. The phones can communicate with H.323 devices such as NetMeeting through a gateway such as Call Manager. More details of the AVVID system are described in *Configuring Cisco AVVID: Architecture for Voice, Video, and Integrated Data* (ISBN: 1–928994–14–8, Syngress Publishing).

Figure 1.20 Call Failure Through a Router Performing NAT

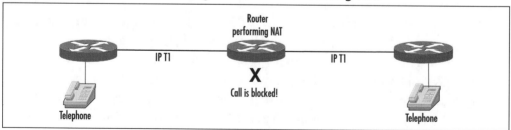

As you will see, the Cisco Call Manager (CM), combined with the Cisco Multimedia Conference Manager (MCM), provides much of the functionality of

a traditional PBX. The purpose of the CM is to provide registration of IP phones as well as directory services for them.

It is also a point where TAPI programs can interface to the network. (We will discuss TAPI applications shortly.) It is important to place any CMs in the right locations on the network. The CMs should be placed in locations that can provide a high level of QoS as well as easy access for repairs and upgrades. Ask yourself this: How often does the PBX fail? The CMs must maintain that level of performance through diligent monitoring and appropriate backup systems such as redundant servers. Call Manager 2.2 provides for a primary and a backup CM. Calls that are in progress will continue. Any transfers, conferences, or calls on hold will fail because the CM is actively managing them. Any idle phones will find the failover CM. Version 3.0 of CCM supports redundant load-sharing servers.

Cisco's MCM provides for management of H.323 conferencing as well as controlling bandwidth for those applications. These might not be considered typical PBX functions, but they are part of the expanded functionality of a network-based PBX. MCM is a software enhancement for the 2500, 2600, 3600, and 3810 series of routers. MCM has the ability to require a login for H.323 conferencing using Radius or TACACS+ accounts. MCM can provide call detail recording (CDR) for tracking usage and possibly for billing purposes. For call routing, MCM can act as an H.323 gatekeeper.

Dial Plan

Taking the time to devise the right dial plan is the key to allowing for growth and ease of manageability. In many cases, the current dial plan can be transitioned to the new system. If the old plan is used, it should be reviewed for growth potential as well as its ability to meet VoIP's unique requirements. A number of extra items should be accounted for:

- Voicemail extensions
- Call parking
- Reserved or preplanned voiceconferencing
- Special outbound gateways
- Third-party TAPI applications that could require dialing numbers

These numbers might not be accounted for with an existing PBX system. If this system is being added to a new WAN that is covering many remote sites, you might need a new dial plan. The gateways and CM have the capability of forwarding calls based on wildcard digits. When you place a call to a remote office, the digits can be forwarded to the gateway once a wildcard for that site has been reached. In our example network, the central site is Baltimore, with a CM. All local inside calls have 2 as the first digit. In Denver, local inside calls start with 3. The CM in Baltimore knows that if it sees a call that starts with 3, it will forward it to Denver. A few numbers, such as 0 and 9, should be reserved for other uses. If you have more than eight sites, you need to move to a two-digit prefix plan instead of one. The total number of digits in an extension also depends on the number of people who will potentially work at each office. If that number will never go over 100 at any office, a three-digit plan would work. In order to avoid headaches down the road, make sure that you plan for more rather than fewer users. Using a four-digit plan to start with is not too taxing on the users and will prevent many headaches down the road (Figure 1.21).

Figure 1.21 A Simple Dialing Plan Between Baltimore and Denver

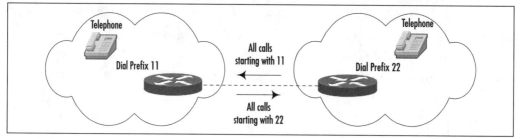

Interactive Voice Response

At some point or even on a daily basis, a call to a business that uses interactive voice response (IVR) systems will be required. We have all had the painful experience of pressing our way through 10 menus before the system finally hangs up, our call unresolved. Obviously, there is a right way to set up an IVR, and as we have all experienced, there is definitely a wrong way. In most typical situations, there is an IVR on any public incoming line. IVRs are useful for routing calls to the appropriate person or department and are less expensive than having an individual do it. Many of Cisco's products now support IVR internally, including the 2600, 3600, and AS5300. This support is achieved with Tool Command Language (TCL) scripts and voice files, which are referenced in the configuration on the router. When a call comes into the router and matches a set of criteria, the script is queried. The script resides on the router's flash. The script runs and, depending on the digits it captures, plays an audio file. This audio file is also stored on the router's flash and is loaded into memory. Cisco provides several standard audio files, but it is recommended that you create your own. The audio files use the standard .AU format. The scripts also have the capability to reroute calls.

Unified Messaging and the Cisco Unity System

Unified messaging is an excellent example of how two typically diverse networks—the phone network and the data network—can come together and provide a better solution. Voicemail and e-mail have always been separate entities. With unified messaging, both systems can fall under one interface. The benefits of this union can be bidirectional. Cisco acquired a small company called Amteva, which produced the Amteva Unified Messaging System (UMS). Now called Cisco Unity, this UMS runs on Windows NT and Solaris platforms. It provides a range of features, such as the following:

- Configuration parameters are stored in Lightweight Directory Access Protocol (LDAP), a standards-based directory structure for organizing information.

- Voicemail and faxes can be accessed through an Internet Message Access Protocol (IMAP) e-mail client. IMAP is a common standard for e-mail retrieval.

- E-mail can be retrieved through any phone.

- It supports numerous types of notification for incoming e-mail, voicemail, and faxes.

- Fax headers can be retrieved through any phone.

- Faxes can be delivered directly to an e-mailbox, viewed from there, and transferred as e-mail.

- It features single number reachability.

- It offers a Web-based management interface.

- It provides excellent scalability.

Configuration parameters are stored via LDAP, a standards-based architecture that has excellent scalability characteristics. LDAP is rapidly growing in popularity due to its capabilities and open standards-based architecture. Using LDAP also allows other applications to have access to some configuration parameters, opening the door even more for third-party programmers.

Voicemail and faxes can be accessed through any IMAP-compliant e-mail system. Unity uses these open standards protocols to convert voicemail and faxes to an SMTP/MIME e-mail format.

Voicemail recordings are stored as .WAV files, and faxes are stored as .TIFF files. With Internet-connected machines popping up everywhere, this flexibility allows anyone to access their voicemail and faxes without having to make a long distance call to the PBX. You could sit down at any multimedia Internet terminal and listen to your voicemail. You could also check to see if your customer faxed back that signed contract you've been waiting for. Once you have looked over your e-mail and faxes, you can send them back out just like e-mail. Consider how many keys it takes to send a voicemail to someone else with a traditional PBX system. Then consider how easy it is to forward an e-mail. Instead of having paper copies of faxes floating around, you could just forward the information to the appropriate people. There is no reason why the e-mail can't be forwarded to any e-mail address. Using standard file formats, the e-mails can be read by anyone.

E-mail can be retrieved from any phone. Let's say you are at the airport and you want to check your e-mail before getting on a plane. You can call into Unity and have your e-mail read back to you. You can even listen to the headers of any faxes you have received.

Unity can be configured to send a notification when a new e-mail, voice-mail, or fax is received. These notifications are configurable for the various types of incoming messages. Notifications can be sent to a pager or to a phone's message-indicator light.

Because the system is based on IP, a Web interface has been designed to allow for remotely managing all configuration parameters. Even voicemails can be accessed directly from the system using the Web interface. Configuration parameters controlling how the mailbox behaves can be set up there as well.

Perhaps one of the most exciting features is single-number reachability, or "find-me, follow-me" service. Many people now carry a cell phone in addition to having a business phone and a home phone. It could be argued that being reachable at all times might not be the best thing, but there is no doubt that more and more people need that kind of access. The problem is that you have to give all your numbers out to everyone, and they have to try each number when they call you. Unity allows you to configure a list of numbers and the times to try them.

When a caller calls your office number and you are not there, the caller hears a message. The message states that you did not answer your phone and that the caller has the option of waiting while the system tries to locate you. The caller can also decide to go directly to voicemail at this time. If the caller decides to wait, the system starts down the list of numbers you have established. If the system can't reach you, it sends the caller to voicemail. If you are at one of the numbers on your list, the call is patched through. This means that you need to give out only one number, and private phone numbers such as your home number remain private.

Driving the growth of many of these systems is the promise of relatively inexpensive scalability. As we will see in the ROI example, upgrading PBXs can be very costly. IP-based PBXs and voicemail systems such as Unity bring the exciting opportunity for rapid inexpensive growth. Through its use of distributed systems and architectures, Unity can support from 50 to 5000 users and more. In today's market of rapid growth, this kind of support can be a key factor in deciding between upgrading/replacing PBXs and installing a packetized voice system.

TAPI Integration

One of the key enablers for this rapid growth of open standards applications will be the functionality of TAPI. TAPI is a standards-based programming interface for telephony applications. It allows programmers to access telephony-specific information supplied by other TAPI applications on the system. This interface has benefits on the workstation and server platforms for different types of applications. On the server, the benefits include diverse types of value-added services, allowing them to integrate with each other. Applications such as voicemail, IVR, and CDR information can be enabled through TAPI. TAPI facilitates design of new applications that could not have been dreamed of with the traditional proprietary PBX programming interfaces. As the standards grow and systems become more robust, TAPI can grow with them.

The other place where TAPI will have an impact is at the workstation. Some TAPI applications that exist now are as simple as phone dialers. Some of the more advanced applications use TAPI for enabling screen pop-ups. As a call comes into the workstation, it registers certain items such as the calling number. With an application that is TAPI enabled, these dialing numbers could be passed through. This is a good application for a call center environment because an operator can get information about the caller before answering the phone. With a well thought out application, a sales call center could instantly have information about the caller: his or her name, buying habits, the last time the caller purchased something, the kind of shipping he or she prefers, and if the caller prefers blue over yellow. In a help desk environment, the operator could instantly have caller-related information regarding the nature of past problems, the level of the service contract, and even the caller's typical demeanor and knowledge level. Then, as the operator passes the call to the next level of support, that person could get a pop-up screen with the same information as well as new information about the particular case. It is quite obvious that the sky is the limit for creative programmers. As the market continues to grow, new ideas will come out of the availability of the open-standard TAPI.

Web Click-to-Talk

You've seen the commercials. A mom is looking at some clothes on the Web and she gets her son to come over and take a look at them. He isn't happy about wasting his time shopping. She sees a shirt she likes and wonders if it is available in other colors, so she clicks the link to customer support. A window pops up with a videoconference to a sales rep who can help.

Until the entire phone system is packetized and IP based, this Web *click-to-talk* or *click-through* scenario might seem like a remote dream. For home consumers, it *will* be a dream, but for business, this scene could happen now. Imagine a large corporation with an entire department dedicated to human resources. An employee decides to take a look at some 401k options, so she pulls up the company intranet on her browser. She clicks over to the 401k section and starts reading. She gets about halfway through and realizes she has more questions than answers. What does she do now? In the traditional scenario, she would pull out the company phone list and search for someone in HR, find a number and call, and no one would answer, so she'd call another number. That person doesn't handle the 401k plan, so she calls another. This person doesn't even work in HR anymore. Now imagine a different ending where the employee clicks a link at the top of the intranet page. This link automatically dials her phone. She picks up the phone and waits for the other end to start ringing. At the other end is the exact person she needs to talk to. The applications for this type of technology are limitless, and the kinds of ideas that have been tossed around regarding web click-through have just scratched the surface.

Once a phone is IP enabled, it is simply a destination address on the IP network. Web click-through is one exciting use for this feature. The hyperlink is configured in such a way that a TAPI application is activated. This application rings the local phone. Once the user has picked up the phone, it begins ringing the destination. Once the person at the destination has picked up, the conversation continues just like any other call (Figure 1.22).

Figure 1.22 The Web Click-Through Call Process

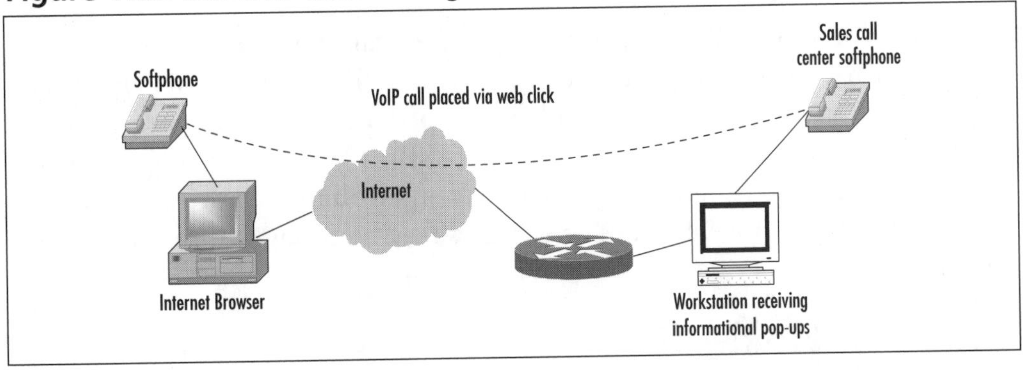

Transfer, Forward, and Conference Capabilities

Transfer, forward, and conference calls are all features found on a typical PBX. Due to the direct point-to-point nature of IP calls, a software solution needs to be implemented.

To provide those three services in a CIPT system, a software-based server is implemented. This is the conference bridge software that works with Cisco Call Manager, and it serves two purposes. The first purpose is for impromptu conferencing; the call has to go through the conference bridge at that point, and the voice traffic is redistributed to all the end points. The second function is *meet-me conferencing* for establishing a prearranged conference call. This technology might be used for a weekly meeting in which all the managers around the country dial in. There are many uses for this type of functionality.

As for transferring and forwarding calls, the CM can handle these features, but the phones have to signal back to the CM to make them happen.

Call Transfer

Cisco IP phones support call transfer. By signaling back to the CM, a call can be transferred to the final destination.

Call Forward

The Cisco IP telephony solution supports three types of call forwarding:

- **Call Forward All** Forwards all calls.

- **Call Forward Busy** Forwards calls only when the line is in use.

- **Call Forward No Answer** Forwards calls when the phone is not answered within a certain configurable number of seconds.

Call Park and Call Pickup

The Call Park feature allows a person to receive a call at another telephone for privacy. A Park soft key allows the receiver to place the caller on hold and dial a designated extension number. At another phone, the extension number can be dialed to pick up the call.

The Call Pickup feature is used to answer an incoming call that is ringing at an unattended telephone. Buttons or soft keys may be configured to activate this function.

Music on Hold

While a caller is on hold, music can be played for the enjoyment of both an on-net or an off-net caller. This feature is known as Music on Hold. The source of the music stream may be a *.WAV file or a fixed external device controlled by the CM.

Conferencing

Two types of conferencing are supported:

- **Ad Hoc Conferencing** Allows a user to add participants to the call by calling new participants and pressing a conference key.

- **Meet Me Conferencing** Allows a user to establish a conference number and advertise it to the participants. Participants join the conference by dialing the conferencing number.

Web Attendant

The Cisco Web Attendant is TAPI software that runs on a Windows PC and allows a receptionist to function as a switchboard operator by providing a Web-based interface. The Web Attendant provides many benefits over traditional operator consoles. With the Web-based interface, every line in the system can be monitored with color-coded display entries. Calls can be efficiently dispatched using a mouse. Point-and-click buttons are used instead of traditional console keys. Call transfer and hold functions can be executed with a simple drag-and-drop operation. The Cisco Web Attendant is scalable and can provide for multiple operators.

Call Detail Recording and Data Mining

Even with the lowered costs associated with using IP-based telephony systems, companies still want complete accounting records. This is true for the business user, as in the smaller company that wants to track where calls are being placed. This is a proactive strategy that emphasizes managed growth. Without understanding where calls are being placed, it is impossible to determine where bandwidth might need to be increased. Accounting records are also a major part of business for companies reselling phone services. A good accounting strategy involves CDR as well as bandwidth analysis obtained from the network. Without both, there is no way to determine if bottlenecks are being caused by voice calls or data traffic.

Call Detail Records

Many of the various pieces of the Cisco voice solution include the ability to capture call detail records. The MCM software can track a number of details and report them to a Radius or TACACS+ server. Those details include:

- Calling number
- Called number
- Call start time
- Call end time
- Bandwidth utilized

Cisco CM also supports output of its CDR to either a Microsoft Access database or an Open Database Connectivity (ODBC) database such as SQL (Figure 1.23).

Figure 1.23 Call Detail from Cisco Call Manager

Call ID	Ascii Date Time Origination	Calling Party Number	IP Address	Cause	Original Called Party	Called Party Number	IP Address	Cause	Ascii Date Time Connect	Disconnect	Call Duration
439	04/07/02 03:02	7734	10.10.10.1	0	7766	7766	10.10.10.40	0	04/07/02 03:02	4/7/02	10301
444	04/07/02 03:02	7734	10.10.10.1	0	7766	7766	10.10.10.40	0	04/07/02 03:02	4/7/02	27
445	04/07/02 03:02	7757	10.10.10.20	16	7777	2001	10.10.10.50	0	04/07/02 03:02	4/7/02	18
451	04/07/02 03:05	7759	10.10.10.30	16	7777	7780	10.10.10.60	0	04/07/02 03:05	4/7/02	0
1	04/07/02 03:06	7757	10.10.10.20	16	7743	7748	10.10.10.70	0	04/07/02 03:06	4/7/02	486
5	04/07/02 03:06	7759	10.10.10.30	16	7752	7752	10.10.10.80	0	04/07/02 03:06	4/7/02	72
3	04/07/02 03:06	7759	10.10.10.30	16	2200	2200	10.10.10.90	0	04/07/02 03:06	4/7/02	1001
7	04/07/02 03:06	7759	10.10.10.30	16	2200	2200	10.10.10.90	0	04/07/02 03:06	4/7/02	8
9	04/07/02 03:07	7734	10.10.10.1	0	2200	2200	10.10.10.90	0	04/07/02 03:07	4/7/02	6
11	04/07/02 03:09	7734	10.10.10.1	0	2200	2200	10.10.10.90	0	04/07/02 03:09	4/7/02	23

Once the data has been compiled to a database, a front-end interface can be designed to format the data in a useful way. In a simple business environment, graphing call trends over a one-month time period could prove very valuable. This type of tracking would allow you to determine such things as whether or not the circuits that are available are being utilized. It could show what departments are making more calls than others, even down to the individual. A trend analysis could be set up to show the duration of calls during a certain time of day. If the CM is being used in a call center environment, the records could show average hold times, dropped calls, and duration of completed calls, among other things. No doubt, if no application is currently using the call record data from CM, there soon will be.

Taking the reporting to the next level are those companies that need to build billing records of call logs. Because CM logs the calls directly into a database format, the front-end interface can pull details from these records and compile them into an automated billing system.

Tracing and Logging

A variety of tracing and logging functions are available for diagnostic purposes. The level of tracing can be configured to provide cursory or detailed information.

Transcoders

Transcoders perform real-time translation of digitized voice from one codec to another. A *codec* is a coding and decoding scheme for converting voice from analog to digital form and back again. Since the various codecs are not compatible with each other, transcoders are used to translate from one codec region to another.

Transcoders are important in conference calling when the participants are not using the same codec. In this example, the conference is conducted in a designated codec, and participants not using that codec will be translated by a transcoder.

Summary

The packetized voice market has many avenues of growth available to it. In this chapter, we looked at some of the basic design considerations for many of them. Although this technology can lead to much excitement about its possibilities, we must keep in mind our current limitations. A good starting point for packetized voice is simple tie-line replacement. Don't get overly ambitious and try a forklift upgrade to the entire PBX system when the situation doesn't warrant it. When the next phone bill comes, you might want to take a look at it. Start building an ROI for replacing a tie line or two. It can be approached as a trial run. You might already use some Cisco 2500s for WAN routers. Calculate how much it would cost to replace them with Cisco 2600s or 3600s and then build the justification off the savings from sending voice over the Frame Relay or HDLC circuit. Do some homework, and make sure there is bandwidth available if you will be using pre-existing circuits. If the circuits aren't there, maybe it is time to enable some file sharing between offices as well as implementing voice technology. The increased benefit of adding data sharing might help in getting the sale. Once you have determined that this will happen, plan the migration carefully. Make sure everything goes off without a hitch and that there won't be any problems adding more sites. Once everything is up as tie-line replacements, you can start talking about PBX replacement.

PBX replacement can involve many stages. The first stage is coexistence. It is unlikely, unless it is a completely new location, that an office won't have a PBX already. It is important to evaluate and understand how the two different PBXs can coexist. This is often the means to getting in the door. You should look at things such as:

- Available capacity
- Growth of the company
- Cost of additional phone sets
- Costs involved in upgrading
- Annual maintenance costs

All of these items can incur cost savings when you're moving to a network PBX. Make sure existing IVR devices are accounted for when you're moving. Try to have a test line on which an IVR can be set up and tested before going into the production environment. Because the IVR is the first point of contact for incoming calls, it is absolutely critical that it is set up correctly. You might want to look at the opportunity to introduce a unified messaging solution. Once a few people are online with this system, the news of its features will spread rapidly. Be prepared for an onslaught of users asking for the same functionality.

Either during the implementation phase or after everything is up and running, the time will come to look at other value-added services. What kinds of third-party software have become available that can enhance the functionality of the system? One of the first things to consider is faxing. Look at the call records associated with the fax machine. Of particular interest are the faxes that are being sent to remote offices. Depending on the call traffic, a solution that implements store-and-forward faxing might be appropriate. If data is already being carried over a WAN to the remote office, it should be relatively easy to devise a faxing alternative. If the organization is a large one or one that has a sales call center, Web click-to-talk could enhance the business. By using the power of the Web, things such as HR queries could be made easier. From a sales perspective, Web click-to-talk allows the customers to interact on a more personal note than the sometimes sterile Web interface. Until voice over the Internet is widely available, that might be difficult. But why not implement it at kiosks? Large department stores could have catalog ordering kiosks that are completely automated until the customer has a question. At that point, the customer could use Web click-to-talk. When will voice over the Internet be viable? That's hard to say. It will probably be sooner rather than later, though. Until then, it might be a good alternative to overseas communications, provided the user is prepared for delays and jitter.

Once everything is in place and running smoothly, don't forget monitoring and maintenance. Part of this task involves looking at the call detail records. Much information can be gleaned from this database. You can determine calling patterns, peak hours, duration of calls, and a laundry list of other things. You can use this information to see where you are saving money and where you might be wasting it. Combining the CDR reports with the corresponding bandwidth utilization on circuit can be quite powerful. Maybe you can determine that the 768Kbps CIR Frame Relay circuit never gets above 256Kbps. Or you might see that the reason the users in Denver are complaining of poor performance is that their circuit is overutilized. Without the details, you have no way of knowing. Despite the fact that many people believe network maintenance is a secret art, if you have good, accurate measures of performance, maintenance becomes almost easy.

Don't forget about VoFR and VoATM. These link layer technologies can be very useful in certain circumstances. VoFR can be quite useful when it is designed as a tie-line replacement. It is simple to implement, takes up very little bandwidth, and requires almost no maintenance. The cost savings can be tremendous for such a simple alternative. VoATM is a great alternative when there is an ATM network in place or going to be installed. The closer that ATM gets to the desktop, the better. Furthermore, VoATM is manageable over smaller circuits, but keep in mind it might not be the best solution.

Cisco's IP Telephony offers a full-featured VoIP solution that can match and surpass the capabilities of the traditional PBX. With an open software-based solution, CIPT is constantly evolving with more powerful features. All the while, it uses the same IP network infrastructure that carries data and can be maintained by the same IP staff. Corporations are finding that CIPT's ROI is compelling.

This chapter should have prepared you with general design concepts and solutions that utilize packetized voice. The market is growing so rapidly that new products are introduced all the time. Within a few months or a year, some of the concepts in this chapter will be much more widespread and easier to implement. It is important to start laying the foundation now. The following chapters address the technical issues involved in making these concepts work. As always, the best place to keep on top of new technologies Cisco offers is the company's Web site. You can be sure that the details in this book will only be supplemented and not replaced over the coming years.

Solutions Fast Track

Introduction to Voice Over IP

- ☑ VoIP adds new and valuable telephony features.
- ☑ VoIP provides toll bypass to lower telephony costs.
- ☑ VoIP is a step toward unified messaging.

Common VoIP Implementation Scenarios

- ☑ VoIP implementations include VoFR, VoATM, and point-to-point links.
- ☑ Cisco's VoIP solution is known as Cisco IP Telephony (CIPT).
- ☑ Corporations are deploying IP-based multimedia technologies, including fax and video.

☑ Carriers are integrating wholesale dial and IP transport into traditional networks.

Basic Toll–Bypass Designs

☑ Tie-line replacement offers a key cost saving.

☑ Merging voice and data networks provides cost savings.

☑ Frame Relay provides a low-cost solution for IP telephony.

☑ ATM provides high QoS with moderate cost savings.

☑ Point-to-point leased lines allow IP staff to manage voice networks.

☑ The ROI of IP telephony is very compelling.

Advanced Features and Integration Possibilities

☑ Cisco's IP telephony system allows PBX replacement with advanced features.

☑ Telephony application program interfaces (TAPI) allow integration of powerful features.

☑ Web click-to-talk functions enhance user convenience and further integrate the Internet with telephony.

☑ VoIP features include call transfer, forwarding, and conferencing.

☑ VoIP auxiliary functions include tracing, logging, and generating call detail records (CDRs).

☑ Transcoders allow the real-time translation of one codec to another to support interoperability.

☑ Methods of providing QoS include classification, queuing, and provisioning.

☑ Unified messaging integrates telephony, e-mail, voicemail, and fax into a common system.

Frequently Asked Questions

The following Frequently Asked Questions, answered by the authors of this book, are designed to both measure your understanding of the concepts presented in this chapter and to assist you with real-life implementation of these concepts. To have your questions about this chapter answered by the author, browse to **www.syngress.com/solutions** and click on the **"Ask the Author"** form.

Q: What types of technologies are available to me today? What will be available tomorrow?

A: Quite a bit is available today. Tie-line replacement is typically the simplest way to start. There is no reason you can't replace the entire PBX right now. Some of the more advanced integration tasks might be difficult to implement today but should be easier in the near future.

Q: Will I be able to sell this technology to my boss and customers?

A: Absolutely! The costs associated with packetized voice are small compared with those f traditional voice solutions. The ROI usually has a pretty quick turnaround.

Q: How do I build an ROI?

A: The first and most important step is to gather as much information as possible and organize it.

Q: I'm not going to lose voicemail, am I?

A: Of course not! Cisco's Unity system gives you a completely unified messaging system.

Q: What is unified messaging?

A: Unified messaging is the integration of e-mail, voicemail and faxing. It allows all these services to be accessed through an e-mail client or a phone.

Q: If my voicemail is treated like e-mail, can I forward it to someone?

A: Yes. You can even forward it to individuals who are not on the Unity system. The voice is treated as a .WAV file attachment. Any multimedia computer should be able to play it.

Q: How can I get my e-mail through a phone?

A: Cisco's Unity will read it to you.

Q: Will this work across the Internet?

A: The best answer is maybe. The Internet is an unpredictable environment, and without control, you have no way of guaranteeing timely arrival of the voice packets. It will work, but it might not work well.

Q: My current PBX has another application that tracks usage and bills my customers automatically. Is there anything that can do the same thing?

A: If the application can use a Microsoft Access or other ODBC-compliant database, the same application will work. It might need some reconfiguring.

Q: The application XYZ that I'm running on my PBX was written by the manufacturer. Will it work on the new system?

A: Probably not. That's one of the major drawbacks to traditional PBXs. Nearly all of them have closed, proprietary systems.

Q: What about 911 calls?

A: If the phone system goes down, that's a problem. There must be something called a *lifeline phone circuit* that can be used in case of an emergency, no matter what happens. A gateway allows the PSTN to be used as a backup in case the IP WAN goes down.

Q: How can I have music on hold?

A: Music on hold (MOH) is available today and streams music to both on-net and off-net users on hold.

Q: How committed is Cisco when it comes to voice? Will the company still be making solutions in a few years?

A: Cisco is very committed! Voice solutions are one of its greatest focuses right now, if not the primary focus.

Q: Is packetized voice really going to be that big a deal?

A: If a company like Cisco is focusing a great deal of its efforts on it, it must be. With open standards and lower costs, packetized voice will do what e-mail has done in becoming ubiquitous across all businesses.

Chapter 2

Traditional Voice Telephony Principles

Solutions in this chapter:

- Analog Systems
- Analog Network Components
- Analog Signaling
- Digital Transmission
- Call Control Signaling
- Analog-to-Digital Conversion

☑ Summary

☑ Solutions Fast Track

☑ Frequently Asked Questions

Introduction

Alexander Graham Bell, a native of Scotland, developed the first practical analog telephone in 1876. Bell's now famous outburst, "Mr. Watson, come here, I want you!" brought his assistant Thomas Watson running. Bell's outburst was the result of spilling acid, a component of the very first impractical telephone, on his pants. Watson's urgency wasn't so much in response to Mr. Bell's distressful outburst but more because Bell's voice had been clearly transmitted and reproduced on a crude yet functional telephone receiver in Watson's office. That's right—the first telephone call was a call for help. This fledgling technology not only spawned one of the largest companies on Earth, American Telephone & Telegraph Company (AT&T), but also MCI, LCI, Sprint, GTE, BellSouth, and all the other U.S.-based and international telephone companies. AT&T alone grew into a huge multibillion dollar company providing well over 1 million telephones to the world.

Another tremendous change is now taking place in the telecommunications industry with the integration of voice and data. This chapter details the principles and concepts of analog and digital signals and basic telephone system operation as a prelude to understanding and implementing VoIP using Cisco's core VoIP products. This chapter includes information on traditional voice networking because, to successfully deploy VoIP in networks, you must consider the characteristics and methods of traditional circuit-switched voice networks.

In the business environment, companies have traditionally supported two separate networks: voice and data. However, with the advent of technology, you can be sure that the world of electronic telephony is going to change. Voice and data transmission, their technologies, and the departments responsible for them are merging and in many instances have already been merged. This merging of the two network types is being dictated by the economic benefits of installing and maintaining a single converged network. Before we discuss why these changes are occurring and how to help your customers benefit from this technological innovation, let's firmly ground your understanding of VoIP by exploring analog signaling, digital transmission, call control signaling, and telephone systems operation. Additionally, voice network planning is introduced, along with Erlang B, a formula used to size trunks or circuits in a voice network.

Analog Systems

Analog refers to transmission of electronic information achieved by adding signals of varying frequency or amplitude to a carrier wave of a given frequency.

Traditional broadcast media such as radio, television, and PSTN use analog technology, typically represented as a series of varying sine waves. The term *analog* can be traced to the similarity between the actual fluctuations of the human voice and the "analogous," or comparable, modulation of a carrier wave. The human voice occupies the 20Hz to 20KHz range, with most energy in the 300–3300Hz range. Viewed graphically (Figure 2.1), both the human voice and a modulated carrier wave display periods of little or no activity followed by periods of activity.

Figure 2.1 Analog Sine Waves

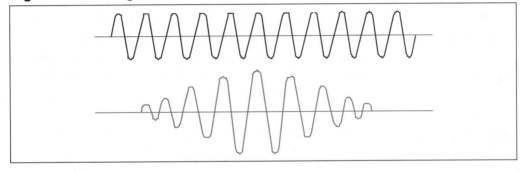

Basic Telephone System Operation

Analog signals are continuous waves that are capable of representing an unlimited number of values. Telephone systems use analog-switched lines to provide voice communications by converting *sound waves*, vibrations that move in the air, into electrical signals. Each telephone handset contains a transmitter covered by a diaphragm and a receiver composed of a coil attached to a speaker cone that vibrates, producing sound waves. When a person lifts the telephone handset to make a call, switchhook contacts are closed, energizing a relay, which prompts a device called a *line searcher* to find an open line. (In the early days, telephone sets had a hook to hold the receiver. Although today's phones no longer have an actual hook to hang the receiver on, the term *switchhook* remains in use.) Then a connection from customer to telephone central office is established and a dial tone is generated. The line finder then prepares the telephone company switching equipment to receive a telephone number.

When a person speaks into a telephone handset, acoustical energy vibrations caused by the person's voice apply varying amounts of pressure to the diaphragm. In response to the natural rise and fall of human speech, the diaphragm in turn converts this pressure into different amounts of current or electrical energy. This variation in the current is in effect an electrical representation of the human voice.

The resulting output of this process is an analog electrical signal. The transmitted signal then flows through the voice coil in the handset of the person receiving the call. The coil attached to the speaker cone in the receiver vibrates in response to the signal to reproduce sound waves, and the person listening to the telephone hears the other person's reproduced voice. To allow the person speaking into the telephone to hear his or her own voice, a small amount of current called a *side-tone* is applied to the transmitting station's receiver; this also helps control the loudness of a person's voice.

Standard telephone cabling is a single pair of twisted-pair copper wiring. The telephone network termination point is an RJ-11 jack. The two–wire connection has two pins, designated *tip* and *ring*. In the early days of the old manual plug-type switchboard, the tip was the tip of the manually inserted plug connector, and the ring was actually the other half of the circuit, just behind the tip of the connector.

Let's do a quick review and break the preceding process down into some simple steps for an analog phone call via a single central office (CO) switch:

1. Both telephone sets are on hook and circuits open.

2. A handset is lifted, causing the switch to close, and current begins to flow. The telephone is then considered to be "off hook." This sends a signal to the telephone company's CO, and the system generates a dial tone.

3. The customer dials a destination telephone number. The resulting signals are received "in band" by the CO switch.

4. The CO that handles the destination phone sends a ringing signal to the destination receiver and a ringing signal to the sender to let him or her know that the call request has been completed and the call is going through.

5. When the call is answered, another signal is sent to the CO to stop ringing and begin the accounting process. The time it takes for the CO to complete the connection between the person calling and the person called is referred to as *call setup time*.

6. When the telephone is put back onto the cradle by either party, the switch is again opened, current ceases, and the dial tone stops. When this occurs, the telephone is considered to be "on hook." The telephone company's CO uses "on-hook/off-hook" information in addition to "called-from" and "called-to" numbers, length of call, and charge per minute or partial minute to generate billing data.

Offices containing more than a few users often use specialized switches designed to share trunk lines to a PSTN. These specialized switches include PBX and key systems. Both these switch types are covered later in the chapter.

Analog Network Components

Let's take a high-level view of a few telephone company components needed to make a connection. We take a more detailed look at analog components later in this book. It is best to start with the end-user instrument, the telephone.

Telephone models come in all shapes, sizes, colors, and prices. A telephone can be a basic push-button wall unit or an integrated system complete with answering machine, stored-number dial, speaker phone, and 900MHz cordless operation. In some countries, telephones are leased, but U.S. consumers usually purchase their phones. Some U.S.-based companies even give away telephones in exchange for fixed-length service contracts.

The next component we need to examine is the connection from the end-user telephone to the telephone pole. This wire or underground cable running from the house to the telephone pole is called a *drop wire*. A commercial business can also have a *demarcation point*, or a point at which personal responsibility for the telephone, line, and equipment ends and the telephone company's responsibility begins. The drop wire coming from a house may then be combined into several distribution cables, called *feeder cables*, for transmission and then connected to the CO. Transmission media to the CO may be guided via twisted-pair, coaxial cable, or fiber, or they can be unguided directional via microwave or satellite or unguided omnidirectional via broadcast or cellular radio. If guided transmission is used via twisted-pair, the feeder cable typically consists of from 4 to 3000 copper-wire pairs varying in size from 16 American Wire Gauge (AWG) with a wire diameter of .05082 inches to 26 AWG with a diameter of .01594 inches. Each individual wire is wrapped in its own polyethylene or polyvinyl insulation.

The CO is the building or buildings containing computerized telephone switching equipment for a predesignated geographical area of responsibility within the greater telephone network. A typical telephone network consists of a multitude of cross-linked and redundantly switched COs, sometimes referred to as *nodes*. Depending on its location in the world, a telephone system node may contain one or more of the telephone switching systems shown in Table 2.1.

Table 2.1 Telephone System Switches

Switch	Description
Basic-NET3	Basic rate switches for the United Kingdom and Europe
Basic-5ESS	AT&T basic rate switches
Basic DMS100	NT DMS-100 basic rate switches
VN2	French VN2 ISDN switches
VN3	French VN3 ISDN switches
NTT	Japanese NTT ISDN switches
Basic-1TR6	German 1TR6 ISDN switches
Basic-NI1	National ISDN-1 switches
Basic-TS013	Australian TS013 switches (obsolete by Basic-NET3)
Primary-4ESS	Lucent 4ESS switch type for the United States
Primary-5ESS	Lucent 5ESS switch type for the United States
Primary-DMS100	Northern Telecom DMS-100 switch type for the United States
Primary-NET5	NET5 switch type for the United Kingdom, Europe, Asia, and Australia
Primary-NI	National ISDN Switch type for the United States
Primary-NTT	NTT switch type for Japan
Primary-QSIG	QSIG switch type
Primary-TS014	TS014 switch type for Australia (obsolete by Primary-NET5)

If a site has more than a few centrally located users, it can use a specialized on-site switch called a *PBX*. A PBX is capable of connecting telephone sets to each other and to a PSTN. Telephones connected to the PBX have a unique extension number enabling intraswitch phone calls, bypassing the need for an external telephone line. Incoming calls may be sent to an onsite operator or automatically routed using dialed-number information provided by the CO switch. PBXs may also be connected to other PBXs over dedicated trunk lines.

An alternative to the PBX is another specialized switch called a *key system*. Key systems are small telephone switches that allow multiple phone sets to share a number of external phone lines. Each line connected to a key system has its own unique number and can be dialed directly from an outside line. Key systems typically connect to standard phone lines from the local CO and provide the same service a standard telephone provides. Additional features are available depending on the sophistication of the key system controller. Individual telephone sets connect to the key system and have a key (button) for each external phone line. To reach an outside line, customers press the corresponding key to make the connection and receive a dial tone. Incoming calls are typically sent to all phones that have a button for that external line, but they could be directed to a single phone or group of phones. Multifeatured key systems often include transfer, speed-dial, memory-dial, park, hold, and paging features.

Let's recall our earlier discussion; for each node to successfully connect and terminate calls, the nodes must communicate with each other and with customer equipment. We defined this communication process as *signaling*. Signaling between and among switches can take place in-band through the same talk channel or out-of-band through some communication path other than the talk channel. In today's telephone network, terminal equipment signaling is generally in-band, whereas signaling between telephone switches is often out-of-band for security and performance reasons.

Each CO is responsible for managing all telephone calls within its area, either switching the call to the called party within the same exchange or switching the call to a trunk and into another CO's area. The side of the CO closest to the local subscriber is called the *line-side interface* or *local loop*. The side of the CO connecting to another CO is called the *trunk-side interface*. Line-side interfaces are primarily responsible for battery feed, over-voltage protection, telephone set ringing, call supervision, signal coding, hybrid two-four wire conversion, and circuit testing.

The battery feed, typically 48 volts DC, coming from the local loop provides power to the customer telephone set, telephone signaling, high AC impedance, and low DC resistance. Most U.S.-based telephone sets require from 10 to 23 milliamps for operation, with 400 ohms of resistance. However, resistance in overseas telephones can and often does vary considerably, ranging from 380 to 800 ohms. Higher or lower resistance demands higher or lower voltages for proper telephone transmitter operation.

Over-voltage protection protects the people using the telephone, as well as the equipment, from transient voltages due to short circuits, lightning surges, and electrical power lines. In addition to over-voltage protection, the CO provides the ringing signal to the subscribers' telephone as an alert for incoming calls. The ringing signal, typically 90 volts rms at 20Hz, is provided after switching completes the connection. Should the connection not go through, the telephone goes off-hook. If the call goes through but the called party hangs up, the CO must sense the absence or presence of current flow and take the appropriate supervisory action.

Designing & Planning…

Network Planning

What factor does an engineer try to optimize when he or she designs a network? For voice networks, the goal has been to minimize cost. For data networks, the first goal is to achieve connectivity and the secondary issue is to minimize delay or to meet some reliability objective. Because the traditional voice network is rich and robust and because connectivity is assumed, economic considerations have always been of the highest importance. The economics of the voice network have always been of paramount importance to voice network operators and customers. Whereas the benefits of new data applications have always dominated, the focus of managers has been on "cost per minute" of voice.

Every startup network begins by having circuits between every pair of nodes. When the network grows beyond seven nodes or so, it becomes unwieldy and uneconomical because some cross-sections of the network have so little demand that some circuits are underused. Then perhaps some connections of the complete topology will not be established, and for this "mesh" network, some arbitrary alternative routing rules will be constructed to accommodate overflows. The dangers of this step in the evolution of a network is that circular routings can occur, it isn't scalable, the network behavior under congestion can become unstable, and the undisciplined routing strategy usually resides in the mind of a single person.

Fixed hierarchical routing (FHR) is a method of implementing hierarchical structures, which produce easy-to-understand, manageable, and highly efficient networks. Most networks in the world use FHR or a variant of it. It protects against cyclic routing and behaves in a sane and predictable way when congestion occurs.

The following is the definition of a classic FHR network: At the highest layer of the hierarchy is a complete graph of final routes, with no alternative routing. Between any two switches in the network, then, there is a unique path along final routes, climbing the hierarchy on one side of the network, crossing at the highest level, and then descending the other side to the destination.

Additionally, if demand warrants it, other routes, called *high-usage routes*, can present. These are tried before final routes and are engineered to overflow onto other high-usage routes or, ultimately, to finals in the busy hour.

Continued

The network is based on a forecast of demand. How much traffic does the network need to carry? The first job is to translate these (probably financial) forecasts into engineering units, whether bits, packets, minutes, or Erlangs. The demand matrix is a point-to-point estimate of where traffic originates and terminates and at what volumes.

Design calculations in the case of a traditional voice network consist of multiple Erlang B (or variant) calculations. For a 20-node network, thousands of such calculations may be performed by an automatic tool, sizing high-usage routes, overflowing traffic onto finals, and so on. The results give trunk quantities for all the final and high-usage trunk groups in the network.

By comparing the design outputs with the existing network, the necessary changes are calculated, then applied in terms of switch or circuit provisioning, routing table updates, and so on.

Finally, the network's database is updated, and measurements are collected and analyzed, so the next iteration will have a better demand matrix on which to operate (that is, not based solely on forecasts).

Voice Encoding: Standards and Techniques

Speech codecs, sometimes called *voice encoders* or *vocoders* if source codecs are used, can be divided into three basic classes: waveform, source, and hybrid. *Waveform codecs* are older, operationally used high bit rates and provide very good-quality speech reproduction. *Source codecs* operate at very low bit rates but tend to produce speech that sounds artificial or tinny. *Hybrid codecs* use techniques from both source and waveform coding, operate at intermediate bit rates, and provide good-quality speech.

Codecs operate by modeling a segment of the speech waveform on the order of 20ms. Speech model parameters are then estimated, quantized (that is, the set of values is limited), coded, and transmitted over a communications channel. The receiver then decodes the transmitted values and reconstructs synthesized speech.

Waveform Encoding

Pulse code modulation (PCM) codecs are the simplest waveform codecs. This approach to voice encoding simply samples and quantizes the input waveform. Narrowband speech is typically sampled 8000 (8KHz) times per second, and each speech sample is quantized. If linear quantization is used, about 12 bits per sample are needed, giving a bit rate of about 96kbps. However, this amount can be easily reduced using nonlinear quantization. For coding speech with nonlinear quantization, 8 bits per sample is sufficient for resulting speech quality nearly indistinguishable from the original signal. That is to say, the typical human ear cannot distinguish a noticeable difference. The preceding example results in a bit rate of 64kbps.

Two nonlinear PCM codecs were standardized in the 1960s: *u-law* in the United States and *A-law* in Europe. Because of their simplicity, excellent quality, and low delay, codecs using these algorithms are still widely used today. One example of PCM use is the .AU audio file format used to transport sounds via the Web. These audio files are PCM-encoded files. PCM codecs are simple, introduce very little delay, and reproduce high-quality speech. The only drawback to PCM codecs is that they require a relatively high bit rate and are highly susceptible to channel or line errors.

Other waveform approaches to speech coding predict the value of the next sample from previous samples. This approach works as a result of repeated vocal patterns present in each speech sample. If predictions are correct, error signals between predicted and actual samples will have lower variance than the original speech samples and the error signal may be quantized with fewer bits than the original speech signal. *Differential pulse code modulation (DPCM)* uses this technique to quantize the difference between original and predicted signals.

Improvements to the preceding codec technique can be made if the algorithm can adapt to match the characteristics of the coded speech. *Adaptive differential PCM (ADPCM)* codecs use this approach, resulting in a 32kbps transmission rate and providing speech quality very near the 64kbps PCM codecs. ADPCM codecs operating at 16, 24, and 40kbps are also now in use.

Source Encoding

Source codecs operate using a model of source signal generation that extracts the model parameters from the signal being coded. Model parameters are then transmitted to the decoder on the receiving end. Sometimes called *vocoders*, source codecs represent the vocal tract as a time-varying filter excited with white noise source for unvoiced speech segments, or a series of pulses separated by the pitch period for vocalized speech. Information sent to the decoder includes filter specification, a voiced/unvoiced flag, the necessary variance of the excitation signal, and the pitch period for voiced speech. This information is continually updated every 10ms to 20ms, following the nonstationary nature of speech.

Vocoders operate at 2.4kbps or less and produce acceptable but far from natural speech. Increasing the bit rate much beyond 2.4kbps is not possible due to limitations in the codec's performance and the simplified source signal model. Vocoders are typically found in military applications for which a very low bit rate is needed to support signal encryption.

The quality of speech generated using analog-to-digital encoding is subjective. That means that the reaction you get will vary depending on individual likes, dislikes, and what a person considers to be normal. To help quantify the quality of a given technique, the mean opinion score (MOS) scale was developed. To compile the MOS numbers, listeners listen to various speech patterns sent through each compression technique. The test listeners then rate the quality of the sound on a scale of 1 to 5, with 5 being the best. The results are averaged to produce the MOS. Table 2.2 includes the current ITU encoding standard compression techniques and each technique's bit rate, MOS, coding delay, and the processing power required for compression.

Table 2.2 Voice Encoding

Coding	ITU-T Standard	Bit Rate (kbps)	OS	MIPS	Frame Size (msec)	Coding Delay (msec)
ACELP	G.723.1	5.3	3.65	16	30	30
MP-MLQ	G.723.1	6.3	3.9	16	30	30
CS-ACELP	G.729a	8	3.7	10.5	10	10
CS-ACELP	G.729	8	3.92	20	10	10
LD-CELP	G.728	16	3.61	33	.625	3-5
ADPCM	G.726	32	3.85	14	.125	1
PCM	G.711	64	4.1	.34	.125	.75

Cisco's voice-enabled routers currently support G.711, G.726, G.728, G.729, G.729a, and G.723.1 coding schemes.

PCM uses the most bandwidth yet receives the best MOS rating. PCM uses the least amount of processing power and introduces the least amount of latency. These factors have made PCM inexpensive to deploy and highly effective in transporting voice traffic over long distance. By contrast, CS-ACELP provides significant bandwidth savings at the expense of increased processing requirements, increased latency, and a lower MOS rating.

Conventionally, the local CO is a two-wire switch permitting conversations in both directions over the same pair of wires. When a signal needs to be transmitted over long distances, the signal must be amplified and transmitted over a four-wire configuration. A hybrid transformer designed to permit full-duplex operation performs two- to four-wire conversion.

Four-wire circuits have two pairs of wires for simultaneous conversations in both directions. Physical separation of the transmitter and receiver are needed to process digital and voice and to permit amplifiers to increase signal level. In addition to two- to four-wire conversion, the CO must conduct loop-side testing. Loop-side testing requires access from the local loop to the CO switch to enable fault detection and permit corrective and preventative system maintenance.

Designed to handle 10,000 telephones or more, a CO is typically identified by the first three numbers of a seven-digit telephone number in the United States. For example, 365-*xxxx* might indicate a CO in Wake County, North Carolina. Should the call require switching between two COs, it would use a line called a *toll trunk line*. The CO is actually designed to handle only a portion of the calls it receives. A CO's design is typically based on the amount of projected or measured traffic received at peak hours, from 10:00 A.M. to 11:00 A.M. and from 2:00 P.M. to 3:00 P.M. Multiple COs are connected to provide redundancy and reliability. When all of an individual CO's facilities are in use, the CO is said to be processing a block of calls, or *blocking*. The grade of service provided by the CO is the proportion of blocked calls to attempted calls expressed as a percentage. Most telephone switching equipment is designed to handle individual telephone calls lasting approximately three minutes. (Dialup Internet access really puts a heavy load on telephone company switches as a result of extended connectivity.) Typical days set aside for blocking are Christmas, Thanksgiving, Father's Day, and Mother's Day. As shown in Figure 2.2, the typical analog telephone network consists of these components:

- Telephone handsets

- Drop wires

- Local loops

- A CO consisting of an electronic switch system (ESS), analog and digital carrier system, DC voltage generation units, and billing, monitoring, and line maintenance computer systems

- Toll trunks

Figure 2.2 Telephone System Components

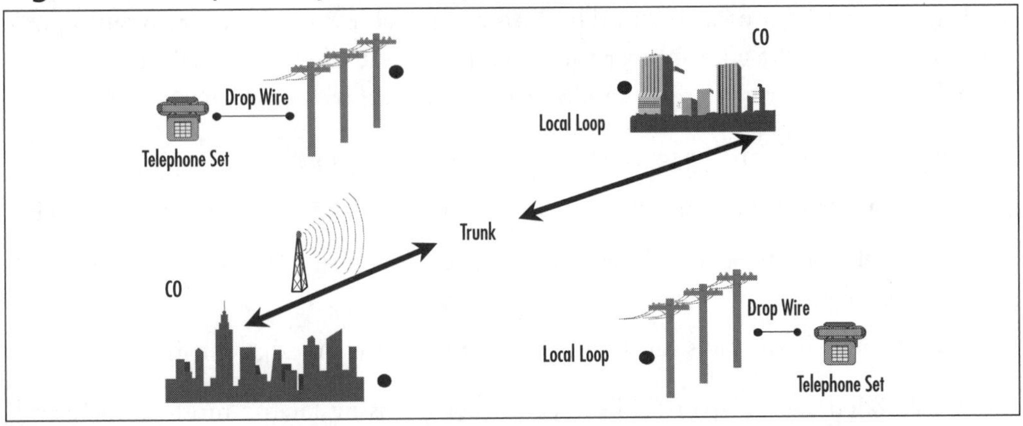

Each telephone CO in North America is described according to an office class and name. Table 2.3 describes a common telephone network hierarchy.

Table 2.3 Telephone Network Exchange Class Hierarchy

Class	Name
1	Regional center
2	Sectional center
3	Primary center
4C	Toll center
4P	Toll point
4X	Intermediate point
5	End office

Long distance switching is normally performed by Class 1, 2, 3, and 4 exchanges, with Class 1 holding the topmost position of the telephone switching tree. A mixture of Class 2, 3, 4, and 5 exchanges may occupy Layer 2 of the hierarchy, with Class 4 and Class 5 variations at the bottom of the tree.

Cabling

Consider some scenarios: It's time to upgrade your current analog voice system, or you've been handed a major project involving voice transmission that involves a state-of-the-art automated assembly plant. A major question to ask yourself is: "What medium should I use: shielded or unshielded coaxial cable, twisted-pair copper, or fiber optic cable?"

Let's look at copper cable. The efficiency of copper has a great deal to do with the length of the cable run. The longer the cable run, the more likely signal distortion will occur. The shorter the cable run, the better the signal quality. Signal distortion across copper cabling can be caused by any of the following:

- **Attenuation** Loss of amplitude or signal strength.

- **Capacitance** The variation in the amount of energy stored in the wire.

- **Delay distortion** Resistance, which can cause frame sequencing problems.

- **Noise** External sounds and/or transmissions on adjacent lines.

Unshielded twisted-pair (UTP) copper wiring is by far the most popular and least expensive copper cabling option. Copper UTP wiring contains eight color-coded conductors (four twisted pairs of copper wires). It offers greatly increased bandwidth, compared with outdated quad wiring often found in old installations. UTP cable is roughly 3/16 inch in diameter, inexpensive, and easily pulled through conduit and overhead trays. Category 5 (Cat 5) is the current standard but will soon be supplanted by even higher-speed versions, known as Category 5E and Category 6. Cat 5 has an approved bandwidth of 100MHz; Cat 6 will likely accommodate approximately 250MHz. Remember, increased bandwidth equates to increased speed. Cat 6 wiring, with encoding, will be able to carry at least 1Gb, or roughly 50,000 text pages, per second. When installing Cat 5 wiring, use these general guidelines:

- Apply 25 to 40 pounds of pull when installing in conduit or plenum.

- Separate data and power cables by at least 6 inches. When it's necessary to cross data and power cables, cross them at 90-degree angles.

- Strip cable sheathing no further than needed, or a maximum of 1.25 inches.

- Untwist wire a maximum of 0.5 inch.

- Bend wiring a maximum radius of 1 inch.

These are just general guidelines. If you need additional information, surf the Web for information on EIA/TIA 568A cabling installation standards.

Cable pathways including underground routes, conduits and tray ways, access flooring, and equipment closets are covered in EIA/TIA 569.

If your project calls for installation of telecommunications cabling in areas with close proximity to electromechanical or high-voltage interference similar to those normally found on the floor of a factory or assembly plant, you can use a fiber optic transmission medium to overcome interference from this type of noise. Fiber optic cabling uses a light-emitting diode (LED) or laser-generated light for voice and data transmission. Fiber optic is an excellent high-speed medium choice, and the installation cost per foot continues to drop.

Fiber optic cabling also has very low signal loss compared to conventional twisted-pair or coaxial cabling. Low signal loss permits greater separation between signal repeaters, resulting in lower equipment cost. Optical fiber does not radiate electrical energy, is noninductive, and does not conduct electricity. Fiber is also free from crosstalk, which can plague twisted-pair installations, and is far more secure because it is not easily tapped without a noticeable drop in signal. In a local area fiber installation multimode (62.5/125 um), fiber optic cable could be used with SC connectors. Beyond 200m, a mixture of single mode (9/125 um) and multimode should be considered.

Have you ever seen the popular "Hear a pin drop …" commercial and wondered how that kind of sound quality is achieved? Let's take a quick look.

Optical fibers guide light rays through the plastic or glass fiber optic material. The speed at which light is propagated through a fiber is dependent on the type of material used. The more pure and exact the material, the faster the propagation. This phenomenon is called *refraction*. Refraction can be measured using Snell's Law, which states: "The ratio of the sine of the angle of incidence to the sine of refraction is equal to the ratio of the propagation velocities of the wave in the two respective media." This is equal to a constant, which is the ratio of the refractive index of the second medium to that of the first:

$$\sin A1/\sin A2 = V1/V2 = K = n2/n1$$

where *A1* and *A2* are the angles of incidence and refraction, respectively; *V1* and *V2* are the velocities of propagation of the wave in the two media; and *n1* and *n2* are the indices of refraction of the two media. Let's put this law in more simple and usable terms: Light introduced into a fiber optic cable will be totally contained within the core of the cable when the angle of incidence is greater than the critical angle.

An optical fiber is a dielectric waveguide consisting of core, cladding, and sheath. A light source (usually an LED or laser) emits light at multiple angles relative to the core of the fiber. The angle at which light enters an optical fiber is called its *mode of propagation*. Therefore, the size of the fiber optic core has direct correlation to whether light rays (voice or data signals) are reflected back at an angle necessary to permit the rays to remain within the fiber and bounce toward their destination or in some cases be absorbed by the cladding. For fiber designed to carry light in several modes of propagation (multimode), the diameter of the core must be several times the wavelength of the light to be carried and the cladding thickness greater than the radius of the core. A typical multimode fiber is 50 um to 100 um in diameter. Rays traveling in a multimode fiber bounce at different angles and arrive at the end of the fiber at different times. An effect called *modal display spreading* can occur as light rays leaving the fiber cross or cancel each other.

Alternatively, a single-mode fiber contains a core only a few times the wavelength of the transmitted light waves. Only one light ray is carried at a time, with none of the previously defined modal display spreading. In addition to this difference, single-mode fibers are prone to permit a large fraction (20 percent) of the light to travel in the cladding near the core, whereas in multimode fibers most of the light travels in the core of the fiber. This is worth mentioning because a significant increase (doubling) in light traveling in a single-mode cable also significantly increases the percentage (50 percent) of light traveling in the cladding. A PSTN uses a combination of twisted-pair and fiber optic cabling within its system to transmit voice signals.

Designing & Planning…

Cabling Standards and References

The PC revolution put a computer, and sometimes two, on every desk, turning each node into a sender and receiver of digitized information. Corporate productivity, and in some cases survivability, is forever tied to the efficiency of this information flow. As you've seen, some of the limitations in our current analog telephone system are a direct result of the cabling found there. Demand for greater bandwidth and higher speeds that support delay-sensitive traffic (such as voice) has also never been greater. Requests for 100Mb to the desktop are commonplace, but because of outdated technology, consumers don't always get what they ask for. Selecting the proper transmission medium is imperative today. To do that you need access to the following cabling standards and references:

Continued

- **ANSI/EIA/TIA 568 A** Commercial building telecommunication wiring standard for building and campus applications up to 10 million square feet and up to 50,000 users. U.S. only.
- **IS 11801** Generic customer premises cabling. International.
- **ANSI/TIA/EIA 569** Commercial building standard for telecommunication pathways and spaces.
- **ANSI/TIA/EIA 606** Administration standard for commercial building telecommunication infrastructure.
- **ANSI/TIA/EIA 607** Commercial building grounding and bonding requirements for telecommunication.
- **BICSI** Building Industry Consulting Service International.

Analog Signaling

The term *signaling* refers to the specific signals transmitted over telephone circuits that are used to pass line control information, user data, and voice conversations. On the PSTN local loop, recall that an open circuit with no current flowing indicates an on-hook condition (telephone handset placed in the cradle). Off-hook (telephone receiver off the cradle) is indicated by a closed circuit with current continuously flowing. Early telephone systems using dial-pulse (DP) technology periodically encountered problems distinguishing off-hook conditions from delayed dial pulses. Dual-tone multifrequency (DTMF) has generally replaced DP, though it is still utilized in more remote areas. DP and DTMF are the address-signaling methods implemented from telephone to switch in the telephone network. Earth and magnet (E&M) signaling is the most commonly utilized method of analog trunking. Start dial supervision is the line protocol that defines how the equipment seizes an E&M trunk and passes the address signaling information such as DP or DTMF. The main start dial signaling protocols used on an E&M circuit are loop and ground start signaling. These signaling protocols are discussed in more depth in this section. We begin with an overview of analog signal composition.

Analog Signal Composition

Analog signals are continuous varying electrical waves that have amplitude, frequency, bandwidth, phase, and period as characteristics. *Amplitude* measures the loudness of the signal in decibels. It can also be thought of as the level of the signal. Signal level is usually expressed in terms of the power the signal delivers to the data load. For example, the power delivered to a balanced-pair transmission line could be expressed in the following equation:

$$Pload = es^{2/z}$$

where

Pload = Power in watts

es = Signal level in volts

Z = Independence in ohms

Each household telephone in the United States requires the use of a single pair of copper wires. A single pair of copper telephone wires has an impedance of 400 ohms. *Impedance* in an alternating current (AC) circuit is similar to resistance in a direct current (DC) circuit. Signal level in telephone circuits is measured in terms of 1 milliwatt of power to the load. If *Pload* = 1 milliwatt (0.001 watt) and *Z* = 400 ohms, then:

$$1mW = es^{2/400 \text{ ohms}}$$
$$400 \text{ X } 1 \text{ X } 10^{-3} = es^2$$
$$0.4 = es^2$$
$$0.633 = es$$

A signal level of .633 volts applied across 400 ohms of resistance produces 1 milliwatt of power. Too much power on the line can cause a single voice signal to interfere with other conversations traveling on the same wire or wires in close proximity. This type of interference is called *crosstalk*. The reverse of this problem—that is, loss of power on a line during a call—is called *attenuation*.

Frequency is essentially the number of vibrations per second. Frequency is typically diagrammed as a sine wave; each complete wave is called a *cycle*. Frequencies are measured in hertz. The human ear can hear frequencies ranging from 20Hz to 15,000Hz. Speech has a frequency ranging from 300Hz to 15,000Hz. The PSTN supporting voice transmission operates in the 300Hz to 3300Hz frequency range.

Bandwidth is the difference between the upper-level and lower-level frequencies. All transmission media have limited frequency bandwidth. These limitations are due to the physical properties of the medium or artificial limitations placed on the medium to prevent crosstalk or interference from other signal sources. Telephone signal bandwidth may be calculated by subtracting the lower frequency range from the upper frequency range. The result will be typical telephone bandwidth.

For example, to calculate telephone bandwidth, we would use this equation:

$$3300Hz - 300Hz = 3000Hz$$

Claude Shannon developed a formula we can use to calculate the maximum capacity of a transmission channel, limited by bandwidth and random noise:

$$C = W \times Log2[1 + (S/N)] \text{ bits per second}$$

where

C = Capacity

S = Power of the signal in watts through the channel

N = Power of the noise in watts out of the channel

W = Bandwidth of the channel in Hertz

Using this formula, we can calculate the "theoretical" limit to binary transmission on a single channel. This is thought of as a theoretical limit due to the formula's inability to incorporate other significant real-world variables such as transmission medium characteristics, distance, and software and hardware enhancements. This formula should be used only as a rough estimate of the capacity of the designated channel due to the variables not taken into account by Shannon's formula. Let's take a look at an example. Given:

S = .0001 watts

W = 3000 Hertz

N = .0000004 watts

$$3000 \times Log2[1 + (.0001/.0000004)] = 24,000 \text{ bits per second}$$

The PSTN is designed to use frequencies as high as 4000Hz but uses only up to 3000Hz to provide a buffer or guard band to help eliminate interference from other signals. *Signal phase* is the relative position of the sine wave measured in degrees. A *phase shift* occurs when a sine wave breaks in the middle of its phase and starts its cycle again. Phase shifts are used more frequently in data-encoding algorithms for data transmission than for voice transmission. A *period* is the time a signal takes to complete one cycle. PSTN uses analog-switched lines to provide voice communications. Data communication over analog lines has limited transmission speed because of the narrow bandwidth of voice lines.

A modem is required to convert digital data signals generated by the computer into analog signals in transmitting data over telephone lines. Analog signals transmitted over long distances are amplified, often distorting and introducing errors into the original data value. When analog data is converted into digital data, it can be transmitted with the use of digital signals faster and without distortion. Discreet and precise samples of binary data make up the content of the payload. Digital data is precise, but it does not have the informational range available in analog transmission.

During transmission of data or voice signals across hardwired copper telephone wires, the transmission can become corrupted by "noise," such as unwanted electrical or electromagnetic energy that degrades the quality of signal and interleaved data. External noise can be picked up from household or industrial electrical appliances in close proximity to the circuit, from high-voltage electrical transformers, from the atmosphere, and even from outer space, where noise can be generated by solar storms or other magnetic phenomena. Normally this noise is of little or no consequence and the system must adjust. However, during severe thunderstorms or in locations where many electrical appliances are in use, external noise can adversely affect communications to the point of making a copper circuit unmanageable. Internet data transfers can be considerably slowed by noise and numerous data retransmissions. The system must also adjust the data transfer rate to compensate for line errors and cyclic redundancy check (CRC) mismatches introduced by external noise. Noise normally has very little impact on voice conversations, often resulting in a rushing or air-like hissing sound before, during, and after the conversation.

Noise is a more significant problem in wireless systems than in hardwired systems. In general, noise originating from outside the system is inversely proportional to the frequency and directly proportional to the wavelength. In other words, at a low frequency such as 300KHz, atmospheric and electrical noise is much more severe than at a high frequency like 700MHz. Noise generated inside wireless receivers, known as *internal noise*, is less dependent on frequency. Engineers are more concerned about internal noise at high frequencies than at low frequencies because the less external noise there is, the more significant the internal noise becomes.

Telecommunications engineers implement innovative improvements to the voice- and data-to-noise ratio by constantly developing new materials, components, and designs to keep pace with the explosion in household, consumer, and commercial automation. The traditional, straightforward method to reduce transmission noise has been to minimize signal bandwidth. The less bandwidth a signal occupies, the less noise is passed. The obvious downside of this approach is that reducing the bandwidth limits the maximum speed at which data can be delivered, and as we know, consumers are demanding faster transmissions, not slower ones.

E&M Signaling

E&M signaling is not as prevalent in carrier networks as it once, but it is still the most prevalent method of providing analog trunking. E&M signaling can also still be found on inter-PBX tie trunks. E&M signaling is commonly called *ear and mouth* or, more correctly, *earth and magnet*. The *earth* portion of this moniker represents electrical ground; the *magnet* portion represents the electromagnet used to generate tone in the telephone handset. E&M signaling provides signaling states indicating on-hook and off-hook conditions, decreasing the likelihood a two-way trunk will be seized simultaneously at both ends. The telephony term for this condition is *glare*.

COs use reverse-battery DC signaling among local and remote CO exchanges to indicate switched-circuit status. The area CO closest to the party requesting the call selects an idle toll trunk circuit. A polarity change on the trunk indicates to the local CO originating the connection that the called phone is on-hook and ringing or is off-hook and busy. The distant-end CO completes the operation by reversing the voltage polarity to indicate that the called party has answered. For two-way switch-to-switch or switch-to-network connections across long inter-CO and short-haul toll trunks, E&M signaling is used. E&M uses an extra pair of wires in the local and distant-end trunk lines with one designated as the *E lead* and one designated as the *M lead*. The E lead receives signals and the M lead transmits signals.

There are five different types of E&M signaling, each using a different method of indicating on-hook and off-hook conditions between the PBX and the CO switch. E&M signaling is supported in both two- and four-wire implementations. Cisco currently supports four of the five E&M signaling types in its VoIP products.

E&M signaling defines a signaling side and a trunking side for each connection. The PBX is the signaling side; the trunking side is the telco, channel bank, or voice-enabled router. The signaling side sends its on-hook/off-hook indicators over the M lead, and the trunking side sends its on-hook/off-hook indicators over the E lead. This system provides each side of the link with a dedicated signaling path.

E&M uses six to eight pins on an RJ-48 jack, depending on the type of E&M signaling used. Off-hook and incoming calls are signaled using one of the five types of E&M signaling. E&M interfaces typically don't use a dial tone but instead use immediate-start, wink-start, or delay-start signaling to indicate an off-hook state or to indicate incoming calls.

Let's take a look at the five types of E&M signaling:

- **Type I** E&M Type I signaling is popular in the United States. During inactivity, the E lead should be open and the M lead should be connected to ground. A PBX indicates an off-hook condition by connecting the M lead to the battery. The router or CO side indicates an off-hook condition by connecting the E lead to ground.

- **Type II** E&M Type II signaling is also used in the United States. During inactivity, both the E and M leads should be open. A PBX indicates an off-hook condition by connecting the M lead to the SB lead, which is connected to the battery at the CO side. The router or CO side indicates an off-hook condition by connecting the E lead to SG, which is connected ground at the PBX side. Type II signaling is symmetrical and allows for signaling nodes to be connected back to back using a crossover cable.

- **Type III** E&M Type III signaling is not commonly used in modern systems. During inactivity, the E lead is open and the M lead is set to ground by connecting it to the SG lead from the CO. A PBX indicates an off-hook condition by disconnecting the M lead from the SG lead and connecting it to the SB lead from the CO. The router or CO side indicates an off-hook condition by connecting the E lead to ground.

- **Type IV** E&M Type IV signaling is not currently supported by Cisco's VoIP router interfaces

- **Type V** E&M Type V signaling is used in the United States and is common in Europe. During inactivity, both the E and M leads should be open. A PBX indicates an off-hook condition by connecting the M lead to ground. The router or CO side indicates an off-hook condition by connecting the E lead to ground. Type V signaling is symmetrical and allows for back-to-back connections using a crossover cable.

Use of the extra wire pair enables both local and distant ends to signal on- and off-hook conditions. With this approach, control signals may be sent in both directions without interfering with control signals going in the opposite direction. Noise problems with common ground may also be avoided by use of two wires for each single signal. E&M signaling states are displayed in Table 2.4.

Table 2.4 E&M Signaling

State	E Lead: Inbound	M Lead: Outbound
On-hook	Open	Ground
Off-hook	Ground	Battery voltage

Signaling rate is the number of times per second a signal on a circuit changes amplitude, frequency, or phase. *Tone signaling* uses single-frequency or multiple-frequency tones to indicate control and line status. The CO sends a continuous or intermittent tone or tones to the calling telephone to indicate call status. To indicate a functioning line in the United States, the CO sends a continuous tone called a *dial tone* by combining a 350Hz tone with a 440Hz tone. To indicate a busy signal or off-hook condition, the CO sends a 480Hz tone combined with a 620Hz tone in intermittent half-second increments. If the receiver remains off-hook for more than a few minutes, the busy signal changes to a much louder 400Hz, 2060Hz, 2450Hz, and 2600Hz combination tone. Table 2.5 shows call progress tones.

Table 2.5 Call Progress Tones

Tone	Frequency	On Time	Off Time
Dial	350 + 440	Continuous	N/A
Busy	480 + 620	0.5 seconds	0.5 seconds
Normal ringback	440 + 480	2 seconds	4 seconds
PBX ringback	440 + 480	1 seconds	3 seconds
Toll congestion	480 + 620	0.2 seconds	0.3 seconds
Local call reorder	480 + 620	0.3 seconds	0.2 seconds
Receiver off-hook	1400 + 2060 + 2450 + 2600	0.1 seconds	0.1 seconds
Number doesn't exist	200 to 400	Continuous frequency modulated at 1Hz	N/A

COs commonly use either in-band or out-of-band tone signaling to indicate signal status. In-band signaling most commonly uses a 2600Hz tone; out-of-band signaling uses a 3700Hz tone. E&M signals use a single-frequency tone for transmission on carrier-based systems. A tone indicates on-hook; a lack of tone indicates off-hook. If multifrequency tone signaling is used, frequencies are used in pairs between toll facilities to indicate numbers 0 through 9 and additional control functions. Multifrequency tones include 700Hz, 900Hz, 1100Hz, 1300Hz, 1500Hz, and 1700Hz.

This type of signaling is rapidly being replaced due to its susceptibility to misuse by hackers, crackers, and phone "phreaks." Perhaps the most famous case of telephone system misuse can be attributed to a man who went by the code name "Captain Crunch." AT&T formerly used a 2600 Hertz (cycles per second) steady signal to indicate a telephone line was not currently in use. No signal on a line could be interpreted to indicate a pause in a voice conversation or a line not in use, so AT&T elected to use a steady 2600Hz signal on all its free lines. It didn't take long for this information to make its way to people determined to circumvent AT&T call charges. These people soon developed a way to use a whistle or other device to generate a 2600Hz tone on a line that was already in use, making it possible to call anywhere in the world on the line without being charged. Cracking the phone system became a hobby for some in the mostly under-20 set who came to be known as *phreaks*.

In the 1960s, Captain Crunch breakfast cereal included a small whistle as a freebie for kids who bought the cereal. By coincidence, the whistle was capable of generating a 2600Hz signal. By dialing a number and then blowing the whistle, you could fool the phone company into thinking the line was not being used while you made a free call to any destination in the world. Thus "Captain Crunch" found a cheap tool to circumvent the telephone company's billing system.

Loop and Ground Start

There are two basic methods for detecting subscriber off-hook and initiating a series called *busy notification* or billing tasks: loop start lines and ground start lines. *Loop start lines* signal off-hook by completing a circuit at the telephone. When the subscriber lifts the handset, current flows from the loop-side battery through the closed switchhook contacts and energizes the line relay. A set of line relay contacts close, signaling that the subscriber desires service. A CO switch called a *line finder* provides dial tone and connects the subscriber into CO switching equipment and onto an available circuit.

Used on local loops to connect PBXs to the CO, *ground start lines* are, in effect, partially operational at all times. Current flows through one-half the line relay as a result of grounding the ring-side path. When a PBX needs connectivity, the CO line finder provides dial tone and connectivity to CO switching equipment. When a dial tone is detected, the ground start contact is opened and the remainder of the line is instantly activated.

Dialing supervision is accomplished through the use of three relays. One of these relays is fast acting and two are slower-acting relays. When dial-pulse signaling is used, it can be very hard to distinguish a dial-pulse signal break and an on-hook situation. To overcome this challenge, the fast-acting relay, which we will call Alpha, energizes when the circuit is closed. The receiver going off-hook closes the circuit. Alpha then mimics each dial pulse by opening or closing as the dial-pulse contacts open and close the circuit. The second relay, which we will call Bravo, energizes when Alpha energizes but is slow to release after the pulse. In fact, the Bravo relay does not release unless the telephone goes on-hook and the Alpha relay has been released for 200 milliseconds. This is how the CO knows when a conversation has ended and the receiver has been placed into the cradle. The last relay, which we will call Charlie, energizes when Alpha and Bravo energize and remains energized as dial pulses are generated. The Charlie relay is used to detect the end of a dial-pulse train and releases only when Alpha remains energized for 200 milliseconds. When dialing is finished, the Alpha relay remains energized for 200 milliseconds. The Charlie relay then releases, indicating that the pulse dial for a single digit is complete. When the call goes through, call answer supervision disconnects the tip ring current (ringing current) and reverses polarity of the wire pair. Call billing typically begins at call *cut through,* or connection to the called party.

Because a portion of the telephone network remains an analog system, some signals must be converted from analog to digital for digital transmission. Voice signals may be coded into serial digital codes for digital transmission, then decoded on the distant end. This function is performed by something called a *codec,* which we discussed earlier in the chapter. To convert an analog code into a digital code, a range of analog voltage levels is divided into individually discrete signal levels. Each level is represented by a unique 8-bit binary code. The original analog signal is sampled for signal levels at precise, regular intervals. The code produced comes out of the codec in parallel each time the input analog signal is sampled. Each signal sample is then converted to its corresponding 8-bit code. Parallel codes are converted into serial form and then transmitted to the distant end. The receiving converter outputs a voltage level for each code received. The voltage level remains constant for each sample period, and the resulting stepped digital square wave is passed through an amplifier and filter to reproduce the original analog signal.

Dial-Pulse Signaling

The telephone network is a system of computerized switching nodes. These nodes communicate with each other in order to coordinate customer call connection, tear-down, and accounting and billing functions. This process is called *signaling.* Two basic methods of address signaling are used to place a telephone call: older and fast-fading dial pulse (DP) and the more popular dual-tone multi-frequency (DTMF).

When you use DP, a circuit opens and closes the exact same number of times as the number of the digit dialed (with just one exception, as we will note later). For example, if someone dials 1-919-555-1212, the switch opens and closes one complete cycle, or about every 100 milliseconds, as follows: once, nine times, once, nine times, five times, five times, five times, once, twice, once, twice. This concept is pretty straightforward so far, but as mentioned earlier, there is one exception to the circuit open/circuit closed rule: When you dial the number 0, up to 10 pulses may be sent to represent the dialed digit. Each open switch period is called a *break interval,* and each closed switch period is called a *make interval.*

Telephone company equipment senses and decodes the number of pulses between numbers dialed based on an incredibly small timed delay between each number dialed. The timed interval between dialed numbers is approximately 700 milliseconds. As a comparison, 1 second is equal to 1000 milliseconds, so the delay between dialed numbers is calculated at 0.7 of a second.

Each time a DP contact interrupts the flow of loop current, a voltage spike occurs. These voltage spikes can cause the telephone bell ringer to ring very softly, or *tinkle.* "Antitinkle" circuits are integrated into the circuitry of a DP system and designed to close when the dial is operated. Often used with a speech-muting circuit designed to eliminate dial-induced clicking on the receiver, an antitinkle circuit shunts a 340-ohm resistor across the ringer coil to prevent dial-produced current from reaching the bell.

Originally conceived and developed to operate electromechanical switches, dial pulses are limited by the mechanical speed of the switch—a very slow operational rate of 8 to 10 dial pulses per second. I can easily recall my grandmother's large black WW II style DP phone and the slow yet sure speed of the rotary dial as it returned to its original location after letting your fingers do the numeric walking. In today's fast-paced telecommunications environment where faster equates to better, this method of signaling and outdated telephone equipment has become far too slow.

Dual-Tone Multifrequency

DP and its associated technology have been almost entirely replaced by DTMF. DTMF uses an audible two-tone signal to indicate a single number. Two audible tones are placed on the line to indicate the key pressed. For instance, if you dial the number 1, the higher-frequency tone placed on the line will be 1209MHz, whereas the lower-frequency tone associated with the number 1 will be 697MHz, as referenced in Table 2.6.

Table 2.6 DTMF Tones

		High-Frequency Tones			
		1209MHz	1336MHz	1477MHz	1633MHz
	697MHz	1	2	3	A
Low-Frequency Tones	770MHz	4	5	6	B
	852MHz	7	8	9	C
	941MHz	*	0	#	D

Telephone company computers decode the signals and make the desired connection, resulting in higher number-dialed to number-connected accuracy, with much quicker call setup and connection time. Additionally, DTMF is humanly faster to dial than DP. Using DTMF, a telephone system can recognize a single digit tone in 50 milliseconds or less with a typical between-digit wait time of another 50 milliseconds or less. The maximum time needed to process a single DTMF digit is 100 milliseconds, or approximately 1/10 of a second. For a DP call, the pulse requires a 60-millisecond break and a 40-millisecond make for each dial pulse, or a total of 100 milliseconds per dial pulse. This becomes significant for high digits in a telephone number such as the extreme example of 999-999-9999. Nine pulses for every digit and a 700-millisecond wait time between digits would result in a significantly longer dial time.

For example, here is a look at a dial-pulse calculation:

(9 pulses per digit) x (100 milliseconds per pulse) x (10-digit number) = 9 seconds

(700 millisecond interdigit wait time) x (10-digit number – 1) = 6.3 seconds

Total dial-pulse time = 9 + 6.3 = 15.3 seconds

Now here is a DTMF calculation:

(10-digit number x 100 milliseconds per number) = 1 second

Total DTMF time = 1 second, or less with improvements in computer processing

Configuring & Implementing...

Erlang B

The unit of volume for telephony traffic is the Erlang, named for A. K. Erlang (1878–1929); it is one hour of two-way conversation in the busy hour. The busy hour is the (usually clock) hour that has the maximum traffic. Data volumes are expressed in terms of bits, bytes, packets, or frames per second. The Erlang B formula is used to dimension trunks in a traditional voice network. The process of dimensioning of trunks should not be confused with determining the number of lines needed; the term *dimensioning* refers to the calculation of trunks needed in a trunk group to carry *x* Erlangs of traffic. A trunk has a switch at both ends, whereas a line has a switch at one end and a telephone at the other end. There is no calculation for number of lines needed, because the carrier is only concerned with the quantity of trunks needed to give the necessary capacity. Because it looks intimidating and because it is hard to calculate from the formula, it has been widely tabulated, and voice traffic engineers have used Erlang B tables for many years. In the United States and Canada, the unit of traffic historically has been (and is still) the CCS or hundred call seconds, which is one thirty-sixth of an Erlang. (3600 call seconds in the busy hour equal 1 hour of conversation in the busy hour, or 1 Erlang.)

Since Erlang B gives the blocking probability when *A* Erlangs of traffic are offered to *S* channels, the practice has been to determine the offered load, then find an *S* giving a sufficiently low value of *B(S,A)*—say, 1 percent. Erlang *B* traffic tables show the number of circuits needed to give a specific blocking probability for the expected offered load.

Offered load in Erlangs is denoted as *A*, the number of voice channels as *S*, and the blocking probability as *B*. Note that *B* depends on both *S* and *A*.

Since *B(S,A)* is the probability of blocking or the proportion of traffic that is blocked when an Erlang of traffic is offered to a group of *S* channels, the offered load multiplied by this probability gives the volume of traffic that is actually blocked. The rest is carried.

The recursion formula for Erlang B is extremely useful. It calculates the blocking probability for *N* channels from the blocking probability for *N-1* channels. So, if you know the blocking probability when 100 Erlangs of traffic are offered to 120 channels, you can use that figure to calculate the blocking probability when that same 100 Erlangs of traffic are

Continued

offered to 121 channels. Of course, the Erlang B formula for 100 Erlangs of traffic offered to 120 channels (expected to be small) is very difficult to calculate. The numerator A to the power S divided by S factorial is 100 to the power 120 divided by 120 x 119 x 118 x 117 x and so on, or 1 followed by 240 zeros divided by 120 x 119 x 118 x and so on. The denominator is a sum of 120 terms that all look like that one! But the recursion helps: It's easy to calculate the blocking probability with zero channels—it's 100 percent. With that, you can calculate blocking with one channel, then that result helps you calculate blocking with two channels, and so on.

For some applications, alternative engineering rules to Erlang B are used. In fact, sophisticated tools use a variant of Erlang B for final trunk group calculations because the overflow loads they are offered are not generated according to a Poisson process but rather according to the superposition of multiple "interrupted" Poisson processes.

Engset accounts for the fact that in a small population of users, if there are calls in process, the arrival rate of new calls must go down— there aren't as many people capable of making calls because they're on the phone already. The Engset model is useful for small key systems or for engineering small wireless base stations for fixed access.

Digital Transmission

Digital transmission has continually increased in use since its introduction in 1962. With a digital transmission (as opposed to analog) system, we are able to manage the quality of the signal by managing the transmission impairments. Digital transmission breaks data down into a series of 0s and 1s. Digital transmission is more robust and of better quality than analog transmission. Although digital transmission requires more bandwidth, digital systems are less expensive than analog transmission, and digital transmission is rapidly replacing analog transmission in voice networks. Time division multiplexing, or TDM, a digital transmission technique, and ISDN signaling are the most common elements of a digital communications network. The most widely used digital transmission formats are provided by the T-carrier system and the E-carrier system.

Time-Division Multiplexing

Time-division multiplexing (TDM) is a digital transmission technique for carrying multiple voice, data, or video signals simultaneously over a single carrier line by interleaving bits of each signal in a time-synchronized string.

The technique of carrying two or more signals over a single carrier line is referred to as *multiplexing*. Telephone companies started multiplexing using *frequency-division multiplexing (FDM)* equipment in the 1930s and 1940s to pass several voice channels over a single carrier line instead of having to string multiple lines. Voice calls transmitted over FDM equipment were noisy as a result of atmospheric noise (pops and clicks) picked up in the transmission medium (cable or microwave) and as a result of amplifier noise (hiss) picked up from the analog electronics.

To solve the problem of noise introduced to voice calls transmitted over analog FDM links, digital TDM was introduced in the mid-1960s. Since TDM transports and regenerates voice digitally, it is immune to noise picked up in the transmission medium.

TDM works by converting all signals to a digital format. With digital transmission, any signal is reduced to a unique bit stream using 1s and 0s. With voice, for example, an analog signal in the range of 300Hz to 3,400Hz bandwidth is converted to a 64,000bps digital channel. Twenty-four such 64Kb channels are then multiplexed together in a T1 at great speed, transmitting all voice and data in a "string." In effect, information from up to 24 different sources is placed on a single digital channel, like train cars on a track.

When computers started to be networked together in the 1970s, people needed a reliable means to send data between them. Originally, analog modems operating at 300bps were used. The telephone companies soon realized that they could take advantage of their TDM digital transmission infrastructure to carry data as well as voice, multiplexing several low-speed data circuits into a single 64Kb channel, which was then transmitted as any other 64Kb channel, or consolidating several 64Kb channels to carry high-speed data. The "trunk" used to carry a digital transmission in North America is called T1, with the electrical interface and framing defined in ANSI T1.403. A T1 line can carry 24 fixed voice and data channels, digitized at 64Kb, for an aggregate carrying capacity of 1.544Mb. Outside North America, the trunk used to carry a digital transmission is called an E1, with the electrical interface and framing defined in ITU-T G.703 and G.704. An E1 line can carry 30 fixed voice and data channels, digitized at 64Kb, for an aggregate carrying capacity of 2.048Mb. This is how TDM is able to simultaneously send any type of information—voice, fax, data, and limited-quality video—across one or more 64Kb channels.

The standard unit of bandwidth used for all digital transmission is 64Kb. It is derived from the fact that the voltage of an analog signal must be sampled in time to be accurately recreated digitally. Specifically, an analog signal is sampled at

256 different voltage levels, 8000 times a second. The resulting signal is then transmitted on a pair of twisted wires as a 64Kb digital bit stream. TDM establishes dedicated, point-to-point bandwidth between a sender and receiver that can be leveraged to carry multiple applications simultaneously across a WAN. Telecommunications service providers use TDM to dramatically leverage the carrying capacity of carrier lines and deliver services more cost-effectively. Corporations that require dedicated bandwidth to support substantial voice and data applications also use TDM to leverage the carrying capacity of dedicated lines. In so doing, they effectively reduce their total line requirements and transmission costs.

Integrated Services Digital Network Signaling

Integrated Services Digital Network (ISDN) technology is standardized according to recommendations of the Commité Consultatif International Telegraphique et Telephonique (CCITT), now the International Telecommunications Union (ITU). These recommendations describe the protocols and architecture to implement a worldwide digital communications network. Generally, ISDN networks extend from the local telephone exchange to the remote user and include all the telecommunications and switching equipment in between. ISDN is based on technology developed during the 1970s that was designed to address the problem of how to transport digital services across a telephony infrastructure based on copper wiring originally intended to carry analog signals only.

The high throughput offered by ISDN, rapid call setup, and the high level of accuracy inherent to digital transmission are the main attractions of ISDN technology. With these attributes, ISDN is able to provide more efficient access to information, enabling many different and novel applications while keeping costs in the range of regular telephone line costs. ISDN provides these advantages without requiring huge new investments by telecommunications carriers because it is a technology that leverages existing switching and wiring investments. In fact, ISDN makes better use of carrier resources by doubling the bandwidth potential of existing wiring to subscribers' homes and businesses (the local loop) and reducing the maintenance costs that are associated with analog carrier equipment. For all its novelty, ISDN is a technology whose viability has already been proven in corporate and academic environments in Europe, Japan, Australia, and North America.

With ISDN, voice and data are carried by bearer channels (known as *B channels*) occupying a bandwidth of 64Kb. Some switches limit B channels to a capacity of 56Kb. A data channel (*D channel*) handles signaling at 16Kb or 64Kb, depending on the service type. There are two basic types of ISDN service: Basic Rate Interface (BRI) and Primary Rate Interface (PRI). BRI consists of two 64Kb B channels and one 16Kb D channel, for a total of 144Kb. This basic service is intended to meet the needs of most individual users. In North America, a PRI consists of 23 64Kb B channels and one 64Kb D channel and gives total available bandwidth of 1.544Mb. In Europe and other parts of the world, an E1 provides 31 64Kb B channels and one 64Kb D channel, providing a total aggregate bandwidth of 2.048Mb.

ISDN Reference Points

ISDN devices include terminals, terminal adapters (TAs), network-termination devices, line-termination equipment, and exchange-termination equipment. ISDN terminals come in two types. Specialized ISDN terminals are referred to as *terminal equipment type 1 (TE1)*. Non-ISDN terminals, such as DTEs that predate the ISDN standards, are referred to as *terminal equipment type 2 (TE2)*. TE1s connect to the ISDN network through a four-wire, twisted-pair digital link. TE2s connect to the ISDN network through a TA. The ISDN TA can be either a standalone device or a board inside the TE2. If the TE2 is implemented as a standalone device, it connects to the TA via a standard physical-layer interface. Examples include EIA/TIA-232-C (formerly RS-232-C), V.24, and V.35.

Beyond the TE1 and TE2 devices, the next connection point in the ISDN network is the network termination type 1 (NT1) or network termination type 2 (NT2) device. These are network-termination devices that connect the four-wire subscriber wiring to the conventional two-wire local loop. In North America, the NT1 is a customer premises equipment (CPE) device. In most other parts of the world, the NT1 is part of the network provided by the carrier. The NT2 is a more complicated device that typically is found in digital private branch exchanges (PBXs) and that performs Layer 2 and 3 protocol functions and concentration services. An NT1/2 device also exists as a single device that combines the functions of an NT1 and an NT2.

ISDN specifies a number of reference points that define logical interfaces between functional groups; such as TAs and NT1s. ISDN reference points include the following:

- **R** The reference point between non-ISDN equipment and a TA.
- **S** The reference point between user terminals and the NT2.

- **T** The reference point between NT1 and NT2 devices.

- **U** The reference point between NT1 devices and line-termination equipment in the carrier network. The U reference point is relevant only in North America, where the NT1 function is not provided by the carrier network.

These ISDN reference points are illustrated in Figure 2.3.

Figure 2.3 ISDN Reference Points

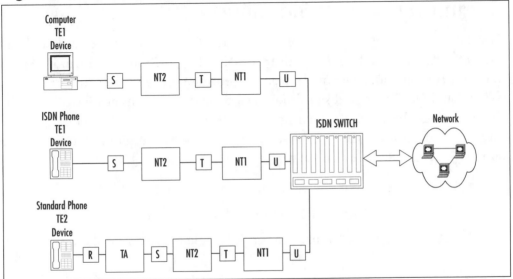

Call Control Signaling

Analog transmission signaling utilizes *Channel Associated Signaling (CAS)*. With the advent of digital transmission, *Common Channel Signaling* (CCS) was developed. This section briefly looks at CAS and provides much more detail on CCS, which is the preferred mode of call control signaling in today's networks.

Channel Associated Signaling

CAS was the only signaling system used until the mid–1970s, although many standards of CAS existed among different countries and within countries. CAS dates back to the early 20th century and was the only form of automatic signaling until 1976, when CCS was introduced. Although CAS is still used today, mostly in underdeveloped countries, it is gradually being replaced by CCS. There are two main characteristics to CAS that differentiate it from CCS:

- CAS signaling is mainly analog.
- CAS signals travel on different paths in the network that carries voice and data services, rather than on a separate network.

CAS is also referred to as *in-band signaling* because signaling information is placed within the actual circuit that is used to carry voice.

Common Channel Signaling

Common channel signaling (CCS), introduced in 1976, was developed as an alternative form of call control signaling for trunks. In CCS, the individual trunks do not carry signaling information. Instead, a signaling network, consisting of signaling data links (SDLs) and signal transfer points (STPs), transfers digital signaling messages between the exchanges. The channel used for CCS does not carry user information. CCS originally evolved from System number 6 to System number 7 as a result of several factors:

- The emergence of digital communication
- The development of intercontinental telephone relations
- The emergence of integrated services digital networks (ISDNs)

Signaling System 7

Signaling System 7 (SS7) is a global standard of CCS for telecommunications that was defined by the ITU Telecommunication Standardization Sector (ITU-T). The standard defines the protocol by which network elements in the PSTN exchange information over a digital signaling network to affect wireless and wireline call setup, routing, and control. The ITU definition of SS7 allows for national variants such as the American National Standards Institute (ANSI) and Bell Communications Research (Telecordia Technologies) standards used in North America and the European Telecommunications Standards Institute (ETSI) standard used in Europe. SS7 defines the architecture, network elements (NE), interfaces, protocols, and management procedures for how a network transports control information between network switches and between switches and databases. The North American version is sometimes called Common Channel Signaling 7 (CCS7).

Signaling across the PSTN is accomplished by two methods: *in-band signaling,* which sends information in the voice band or voice channel, and *out-of-band signaling,* which uses a separate 64Kb data channel. Until the last 10 or 12 years, CAS was the state-of-the-art method used to communicate between switches for the setup and teardown of telephone calls, and it utilized in-band signaling. SS7 is an out-of-band signaling protocol that uses separate data links to support packet signaling between switches and databases (for network services such as the 800 service) and is the preferred signaling protocol of the past dozen years or so.

One of the most powerful capabilities of the SS7 signaling protocol is its ability to deliver additional call-related information across the network. One example of this information is the calling party identification (CPID), which is the telephone number of the party placing the call. If CPID is delivered to the destination office, enhanced call features such as call forwarding, calling party name and number display, and three-way calling are possible. Increased network efficiency is another advantage of SS7. SS7 enables calls to be set up and torn down faster than with CAS, thus utilizing the network more efficiently. Previously, establishing a long distance call involving multiple switches could take 15 to 30 seconds or more, but with SS7 such a call can be reduced to a few seconds or less, thereby providing a higher quality of service and increasing the efficiency of the network. Expensive long-haul trunks are no longer tied up for many seconds during call setup. Additionally, out-of-band signaling eliminated blue-box phone fraud as a source of revenue loss for the phone companies. As we saw earlier, this was an issue because in-band signaling allowed tapping into the signaling and sending tones that would "trick" the network into thinking the call had gone on-hook, thus terminating billing but allowing for continuance of the call.

Signaling Points

Each signaling point in the SS7 network is uniquely identified by a numeric point code. Point codes are carried in signaling messages exchanged between signaling points to identify the source and destination of each message. Each signaling point uses a routing table to select the appropriate path for each message.

There are three kinds of signaling points in the SS7 network:

- Service switching point (SSP)
- Signal transfer point (STP)
- Service control point (SCP)

SSPs are switches (such as DMS-100, 5ESS, GTD-5, AXE, or EWSD) that originate, terminate, or tandem calls. SSPs are a switching system, including any remote modules hosted by the system, that are equipped with SS7 hardware, software, and signaling links. An SSP sends signaling messages to other SSPs to set up, manage, and release voice circuits required to complete a call. An SSP may also send a query to a centralized database (SCP) to determine how to route a call.

STPs are high-speed, ultra-reliable, special-purpose packet switches for signaling messages in the SS7 network. Network traffic between signaling points may be routed via STPs. Network switches and SCPs connect directly to STPs for message routing. An STP routes each incoming message to an outgoing signaling link based on routing information contained in the SS7 message. Because an STP acts as a network hub, it provides improved utilization of the SS7 network by eliminating the need for direct links between signaling points. STPs perform global title translation, a method by which the destination signaling point is derived from the digits in the signaling message. For reliability purposes, STPs are always deployed in mated pairs. Additionally, carriers typically interconnect their SS7 networks via STPs.

SCPs are highly reliable computer and database systems that run service logic programs (SLP) to provide customer services through SSPs. Initially, supporting a database the size and complexity in each switching system in the network was not practical. The local exchange carriers (LECs) decided instead to build centralized databases that could be accessed over the SS7 network to provide 800-number translation functionality. The deployment of these databases form the basis for what is called *advanced intelligent networks (AINs)*. Using the SS7 network as a transport vehicle, the local switches are able to momentarily suspend call processing on a particular call and access application software called SLPs on a SCP. The SLPs instruct the SSP how to proceed with processing the call. In the case of 800-number portability, the local SSP suspends call processing, sends the dialed 800 number to the SCP, and receives the identity of the interexchange carrier (IXC) that should handle the call.

Signaling Links

All SS7 signaling points are interconnected via signaling data links. SS7 messages are exchanged between network elements over 56Kb or 64Kb bidirectional channels called *signaling links*. Signaling links are logically organized by link type (A through F) according to their use in the SS7 signaling network, as illustrated in Figure 2.4.

Figure 2.4 SS7 Signaling Points

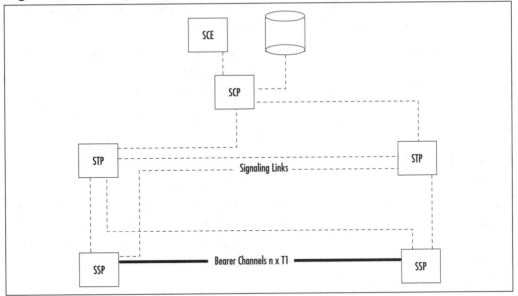

As previously stated, signaling links are logically organized by link type A through F according to their use in the SS7 signaling network. Here are brief descriptions of these link types:

- *Access (A) links* are used between the SSP and the STP, SCP, and STP. These links provide access to the network and to databases through the STP.

- *Bridge (B) links* are used to connect mated STPs to other mated STPs at the same hierarchical level. Bridge links are deployed in a quad fashion.

- *Cross (C) links* connect an STP to its mate STP. They are always deployed in pairs, to maintain redundancy in the network. Normal SS7 traffic is not routed over these links except when congestion on the network exists.

- *Diagonal (D) links* are used to connect mated STP pairs at a primary hierarchical level to another STP mated pair at a secondary hierarchical level. Not all networks deploy D links, since not all networks use a hierarchical network architecture.

- *Extended (E) links* are used to connect to remote STP pairs from an SSP. The SSP connects to its home STP pair but, for diversity, may be connected to a remote STP pair as well, using E links.

- *Fully associated (F) links* are used when a large amount of traffic exists between two SSPs or when an SSP cannot be connected directly to an STP. F links allow SSPs to use the SS7 protocol and access SS7 databases when it's not economical to provide a direct connection to an STP pair.

SS7 Protocol Stack

The SS7 protocol stack is made up of the Message Transfer Part (MTP), the Signaling Connection and Control Part (SCCP), and the Transaction Capabilities Application Part (TCAP). North American networks use the ISDN (ISUP), whereas European networks use the Telephony User Part (TUP). The SS7 protocol elements as dictated by the International Organization for Standardization (ISO) are depicted in Figure 2.5.

Figure 2.5 SS7 Protocol Elements

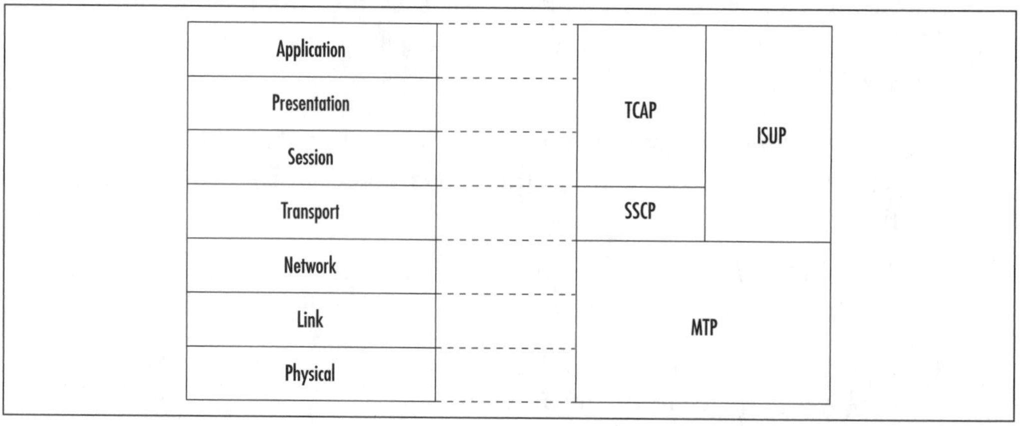

The Message Transfer Part

The MTP is divided into three levels. MTP Level 1, the lowest layer, is equivalent to the OSI physical layer and defines the physical, electrical, and functional characteristics of the digital signaling link. Physical interfaces defined include E-1 (2048kbps; 32 64kbps channels), DS-1 (1544kbps; 24 64kbps channels), V.35 (64kbps), DS-0 (64kbps), and DS-0A (56kbps).

Because central offices are already using DS-1 and DS-3 facilities to link one another, the DS-0A interface is readily available in all central offices and is preferred in the SS7 network. As the demands on the SS7 network increase (local number portability) and as the industry migrates toward ATM networks, the DS1 interface will become the link interface.

The data link level (MTP Level 2) provides the network with sequenced delivery of all SS7 message packets. Like the OSI Data Link layer, it is concerned only with the transmission of data from one node to the next, not to its final destination in the network. Sequential numbering is used to determine if any messages have been lost during transmission. Each link uses its own message-numbering series independent of other links.

SS7 uses CRC-16 error checking of data and requests retransmission of lost or corrupted messages. Length indicators allow MTP Level 2 to determine the type of signal unit it is receiving and how to process it.

MTP Level 3 provides message routing between signaling points and controls traffic when congestion occurs. This is accomplished due to the fact that it also includes mechanisms for flow control and congestion control and procedures for changeover and changeback to enhance reliability. MTP Level 3 is equivalent to the OSI Network layer.

The ISDN User Part

The ISUP defines the protocol to set up, manage, and release trunk circuits that carry voice and data between terminating line exchanges (i.e., between a calling party and a called party). ISUP is used for both ISDN and non-ISDN calls. However, calls that originate and terminate at the same switch do not use ISUP signaling. ISUP includes support for ISDN supplementary voice services and interoperates with Q.921 and Q.931. ISUP supports both basic bearer services and supplementary services for voice and nonvoice applications. In addition, circuit-switched telephone service and data services are also supported. ANSI adopted ISUP to replace the TUP. The TUP does not support data transmission or digital circuits. The ISUP added the parameters necessary to support digital circuits and data transmission.

The ISUP does not support broadband technologies such as Frame Relay and ATM. Broadband ISUP (B-ISUP) addressed these technologies. To support the new broadband ISDN (B-ISDN) and ATM architectures, the ISUP protocol was modified. The most significant difference between the ISUP and the B-ISUP protocols is in the circuit assignment and the type of circuits supported. ATM and broadband ISDN circuits are virtual circuits rather than physical circuits. The network must be capable of assigning and maintaining these virtual circuits. Because of the number of circuits available in broadband networks, a new circuit-numbering convention was adopted.

The Transaction Capabilities Application Part

The TCAP, probably the most versatile of all the SS7 protocols, provides a structured method to request processing of an operation at a remote node, defining the information flow to control the operation and the reporting of its result.

Operations and their results are carried out within a session known as a *dialogue* or a *transaction*. Within a dialogue, many operations may be active and at different stages of processing. The operations and their results are conveyed in information elements known as *components*. The operation of the TCAP is to store components for transmission received form the higher layers until a dialogue-handling information element is received, at which time all stored components are formatted into a single TCAP message and sent through SCCP to the peer TCAP. A network entity does not have to be a switch. Any network device, provided it is equipped with the proper interfaces and can provide all four levels of SS7 support, can be accessed by this protocol.

The Signaling Connection and Control Part

The SCCP is an enhancement of transport oriented MTP functions. Applications that require enhanced transport capabilities are users of the SCCP. These include end-to-end routing, which is not possible with MTP. SCCP provides the means for routing a message transparently through the network using intermediate nodes as routers without the need to know the individual addresses of each of the intermediate nodes.

Two key additions to the SCCP are extended addressing capability and the ability to provide both connectionless and connections-oriented service.

Due to the use of a 4-bit service indicator for addressing, the number of users of the MTP is limited to 16 (0 through 15). The MTP at any node is concerned only with getting the message to the next node. For this reason, it only uses the SCPs of the adjacent nodes. SCCP provides for up to 255 users by employing subsystem numbers. This enhancement allows the SCCP to provide end-to-end routing as it makes use of all the SCPs for all locations in the network, whether linked to its local node or not.

The second key enhancement is the ability for SCCP to provide users with four service classes. This feature differs from the single connectionless service offered by MTP. SCCP provides the following classes of service:

- **Class 0** Basic connectionless service.
- **Class 1** Connectionless service with sequence control.
- **Class 2** Basic connection-oriented service.
- **Class 3** Connection-oriented service with flow control.

In connectionless services, the SCCPs at the signaling points of the two subsystems involved in a transaction are not aware of the transaction. In a connection-oriented service, a virtual signaling connection between the SCCPs is established first, making both SCCPs aware of the transaction. At the end of the transaction, the signaling connection is released.

The Telephone User Part

The TUP is an analog protocol that performs basic telephone call connects and disconnects. It has been replaced by ISUP but is still used in some parts of the world, such as China.

The TUP provides conventional PSTN telephony services across the SS7 network. TUP was the first Layer 4 protocol defined by the standards bodies; as such, it did not provision for ISDN services. Prior to the introduction of ISUP, national variants of TUP evolved, providing varying degrees of support for ISDN.

Analog-to-Digital Conversion

Why can't a digital signal from a computer be transmitted over a telephone line without being turned into an analog signal? As stated earlier in this chapter, voice channel bandwidth ranges from 300Hz to 3400Hz. Digital signals generated by computers are *unipolar*—that is, they have a range of 0 to 1, either on or off. In addition, the change from 0 to 1 and back again is very fast, resulting in high-frequency signals. As a result, computers generate both very low frequencies, below 300Hz, and very high frequencies, above 3300Hz. The typical voice channel will simply not handle the frequency range needed to transmit digitized computer data. To overcome this problem, the digital signal must be transformed into a signal compatible with the channel capacity (bandwidth) of a voice circuit. The methodology used to transform the signal from digital to analog is called *modulation*. Modulation is the process of changing the carrier wave in response to a change in the modulating signal within the 300Hz to 3400Hz voice circuit frequency range.

Modems commonly use three methods to modulate a digital signal: amplitude, frequency, and phase modulation. The word *modem* is an acronym for *modulator/demodulator*. Modems accept digital data from a computer and convert it to a modulated analog waveform for transmission over a normal analog phone line. The inverse of this operation is that the modem accepts the modulated analog wave from the telephone line, converts it into a digital form, and then passes it to a computer. *Amplitude modulation* uses a full sine wave or signal peak to a predesignated high to indicate a 1, and a drop in the sine wave or return in the wave to a flat or null signal to indicate a 0. Amplitude modulation is actually seldom used by itself for data transfers due to amplitude transmission sensitivity to electrical noise and interference.

Frequency modulation uses a change in the frequency with which the signal is repeated (measured in cycles per second) to indicate a 0 or 1. A separate lower-frequency value might indicate a 0, and another, higher frequency would indicate a 1. This technique is called *frequency shift keying (FSK)*, or, if it's used in the voice band, it is called *audio frequency shift keying (AFSK)*.

The last modulation technique, *phase modulation*, uses a shift in phase of the signal in reference to another wave of the same frequency, either rising or falling, to indicate a 1. The phase of the signal, however, is not shifted for 0. The phase of the wave is measured relative to the phase of the wave during the previous signal that registered a 1.

Since most circuits available today are voice grade, considerable time, effort, and money has gone into developing modems, units designed to modulate digital signals into analog signals and demodulate analog signals into digital signals, at ever-increasing rates. The 1s and 0s in a computer's data stream coming from the data terminal equipment (DTE) are converted to analog sine waveforms with frequencies between 300Hz and 3000Hz. As stated earlier, voice-grade circuits are limited in range from 300Hz to 3000Hz.

The maximum signaling rate is fixed by the channel bandwidth and the signal-to-noise ratio. This means a voice-grade signal will have a maximum baud rate of approximately 2400 baud. To speed things up, we need to stuff more bits into a single signal or, to state the concept in another way, transmit multiple bits per baud.

Modems

Traditional modem standards assume that both ends of a modem session have an analog connection to the PSTN. Data signals are converted from digital to analog and back again, limiting transmission speeds to 33.6Kbps with V.34 modems. Due to limitations of the PSTN, the theoretical maximum speed that can be gained over a standard phone line is 35Kbps. Now with V.92 technology a different assumption is made: that one end of the modem session has a pure-digital connection to the phone network (which ISPs and corporations already use for remote access) and takes advantage of that high-speed digital connection. V.92 is a new standard for dialup communications that offers several important improvements over the existing V.90 standard. These improvements are intended to make communications faster, easier, and more enjoyable. V.92 and its companion compression standard, V.44, have been officially adopted by the ITU. Additionally, the V.92 standard allows your ISP to put your data connection "on hold" while you pick up a voice call using your call-waiting service. When you finish with the voice call, you can instantly resume the original connection as though you had never left it.

By viewing the PSTN as a digital network, V.92 technology is able to accelerate data downstream from the Internet to your computer at speeds of up to 56Kbps. In this way, V.92 technology is different from other standards of today because it digitally encodes downstream data instead of modulating it as analog modems do. The data transfer is done in an asymmetrical fashion, so upstream transmissions (mostly keystroke and mouse commands from your computer to the central site, which require less bandwidth) continue to flow at the conventional rates of up to 33.6Kbps. That is, upstream data (data sent from your modem) is sent as an analog transmission that mirrors the V.34 standard. Only the downstream data transfer takes advantage of the high-speed V.90 rates. The V.92 standard increased the upstream data rate to up to 48Kbps.

V.92 technology is ideal for Internet users because they really need the 56Kbps speed for downloading Web pages with sound, video, and other large files. All that is needed is for the user's V.92 modem to be connected to an ISP or corporate site using V.92 technology over its digital lines to the network.

In V.92 architecture, most ISPs connect directly to the phone company's digital backbone. Data coming from an ISP need never undergo an analog-to-digital conversion. Instead, the data can be encoded using PCM so that it remains an entirely digital signal until it gets to the central office. Once it arrives at the CO, the data is put through a digital-to-analog conversion before being sent across the analog phone lines to the user's modem. Furthermore, since digital-to-analog conversions aren't affected by quantization noise, the result, in theory at least, is throughput as high as 56Kb from ISP to user modem.

Modems can receive data at speeds of up to 56Kbps, but due to Federal Communications Commission (FCC) rulings on maximum permissible transmit power levels during download transmissions, speeds of 54Kb are the mandated as the maximum for the United States. Actual data speeds received will vary depending on line conditions.

Factors That Affect V.92 Throughput

Many factors can affect modem performance. Line conditions greatly affect V.92 throughput. Such factors such as ISP connection to telephone company CO, telephone company central office switch, and digital loop carrier (DLC) determine actual throughput. Let's look at these factors in more detail.

The Internet Service Provider

The ISP should have a fully digital connection to the telephone company's CO for V.92 technology to work. This means that ISP must have either ISDN or a T1/E1 or T3/E3 circuit. In the case of V.92 technology, ISDN has an advantage over T1/E1. ISDN generally uses out-of-band signaling in which a separate channel is used to synchronize the flow of data and set up the call, thereby freeing the line's entire bandwidth for sending data. T1 lines use what is known as *robbed-bit signaling*. In that method, a bit of incoming data is stripped off to indicate the status of an incoming or outgoing call and to synchronize the data flow, slightly reducing maximum throughput.

The Telephone Central Office Switch

Connections between local CO switches can sometimes be a problem. Old equipment could require analog terminations, resulting in an analog-to-digital conversion as the call goes through to the next switch. If a local call to an ISP gets routed through these partially analog switches, it will lose V.92 capability. The telephone company might be able to tell which type of switches a call gets routed through on the way to the ISP.

Regardless of whether it is a long distance call or not, the call must only travel through digital switches to get V.92 capabilities.

The Digital Loop Carrier

A number of problems can occur as data makes its way from the local CO to your home. Although older telephone lines connect directly to the switch at the CO, newer lines go through a DLC. These devices can combine 96 separate lines into one before they reach the CO switch. When it uses a DLC, the phone company doesn't have the expense of buying as much copper wire, which not only saves money but also increases connection reliability. DLCs, however, can wreak havoc with V.92. If the DLC is digitally connected to the switch, there is no problem. However, if it uses a universal connection, an analog-to-digital conversion will occur, rendering your modem's 56Kbps capabilities useless.

There may also be a pad between you and the CO. A pad balances the volume on both ends of the line when you make a call. If the pad occurs before the signal is converted to analog, you'll see only a slight degradation in V.92 performance.

Some local lines also run through an amplifier called a *load coil* to boost the signal rates across longer distances. Load coils cause some signal distortion and will affect V.92 throughput.

Summary

With Alexander Graham Bell's invention of the first practical analog phone in 1876, the telephone system has seen many advances in equipment and networking technology that bring us to today's present iteration of the PSTN, digital transmission allowing for both the transport of both data and voice. Initially, the PSTN's use was strictly limited to the transport of voice calls. Today's networks see a coming together of both data and voice networks into a single converged network. This migration is being led by the advent of VoIP.

From its inception through the 1960s, the PSTN was strictly an analog network. The term *analog* can be traced to the similarity between the actual fluctuations of the human voice and the *analogous*, or comparable, modulation of a carrier wave. We discussed typical analog components required to create and pass analog voice traffic. PBXs, telephone handsets, switches, and cabling make up the basic foundation of the PSTN.

As discussed in the chapter, analog signals are continuous electrical waves that have as characteristics amplitude, frequency, bandwidth, phase, and period. With analog signaling, we touched on the basic methods implemented to pass control signaling and user data. The most common form of analog trunking is E&M signaling. Although not as prevalent as in early days, it is still widely used in today's networks. The basic line protocols used in addressing a call are the older DP and the technically advanced and more widely used DTMF.

With the inception of digital transmission during the 1960s, the PSTN has seen its greatest changes. Digital transmission requires more bandwidth, but digital systems are less expensive than analog transmission. The most widely deployed form of digital transmission is the T-carrier system used in conjunction with TDM switching technology, which allows for the carrying of multiple voice, data, or video signals simultaneously over a single carrier line by interleaving bits of each signal in a time-synchronized string. Since TDM transports and regenerates voice digitally, it is immune to noise picked up in the transmission medium. We also discussed Integrated Services Digital Network (ISDN) and described the protocols and architecture to implement a worldwide digital communications network.

This chapter touched briefly on call control signaling. Initially, the standard for signaling was Channel Associated Signaling (CAS). Common Channel Signaling (CCS) has widely replaced CAS, but CAS is still used in the PSTN. The main difference between CAS and CCS is that whereas CAS utilizes in-band signaling, CCS uses out-of-band signaling and thus provides more security on the network, addressing the issue of hackers placing voice calls and not being billed for them.

This chapter finished with a discussion of analog-to-digital conversion, which is a technique utilized by modems. The word *modem* comes from the term *modulator/demodulator*. Analog-to-digital conversion occurs when a modem receives a digital transmission from your computer and converts it to an analog signal for transport across the PSTN. The far-end modem then converts this analog signal back to a digital signal and passes it to the computer on the far end. Previous modem standards allowed for maximum data transfer rates of 33.6Kbps due to the characteristics of analog signals. Technology advancements have led to the creation of V.92, which has increased transmission speeds to 56Kbps. This increase in speed is based on the premise that there is only one analog-to-digital conversion leg between two modems.

Although we could dedicate several more chapters, and possibly several books, to the topic of traditional voice telephony principles, the basic concepts are briefly outlined in this chapter. This information on traditional voice networking is required because successful VoIP deployments in networks must consider the characteristics and methods of traditional circuit-switched voice networks.

Solutions Fast Track

Analog Systems

- ☑ The term *analog* can be traced to the similarity between the actual fluctuations of the human voice and the *analogous*, or comparable, modulation of a carrier wave. The human voice occupies the 20Hz to 20KHz range. Analog signals are continuous waves that are capable of representing an unlimited number of values.

- ☑ If a site has more than a few centrally located users, they can use a specialized on-site switch called a *private branch exchange,* or *PBX*. A PBX is capable of connecting telephone sets to each other and to a PSTN. A PBX eliminates the need to utilize an external phone line to place calls within that location utilizing extensions. These calls are never routed out to the PSTN.

Analog Network Components

☑ A typical analog phone system consists of telephone handsets, drop wires, local loops, CO, and toll trunks. Drop wires extend from the house to the telephone pole and are combined into feeder cables, then terminated at the nearest CO. Drop wires and feeder cables combined are referred to as the *local loop*. The CO is the building or buildings containing computerized telephone switching equipment for a predesignated geographical area of responsibility. Toll trunks then connect COs in other exchange regions.

☑ Each CO is responsible for managing all telephone calls within its area, either switching the call to the called party within the same exchange or switching the call to a trunk and into another CO's area. The side of the CO closest to the local subscriber is called the *line-side interface,* or *local loop.* The side of the CO connecting to another CO is called the *trunk-side interface.*

☑ The efficiency of copper has a great deal to do with the length of the cable run. The longer the cable run, the more likely signal distortion will occur. The shorter the cable run, the better the signal quality. Attenuation, capacitance, delay distortion, and noise can cause signal distortion across copper cabling.

☑ Codecs are used to synthesize speech on the voice network. Waveform encoding is the most widely used class of codec. Within waveform encoding are pulse code modulation (PCM) and adaptive pulse code modulation (ADPCM). Standardized in the 1960s, these forms of modulation are still widely used due to their simplicity, excellent quality, and low delay.

Analog Signaling

☑ Analog signals are continuous electrical waves having amplitude, frequency, bandwidth, phase, and period as characteristics. Amplitude measures the loudness of the signal in decibels. Frequency is essentially the number of vibrations per second. Bandwidth is the difference between the upper-level and lower-level frequencies. Signal phase is the relative position of the sine wave, measured in degrees. A period is the time it takes to complete one cycle.

☑ The most common form of analog trunking utilizes E&M signaling. Analog circuits connect automated switching systems such as PBXs to a CO. E&M signaling defines a signaling side and trunking side for each connection. The PBX is the signaling side; the trunking side is the CO. There are five different types of E&M signaling interfaces, designated as Types I through Type V.

☑ Start-dial supervision is the line protocol that defines how the equipment seizes an E&M trunk and passes the address signaling information such as DP or DTMF. The main start-dial signaling protocols used on an E&M circuit are loop- and ground-start signaling.

☑ Address signaling typically represents the digits dialed. Two options are used to pass address information. Either dial-pulse signaling (rotary dialing) or dual-tone multifrequency (DTMF) signaling can be used. DTMF has replaced DP in most places but is still used in some remote areas.

Digital Transmission

☑ Digital transmission requires more bandwidth than analog, but digital systems are less expensive than analog transmission, and digital transmission is rapidly replacing analog transmission in voice networks. Digital transmission breaks data down into a series of 0s and 1s.

☑ The most widely used formats of digital transmission are the T-carrier system and the E-carrier system. The T-carrier system was introduced in the United States by Bell Telephone in the 1960s. It was the first successful system that supported digitized voice transmission. The equivalent of this standard in Europe is the E-carrier system. A T1 has 24 64Kb channels producing 1.544Mb of bandwidth, whereas an E1 has 32 64Kb channels producing 2.048Mb of bandwidth.

☑ Time-division multiplexing (TDM) is a digital transmission technique for carrying multiple voice, data, or video signals simultaneously over a single carrier line by interleaving bits of each signal in a time-synchronized string. TDM works by converting all signals to a digital format. To solve the problem of noise introduced to voice calls transmitted over analog FDM links, digital TDM was introduced in the mid-1960s. Since TDM transports and regenerates voice digitally, it is immune to noise picked up in the transmission medium.

☑ Integrated Services Digital Network (ISDN) technology is standardized according to ITU recommendations that describe the protocols and architecture to implement a worldwide digital communications network. There are two basic types of ISDN service: Basic Rate Interface (BRI) and Primary Rate Interface (PRI). BRI consists of two 64Kb B channels and one 16Kb D channel, for a total of 144Kb. This basic service is intended to meet the needs of most individual users. A PRI in North America consists of 23 64Kb B channels and one 64Kb D channel. In other countries (Europe and Australia), a PRI consists of 31 64Kb B channels and one 64Kb D channel.

Call Control Signaling

☑ Until the mid 1970s, Channel Associated Signaling (CAS) was the only signaling system utilized on the voice network. Common Channel Signaling (CCS) has gradually replaced it. CAS signaling is analog, and signaling information is passed within the actual circuit, which is referred to as *in-band signaling*.

☑ CCS was developed to support the enhanced services offered with the emergence of digital communications and ISDN. Because signaling information is carried on a separate network, CCS is referred to as *out-of-band signaling* and uses a separate 64Kb data channel for passing control information. The most widely deployed form of CCS is Signaling System 7 (SS7).

Analog-to-Digital Conversion

☑ Voice channel bandwidth ranges from 300Hz to 3400Hz. Digital signals are generated as a series of 0s (on) and 1s (off). As a esult, computers generate both very low frequencies (below 300Hz) and very high frequencies (above 3400Hz). To overcome this issue, the digital signal is transformed into an analog signal.

☑ Modulation is the process of changing the carrier wave in response a change in the modulating signal within the 300Hz to 3400Hz voice frequency range. Three common methods are used to modulate a digital signal: amplitude, frequency, and phase modulation.

☑ The word *modem* is an acronym for *modulator/demodulator*. Traditional modem standards assume that both ends of a modem session have an analog connection to the PSTN. Converting signals from data to analog and back again limits transmission speeds to 33.6Kbps with V.34 modems.

☑ V.92 technology is the newest standard for dialup communications. Downstream speeds have been increased to 56Kbps. Upstream transmission speeds have been increased to 48Kbps. A further enhancement to V.92 technology allows an ISP to put your data connection "on hold" while you pick up a voice call.

☑ Many factors influence and affect modem performance. Line conditions greatly affect transmission speeds. Factors such as ISP connection to the PSTN company's CO, the telephone company CO switch, and digital loop carriers determine actual throughput.

Frequently Asked Questions

The following Frequently Asked Questions, answered by the authors of this book, are designed to both measure your understanding of the concepts presented in this chapter and to assist you with real-life implementation of these concepts. To have your questions about this chapter answered by the author, browse to **www.syngress.com/solutions** and click on the **"Ask the Author"** form.

Q: Which is better, analog or digital transmission? What is the difference?

A: My favorite engineering answer applies here: "It depends." Analog transmission has a greater informational range than digital, but analog transmission is not as precise as digital transmission. Analog transmission over long distances is prone to pick up noise and amplify it. Digital technology uses binary codes (0 or 1) to represent information. Digitally transmitted information has two major benefits:

■ The signal can be reproduced precisely. In long telecommunications transmission circuits, the signal progressively loses strength and picks up electromagnetic static and electrical interference. Using digital transmission, the signal is regenerated and reconstructed to an exact replica of the original signal, minus the noise.

- Technology needed to reproduce signals digitally has become considerably less expensive and more powerful.

Q: Is it true that a PC modem converts digital data to analog, then sends the data over twisted pairs of copper wire?

A: Yes. When you use a PC connected to a modem to dial into the Internet or call another computer system, the data is typically sent over the standard telephone connection between your residence and the telephone company. Most connections to and from residences consist of twisted-pair copper wire.

Q: Do individual phone lines always connect to a T1 line?

A: No. Individual phone lines connect to a telephone switch such as Basic-NET3, Basic-5ESS, or Basic DMS100. T1 lines are digital circuits typically used to interconnect these telephone switches. Interswitch connections are sometimes referred to as *digital trunks*.

Q: Do V.34 and V.42 modems have the capability to exceed analog phone-line bandwidth limitations?

A: Yes. High-speed V.34 and V.42 modems compress the data they transmit. Usually a 2:1 or 4:1 ratio is achieved, depending on file type and characteristics. Due to data compression and the modem's use of codes to represent data bit patterns, the modem actually stuffs more information into the data it transmits.

Q: What is the bandwidth limitation of today's analog telephone circuits?

A: The telephone signal bandwidth can be calculated by subtracting the lower-frequency range from the upper-frequency range. The result is typical telephone bandwidth. For example, to calculate telephone bandwidth, you would use the following equation:

$$3300Hz - 300Hz = 3000Hz$$

Chapter 3

VoIP Signaling and Voice Transport Protocols

Solutions in this chapter:

- An Overview of IP Networks
- VoIP Signaling, Addressing, and Routing
- Introducing H.323
- H.323 Protocol Stack
- H.323 Call Stages
- Session Initiation Protocol
- Media Gateway Control Point
- The Role of QoS in Packet-Switched Voice Networks

☑ Summary

☑ Solutions Fast Track

☑ Frequently Asked Questions

Introduction

In the last two years, VoIP solutions have gone from being often unreliable and sometimes annoying solutions to a "New Age," widely accepted, and growing technology. Although several factors could be cited as the reasons for the increasingly rapid adoption of VoIP solutions, the simplest explanation is that the technology has substantially improved. Calls that, not too long ago, were choppy and unintelligible are now clear and understandable. This change in both technology and perception can most definitely be contributed to improvements in the overall VoIP technology family. VoIP signaling protocols fill a vital and fundamental role in improving the overall reliability of VoIP and related technologies. VoIP signaling protocols not only enable VoIP to work, they control all facets of the connections across a network, creating a fixed and reliable communications path across an unreliable network.

The goal of this chapter is to provide an in-depth and thorough investigation of these protocols as well as to explain the fundamental technologies and concepts behind them. Our discussion begins with an introduction to the TCP/IP protocol, providing an overview of the TCP/IP Department of Defense (DoD) protocol stack as well as the International Organization for Standardization (ISO) protocol stack. We then discuss some of the fundamental concepts of IP addresses, including IP addressing, address classes, private addressing, subnetting, supernetting, fixed-length subnet masking, and variable-length subnet masking. For experienced networking professionals, this discussion serves as a brief review of these fundamental concepts; for traditional voice and PBX professionals, it serves as an excellent introduction to the fundamentals of TCP/IP.

Our discussion then turns to the basics of VoIP signaling and an introduction to VoIP signaling, addressing, and routing. The focus of this section is to introduce the basic concept of how an end-to-end VoIP call is completed and some of the protocols that come into play in making a call happen.

H.323 is one of the most widely deployed and supported VoIP and video over IP protocols deployed in converged networks today. H.323 is one of the oldest and most stable VoIP protocols in use today. For that reason, a good portion of this chapter is devoted to providing a clear and accurate discussion of the H.323 protocol, its components, terminals, gateways, gatekeepers, and multipoint control units (MCUs), H.323 protocol stack, and H.323 call stages.

Session Initiation Protocol (SIP) is a relatively new standards-based VoIP protocol that is gaining wide acceptance and support. SIP is much younger than the

H.323 protocol and therefore does not enjoy the same widespread support and acceptance as H.323. However, due to SIP's scalability, interoperability, and simplicity, it is and will continue to become more prevalent in VoIP deployments. We focus on fully introducing you to this protocol and explaining the components as well as the benefits of deploying SIP in your VoIP network.

Media Gateway Control Protocol (MGCP) is a VoIP control protocol most often used to control gateway devices in a VoIP network. A relatively new protocol, MGCP is gaining wide acceptance as a part of the Cisco Architecture for Voice, Video, and Integrated Data (AVVID). AVVID most commonly uses MGCP in Call Manager deployments to control VoIP gateway devices. Our discussion of MGCP introduces the specifics of the protocol and explains its various components. We also discuss the emerging MeGaCo standard.

Our discussion of VoIP protocols concludes with the role and importance of QoS techniques in VoIP and packet-switched networks. Many of the improvements in the quality and reliability of VoIP solutions can be attributed to improvements in QoS technologies. Entire books have been written on QoS, a very important function in all facets of networking, especially in dealing with the real-time requirements of a converged infrastructure. Due to this importance, we focus on introducing and discussing the basic concepts of QoS.

NOTE

For more information on QoS, review *Administering Cisco QoS for IP Networks* (ISBN: 1-928994-21-0), also available from Syngress Publishing (www.syngress.com).

An Overview of IP Networks

Unlike Frame Relay and ATM connection-oriented networks, Internet Protocol (IP) is a connectionless network protocol that uses variable-length bit streams. In a connectionless network protocol, information is transferred between two entities without first establishing a connection. Upper-layer protocols may be connectionless or connection-oriented. IP is a network layer protocol (Layer 3 of the Open Systems Interconnection (OSI) model, shown in Figure 3.1). It contains the addressing and control information that enables datagrams to be routed and thereby provides connectionless best-effort delivery of datagrams through an internetwork. A message can be transmitted as a series of datagrams that are reassembled at the receiving location. Typically, IP traffic has been transmitted on a first-in, first-out (FIFO) basis. Packets have been variable in nature, allowing large file transfers to utilize the efficiency with large associated packet sizes.

Figure 3.1 Internet Protocol Mapped to the OSI Reference Model Protocol Stack

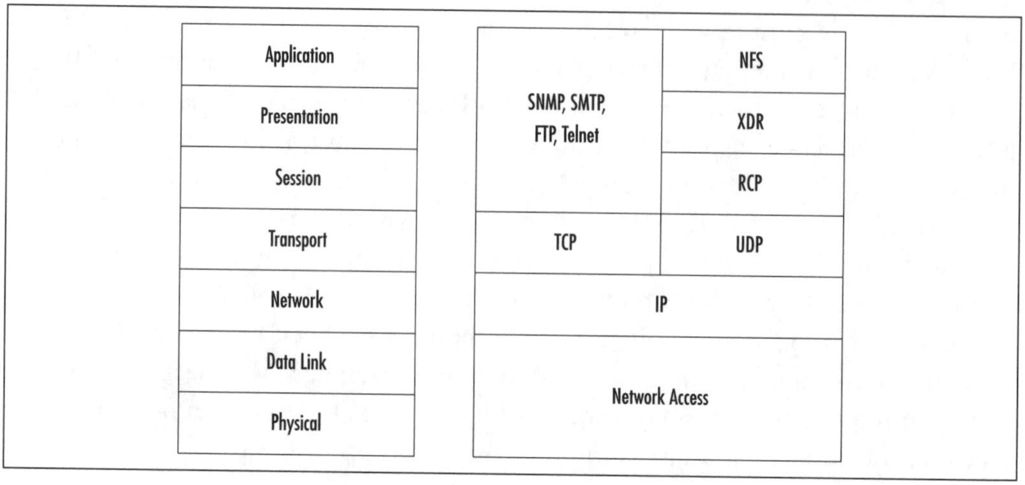

Application	SNMP, SMTP, FTP, Telnet	NFS
Presentation		XDR
Session		RCP
Transport	TCP	UDP
Network	IP	
Data Link	Network Access	
Physical		

The Internet is a "best effort" internetwork, meaning that network nodes make every effort to forward packets to their destination, but make no guarantees that packets will be forwarded. Additionally, there are no guarantees of bandwidth, delay or jitter. Many corporate networks also operate in a "best effort" manner and, as a result, cannot deliver the same quality for voice traffic as that provided by the PSTN. IP provides for addressing within the Internet. Each packet sent on the Internet contains both a destination address and a source address. The IP network may be the public Internet or a private IP-based network. The IP network supports real-time services via the following protocols:

- Resource Reservation Protocol (RSVP)
- Differentiated Services (DiffServ)
- Real-time Transport Protocol (RTP)
- Real-time Control Protocol (RTCP)

Transmission Control Protocol (TCP) is a connection-oriented protocol responsible for dividing a message into IP-manageable packets and then reassembling the packets into a complete message at the other end. TCP is considered a reliable transport service. It is a Layer 4, end-to-end protocol that provides virtual connection reliability. *Virtual connection* is simply an association between processes on two machines. TCP is not processed at the network routers or switches but instead at the endpoints. It provides the application with reliable virtual circuit and flow control, and it determines and adapts to network congestion. TCP is responsible for providing reliable transmission of data over the network by providing the following services:

- Streamed data transfer

- Multiplexing (numerous upper-layer conversations can be transferred simultaneously over a single connection)

- Efficient flow control

- Reliability

- Full-duplex operations

Streamed data transfer delivers data as a steady and continuous stream of bytes. A sequence number identifies each byte so that applications do not have to segment data into manageable blocks before handing the data to TCP.

When TCP receives the byte stream, it groups it into segments and sends the segments to IP for delivery. Each packet contains a forward acknowledgment number that indicates to the receiver which segment number is expected next by the transmitter. TCP has the ability to recover from lost and delayed packets.

The User Datagram Protocol (UDP) is another Layer 4 protocol. It is a connectionless protocol that sends data (datagrams) from one computer to another. UDP has no mechanisms for ensuring packet delivery and is, therefore, not considered reliable. UDP is different from TCP and more appropriate to applications for which acknowledgments are unnecessary or retransmission is not appropriate—for example, Domain Name Service queries and Internet telephony. UDP provides so-called *unreliable* transport layer service to the application because there are no acknowledgments. Essentially, UDP adds Layer 4 port numbers.

UDP is used for VoIP and is a simple protocol that exchanges datagrams without acknowledgements or guaranteed delivery. It requires that error processing and retransmission be handled by other protocols. UDP adds no reliability, flow control, or recovery functions to IP. It simply acts as an interface between IP and upper-layer processes.

UDP's header contains fewer bytes and consumes less network overhead than TCP, and because UDP does not handshake with the receiving end, the initiation and sending process is faster than for TCP. This speed makes UDP a logical transport protocol for VoIP.

To successfully integrate connection-oriented voice traffic in a connection-less-oriented IP network, enhancements to the signaling stack are required. In some manner, we must make this connectionless network appear connection-oriented.

IP Addressing Overview

As we discussed in the previous section, IP addressing is a logical construct. Unlike Layer 2 addresses such as Ethernet Media Access Control (MAC) addresses, which are burned into individual adapters and so cannot be changed, IP addresses are completely logical and therefore completely configurable.

TCP/IP has a very long and prestigious history dating back to the late 1960s and early 1970s, when it was the proposed standard for addressing in the Defense Advanced Research Projects Agency (DARPA) project. What we know today as the Internet also saw its origin at this time. The original Internet, a far cry from what we know today, was intended to have only tens of networks with hundreds of hosts, not the thousands of networks with millions of hosts that it has today.

Currently, IP is on its fourth version, referred to as *IPv4*. This standard describes a 4-octet, 32-byte address that contains two parts, a network address and a host/node address. This address is represented by a series of numbers separated by periods, such as 10.10.10.1. No octet can exceed the value of 255. To understand IP addresses, it is important to know how to read the address. For the example network address 10.10.10.1, we chose to present it in decimal or number format, but for a real understanding of IP addressing, an understanding of binary numbering is important. Binary numbering uses only two values, either 0 or 1, or off and on. So, in binary, the example address would be represented as 00001010.00001010.00001010.00000001. In binary numbering, you count from right to left, and the value of each bit position doubles every digit up to 128. The progression is as follows: 128, 64, 32, 16, 8, 4, 2, 1.

The decimal value is derived from adding the values from right to left. So, the lowest-value bits are to the right and the highest-value bits are to the left. Table 3.1 offers a binary-to-decimal conversion.

Table 3.1 Binary-to-Decimal Conversion

Binary	Decimal
00000000	0
00000001	1
00000011	3
00000111	7
00001111	15
00011111	31
00111111	63
01111111	127
11111111	255

Remember; even though a number is 255, there are actually 256 values because 0 is also considered a number in binary numbering.

Since IP addressing is used for the global Internet, these addresses are public addresses. Due to the mathematical limitation of the IPv4 standard, there is a finite number of IP addresses. Since these addresses are public and finite, it is also very important to note that the same IP address cannot exist on two nodes at the same time. If it did, it could have dire consequences. (There is a workaround to this issue in the form of private addresses, which we discuss later in the chapter.) For this reason, the assignment of IP addresses is policed. In order to get a valid IP network address, an organization generally goes through an Internet service provider (ISP).

IP addresses are divided into a system known as *address classes*. There are currently five address classes, A through E. Address classes are important to note because the address class to which a particular range of addresses belongs determines the number of networks within that class as well as the number of hosts within a given network. Remember, all IP addresses are of fixed length—32 bytes, or four octets—so in order to support different classes of address, the address must be split into a host network portion. For the different classes of address, this split in address is moved.

Address Classes

The first class of network is Class A. A Class A address uses the entire first octet of an IP address. So, 10.0.0.1 is a valid Class A address. An IP address class is determined by looking at the leftmost, or high-order, bits of an IP address.

TCP/IP's designers determined that all Class A addresses should have a 0 as the first bit in a Class A IP address. With that 0 in the 128-bit position of the address, the valid range of address was left with only 7 bits to work with. Thus, there are 127 possible networks in a Class A address. Valid numbers for this space are between 0 and 127; however, 127 is unavailable because it is used as a local machine loopback address. Therefore, in reality the valid address range is between 0 and 126. The number of remaining octets left in the IP address determines the number of hosts per network.

Since Class A addresses use only the first octet of the IP address, the remaining three octets are available for host addresses. The calculation to determine this number is $2^{remaining\ bytes\ available}$, in this case 24. This equates to a Class A address having 16,777,216 available addresses. This number then needs to be reduced by two to 16,777,214 because one address, 0, represents the network, and the 255.255.255 address represents a broadcast address for the network. Therefore, the valid Class A network address space is 1.0.0.0 to 126.255.255.255. Needless to say, any organization that would require 16,777,214 hosts would be a very large organization indeed. No Class A networks are available today; the majority of these address spaces are controlled by the government and service provider networks.

The second class of network is Class B. Class B networks use the first two octets of the IP address in order to determine the network address. Like Class A addresses, Class B addresses have restrictions regarding the first bits of the IP address. The designers of the TCP/IP protocol determined that that the first bit of a Class B address should be a 1; however, the second bit must be a 0. Therefore, the bit space available for Class B network address space was reduced by two bits, so the number of Class B networks is 2^{14}, or 16,384. The valid range of Class B network numbers in the first octet is between 128 and 191. This leaves two full octets available for host addressing (2^{16}), so the total number of host addresses available to a given class B network is 65,536 minus 2 for network and broadcast addresses for a grand total of 65,534 possible addresses in a given network. Class B networks were originally envisioned to provide service for midsize organizations, but, with 65,534 possible hosts; they could scale to meet the needs of very large organizations. As with Class A addresses, very few if any Class B networks are available to be assigned.

The third class of network is Class C. Similar to Classes A and B, a restriction was placed on the addressing range of Class C addresses in that the IP address must begin with 110 as the first three bits. Class C networks use the first three octets for the network address minus three bits, or 21 bit positions. So the total number of Class C networks is 2^{21}, or 2,097,152. The range of addresses in the first octet for Class C networks is between 192 and 223. Because only one octet is available for host addresses, a total of 256 addresses are possible between 0 and 255, minus two addresses for network and broadcast addresses, for a total of 254 possible hosts on a Class C network. Class C networks are the most widely deployed and available. With only 254 possible addresses per network, Class C networks were only originally envisioned for small organizations.

The fourth class of networks is the Class D address range. The Class D address range is used exclusively for multicast traffic and is not used in unicast IP addressing. The range of Class D addresses is between 224 and 239.

The fifth and final class is the Class E address space, covering the address spaces between the 240 and 255 ranges. The Class E address range is not available for public use; it is reserved for developmental purposes.

Private Address Space

The early to mid-1990s saw explosive growth of networking and Internet usage, to a point where the finite amount of available IP addressing space began to deplete at an alarming rate. In order to combat this trend, RFC 1918 was proposed. This RFC outlines the use of private address space for use within private networks. This RFC outlines three address ranges that can be used solely within an organization. This private address space is as follows:

- One Class A network address 10.0.0.0 with 16,277,214 possible host addresses

- 16 Class B network addresses, 172.16.0.0 through 172.31.0.0, each with 65,524 possible host addresses

- 256 Class C network addresses, 192.168.0.0 through 192.168.255.0, each with 254 possible host addresses

This address space is available to any organization that wants to use it. In fact, if your organization is medium-sized to large, you are very likely utilizing one of these address spaces already. A couple of key points to remember when utilizing this private address space are:

- These addresses *cannot* be advertised on the Internet or to other outside networks. Although almost every service provider has provisions and safeguards built into its networks to prevent such an occurrence, imagine the traffic that an organization would face if it received all the traffic destined for these generic private networks.

- To communicate to outside networks, a device capable of performing Network Address Translation (NAT) must be incorporated to translate private addresses to valid global IP addresses. This device can come in the form of a router or firewall.

- Devices outside the internal network will not be able to see resources such as Web or e-mail servers and will require utilization of NAT coming into the network or use of a "demilitarized zone" (DMZ) between the internal and external networks.

Subnetting and Supernetting Review

Subnetting is a unique and powerful feature that is exclusive to the TCP/IP protocol and is one of the reasons TCP/IP offers great scalability. Subnetting allows a network address to be further divided, apart from the already established classful boundaries, into smaller, more manageable networks. This division provides for unparalleled scalability and hierarchy and gives a network administrator benefits such as reduced network traffic, less susceptibility to broadcast traffic, network optimization, and greater ease of management. In the following sections, we discuss this process and several of its components such as the subnet mask, the process of calculating subnetting, fixed-length and variable-length subnet masking, and the process of supernetting.

Subnet Mask

As we discussed in the previous section, there are two parts to the IP address, the network portion and the host portion. Although we know this, the node assigned that IP address as well as other nodes that must communicate with it have no idea of the location of the line between host and network portions of the address. The subnet mask provides the answer to this dilemma. The subnet mask follows the IP address and details the line indicating where the network portion of the address ends and the host portion begins. Like the IP address, the subnet mask is in a 4-octet, 32-byte format. An example of a subnet mask is 255.0.0.0. Recall from our discussion of binary numbering that 255 is equivalent to 11111111 in binary. In other words, a value of 255 means match all. Each of the three configurable IP address classes has a default subnet mask:

- **Class A** 255.0.0.0
- **Class B** 255.255.0.0
- **Class C** 255.255.255.0

Notice from these examples that the 255 values correspond to the number of octets that each class uses for its network address. If we were to follow the strictly class-based usage of subnet masks, there would be little point in having the subnet mask. Rather, you could just build the delineation directly into the address itself, but the subnet mask becomes an invaluable part of subnetting, which we discuss next.

Subnetting

Subnetting is a feature of TCP/IP that makes IP addressing a more realistic and scalable solution. As we just discussed, each class of address has a certain set number of host addresses per class, and the subnet mask decides the delineation between the network address and the host addresses. Subnetting allows us to break that number of host addresses into smaller, more manageable networks. Imagine a single Class A network with 16,777,214 hosts. The broadcast traffic alone could kill the entire network. Just imagine the administrative nightmare of that many hosts on a single network.

Subnetting creates subnetworks by "borrowing" bits from the host portion of the IP address, thus increasing the number of networks by reducing the number of hosts. This borrowing is done directly after the network address by manipulating the zero-value octets of the subnet mask. Unlike IP addressing, this is done from left to right, not right to left. So if you wanted to create two subnets, you would borrow one bit from the leftmost portion of the host address space. Why one, why not two? Remember, in binary math, each bit position has two possible values, 0 and 1. If you wanted to create four subnets, you would borrow two bits; to create eight subnets, you'd borrow three bits, and so on. The subnet mask is then changed to reflect the number of bits that you have borrowed from the host portion of the address.

For instance, if you were to borrow 1one bit from the host portion of a Class B network, your subnet mask would be 255.255.128.0. Remember, you borrow bits from left to right, but those bit positions still hold their original values, so the rightmost bit would be valued at 128. If you wanted to create four subnets, your subnet mask would read 255.255.192 because you have now borrowed two bits, one valued at 128 and another valued at 64. So, 128 + 64 = 192. Table 3.2 outlines conversion of subnet masks to number of networks.

Table 3.2 The Conversion of Subnet Masks to Number of Networks

Subnet Mask	Binary	Number of Networks
0	00000000	1
128	10000000	2
192	11000000	4
224	11100000	8
240	11110000	16
248	11111000	32
252	11111100	64
254	11111110	128
255	11111111	256

The subnet mask tells us how many networks that we will have. However, we need to determine which host addresses are in a given network range. Although there are complex formulas for figuring this out, the simplest way to do it is to divide the total number of host address spaces available by the number of subnets that have been created. For example, if we subnetted a Class C address with a 192 subnet mask, which would read 255.255.255.192, we would have created four subnets. Then we divide 256 by 4 for a result of 64, so in this case the valid subnet address ranges would be:

- 0 through 63
- 64 through 127
- 128 through 191
- 192 through 255

However, since we have now created four new networks, we must remember that each network needs the network address (all 0s), as well as the broadcast address (all 1s), so in actuality, our available address range for host IP network address assignment is:

- 1 through 62
- 65 through 126
- 129 through 190
- 193 through 254

In essence, you sacrifice two possible IP addresses per subnet in order to more granularly define your network.

Fixed-Length Subnet Masking

The process that we have just described is part of a standard known as *fixed-length subnet masking (FLSM)*. Because of the inherent limitations in classful routing protocols, routing protocols that do not carry subnet mask information, such as RIP and IGRP, we are often faced with the situation of requiring that subnet mask be uniform across the entire network. If every subnet had the exact number of hosts per subnet, this would not be a problem; unfortunately, this is rarely the case. In deciding on the appropriate subnet mask to use for a network, you must choose a subnet mask that will support the subnet with the largest number of hosts. For instance, if you are given a Class C address and have one location with 56 users and another with only 14 users, you must specify a 255.255.255.192 subnet mask to allow for 64 users at each site. Then, at the second site, 49 IP addresses are wasted. You can see that this is not at all an efficient method of assigning and managing IP addresses. There is, however, a much more efficient method of IP address allocation, known as *variable-length subnet masking (VLSM)*.

Variable-Length Subnet Masking

VLSM provides a solution to the inefficient address allocation caused by standard FLSM addressing practices. VLSM provides a network administrator the ability to use differing subnet masks throughout the network. VLSM is not supported by classful routing protocols such as RIP and IGRP, because these protocols do not carry subnet information in their routing updates. Rather, VLSM is supported by classless routing protocols—routing protocols that carry subnet masks in routing updates, such as OSPF and EIGRP. Using our example of the site with 56 users and 14 users, one site could be assigned a .192 mask and the other could be assigned a .240 mask, thus preserving 48 of those wasted IP addresses. Two important design notes to make when utilizing VLSM are that the dynamic routing protocols in use must support VLSM and you must not allow your address spaces to overlap when using different subnet masks.

Supernetting and Classless Interdomain Routing

When we utilize subnetting, we "borrow" bits from the host portion of the IP address in order to create several smaller networks within the given address space. *Supernetting*, also known as *classless interdomain routing (CIDR)*, does nearly the opposite. Supernetting takes multiple small networks and, through manipulation of the rightmost bits of the network portion of the subnet mask, creates a larger network out of smaller networks. For instance, if we had four class C networks—192.16.128.0, 192.16.129.0, 192.16.130.0, and 192.16.131.0—each of these networks would have 24-bit subnet mask, 255.255.255.0. Instead of representing these networks as four individual Class C networks, we could represent them as a single subnet in a larger Class B network. In order to do this, we would select the lowest-numbered Class C address and represent it with a Class B subnet mask that would include only those three networks. In this case, since there are three networks, we would have to include two bit positions in order to allow for the four networks, or a 255.255.252.0 subnet mask.

Three important considerations must be made in dealing with supernetting or CIDR. The first of these considerations is the use of classless routing protocols. In order for supernetting or CIDR to work, the subnet mask must be carried in the routing protocol updates. The second consideration is that of address overlap. When you supernet, you must take care that when selecting your given subnet mask, all the networks are included in that subnet. In our example, we chose to use the subnet mask of .252. In doing so, we created 64 subnets—0–3, 4–7, and so on up to 128–131—as a valid range. If one of the ranges had been 129–132, we would have had to use a smaller subnet mask in order to reduce the number of subnets and increase the number of hosts within each one, thus including a greater range. The final consideration is that in order for supernetting or CIDR to work effectively, the networks must be sequential, such as 192.16.128.0, 192.16.129.0, 192.16.130.0, and 192.16.131.0. You cannot supernet nonsequential address spaces.

Often the terms *CIDR* and *supernetting* are used synonymously. In fact, the two terms refer to the same idea, but CIDR further refers to the ability of Border Gateway Protocol (BGP) to summarize lower-level networks in order to reduce the size and number of routing table entries when advertising autonomous system (AS) information between peers.

VoIP Signaling, Addressing, and Routing

VoIP signaling is most commonly used in three distinct areas: signaling from the PBX to the router, signaling between routers, and signaling from the router to the PBX. In the following sections we discuss the specifics of each of these signaling types and their importance to the overall success of a VoIP connection. We begin by discussing the signaling and connection requirements between routers and traditional PBX systems and then move on to a discussion of VoIP signaling.

Signaling Between Routers and PBXs

When signaling from PBX to router, the user picks up the handset, signaling an off-hook condition. The connection between the PBX and router appears as a trunk line to the PBX, which signals the router to seize the trunk. Once a trunk is seized, the PBX forwards the dialed digits to the router in the same manner the digits would be forwarded to a telephone company switch or another PBX. The signaling interface from the PBX to the router may be any of the common signaling methods used to seize a trunk line, such as FXS, FXO, E&M, or T1/E1 signaling.

The PBX then forwards the dialed digits to the router in the same manner as the digits would be forwarded to a telco switch. As you can see in Figure 3.2, the PBX seizes a trunk line to the router and forwards the dialed digits. Within the router, the dial plan mapper maps the dialed digits to an IP address and initiates a Q.931 call establishment request to the remote peer router that is indicated by an IP address. Figure 3.3 shows this process. Meanwhile, this control channel is used to set up the Real–Time Protocol (RTP) audio streams, and the RSVP protocol may be used to request a guaranteed QoS.

Figure 3.2 PBX-to-Router Signaling

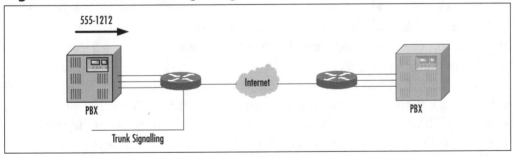

Figure 3.3 Router-to-Router Signaling

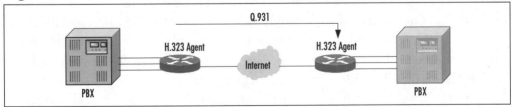

When the remote router receives the Q.931 call request, it signals a line seizure to the PBX. After the PBX acknowledges this seizure, the router forwards the dialed digits to the PBX and signals a call acknowledgment to the originating router. Figure 3.4 shows this line seizure.

Figure 3.4 Router-to-PBX signaling

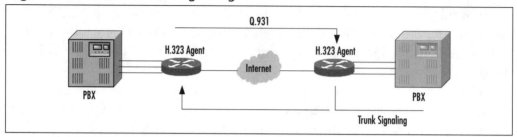

VoIP Signaling

In connectionless network architectures such as IP networks, the responsibility for session establishment and signaling resides in the end stations. To successfully emulate voice services across an IP network, enhancements to the signaling stacks are required.

For example, an H.323 agent is added to the router for standards–based support of the audio and signaling streams. The Q.931 protocol is used for call establishment and tear-down between H.323 agents or end stations. H.225 is essentially the same as Q.931.

Real–Time Control Protocol (RTCP) provides for reliable information transfer once the audio stream has been established. A reliable session–oriented protocol such as TCP is deployed between end stations to carry the signaling channels. RTP, which is built on top of UDP, is used to transport the real–time audio stream. RTP uses UDP as a transport mechanism because it has lower delay than TCP and because actual voice traffic, unlike data traffic or signaling, tolerates low levels of loss and cannot effectively exploit retransmission.

H.245 control signaling is used to negotiate channel usage and capabilities. H.245 provides for capabilities' exchange between endpoints so that codecs and other parameters related to the call are agreed upon between the endpoints. It is within H.245 that the audio channel is negotiated.

This section is meant to only briefly introduce the H.323 protocol and its subprotocols; the next section focuses solely on this important and complex protocol.

tionship between the ISO reference model and the

;ents.

odel and H.323 Standards

Standard
G.711, G.729, G.729a, etc.
H.323, H.245, H.225, RTCP
RTP,UDP
IP, RSVP, WFQ
RFC1717(PPP/ML), Frame, ATM, etc.

intranet, an IP addressing plan will be in place. To the

voice interfaces will appear as additional IP hosts,

e existing scheme or with new IP addresses. The dial

lation of dial digits from the PBX to the far-end IP

P router. When the originating router receives the

ompares this number to those defined in the router

he call is routed to the appropriate far-end router.

IP is the maturity and sophistication of its routing

protocols. A modern routing protocol, such as EIGRP, can take delay into consideration when calculating the best path. These are also fast-converging routing protocols, which allow voice traffic to take advantage of the self-healing capabilities of IP networks. Advanced features, such as policy routing and access lists, make it possible to create highly sophisticated and secure routing schemes for voice traffic. RSVP can be automatically invoked by Cisco's VoIP gateways to ensure that the appropriate bandwidth and delay characteristics are provided in the IP network to transport voice with a high level of QoS. One of the most interesting developments in IP routing is the development of tag switching and other IP switching disciplines. Tag switching provides a way of extending IP routing, policy, and QoS features over ATM and other high-speed transports. Another benefit of tag switching is its traffic engineering capabilities, which are needed for the efficient use of network resources. Traffic engineering can also be used to shift traffic load based on various predicates, such as time of day.

Introducing H.323

H.323 is probably the most important standard supporting packetized voice technology. During the 1990s, the H.320 standard was defined for ISDN BRI videophones and videoconferencing systems. The initial H.323 (H.323v.1) recommendation in October 1996 was heavily weighted toward communications in a LAN environment, but experiments with voice communications over the Internet were already underway. H.323 v.1 was mainly developed for multimedia LANs without packet-based QoS. These initial attempts were based on proprietary methods for setting up calls, compressing voice, locating and alerting endpoints, and so on.

As VoIP became more commonplace, the need for a standard method of providing voice communications over the Internet became apparent. In 1998, experiments with sending voice over the Internet led to the need for new standards and new applications, such as PC-based phones calling analog phones. H.323 is an ITU-T recommendation umbrella set of standards that defines the components, protocols, and procedures necessary to provide multimedia (audio, video, and data) communications over *IP-based* networks. Essentially, H.323 provides a method to enable other H.32X-compliant products to communicate. It is today's most mature VoIP protocol, and it has widespread industry support. In addition to *control* and *call setup* standards, H.323 encompasses protocols for audio, video, and data as follows:

- **Audio** The compression algorithms H.323 supports for audio are all proven International Telecommunications Union (ITU) standards (G.711, G.723, and G.729). Because audio is the minimum service provided by the H.323 standard, all H.323 terminals must have support for at least one audio codec support, as specified by G.711.

- **Video** Video capabilities for H.323 are optional. However, any video-enabled H.323 terminal must support the ITU-T *H.261* encoding and decoding recommendation. (H.263 is optional.)

- **Data** H.323 references the T.120 specifications for data conferencing. An ITU standard, T.120 addresses point-to-point and multipoint data conferences. It provides interoperability at the application, network, and transport levels.

Figure 3.5 shows the roles and interoperability of the various H.323 protocols.

Figure 3.5 H.323 Protocol Interoperability

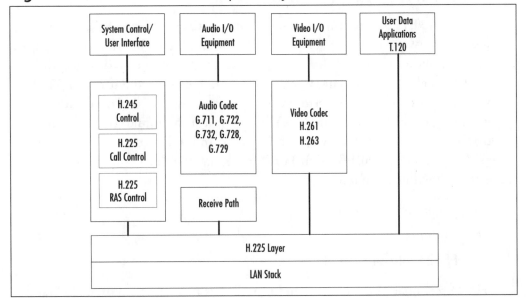

H.323 Components

Now that you have been properly introduced to the overall H.323 protocol, let's turn our attention to the components that make up the H.323 protocol. In order to truly understand and work with the H.323 protocol, a solid understanding of these components, their functions, and their importance is paramount. Although the H.323 protocol is used for numerous applications such as VoIP, videoconferencing, and the like, all devices that fall within the H.323 protocol stack can be categorized as one of four types of devices. These device types are terminals, gateways, gatekeepers, and multipoint control units (MCUs).

Terminals, also referred to as *endpoints*, provide the user interface into the H.323 protocol and provide real-time, two-way multimedia communications. All endpoints must support voice communications and can optionally support video or data communications. Gateways work as a translator to allow communications between H.323 and non-H.323 entities (for instance, between H.323 terminals and telephones on the circuit-switched network). Gatekeepers provide call control functions such as address translation and bandwidth management and are often considered to be the most important component in the H.323 stack. MCUs provide conference facilities for users who want to conference three or more endpoints together.

H.323 Terminals (Endpoints)

As we discussed, H.323 terminals, or endpoints as they are often called, provide the user-to-network interface for the H.323 protocol. This interface is contingent upon the application for which H.323 is being used. In the case of voice, the H.323 terminal is generally an IP telephone. In the case of video, the H.323 terminal is a videoconferencing terminal. H.323 is also widely deployed on PCs. A very common application of the H.323 protocol can be found in the Microsoft NetMeeting software that allows for both voice and video transmissions on a user's PC. In order to qualify as an H.323 terminal, the device in question must have the following three items:

- A network interface
- Audio codecs
- H.323 software

H.323 terminals must support audio (G.711 is mandatory, and G.723.1 and G.729 are recommended for networks of low bandwidth). Video and data support is optional; H.261 is mandatory when video is supported. H.245 and H.225 are required for control functions, and RTP is required for sequencing media packets.

H.323 Gateways

Gateway devices are also looked at by the H.323 protocol as endpoints. However, instead of providing an interface for users, H.323 gateways provide a means for an H.323 network to communicate to other networks, most typically the PSTN or PBX systems. In order to provide this interoperability, gateways provide for translation and call control functions between the two dissimilar network types. Encoding, protocol, and call control mappings occur in gateways between two endpoints. Gateways provide many functions, including:

- **Translating protocols** The gateway acts as an "interpreter," allowing the PSTN and the H.323 network to talk to each other to set up and tear down calls.

- **Converting information formats** Different networks encode information in different ways. The gateway converts this information so that both networks can freely exchange information such as speech and video.

- **Transferring information** The gateway is responsible for transferring information between different networks, such as the PSTN and the Internet.

In either a traditional VoIP infrastructure or an IP telephony environment, gateway functionality is generally provided by a router, such as the 2600 or 3600 series, a Catalyst gateway module such as the 6000 T1 gateway module, or dedicated gateway devices such as the VG200 and DT-24+.

H.323 Gatekeepers

Let's move on to a discussion of the H.323 gatekeeper. The gatekeeper performs the call control functions and administration of policy for registered H.323 endpoints. Many people consider gatekeepers to be the "brains" of the H.323 network. *Gatekeepers in H.323 networks are optional.* However, if they are present, it is mandatory that endpoints use their services. The H.323 standards define several mandatory services that the gatekeeper *must* provide and specify other optional functionality. The following services are mandatory:

- **Address translation** The gatekeeper must be able to translate an alias address into a transport address. This function is particularly important in scenarios in which a phone on the circuit-switched network is attempting to call a PC on an IP network. (An E.164 number such as 212-555-2121 will be translated into an IP network address such as 180.23.12.78.)

- **Admissions control** H.323 defines the Registration, Admission, and Status (RAS) messages necessary to authorize network access but does not define the rules or policies used to authorize access to network resources. To do that, the gatekeeper can interface with an existing authorization mechanism.

- **Bandwidth control and management** Gatekeepers must support RAS bandwidth messages. However, the way they provide the bandwidth access or bandwidth management is left to the provider. The H.323 standards have yet to define a mechanism for enforcing bandwidth control. A gatekeeper may also determine that there is no bandwidth available for a call or no additional bandwidth available for an ongoing call requesting an increase. The gatekeeper can instruct an ongoing call to reduce its bandwidth usage. All these decisions are outside the scope of the H.323 standards and are, therefore, left to the discretion of the H.323 provider.

- **Zone management** An H.323 "zone" is the collection of all components—terminals, gateways, and MCUs—managed by a single gatekeeper. Within its zone, a gatekeeper must provide required functions (for example: address translation, admissions control, bandwidth control) to all endpoints that have registered with it.

The gatekeeper can also perform some optional functions, such as:

- **Call authorization** The gatekeeper can decide to authorize or reject a given call; the provider of the H.323 service specifies the reasons for authorization and rejection. Reasons may include the time of day, type of service subscription, desire to access a restricted gateway, or lack of available bandwidth.

- **Call control signaling** A gatekeeper can decide that it will process all call signaling associated with the endpoints registered with it or allow the call-signaling messages to pass directly between the endpoints. The first method is commonly referred to as *gatekeeper routed call signaling*.

- **Call management** The gatekeeper may provide intelligent call management. For instance, it could be known that a requested terminal is currently engaged in a call. The gatekeeper can choose to redirect the call or, at a minimum, save the call setup time by not attempting to establish a call to a busy terminal. The call management may be based on address translation functions providing call screening, call forwarding/redirection, and call routing based on time of day, network congestion, or least-cost path.

As with gateways, routers are typically incorporated to provide gatekeeper functionality.

Multipoint Control Units

MCUs provide a unique function to the H.323 protocol in that they do not provide a direct interconnection to the H.323 protocol stack. Rather, they provide a method for H.323 to interconnect voice and videoconferencing.

MCUs provide conference support for three or more endpoints. All terminals participating in the conference establish a connection with the MCU. It manages conference resources and negotiations between endpoints to determine which audio or video codec to use. The MCU might or might not handle the media stream. An MCU has two functional components:

- A multipoint controller (MC) that performs conference control by controlling what media streams go where. The MC has a reconciliation capability (common mode) and may be located in the terminal, gateway, or gatekeeper. The MC is required for all conferences.

- A multipoint processor (MP) that mixes, switches, and processes media streams, including some or all of the streams in the conference call (video, data, or audio). The MP is not required, but its absence can put a burden on a terminal.

The H.323 Protocol Stack

In our discussion of the H.323 protocol, to this point we have referred to it as a single protocol that performs several functions. This is not the case. Just as with the TCP/IP protocol, the H.323 protocol is actually a suite of protocols that work together to provide end-to-end call functionality in a converged network. However, the H.323 protocol also relies heavily on the services provided by other protocols such as TCP, IP, and UDP as well as RTP. The protocols that make up the H.323 protocol are Registration, Admission, and Status (RAS), H.245, and H.225. Let's take a few moments and discuss each of the protocols that go into making the H.323 protocol able to provide end-to-end call functionality.

IP, TCP, and UDP

The first protocols that we discuss are not truly part of the H.323 protocol stack. Rather, they are three of the key protocols of the TCP/IP protocol stack. However, each of these protocols provides crucial functionality to the H.323 protocol as well as the other VoIP protocols that we discuss in this chapter. We begin this discussion with IP.

Internet Protocol

As with any other network that uses the TCP/IP protocol, IP provides a hierarchical addressing scheme for the H.323 protocol. Each H.323 endpoint, gateway, gatekeeper, and MCU must have a valid and unique IP address. This also holds true for PCs with applications that use the H.323 protocol. IP provides each H.323 node an address and provides the mechanism to route H.323 packets across a network. A design consideration to make regarding IP addresses in an H.323 network is that it is advisable to utilize private addressing space, discussed earlier in this chapter, when assigning IP addresses in a VoIP environment.

Transmission Control Protocol

As we know from our discussion earlier in the chapter, TCP is responsible for providing a reliable transmission control mechanism over the unreliable IP protocol. In order to do so, TCP incorporates such mechanisms as sequencing, windowing, and reassembly of packets. In an H.323 environment, TCP is used to provide initial connection setup between H.323 endpoints and gateways/gatekeepers.

User Datagram Protocol

In sharp contrast to the reliable, connection-oriented protocol provided by TCP, UDP offers an unreliable, unsequenced, connectionless protocol that sacrifices reliability for speed. UDP relies on higher-layer protocols to provide sequencing and reliability and, as such, provides a much faster and lower-level transport protocol than TCP can. For this reason, UDP is used for the actual payload for VoIP calls. If a voice packet is for some reason lost or dropped, UDP disregards the lost packet, simply because delivering a lost voice packet out of sync will hinder rather than aid a call.

H.225

H.225 provides call setup and control with all signaling necessary to establish a connection between two H.323 endpoints. The ITU Q.931 provides a means to establish, maintain, and terminate network connections across ISDN. It is defined as the basic call setup protocol for an ISDN. In the Blue Book (1988), Q.931 uses 22 messages, and 29 in case of Q.932. H.225 adopted a subset of Q.931 messages and parameters. The H.323 mandatory messages are Alerting, Call Processing, Connect, Setup, Release Complete, Status, Status Inquiry, and Facility (Q.932).

H.245

H.245 control signaling is used to negotiate channel usage and capabilities. H.245 exchanges end-to-end control messages managing the operation of the H.323 endpoint. Control messages carry information related to:

- Capabilities exchange

- Opening and closing logical channels used to carry media streams

- Flow control messages

- General commands

After call setup, all communications are over logical channels. H.245 defines procedures for mapping logical channels. (Logical channel 0 is for H.245 control—open for the duration of the call—and multiple logical channels of varying types, such as video, data, voice, are allowed for a single call.) H.245 defines the protocol for accomplishing specific tasks such as signaling entities.

The H.245 Capability Exchange Signaling Entity identifies the capabilities of participating entities and may identify options and valid combinations of capabilities: one video channel (H.261) and one audio channel (G.711 or G.723).

The H.245 Master/Slave Determination Signaling Entity identifies the entity that will act as MC; deterministic rules apply, based on hierarchy of capabilities and entity types.

Registration, Administration, and Status

RAS is a protocol used between endpoints (terminals and gateways) and gatekeepers. It is used to perform registration, admission control, bandwidth changes, and status and to disengage endpoints from gatekeepers. RAS uses UDP port 1719.

Real-Time Transport Protocol

RTP provides end-to-end network transport functions suitable for applications transmitting real-time data such as audio, video, or simulation data, over multicast or unicast network services. It is used to transport data via UDP. RTP does not address resource reservation and does not guarantee QoS for real-time services. The data transport is augmented by a control protocol (RTCP) to allow monitoring of the data delivery in a manner scalable to large multicast networks and to provide minimal control and identification functionality. RTP and RTCP are designed to be independent of the underlying transport and network layers. The protocol supports the use of RTP-level translators and mixers.

RTCP provides a control transport for RTP. RTCP provides feedback on the quality of data distribution and carries a transport-level identifier for an RTP source used by receivers to synchronize audio and video.

Codecs

Coder/decoders (codecs) are used by not only the H.323 protocol but by all VoIP protocols to define the degree of compression and decompression algorithms that will be used to transport either a voice or video transmission across a converged network. H.323 supports most of the standard voice and video codecs, including:

- **G.7XX** ITU series of audio codecs (G.711, G.723, G.729).
- **H.26X** ITU series of video codecs (H.261, H.263). H.26x series describe a video stream for transport using RTP with any of the underlying protocols that carry RTP.

Figure 3.6 demonstrates how the H.323 protocols interrelate with one another.

Figure 3.6 The H.323 Protocol Stack

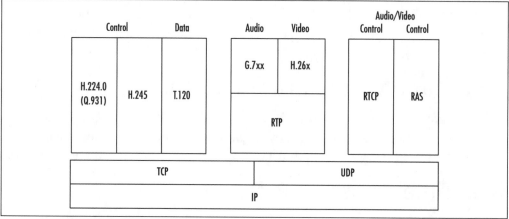

H.323 Call Stages

The process of establishing and maintaining an H.323 call is a very complex one. In the following sections we break this process down into a logical and hierarchical order of events to help you understand what is taking place at each stage and the requirements and resources used for each stage of an H.323 call. After reading this section, you should have a solid understanding of the H.323 call process.

H.323 Discovery and Registration

Now that you have an understanding of the devices involved in an H.323 environment as well as the protocols that make the H.323 protocol function, let's focus on the actual stages of an H.323 call and examine the details of each of these connections. The connection procedures involved in creating an H.323 call can be grouped into five stages:

1. Discovery and registration
2. Call setup

3. Call-signaling flows

4. Media stream and media control flows

5. Call termination

A lot is happening within each of these stages, from the time the call is requested to the time it is terminated. In the following sections we look at each of these steps in detail.

Device Discovery and Registration

During the discovery and registration stage of the H.323 call, the gatekeeper initiates a "discovery" process to determine the gatekeeper with which the endpoint must communicate. This discovery can be either a statically configured address or through multicast traffic. Once this is determined, the endpoint or gateway registers with the discovered gatekeeper.

Registration is used by the endpoints to identify a zone with which it can be associated. (A *zone* is a collection of H.323 components managed by a single gatekeeper.) H.323 can then inform the gatekeeper of the zones' transport address and alias address. Figure 3.7 shows the process of intrazone call placement.

Figure 3.7 H.323 Gatekeeper Call Control/Signaling: Discovery and Registration

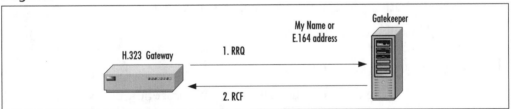

In Figure 3.7, two distinct actions are occurring:

1. An H.323 gateway (or terminal) sends a request to register (RRQ) message using H.225 RAS on the RAS channel to the gatekeeper.

2. The gatekeeper confirms the registration by sending a registration confirmation (RCF) or a "Reject registration" message back to the gateway.

Intrazone Call Placement

Let's assume that the gateways (or terminals) are already registered. In the case where Gateway X (Figure 3.8) wants to place a call to a terminal connected to

Gateway Y, Gateway X sends an ARQ message to the gatekeeper requesting permission to place a call to a phone number serviced by Gateway Y. Figure 3.8 helps us visualize this process.

Figure 3.8 H.323 Gatekeeper Call Control/Signaling: Call Placement (Intrazone)

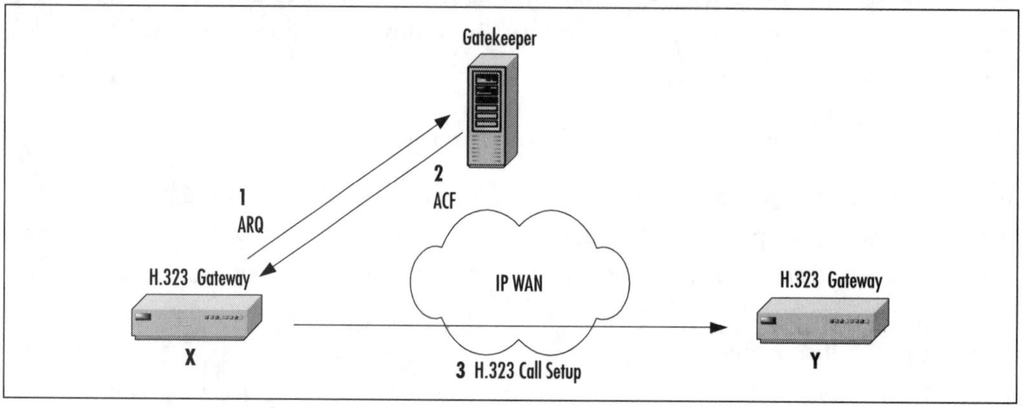

In Figure 3.8, the following is occurring:

1. Gateway X sends an admission request (ARQ) message using H.225 RAS on the RAS channel to the gatekeeper.

2. The gatekeeper requests the direct call signaling by sending an admission confirmation (ACF) message back to Gateway X.

3. H.323 call setup is then initiated.

Interzone Call Placement

The process of placing an interzone call versus an intrazone call is somewhat more complicated and resource intensive. In this case, we assume that the network is relatively large and divided into different zones (two zones in this example). Gatekeeper A controls Zone A, and Gatekeeper B controls Zone B. Gateway X (or Terminal X) is registered with Gatekeeper A, and Gateway Y is registered with Gatekeeper B (Figure 3.9).

Gateway X wants to place a call to a terminal connected to Gateway Y. Gateway X sends an ARQ message to the gatekeeper requesting permission to place a call to a phone number serviced by Gateway Y. Since Gateway Y is not registered with the gatekeeper in Zone A, we assume that the gateways (terminals) are already registered. Figure 3.9 takes a look at this process.

Figure 3.9 H.323 Gatekeeper Call Control/Signaling: Call Placement (Interzone)

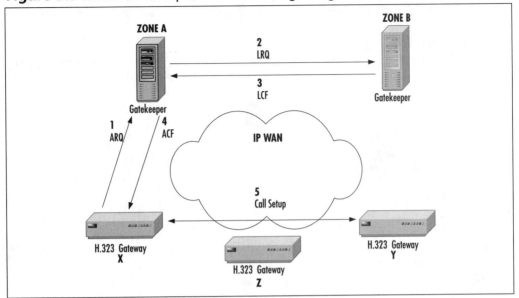

Figure 3.9 reveals five distinct phases in an interzone call placement. These stages are:

1. **Admission request (ARQ)** Gateway X is requesting a connection to Gateway Y from its local gatekeeper.

2. **Location request (LRQ)** The local gatekeeper for Gateway X does not know the IP address of Gateway Y and is requesting the address from Gateway Y's local gatekeeper.

3. **Location confirm (LCF)** Gateway Y's local gatekeeper responds to Gateway X's local gatekeeper with the IP address of Gateway Y.

4. **Admission confirm (ACF)** The local gatekeeper responds to Gateway X's request and provides the remote IP address of Gateway Y.

5. **Call established** The H.323 call is established between Gateway X and Gateway Y.

H.323 Call Setup

Once discovery and registration and then call placement are successfully completed, the H.323 call moves to the *call setup* stage. Within this stage, the gateways are communicating directly to set up the connection. An alternate method of call setup is *gatekeeper-routed call signaling,* where all the call setup messages traverse the gatekeeper. Figure 3.10 helps us conceptualize this process. The setup protocol is based on Q.931, and the setup message includes caller name and IP address.

Figure 3.10 Call Setup

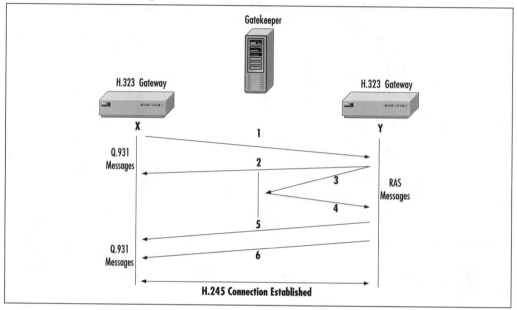

The call setup is based on the ITU–Q.931 (H.225 is a subset of Q.931), which provides a means to establish, maintain, and terminate network connections across an ISDN. This process comprises six distinct phases:

1. Gateway X sends an H.225 call-signaling setup message to Gateway Y to request a connection.

2. Gateway Y sends an H.225 message back to Gateway X, advising that it may proceed with the call.

3. Gateway Y sends an RAS message (ARQ) on the RAS channel to the gatekeeper to request permission to accept the call.

4. The gatekeeper confirms that the call can be accepted by sending a message (ACF) back to Gateway Y.

5. Gateway Y sends an H.225 message to Gateway X, alerting that the connection has been established.

6. Gateway Y sends an H.225 message to Gateway X, confirming the call connection, and the call is established.

Logical Channel Setup

After call setup, all communications traverse over logical channels. The H.245 protocol is now used to define procedures for managing these logical channels. Multiple logical channels of varying types (video, audio, and data) are allowed for a single call.

The H.245 Logical Channel Signaling Entity (LCSE) opens a logical channel for each media stream. Channels may be unidirectional or bidirectional. Figure 3.11 helps us visualize how the H.323 utilizes virtual channels.

Figure 3.11 Media Channel Setup

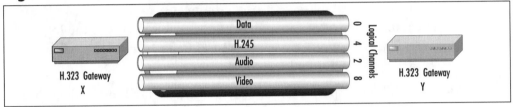

NOTE

An H.245 logical channel number identifies a single, unidirectional media channel.

Let's see how this logical channel setup fits within the flow of this H.323 call. The H.245 control channel is established between Gateway X and Gateway Y. Gateway X uses H.245 to identify its capabilities by sending a Terminal Capability Set message to Gateway Y. The media channel setup flow is as follows:

1. Gateway X exchanges its capabilities with Gateway Y by sending an H.245 Terminal Capability Set message.

2. Gateway Y acknowledges Gateway X's capabilities by sending an H.245 Terminal Capability Set Acknowledge message.

3. Gateway Y exchanges its capabilities with Gateway X by sending an H.245 Terminal Capability Set message.

4. Gateway X acknowledges Gateway Y's capabilities by sending back an H.245 Terminal Capability Set Acknowledge message.

5. Gateway X opens a media channel with Gateway Y by sending an H.245 Open Logical Channel message and includes the transport address of the RTCP channel. (The media stream is managed by RTCP.)

6. Gateway Y acknowledges the establishment of the logical channel with Gateway X by sending an H.245 Open Logical Channel Acknowledge message, including:

   - The RTP transport addresses (which will be used for sending the RTP media stream) allocated by Gateway Y

   - The RTCP address previously received from Gateway X

7. Gateway Y then opens a media channel with Gateway X by sending an H.245 Open Logical Channel message and includes the transport address of the RTCP channel.

8. To complete the establishment of the bidirectional media stream communication, Gateway A acknowledges the establishment of the logical channel with Gateway Y by sending an H.245 Open Logical Channel Acknowledge message and includes:

   - The RTP transport addresses (which will be used for sending the RTP media stream) allocated by Gateway X

   - The RTCP address previously received from Gateway Y

Figure 3.12 highlights this process.

Figure 3.12 Media Channel Setup Call Flow

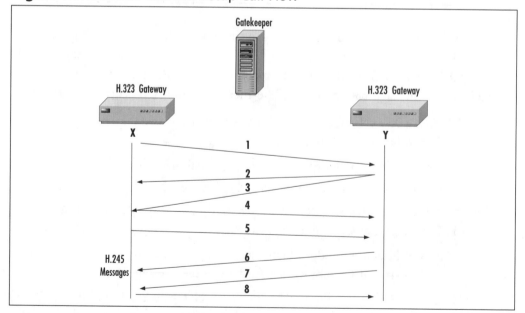

Media Stream and Media Control Flows

In Cisco VoIP gateways, RTP media streams are transported over UDP ports 16384 through $16384 + 4x$ (where x is the number of voice ports on the gateways). For example, a Cisco 3620 router with four E&M ports would use UDP ports 16384–16400 for RTP flows.

Media streams in the H.323 call flow are managed by RTCP. This protocol provides for QoS feedback from receivers. The source may use this information to adapt encoding or buffering schemes. RTCP uses a dedicated logical channel for each RTP media stream. Let's briefly review the steps in this stage of the H.323 call flow. Figure 3.13 demonstrates this process.

Figure 3.13 Media Stream Communication

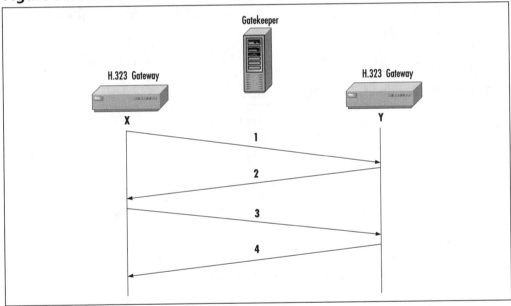

In the example shown in Figure 3.13, four actions are occurring:

1. Gateway X sends the RTP encapsulated media stream to Gateway Y.
2. Gateway Y sends the RTP encapsulated media stream back to Gateway X.
3. Gateway X sends the RTCP messages to Gateway Y.
4. Gateway Y sends the RTCP messages back to Gateway X.

Endpoints may seek changes in the amount of bandwidth initially requested and confirmed. The gatekeeper must be asked for bandwidth increases and may be asked for bandwidth decreases. Endpoints must comply with gatekeeper responses and requests. The bandwidth change flow is diagramed in Figure 3.14. This process consists of six stages:

1. The initiating gateway sends a bandwidth request (BRQ) to the gatekeeper to request the desired bandwidth.

2. The gatekeeper responds with a bandwidth confirmation (BCF) message for the requested bandwidth.

3. A logical channel is established between the two gateways with the specified bandwidth.

4. A BRQ is sent from the remote router to the gatekeeper to change the bandwidth of the connection.

5. The gatekeeper responds to the gateway with a BCF to confirm the new bandwidth.

6. The logical channel is re-established with the new bandwidth.

Figure 3.14 Bandwidth Change Request

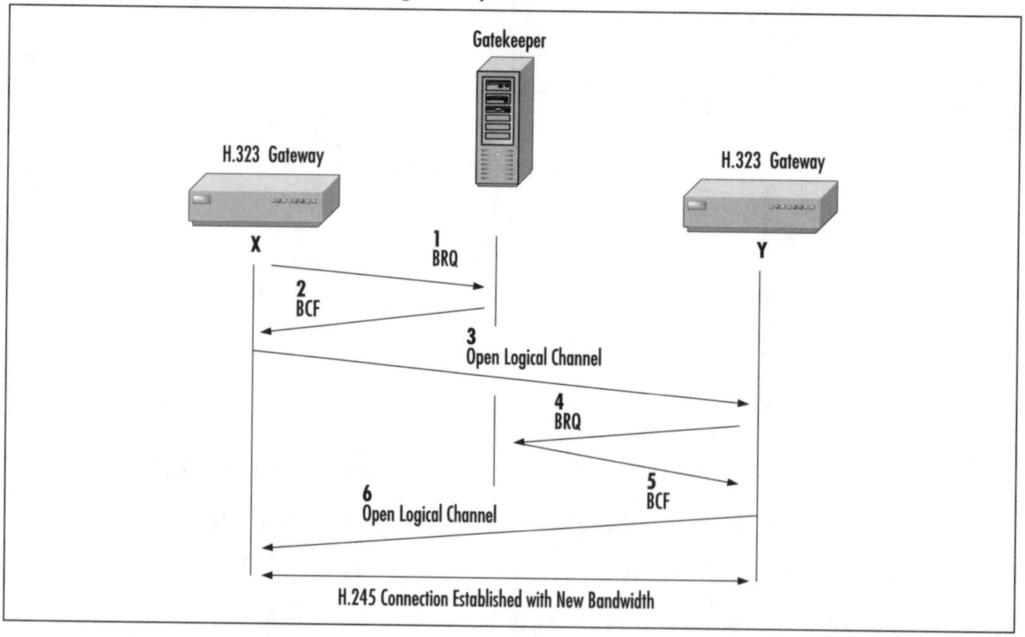

Call Termination

Call termination stops the media streams and closes the logical channels. It may be requested by any endpoint or by a gatekeeper. Call termination also ends the

H.245 session, releases H.225/Q.931 connections, and provides disconnect confirmation to the gatekeeper via RAS. Figure 3.15 shows call termination flow and is described as follows:

1. Gateway Y initiates the call termination by sending an H.245 End Session Command message to Gateway X.

2. Gateway X releases the call endpoint and confirms the release by sending an H.245 End Session Command message back to Gateway Y.

3. Gateway Y completes the call release by sending an H.245 Release Complete message to Gateway X.

4. Gateway X and Gateway Y disengage with the gatekeeper by sending a RAS DRQ message.

5. The gatekeeper disengages and confirms by sending DCF messages to both Gateway X and Gateway Y.

Figure 3.15 Call Termination (H.245/H.225/Q.931/RAS)

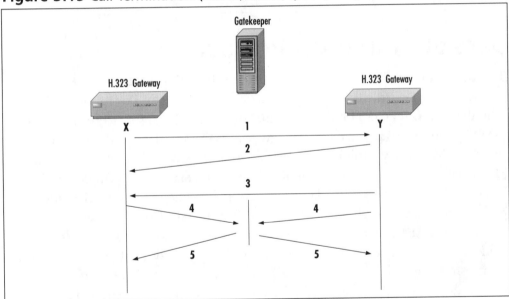

H.323 Endpoint-to-Endpoint Signaling

Assuming that endpoints (clients) know each other's IP addresses, the H.323 signaling is shown in Figure 3.16. This figure is based on the steps described in the previous section, "Call Termination."

Figure 3.16 H.323 Endpoint-to-Endpoint Signaling

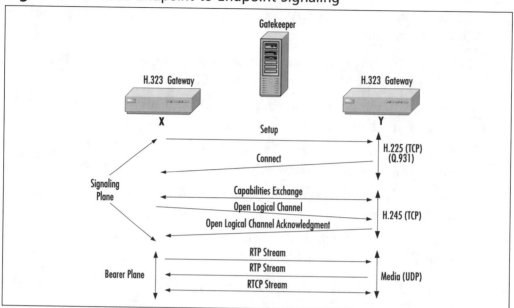

Session Initiation Protocol

The next protocol for discussion is the Session Initiation Protocol, or SIP. SIP is a simple signaling protocol used for Internet conferencing and telephony. SIP is fully defined in RFC 2543. Based on the Simple Mail Transport Protocol (SMTP) and the Hypertext Transfer Protocol (HTTP), SIP was developed within the IETF Multiparty Multimedia Session Control (MMUSIC) working group. SIP specifies procedures for telephony and multimedia conferencing over the Internet. SIP is an application-layer protocol independent of the underlying packet protocol (TCP, UDP, ATM, X.25). SIP is based on a client/server architecture in which the client initiates the calls and the servers answer the calls. By conforming to these existing text-based Internet standards (SMTP and HTTP), troubleshooting and network debugging are facilitated, since the protocol can be read in the clear without decoding the binary ASN.1 payload required in non-text-based protocols such as H.323. Because it is an open, standards-based protocol, SIP is widely supported and is not dependent on a single vendor's equipment or implementation.

SIP is a newer protocol than H.323 and does not have maturity and industry support at this time. However, because of its simplicity, scalability, modularity, and ease with which it integrates with other applications, this protocol is attractive for use in packetized voice architectures. Some of the key features that SIP offers are:

- Address resolution, name mapping, and call redirection
- Dynamic discovery of endpoint media capabilities by use of the Session Description Protocol (SDP)
- Dynamic discovery of endpoint availability
- Session origination and management between host and endpoints

Key Benefits of Session Initiation Protocol

SIP is complementary to MGCP in that MGCP provides for device control while SIP handles session control. Some of the key benefits of SIP are:

- **Simplicity** SIP is a very simple protocol. Software development time is very short compared with that of traditional telephony products. Due to SIP's similarity to HTTP and SMTP, code reuse is possible.

- **Extensibility** SIP has learned from HTTP and SMTP and has built a rich set of extensibility and compatibility functions.

- **Modularity** SIP was designed to be highly modular. A key feature is its independent use of protocols. For example, SIP issues invitations to called parties, independent of the session itself.

- **Scalability** SIP offers two scalability benefits:

  - **Server processing** SIP has the ability to be either *stateful* or *stateless*.

  - **Conference sizes** Since there is no requirement for a central multipoint controller, conference coordination can be fully distributed or centralized.

- **Integration** SIP has the capability to integrate with the Web, e-mail, streaming media applications, and other protocols.

- **Interoperability** Because it is an open, RFC-based standard, SIP can offer interoperability between different vendors platforms seamlessly.

Session Initiation Protocol Components

The SIP system contains two components: user agents and network servers. A *user agent (UA)* is SIP's endpoint, which makes and receives SIP calls.

- The client is called the *user agent client (UAC)* and is used to initiate SIP requests.

- The server is called the *user agent server (UAS),* receiving the requests from the UAC and returning responses for the user.

SIP clients can include:

- IP telephones acting in the capacity as either UACs or UASs.

- Gateways. As we know from our discussion of H.323, a gateway provides call control for a VoIP environment. In a SIP implementation, gateways provide conferencing and translation functionality.

There are three kinds of SIP servers:

- **Proxy server** Proxy servers decide to which server the request should be forwarded and then forward the request. The request can actually traverse many SIP servers before reaching its destination. The response then traverses in the reverse order. A proxy server can act as both a client and server and can issue requests and responses.

- **Redirect server** Unlike the proxy server, the redirect server does not forward requests to other servers. Instead, it notifies the calling party of the actual location of destination.

- **Registrar server** Provides registration services for UACs for their current locations. Registrar servers are often placed with proxy and redirect servers.

We also can talk about the SIP terminal, which can support real-time, two-way communication with another SIP entity. SIP terminal supports both signaling and media, similar to H.323 terminal. The SIP terminal contains the UAC. Figure 3.17 looks at the interaction between SIP components.

Figure 3.17 SIP Components

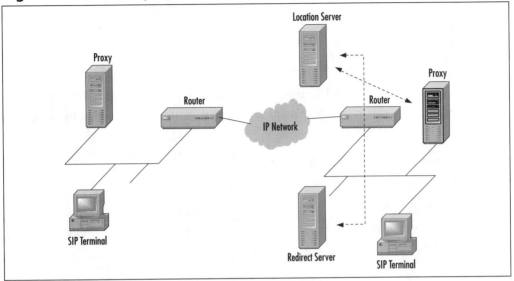

Session Initiation Protocol Messages

SIP works on a simple premise of client/server operation. Clients or endpoints are identified by unique addresses. These addresses come in a format very similar to that of an e-mail address: user@domain.com. Let's take a look at some points to remember when we're discussing SIP addresses:

- SIP addresses are always user@host.
- User: name, telephone (E164 address), number.
- Host: domain, numeric network (IP) address.

The users or clients register with SIP servers to provide location contact information.

SIP uses *messages* for call connection and control. There are two types of SIP message: requests and responses. SIP messages are defined as follows:

- **Invite** Used to initiate a user to a call. Header fields contain:
  - Addresses of the caller and the person being called
  - Subject of the call
  - Call priority

- Call routing requests
- Caller preferences for the user location
- Desired features of the response

- **Bye**   Used to terminate a connection between two users.

- **Register**   Conveys location information to a SIP server, allowing a user to tell the server how to map an incoming address into an outgoing address that will reach the user.

- **ACK**   Confirms reliable message exchanges.

- **Cancel**   Cancels impending requests.

- **Options**   Solicits information about the capabilities of the end being called, such as the difference between a plain old telephone handset and a fully featured multimedia phone.

Media Gateway Control Protocol

The final protocol that we discuss in this chapter is Media Gateway Control Protocol (MGCP). MGCP is a relatively new protocol compared with its predecessors H.323 and SIP, and as such, it is not as widely deployed. This is especially true when we compare MGCP to H.323. However, MGCP offers many key benefits and is growing in popularity, especially in Cisco Call Manager deployments.

MGCP is presented as a merger of the Simple Gateway Control Protocol (SGCP) and the Internet Protocol Device Control (IPDC). SGCP is very similar to MGCP in that it also calls for a simplified design and a centralized intelligent call control. However, it does not offer many of the features and functionality of MGCP. SGCP was developed through a partnership between Cisco Systems and BellCore. IPDC was designed to provide a medium to bridge VoIP networks and traditional telephony networks. Like SGCP, IPDC also operated on the idea of centralized call control and simplified design. Ascend, Nortel, and Level 3 created IPDC. These organizations had the foresight to merge two similar protocols and move toward a single protocol. MGCP is a media control protocol, suited for large-scale IP telephony deployment, and supports VoIP only. MCGP is fully defined in RFC 2705.

MGCP incorporates devices known as *media gateway controllers (MGCs),* also referred to as *call agents*, in order to perform all call connection and call control within an MGCP network. These MGCs signal to, and control, media gateways

(MGs) in order to connect and control VoIP calls. All the information for making and completing a VoIP call is held in the MG. MGs have very little intelligence and receive all their marching orders from the MGC; for this reason, an MG cannot function without a MGC to control it. In a Cisco Call Manager deployment, the MGC is often a Call Manager server and the media gateway is a router used to connect to a dissimilar network. Examples of gateway applications are:

- **Trunking gateways** Interfaces between the telephone network and a VoIP network. Such gateways typically manage a large number of digital circuits.

- **Voice over ATM gateways** Operate much the same way as VoIP trunking gateways, except that they interface to an ATM network.

- **Residential gateways** Provide a traditional analog (RJ11) interface to a VoIP network. Examples of residential gateways include cable modem/ cable set-top boxes, xDSL devices, and broadband wireless devices.

- **Access gateways** Provide a traditional analog (RJ11) or digital PBX interface to a VoIP network. Examples of access gateways include small-scale VoIP gateways.

- **Business gateways** Provide a traditional digital PBX interface or an integrated "soft PBX" interface to a VoIP network.

- **Network access servers** Can attach a modem to a telephone circuit and provide data access to the Internet. We expect that in the future, the same gateways will combine VoIP services and Network Access Services.

When a gateway device detects that an end-user phone connection goes off-hook, it, at the direction of the MGC, provides dial tone to the phone and receives the dialed digits and forwards them to the MGC for call processing.

MGCP Connections

In an MGCP connection, there are two basic types of logical devices: endpoints and connections. *Endpoints* are the physical, or at times, logical interfaces that either initiate or terminate a VoIP connection. Endpoints are most often analog or digital ports in routers acting as gateway devices or digital interfaces into a PBX system. *Connections* are temporary logical flows that are established solely for the purpose of establishing, maintaining, and terminating a VoIP call. Once the call is complete, the connection is torn down and the resources that were allocated for that connection can be reused to support another connection. Think of this process as very similar to the way that a TCP/IP virtual connection works. There are two flavors of connections: one-to-one and multipoint. A *one-to-one connection* is really a point-to-point connection; a single endpoint signals to another single endpoint for the purposes of completing a single VoIP connection. *Multipoint calls* are used for conferencing and broadcast to multiple endpoints simultaneously.

MGCs are solely responsible for the management of connections in an MGCP network. In order to accomplish this command and control, a protocol known as Session Description Protocol (SDP) is incorporated. SDP uses ASCII commands over IP/UDP to perform all call management functions. A series of eight connection messages is used by the MGC in order to control endpoints. These messages are:

- CreateConnection

- ModifyConnection

- DeleteConnection

- NotificationRequest

- Notify

- AuditEndpoint

- AuditConnection

- RestartInProgress

MeGaCo/H.248

MeGaCo is a new evolution of the MGCP standard. Currently, MeGaCo is also known as ITU designation H.248 and is fully defined in RFC 3015. Although very similar to the MGCP standard in many ways, MeGaCo offers several enhancements and features that MGCP does not. MGCP was built on a simple premise of centralizing call control to a central, intelligent media gateway controller (MGC) and having several "dumb" media gateways (MGs) perform low-level connections and terminations. The MeGaCo standard proposes several changes to this concept.

One of the most exciting of these changes is the ability for MGCs to interact with the media stream directly from an end-user telephone. Under the current MGCP standard, the dialed digits are terminated by the gateway device and then forwarded to the MGC for appropriate call processing. Although efficient, this method greatly limits MGCP to performing only call processing. MeGaCo changes this situation by allowing the MGC to directly listen to the dialed digits from the end-user telephone. What does this capability afford a MeGaCo-enabled infrastructure? It allows a MeGaCo-enabled infrastructure to provide sophisticated voice-conferencing capabilities based on dialed digits as well as the ability to interact with interactive voice response (IVR) systems. Every protocol that we have discussed thus far in this chapter has centered on VoIP and was designed to support only VoIP; MeGaCo is the exception to this rule. Even though similar to the other protocols, MeGaCo was designed to work with VoIP and offers the ability work with VoATM and VoFR networks. It can provide a translation mechanism between the dissimilar network types. This is a function that no other protocol currently offers.

Currently, a debate rages as to whether or not MeGaCo will be a viable solution for VoIP deployments and whether or not it should completely replace or merely augment the current MGCP standard. Currently, vendor support for the MeGaCo standard is sparse at best, but with the advanced functionality and features provided by this protocol, it could provide a great solution for converged infrastructures. Only time will tell.

Designing & Planning...

So Many Protocols

H.323, SIP, MGCP, MeGaCo—which protocol is the right one to use? You are not alone in asking this question. This question is not only plaguing organizations that want to deploy VoIP solutions—it is currently being asked by the entire industry. All these protocols offer several benefits and some limitations. The question "Which protocol is right for my network?" can be answered only after careful examination of your network, potential growth, and several other factors. Let's look at the type of deployment in which each protocol could be found:

- **H.323** H.323 is the oldest and most stable of the protocols that we have discussed thus far. You will most likely find it in use in organizations that have employed VoIP technologies and solutions for some period of time. H.323 offers a great deal of scalability and reliability; because it is an open

Continued

standard, it offers vendor interoperability and integration. H.323 is suited to midsize to large deployments.

- **SIP** Like H.323, SIP is an open standards-based protocol that offers vendor interoperability and integration. However, SIP is a much lower-overhead protocol and is based on a completely different standard than H.323. Because of the newness of the protocol and the dominance of H.323, SIP is not currently in wide deployment. However, due to its low overhead and scalability, SIP could be implemented in a network of any size.

- **MGCP** Like SIP, MGCP departed from the model set forth by the H.323 protocol. MGCP, like the other two protocols, is a completely open standard offering interoperability between different vendors' equipment. MGCP works on a simplified, centralized call-processing model, with all call-processing intelligence contained in the MGC. MGCP has met with a good deal of popularity in Cisco AVVID Call Manager deployments as a means of controlling gateway devices. As such, MGCP is a good solution for a greenfield IP telephony deployment.

The Role of QoS in Packet-Switched Voice Networks

At the beginning of this chapter we discussed how, in recent years, VoIP has gone from being something that was rarely deployed to a viable and reliable solution for organizations for varying sizes. A great deal of this change in perceptions and ability can be attributed to the improvements made in QoS. QoS is not really a technology of sorts, nor is it a single protocol; rather it is a set of ideas, procedures, practices, and numerous protocols that provide for reliable and efficient transportation across data networks. In this section we introduce some of the concepts and protocols that make up QoS as well as discuss the importance of QoS in a packet-switched network. This discussion serves as only an introduction to QoS; entire books have been written on this subject, and it is of fundamental importance to a converged infrastructure. Chapter 6 discusses QoS in much greater detail.

What Is Quality of Service?

QoS is a set of tools and mechanisms available to network administrators to provide predictable service levels to IP packets as they transverse an IP network. Many protocols and applications are not critically sensitive to network congestion. File Transfer Protocol (FTP), for example, has a rather large tolerance for network delay or bandwidth limitation. To the user, FTP simply takes longer to download a file to the target system. Although annoying to the user, this slowness does not normally impede the operation of the application.

On the other hand, applications such as voice and video are particularly sensitive to network delay. If voice packets take too long to reach their destinations, the resulting speech sounds choppy or distorted. QoS can be used to provide predictable service levels to these applications. Critical business applications can also use QoS. Companies whose main business focus relies on Systems Network Architecture (SNA)-based network traffic can feel the pressures of network congestion. SNA's handshake protocol is very sensitive to delay and normally terminates a session when it does not receive an acknowledgment in time. Unlike TCP/IP, which recovers well from a missed acknowledgment, SNA does not operate well in a congested environment. In these cases, providing low latency treatment for SNA traffic could be a proper approach to QoS.

Applications for Quality of Service

When would a network engineer consider designing QoS into a network? Here are a few reasons to deploy QoS in a network topology:

- To give priority to certain mission-critical applications in the network

- To maximize the use of the current network investment in infrastructure

- To provide better performance for delay-sensitive applications such as voice and video

- To respond to changes in network traffic flows

Often we find that the simplest method for achieving better performance on a network is to throw more bandwidth at the problem. In this day and age of Gigabit Ethernet and optical networking, higher capacities are readily available. More bandwidth does not, however, always guarantee a certain level of performance. It may well be that the very protocols that cause the congestion in the first place will simply eat up the additional bandwidth, leading to the same congestion issues experienced before the bandwidth upgrade.

A more judicious approach is to analyze the traffic flowing through the bottleneck, determine the importance of each protocol and application, and determine a strategy to prioritize the access to the bandwidth. QoS allows the network administrator to have control over bandwidth, latency, and jitter within the network.

Deploying certain types of QoS techniques can control four parameters (bandwidth, latency, jitter, and packet loss). Within many corporate networks today, QoS is not widely deployed. With the push for applications such as multicast, streaming multimedia, and VoIP, the need for certain quality levels is more inherent, especially because these types of applications are susceptible to jitter and delay. Poor performance is immediately noticed by the end user. End users experiencing poor performance typically generate trouble tickets, and the network administrator is left troubleshooting the performance problem. A network administrator can proactively manage new, sensitive applications by applying QoS techniques to the network. It is important to realize that QoS is not the magic solution to every congestion problem. It may very well be that upgrading the bandwidth of a congested link is the proper solution to the problem. However, by knowing the options available, you will be in a better position to make the proper decision to solve congestion and quality issues.

Three Levels of QoS

QoS can be broken into three different levels, also referred to as *service models*. These service models describe a set of end-to-end QoS capabilities. *End-to-end QoS* is the network's ability to provide a specific level of service to network traffic from one end of the network to the other. The three service levels are best-effort service, integrated service, and differentiated service. Here we examine each service model in greater detail.

Best-Effort Service

Best-effort service, as its name implies, is when the network will make every possible attempt to deliver a packet to its destination. With best-effort service, there are no guarantees that the packet will ever reach its intended destination. An application can send data in any amount, whenever it needs to, without requesting permission or notifying the network.

Certain applications can thrive under this model. FTP and HTTP, for example, can support best-effort service without much hardship. However, it is not an optimal service model for applications that are sensitive to network delays, bandwidth fluctuations, and other changing network conditions. Network telephony applications, for example, might require a more consistent amount of bandwidth in order to function properly. The results of best-effort service for these applications could be failed telephone calls or interrupted speech during the call.

Integrated Service

The integrated service model provides applications with a guaranteed level of service by negotiating network parameters end to end. Applications request the level of service necessary for them to operate properly and rely on the QoS mechanism to reserve the necessary network resources prior to the application beginning its transmission. It is important to note that the application will not send the traffic until it receives a signal from the network stating that the network can handle the load and provide the requested QoS end to end. To accomplish this task, the network uses a process called *admission control*.

Admission control is the mechanism that prevents the network from being overloaded. The network will not send a signal to the application to start transmitting the data if the requested QoS cannot be delivered. Once the application begins transmitting data, the network resources reserved for the application are maintained end to end until the application is done or until the bandwidth reservation exceeds what is allowable for this application.

Cisco IOS has two features to provide integrated service in the form of controlled load services. They are Resource Reservation Protocol (RSVP) and intelligent queuing. RSVP is currently in the process of being standardized by the IETF in one of its working groups. Intelligent queuing includes technologies such as Weighted Fair Queuing (WFQ) and Weighted Random Early Detection (WRED).

RSVP is a Cisco proprietary protocol used to signal the network of an application's QoS requirements. It is important to note that RSVP is not a routing protocol. RSVP works in conjunction with the routing protocols to determine the best path through the network that will provide the QoS required. RSVP-enabled routers actually create dynamic access lists to provide the QoS requested and ensure that packets are delivered at the prescribed minimum quality parameters. RSVP will be covered in greater details later in this book.

Differentiated Services

The last model for QoS is the Differentiated Services (DiffServ) model. DiffServ includes a set of classification and marking tools, queuing mechanisms and other components to provide for the differentiated treatment of traffic, based on the marking given to various packets. The DiffServ model suggests that edge routers should perform the classification and marking of the various types of traffic (packets) traversing the network. Network traffic can be classified by network address, protocols and ports, ingress interfaces, or in a variety of other ways.

Configuring & Implementing...

QoS versus Queuing

When many individuals, even the most experienced networking professionals, hear the term QoS, they automatically assume that you are referring to queuing. This assumption is not without base due to the fact that until recently, there were very few QoS tools and features other than queuing. With the recent advances in QoS technology, many new solutions have become available. While we are on the subject, however, let's briefly discuss queuing technologies and the various types of queuing available to you.

As its name implies, *queuing* is the ordering of packets that arrive on a router's interfaces. The method of queuing used determines how specific types of traffic will be handled. Several queuing methods are available to Cisco routers. Let's discuss some of the more common of them now:

- **Weighted fair queuing** WFQ is the default queuing method on all Cisco router interfaces that are 2Mb or slower. WFQ uses an algorithm that divides all traffic into flows based on the IP type of service (TOS) and gives low-volume traffic priority over higher-volume traffic.

- **Priority queuing** Priority queuing (PQ) allows an administrator to establish four queues: high, medium, normal/ default, and low. PQ is one of the simplest of the queuing

Continued

techniques. In servicing the queues, the router services the high queue until it is empty and then moves onto the medium queue and so forth. PQ allows the administrator to give absolute priority to a given traffic class, but if that queue is too large, the other queues could be starved for bandwidth.

- **Custom queuing** Custom queuing (CQ) allows an administrator to create 16 custom queues for each interface on the router. Each queue is assigned a byte count. Each queue is then serviced by the router in a round-robin fashion, one after the other. Custom queuing is advantageous in that it prevents starvation for any one given queue, but it is difficult to guarantee priority for a specific class of traffic.

- **Class-based weighted fair queuing** Class-Based Weighted Fair Queuing (CBWFQ) is loosely based on the WFQ algorithm, but combines the functionality of WFQ with that of CQ and is, therefore, sometimes called a hybrid congestion management mechanism.

- **IP RTP priority queuing** IP RTP priority is a combination of WFQ and PQ. In IP RTP priority queuing, a range of RTP port numbers is given strict priority over all other traffic types and transmitted first before any other traffic. This type of queuing is available only on serial and Frame Relay interfaces.

This is a brief introduction to queuing technologies. Chapter 6 gives a much more in-depth discussion of QoS and covers each of these queuing methods in much greater detail.

Why QoS Is Essential in VoIP Networks

Now that we have an understanding of what QoS is and some of the components that make up QoS, let's discuss the importance of QoS in a packet-switched network. The existing worldwide telephone system is based on a century-old idea that provides for a fixed amount of bandwidth (64kbps) available to every telephone in a given system, whether a PBX or the legacy PSTN. This system was, and still is, most concerned with availability and reliability. You will face a great challenge in finding a more reliable and available infrastructure anywhere than the legacy telephone system. However, by dedicating 64kpbs at all times, regardless of whether or not a telephone line is in use, is a vast underutilization of resources.

Packet-switched networks (which are the networks that carry VoIP) seek to address this underutilization of resources by offering a converged infrastructure for all voice and data traffic by more efficiently allocating this bandwidth on a dynamic basis. But as we discussed, what makes the legacy system so popular is its reliability and availability, so the challenge facing a converged infrastructure is to provide the efficiency of a packet-switched network with the reliability of a legacy network. This is the role that QoS fills.

QoS, through a variety of methods, gives reliability and availability to a converged infrastructure and still affords it the same benefits of efficient utilization of resources by providing the following:

- Managed response times

- Jitter (variation in delay) control

- Prioritization of delay-sensitive traffic

- Congestion management

- Congestion avoidance

- Support and enforcement of dedicated bandwidth requirements

- Management of packet loss

With QoS, converged infrastructures can provide end users with a convenient, low-cost, scalable, and above all reliable solution for the majority of their communications. Without QoS, a converged infrastructure would be comparable to anarchy, with little to no reliability, convenience, or scalability—to a level where a single FTP session could shut down your entire VoIP infrastructure. In short, QoS is not an option; it is a necessity.

Summary

In this chapter, we discussed the concepts surrounding VoIP signaling protocols. We began our discussion with an overview of TCP/IP and it's addressing. Internet Protocol (IP) is a connectionless protocol that provides Layer 3 logical addressing to nodes in a TCP/IP network. Transmission Control Protocol (TCP) provides a reliable, Layer 4 transport protocol to IP. User Datagram Protocol (UDP) serves many of the same functions as TCP, but it is not considered reliable because it does not provide many of the service assurance measures that TCP does. UDP has a much smaller packet size and provides faster transmission than TCP and so is commonly used in many VoIP protocols.

An IP address is a 32-byte (4-octet) number that represents a logical IP address. IP addressing is based on the binary numbering system. There are five classes of IP address, A to E; classes A to C are available for node addressing, class D is used for multicast purposes, and Class E is reserved for test purposes. Subnetting allows an IP network to be broken into smaller networks by "borrowing" bits from the host portion of the address and using them to create smaller networks. The subnet mask is used to determine where the line exists between the network portion of an IP address and the host portion of the IP address. Supernetting performs the opposite of subnetting by taking several smaller, contiguous networks and representing them as a larger, single network.

VoIP signaling takes place in three distinct areas: between PBX systems and routers, router to router, and router to PBX. When signaling from PBX to router, the user picks up the handset, signaling an off-hook condition. The connection between the PBX and router appears as a trunk line to the PBX, which signals the router to seize the trunk. Once a trunk is seized, the PBX forwards the dialed digits to the router in the same manner as the digits would be forwarded to a telephone company switch or another PBX. The routers in question use the Q.931 protocol for all call functions between the routers and incorporate dial plans to decide to which router on the far end of the connection a connection should be established. When the remote router receives the Q.931 call request, it signals a line seizure to the PBX. After the PBX acknowledges this seizure, the router forwards the dialed digits to the PBX and signals a call acknowledgment to the originating router. VoIP signaling incorporates several protocols to make reliable connections. Some of these protocols are Real-Time Protocol (RTP), Real-Time Control Protocol (RTCP), and Resource Reservation Protocol (RSVP).

H.323 is one of the oldest and most widely deployed VoIP signaling protocols in existence. H.323 is a derivative of the original H.320 protocol, designed to support video over ISDN. H.323 supports both voice and video of packet-switched infrastructures. The H.323 specification classifies devices into four types: terminals (endpoints), gateways, gatekeepers, or multipoint control units (MCUs). Terminals provide the user-to-network interface in an H.323 environment. They are most commonly IP telephones and PCs running H.323-compliant software. Gateways provide the H.323 network an interface to dissimilar network types such as the PSTN. Gateways are often routers with gateway modules installed. Gatekeepers perform call control function and administration for H.323 end-points and gateways. They are considered by many to be the most important element in an H.323 network. Routers and gateway devices often provide gatekeeper functionality in an H.323 network. MCUs provide conference capabilities to three or more voice conferences. The H.323 protocol stack incorporates IP for addressing, TCP for connection establishment, and UDP for low-overhead transport.

H.225 provides call setup and control for all session establishment between H.323 endpoints. H.245 is used for control signaling, including capabilities exchanges, logical channel establishment and tear-down, flow messages, and general commands. Registration, Administration, and Status (RAS) provides registration, admission control, bandwidth changes, status, and disengaging endpoints from gatekeepers. RTP provides end-to-end network transport functions suitable for applications transmitting real-time data, such as audio, video, or simulation data, over multicast or unicast network services. H.323 supports the majority of the standard voice and video codes. There are five stages of an H.323 call: discovery and registration, call setup, call-signaling flows, media stream and media control flows, and call termination.

Session Initiation Protocol (SIP) is a newer and simpler protocol than H.323. SIP, based on SMTP and HTTP, is a completely open standards-based protocol. SIP offers several advantages: simplicity, extensibility, modularity, scalability, integration, and interoperability. SIP has two major components: a user agent client (UAC), which is used to initiate SIP requests, and user agent servers (UAS), which are used to answer requests and provide resources to UAC requests. SIP clients include IP telephones and gateways. There are three types of SIP server: proxy servers, redirect servers, and registrar servers. SIP addresses are similar in format to an e-mail address, following a *user@host* format. SIP addresses can be either user addresses or E164 addresses. SIP uses six message types in communications: Invite, Bye, Register, ACK, Cancel, and Options.

MGCP is a new protocol in comparison to H.323 and as such is not as widely deployed as H.323. MGCP is built on a premise of centralized intelligent call management with dumb gateway devices. MGCP incorporates two device types. The first is known as the media gateway controller (MGC), which is also referred to as the *call agent*. MGCs provide all the intelligence in an MGCP network by performing all call control and processing functions. The second device type is known as the media gateway (MG) and, as its name implies, it provides gateway functionality to the MGCP protocol. The media gateway has no call-processing capabilities. MGCP also incorporates two types of logical devices: endpoints and connections. Endpoints are the physical or logical interfaces that initiate or terminate a VoIP call. Connections are the temporary, virtual channel setups between endpoints for the duration of the call. MeGaCo is a new protocol that improves upon the MGCP standard and provides several enhancements, such as the ability to interact with IVR applications as well as the ability to directly interconnect with VoFR and ATM networks.

QoS is vital to the successful deployment of a converged infrastructure. QoS is simply a set of tools available to network administrators to enforce certain assurances that a minimum level of services will be provided to certain traffic. QoS can provide guaranteed network resources to critical and delay-sensitive applications and offers a sensible and economical alternative to increasing bandwidth. There are three levels of QoS deployment: Best Effort Service, Integrated Services (InterServ), and Differentiated Services (DiffServ). QoS affords a converged network the reliability of a legacy TDM-based network with the scalability and efficiency of a packet-switched network.

Solutions Fast Track

An Overview of IP Networks

☑ IP is a connectionless, logical addressing protocol. TCP provides a reliable, Layer 4 transport protocol for IP.

☑ There are five classes of IP address, A to E. Classes A to C are available for host address assignment.

☑ Subnetting allows a network administrator to subdivide an IP network into several smaller networks. The subnet mask determines the division between the network and host portions on an IP address.

VoIP Signaling, Addressing, and Routing

☑ PBX-to-router signaling begins when the telephone handset goes into an off-hook condition. When this happens, the PBX signals the router and the router seizes a trunk.

☑ Router-to-router signaling is carried out through use of dial peers and the Q.931 protocol. RTP and RSVP are also used in this process.

☑ Router-to-PBX signaling is the last step of a VoIP call connection. In this phase, the receiving router indicates an incoming call to the PBX and the PBX system seizes the trunk for the call.

Introducing H.323

☑ H.323 is one of the most widely deployed and oldest VoIP protocols in use. It provides an open, vendor-independent standard.

☑ H.323 is capable of transmitting voice, video, and data traffic across a packet-switched network.

☑ H.323 is based on the legacy H.320 protocol for video over ISDN traffic.

H.323 Components

☑ Terminals (endpoints) provide the user-to-network interface in an H.323 environment. They are most often IP phones and PCs running H.323 software.

☑ Gateways provide an interface into non-H.323 networks such as the PSTN.

☑ Gatekeepers are the brains of an H.323 network and provide call control and administration for H.323 endpoints.

☑ MCUs provide voice and videoconferencing facilities for three or more conferences at a time.

H.323 Protocol Stack

☑ H.323 uses IP/TCP/UDP for addressing, connection establishment, and voice transport.

☑ H.225 is used to provide call setup and control between two H.323 endpoints.

☑ H.245 is used to negotiate channel usage and capabilities as well as provide control messages.

☑ Registration, Admission, and Status (RAS) is used to perform registration, admission control, bandwidth changes, and status and to disengage endpoints from gatekeepers.

☑ The Real-Time Transport Protocol (RTP) provides end-to-end network transport functions suitable for applications transmitting real-time data such as audio, video, or simulation data over multicast or unicast network services.

H.323 Call Stages

☑ Registration is used by the endpoint to identify a zone with which it can be associated.

☑ Call setup establishes a reliable connection between the H.323 endpoints.

☑ In Cisco VoIP gateways, RTP media streams are transported over UDP ports 16384 through 16400.

☑ Call termination stops the media streams and closes logical channels. Termination can be requested by any endpoint or by a gatekeeper.

Session Initiation Protocol

☑ The Session Initiation Protocol (SIP) is a simple signaling protocol used for Internet conferencing and telephony.

☑ The SIP system contains two components: user agents and network servers. A user agent (UA) is SIP's endpoint that makes and receives SIP calls.

☑ SIP clients can be either IP telephones or gateways.

☑ There are three types of SIP server: proxy servers, redirect servers, and registrar servers.

Media Gateway Control Point

☑ MGCP is a relatively new protocol compared with its predecessors H.323 and SIP, and as such, it is not as widely deployed.

☑ MGCP incorporates devices known as media gateway controllers (MGCs), also referred to as *call agents*, in order to perform all call connection and call control within an MGCP network. These MGCs signal to and control media gateways (MCs) in order to connect and control VoIP calls.

☑ MeGaCo offers several enhancements and features that MGCP cannot, such as interoperability with IVR applications as well as the ability to interact with non-VoIP networks.

The Role of QoS in Packet-Switched Voice Networks

☑ QoS is simply a set of tools available to network administrators to enforce certain assurances that a minimum level of services will be provided to certain traffic.

☑ There are three levels of QoS: best-efforts service, integrated services, and differentiated services.

☑ QoS allows packet-switched networks to provide service level guarantees for resources such as bandwidth, delay, jitter and packet loss.

Frequently Asked Questions

The following Frequently Asked Questions, answered by the authors of this book, are designed to both measure your understanding of the concepts presented in this chapter and to assist you with real-life implementation of these concepts. To have your questions about this chapter answered by the author, browse to **www.syngress.com/solutions** and click on the **"Ask the Author"** form.

Q: What is the purpose of private addressing, and can I use it?

A: Private addressing was a mid-1990s movement to combat the rapidly depleting number of available IP addresses. Private addressing created a set of private Class A, B, and C networks that any organization can deploy within its internal network. However, private addresses cannot be used on the public Internet. See RFC 1918 for more details.

Q: What is the difference between a gateway and a gatekeeper in an H.323 network?

A: A gateway provides a connection between the interface of an H.323 network and a dissimilar network such as the PSTN. A gatekeeper provides overall call control and administration to an H.323 network. Although they sound alike, the tasks are very different. However, often the functions of a gateway and a gatekeeper are provided by the same piece of equipment.

Q: Why would a VoIP call use UDP as a transport mechanism? Isn't TCP much more reliable?

A: True—TCP, incorporating techniques such as synchronization and windowing, is more reliable than UDP, but UDP is used because of its low overhead. Additionally, if packets are lost, you do not want them to be retransmitted. Doing so would cause more confusion to the end user than not receiving them at all.

Q: What is the purpose of a proxy server in a SIP network?

A: Proxy servers decide to which server the request should be forwarded and then forward the request. The request can actually traverse many SIP servers before reaching its destination.

Q: How does MGCP interoperate with a Call Manager deployment?

A: MGCP is a popular protocol with deployments of the Cisco Call Manager solution. In such a deployment, the Call Manager server(s) would act as an MGC and would direct its gateway routers acting as MCs.

Q: Does quality of service depend on the type of network I am using, such as ATM or Frame Relay?

A: Although it is true that certain types of network media do lend themselves more to QoS than others (such as ATM's inherent QoS features), all media types can support some form of QoS. As with any other network decisions, the type and breadth of your QoS deployment should be dependent on your individual network and its needs.

Q: Which form of queuing will work best for my network?

A: QoS design, like any other network design consideration, depends on the network in question. In order to determine the QoS strategy to use for your network, you must complete a through investigation of the traffic types in question and your network's goals.

An Overview of Cisco's VoIP Components

Introduction

This chapter introduces the various Cisco components used to implement a VoIP solution. Implementing such a solution can be quite a daunting task, depending on the type of environment for which it is needed. These environments can include small offices, branch offices, and widely dispersed enterprises. Numerous voice-related components are required to complete a total VoIP solution, but the goal of this section is to cover the infrastructure components: voice network modules (VNMs), voice interface cards (VICs), and a few of the Cisco routers and switches used for supporting voice traffic.

Companies are realizing the need to upgrade aging legacy equipment with networking equipment that can support voice and video while also transporting existing data traffic. Cisco has long been a leader in the VoIP market and is constantly developing equipment to keep up with this demand. Cisco has a broad portfolio of routers, switches, and access gateways used to complete the convergence of voice, video, and date networks.

This chapter also includes a VoIP terminology section to help identify some of the common terms and acronyms used in modern voice networking. As stated earlier, the task of implementing an efficient, reliable VoIP network can be difficult. With a good understanding of the current Cisco voice products available, this difficulty can be lessened and an infrastructure can be chosen to support the many applications required of a modern converged network.

Exploring the Types of Voice Ports

This section discusses the various types of voice ports available to allow a voice call to occur. These ports are necessary to allow connections from basic telephone equipment to the PSTN. This section also discusses the hardware components required to support these voice ports and highlights the subsequent components required for the delivery of voice from a packet-switched (VoIP) network to a circuit-switched (PSTN) network and back.

Foreign Exchange Station Interface

The *foreign exchange station (FXS)* port is used to connect the router to standard telephony devices and endpoint stations, such as basic telephone equipment, keysets, or fax machines. The FXS port can supply ring voltage, dial tone, and other basic signaling to an end station. The FXS port is configured with a standard RJ-11 connection port (see Figure 4.1 and Table 4.1).

Figure 4.1 An RJ-11 Pinout

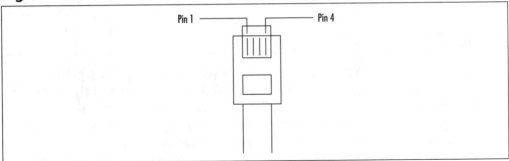

Table 4.1 RJ-11 Pinout Signals

Pin	Signal
1	–
2	–
3	Ring
4	Tip

WARNING

Do not connect an FXS port to the PSTN. The FXS interface emulates the CO switch to the endpoint device by providing dial tone and ring voltage. If an FXO was inadvertently used in place of the FXS, the endpoint may receive signaling but will be unable to ring the phone to alert the user of an incoming connection.

Foreign Exchange Office Interface

The *foreign exchange office (FXO)* port is also configured with an RJ-11 connection port (refer back to Figure 4.1 and Table 4.1). However, rather than supplying the signaling and voltage needed for basic telephony equipment, FXO ports are used to connect the IP network to off-premises equipment such as a PSTN CO or to a PBX tie-line interface. The FXO port is plugged directly into the line side of the switch, which allows the switch to think it is connected to a telephone. You can set several parameters that are compatible with tie-line features on a PBX.

> **WARNING**
>
> Connect only an FXO port approved for your country to the PSTN. Otherwise, connect an FXO port only to a PBX (connections from the PBX to the PSTN are permitted). The FXO interface emulates the operation of a handset waiting for ring voltage from the CO switch. If the FXS is inadvertently used in place of the FXO, it will not anticipate this ring voltage on the line, thus it will be unable to close the loop to complete the connection.

E&M Interface

The ear and mouth, or earth and magnet (E&M), interface is a RJ-48C type connector (see Figure 4.2) that allows for connections specifically to PBX trunk lines (otherwise known as *tie-lines*) between PBXs. The E&M interface can be programmed with special attenuation, gain, and impedance settings that can conform to the specific attributes of different PBX systems. E&M is a signaling technique for two-wire and four-wire telephone and trunk lines. The connections and pinout specifications are listed in Table 4.2.

Figure 4.2 An RJ-48C Pinout

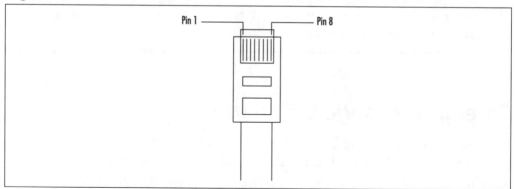

Table 4.2 E&M Pinouts

Pin	Signal	Description	Two-Wire Operation, Type				Four-Wire Operation, Type			
			1	2	3	5	1	2	3	5
1	SB	–48V signaling battery	–	SB	SB	–	–	SB	SB	–
2	M-lead	Signaling input	M	M	M	M	M	M	M	M
3	R	Ring, audio input	–	–	–	–	R	R	R	R
4	R or R1	Ring, audio input/output or output	R	R	R	R	R1	R1	R1	R1
5	T or T1	Tip, audio input/output or output	T	T	T	T	T1	T1	T1	T1
6	T	Tip, audio input	–	–	–	–	T	T	T	T
7	E-lead	Signaling output	E	E	E	E	E	E	E	E
8	SG	Signaling ground return	–	SG	SG	–	–	SG	SG	–

171

WARNING

Do not connect an E&M port to the PSTN. Doing so can cause disruptions and unpredictable results at the PSTN's CO. This is due to the fact that E&M ports use up to four pairs of wires for signaling and ground, compared with FXS and FXO, which use only one pair. This allows for better answer and disconnect supervision of trunk-to-trunk and switch-to-switch calls.

E1/T1 Voice Connectivity

Digital E1 and T1 connectivity allows Cisco series routers and switches to provide E1 or T1 voice connectivity to PBXs or to a CO. T1 voice connections are available for various routers and switches, including, but not limited to, Cisco 1700, 2600, 3600, 3700, MC3810, 7200, 7500, AS5300, AS5800, and Catalyst 4000 and 6000 series equipment. Additional platforms are discussed later in this chapter.

The 7200, 7500 series, and AS5300 series are primarily used as tandem switch points from T1 tie lines to PBXs and the PSTN to the IP internal network. An example of tandeming is receiving a voice call on one VoIP interface and switching it back out another VoIP interface to its final destination. The 1700, 2600, and 3600 router series are now also capable of performing this function because support for voice T1/E1 interfaces with up to two T1/E1 circuits per card has been added. The T1/E1 enhanced voice port adapter is used in the 7200 and 7500 series routers and can support up to two T1s per card. The AS5300 series access switch uses the T1 carrier card that can support up to four T1s.

The 7200, 7500, and AS5850 can be used to perform the function of T1 termination for voice traffic into the WAN and can forward the signals and transmissions to the 1700, 2600, 3600, and AS5300 series routers for complete processing.

The Catalyst 4000 series utilizing the Access Gateway Module (WS-X4604-GWY) can support up to three VICs for T1/E1 voice connectivity. The Catalyst 6000 series utilizing the T1 Service Module (WS-X6608-T1) can support up to eight T1s for voice connectivity.

Voice Modules and Cards

In order to implement VoIP on Cisco routers and switches, you first need to understand the various types of hardware and router/switch ports required to use the VoIP technology. Routers and switches use voice network modules to transform voice signaling to a form that can be transported across the IP network and to use VICs to provide connectivity to the telephone equipment. Routers such as the Cisco 1751 and 1760 use the Cisco IOS to provide the signal processing, so they only require VICs. The Catalyst 4000 uses an access gateway module, which is similar in function to the voice network module but includes some additional features.

VNMs and VICs use Cisco IOS VoIP commands to enable voice communications on Cisco routers. There may be slight differences in command syntax and structure, depending on which Cisco IOS release is used; therefore, prior to completing a new installation, it is a good idea to refer back to an IOS configuration guide for the chosen release.

Digital signal processors (DSPs) are used in various Cisco voice-enabled routers in order to convert analog voice signals to digital for transmission across an IP network and to convert back to analog once the packet has arrived at the destination router. DSPs can be found as modules inserted onto the motherboard, as on the 1700 series routers, or as slots built onto a VNM that is placed in the router. (Further information on DSP modules as they relate to the 1700 series appears later in this chapter.)

Voice Network Modules

In order to install voice ports on the 2600, 3600, and 3700 series routers, equipment must be installed that can interpret analog signals to digital format for transmission over the IP network as well as to provide additional capabilities. VNMs are designed to serve this purpose, and at least one VNM is needed to enable the router to handle voice traffic. VNMs come in three different models for the 2600/3600 series routers.

NOTE

The NM-1V/2V does not support WAN interface cards. Only VICs are supported in the carriers with a *V* in the name. WAN interface cards (WICs) require a carrier with a *W* in the name, such as NM-1W.

Figure 4.3 shows an NM-1V—a one-slot VNM. You can install one VIC in the NM-1V, providing up to two voice ports.

Figure 4.3 An NM-1V Voice Network Module

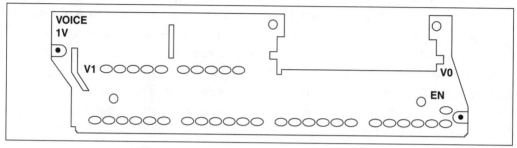

Figure 4.4 is a NM-2V—a two-slot version of the VNM. You can install up to two VICs in the NM-2V, providing up to four voice ports. Table 4.3 shows the supported platforms and IOS versions.

Figure 4.4 An NM-2V Voice Network Module

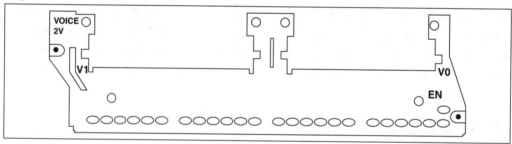

Table 4.3 Supported Platforms and IOS Versions

Cisco IOS Support	2600	3620, 3640	3660
NM-1V	All IOS versions	11.3(1)T, 12.0, 12.0T, 12.0XK, 12.1, 12.1T	All IOS versions
NM-2V	All IOS versions	11.3(1)T, 12.0, 12.0T, 12.0XK, 12.1, 12.1T	All IOS versions

Figure 4.5 is a diagram of an NM-HDV high-density VNM. This network module consists of five slots, one for the voice WIC (VWIC) and four for the packet voice DSP modules (PVDM). You can install one VWIC in the NM-HDV, providing up to two voice ports.

Figure 4.5 An NM-HDV High-Density Voice Network Module

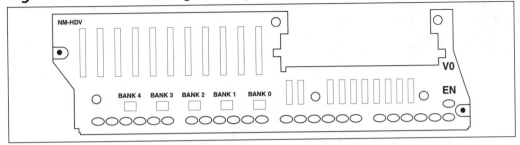

Figure 4.6 shows the top view of the NM-HDV from Figure 4.5, illustrating the packet voice DSP slots. Table 4.4 shows the supported platforms and Internetwork Operating System for the NM-HDV.

Figure 4.6 Top View of an NM-HDV High-Density Voice Network Module

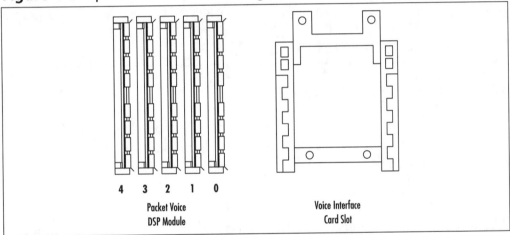

Table 4.4 Supported Platforms and Internetwork Operating System for the NM-HDV

Cisco IOS Support	2600	3620, 3640	3660
NM-HDV-1E1-30	12.0(7)XK, 12.1(2)T	12.0(7)XK, 12.1(2)T	12.0(7)XK, 12.1(2)T
NM-HDV-1E1-30E	12.0(7)XK, 12.1(2)T	12.0(7)XK, 12.1(2)T	12.0(7)XK, 12.1(2)T
NM-HDV-2E1-60	12.0(7)XK, 12.1(2)T	12.0(7)XK, 12.1(2)T	12.0(7)XK, 12.1(2)T

Continued

Table 4.4 Continued

Cisco IOS Support	2600	3620, 3640	3660
NM-HDV-1T1-24	12.0(5)XK, 12.0(7)T, 12.1, 12.1T	12.0(5)XK, 12.0(7)T, 12.1, 12.1T	12.0(5)XK, 12.0(7)T, 12.1, 12.1T
NM-HDV-1T1-24E	12.0(5)XK, 12.0(7)T, 12.1, 12.1T	12.0(5)XK, 12.0(7)T, 12.1, 12.1T	12.0(5)XK, 12.0(7)T, 12.1, 12.1T
NM-HDV-2T1-48	12.0(5)XK, 12.0(7)T, 12.1, 12.1T	12.0(5)XK, 12.0(7)T, 12.1, 12.1T	12.0(5)XK, 12.0(7)T, 12.1, 12.1T
NM-HDV	12.0(5)XK, 12.0(7)T, 12.1, 12.1T	12.0(5)XK, 12.0(7)T, 12.1, 12.1T	12.0(5)XK, 12.0(7)T, 12.1, 12.1T
PVDM-12	12.0(5)XK, 12.0(7)T, 12.1, 12.1T	12.0(5)XK, 12.0(7)T, 12.1, 12.1T	12.0(5)XK, 12.0(7)T, 12.1, 12.1T

Voice Interface Cards

Several VIC modules work with the VNM to provide multiple types of functionality. The types of voice modules that are currently available, as well as some specifications used to differentiate them in the router, are described in this section.

VIC-2E/M

The two-port E&M module VIC-2E/M is typically used to connect an IP network directly to a PBX system. It is capable of being configured for special settings associated with tie-line ports on most PBXs. E&M ports are always color-coded brown. A VIC-2 port E&M is shown in Figure 4.7.

Figure 4.7 A VIC-2E/M

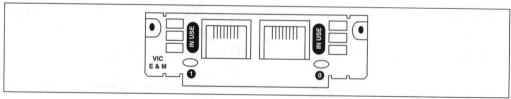

VIC-2FXS

The two-port FXS module VIC-2FXS is used to connect directly to endpoint equipment such as a telephone, keypad, or fax. These ports provide special connectivity by providing ringing voltage, dial tone, and other endpoint specific functionality. FXS ports are always color-coded gray. A VIC-2FXS is shown in Figure 4.8.

Figure 4.8 A VIC-2FXS

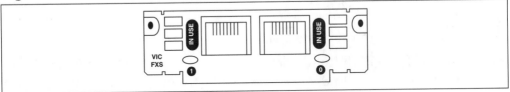

VIC-2FXO

The two-port FXO module VIC-2FXO is typically used to connect to a PBX or PSTN. This is the type of interface that a standard telephone provides. FXO ports are always color-coded pink. Other types of FXO cards for use outside North America are capable of providing switching and signaling techniques used in other geographic regions; VIC-2FXO-EU is intended for use in Europe, and VIC-2FXO-M3 is intended for use in Australia. A VIC-2FXO can be seen in Figure 4.9.

Figure 4.9 A VIC-2FXO

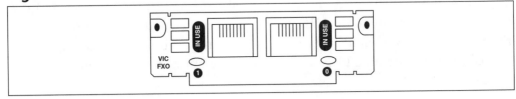

VWIC-2MFT-T1

The two-port VWIC multiflex trunk interface card is a two-port card that can be used for voice, data, and integrated voice/data applications. The multiflex VWIC can support data-only applications as a WAN interface on the Cisco 1700, 2600, or 3600. It can also then be reused to integrate voice and data with the Drop and Insert multiplexer functionality and/or configured to support packetized voice

(VoIP) when in the digital T1/E1 network module. A VWIC-2MFT-T1 is shown in Figure 4.10.

Figure 4.10 A VWIC-2MFT-T1

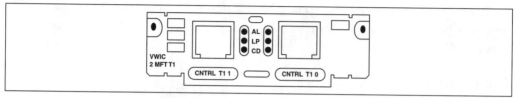

Two-Port ISDN BRI Card

Two two-port ISDN BRI VICs are available for the Cisco 1700, 2600, and Cisco 3600 series routers. These cards are available as ISDN BRI S/T or NT interfaces for terminating to an ISDN telephone network. A two-port ISDN BRI is shown in Figure 4.11.

Figure 4.11 A Two-Port ISDN BRI Card

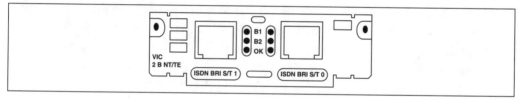

Four-Port Analog DID/FXS VICs

Two direct inward dial interface cards are available. The first card (not shown) is a two-port RJ-11 that supports DID only. The second card, the four-port DID/FXS card, is shown in Figure 4.12. Both cards are used for providing DID service to extensions on a PBX so that users may transparently dial directly to extensions.

Figure 4.12 A Four-Port Analog DID/FXS VIC

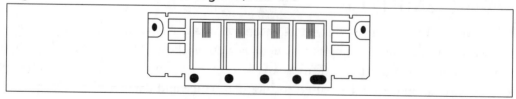

Connecting VNMs and VICs to the Router

The new Cisco router standard is to use a chassis-based hardware format that can be customized to meet the needs of any business and scaled to any level of functionality. Depending on an individual business's needs, it can choose from a variety of chassis formats to accommodate VoIP installations. The types of router chassis are listed in this section along with information on how VNMs, VICs, and additional voice port adapters are installed on the various platforms.

> **NOTE**
>
> When deploying or designing new voice-enabled networks, ensure that you complete a gap analysis between the current network infrastructure and the proposed design so that existing equipment that is voice capable is upgraded before you make an investment in unnecessary new equipment.

1700 Series Router Configurations

The 1700 series modular access routers are designed primarily for small to medium-sized businesses and small enterprise branch offices. The 1700 family has several chassis for different applications, but the two that were designed specifically for voice applications are the 1751 and the 1760. These two modular chassis use the Cisco IOS along with various VICs to support analog and digital voice traffic over the IP network.

Cisco 1751 Modular Access Router

The Cisco 1751 is a standalone chassis with three voice interface slots. It comes in two models: A base model suited primarily for data but with an easy upgrade path to voice and a multiservice model (identified with a *V*) that includes all features for immediate integration of data and voice. Both models include three slots for data/voice interface cards as well as a 10/100 Ethernet port, a console port, and an auxiliary port. The 1700 series VICs are interchangeable with the Cisco 2600 and 3600 series routers. Table 4.5 shows the available VICs for the 1751 router.

WARNING

WICs and VICs are *not* field upgradeable for the Cisco 1751. If an upgrade is completed in the field, the Cisco 1751 must be completely powered down to perform the upgrade. Data and voice traffic will be halted for the length of the upgrade.

Table 4.5 Voice Interface Cards for the Cisco 1751

VIC Model	Description
VIC-2FXS	Two-port FXS voice/fax interface card for voice/fax network module
VIC-2DID	Two-port DID voice/fax interface card
VIC-2FXO	Two-port FXO voice/fax interface card for voice/fax network module
VIC-2FXO-EU	Two-port FXO voice/fax interface card for Europe
VIC-2FXO-MI	Two-port FXO voice/fax interface card with battery-reversal detection and caller ID support (for U.S., Canada, and others); enhanced version of the VIC-2FXO
VIC-2FXO-M2	Two-port FXO voice/fax interface card with battery-reversal detection and caller ID support (for Europe); enhanced version of the VIC-2FXO-EU
VIC-2FXO-M3	Two-port FXO voice/fax interface card for Australia
VIC-2E/M	Two-port E&M voice/fax interface card for voice/fax network module
VIC-2BRI-NT/TE	Two-port network-side ISDN BRI interface
VWIC-1MFT-T1	One-port RJ-48 multiflex trunk—T1
VWIC-2MFT-T1	Two-port RJ-48 multiflex trunk—T1
VWIC-2MFT-T1-DI	Two-port RJ-48 multiflex trunk—T1 with drop and insert
VWIC-1MFT-E1	One-port RJ-48 multiflex trunk—E1
VWIC-2MFT-E1	Two-port RJ-48 multiflex trunk—E1
VWIC-2MFT-E1-DI	Two-port RJ-48 multiflex trunk—E1 with drop and insert
VWIC-1MFT-G703	One-port RJ-48 multiflex trunk—E1 G.703
VWIC-2MFT-G703	Two-port RJ-48 multiflex trunk—E1 G.703

Pictured in Figure 4.13 is the rear view of the Cisco 1751 modular access router. The 1751 has three slots for VICs, with Slot 2 used *only* for VICs. The slots are labeled Slot 0, Slot 1, and Slot 2. To install the VIC or WVIC, follow these steps:

1. Disconnect power to the router.

2. Use a Phillips or flat-blade screwdriver to remove the filler panel from the VIC slot.

3. Align the card with the guides and slide it gently into the VIC slot.

4. Push the card until you feel it connect securely in the router chassis.

5. Fasten the screws into the holes in the module, using the Phillips or flat-blade screwdriver.

6. Connect cabling and power up.

7. Verify that the slot you placed the VIC in states "OK" on the LED on the back of the router.

Figure 4.13 Cisco 1751, Rear View

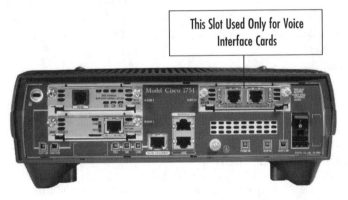

The Cisco 1751 includes one PVDM-256K-4 (one DSP) that supports one analog VIC. If two analog VICs or one or more digital ISDN VICs are used, additional DSPs are required. The Cisco 1751 has two DSP slots to support additional voice channels. See Figure 4.14 for DSP placement on motherboard, Table 4.6 for a complete list of DSP modules, and Table 4.7 for the minimum IOS release.

Figure 4.14 PVDM Slot Locations on a Cisco 1751 Router Motherboard

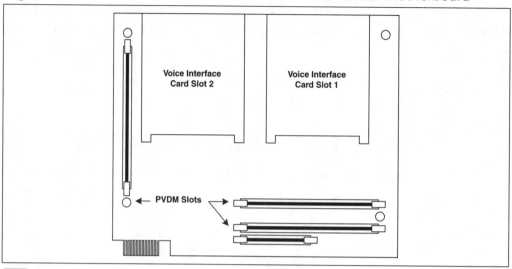

WARNING

A PVDM is required to support VICs on the Cisco 1750 and 1760 routers. These two chassis require PVDMs to be placed on the motherboard, unlike the Cisco 2600, 3600, and 3700 routers, which have DSP support on the VNMs.

Table 4.6 Cisco 1751 DSP Modules

Module Number	Description
PVDM-256K-4	A 4-channel packet voice/fax DSP module (one DSP)
PVDM-256K-8	An 8-channel packet voice/fax DSP module (two DSPs)
PVDM-256K-12	A 12-channel packet voice/fax DSP module (three DSPs)
PVDM-256K-16	A 16-channel packet voice/fax DSP module (four DSPs)
PVDM-256K-20	A 20-channel packet voice/fax DSP module (five DSPs)

Table 4.7 Cisco 1751 Minimum Supported Software Release

Module Number	Description
PVDM-256K-12	12.1(5)YB, 12.2(2)XH, 12.2(2)XJ, 12.2(2)XK, 12.2(2)XQ, 12.2(4)T
PVDM-256K-16	12.1(5)YB, 12.2(2)XH, 12.2(2)XJ, 12.2(2)XK, 12.2(2)XQ, 12.2(4)T
PVDM-256K-20	12.1(5)YB, 12.2(2)XH, 12.2(2)XJ, 12.2(2)XK, 12.2(2)XQ, 12.2(4)T
PVDM-256K-4	12.1(5)YB, 12.2(2)XH, 12.2(2)XJ, 12.2(2)XK, 12.2(2)XQ, 12.2(4)T
PVDM-256K-8	12.1(5)YB, 12.2(2)XH, 12.2(2)XJ, 12.2(2)XK, 12.2(2)XQ, 12.2(4)T
VIC-2BRI-NT/TE	12.1(5)YB, 12.2(2)XH, 12.2(2)XJ, 12.2(2)XK, 12.2(2)XQ, 12.2(4)T
VIC-2DID	12.2(2)XJ, 12.2(2)XK, 12.2(4)T
VIC-2E/M	12.1(5)YB, 12.2(2)XH, 12.2(2)XJ, 12.2(2)XK, 12.2(2)XQ, 12.2(4)T
VIC-2FXO-EU	12.1(5)YB, 12.2(2)XH, 12.2(2)XJ, 12.2(2)XK, 12.2(2)XQ, 12.2(4)T
VIC-2FXO-M1	12.2(2)XJ, 12.2(2)XK, 12.2(4)T
VIC-2FXO-M2	12.2(2)XJ, 12.2(2)XK, 12.2(4)T
VIC-2FXO-M3	12.1(5)YB, 12.2(2)XH, 12.2(2)XJ, 12.2(2)XK, 12.2(2)XQ, 12.2(4)T
VIC-2FXO	12.1(5)YB, 12.2(2)XH, 12.2(2)XJ, 12.2(2)XK, 12.2(2)XQ, 12.2(4)T
VIC-2FXS	12.1(5)YB, 12.2(2)XH, 12.2(2)XJ, 12.2(2)XK, 12.2(2)XQ, 12.2(4)T
VWIC-1MFT-E1	12.2(4)YB
VWIC-1MFT-T1	12.2(4)YB
VWIC-2MFT-E1-D1	12.2(4)YB
VWIC-2MFT-E1	12.2(4)YB
VWIC-2MFT-T1-D1	12.2(4)YB
VWIC-2MFT-T1	12.2(4)YB

The Cisco 1760 Modular Access Router

The Cisco 1760 is a 19-inch rack-mount chassis with four slots for VICs. It comes in two models: A base model suited primarily for data but with an easy upgrade path to voice and a multiservice model (identified with a *V*) that includes all features for immediate integration of data and voice. Both models include four slots for data/voice interface cards as well as a 10/100 Ethernet port, a console port, and an auxiliary port. The 1700 series VICs are interchangeable with the Cisco 2600 and 3600 series routers. Unlike the 1751, the 1700 series VICs are field upgradeable. Table 4.8 shows the available VICs for the 1760 router.

Table 4.8 Voice Interface Cards for the Cisco 1760

VIC Model	Description
VIC-2E/M	Two-port E&M voice/fax interface card for voice/fax network module
VIC-2FXO	Two-port FXO voice/fax interface card for voice/fax network module
VIC-2FXS	Two-port FXS voice/fax interface card for voice/fax network module
VIC-2FXO-M1	Two-port FXO voice/fax interface card for North America
VIC-2FXO-M2	Two-port FXO voice/fax interface card for Europe
VIC-2FXO-M3	Two-port FXO voice/fax interface card for Australia
VIC-2DID	Two-port analog DID voice interface card
VIC-2FXO-EU	Two-port FXO voice/fax interface card for Europe
VIC-2BRI-NT/TE	Two-port network-side ISDN BRI VIC
VWIC-1MFT-T1	One-port FJ-48 multiflex trunk—T1
VWIC-2MFT-T1	Two-port RJ-48 multiflex trunk—T1
VWIC-2MFT-T1-DI	Two-port RJ-48 multiflex trunk—T1 with drop and insert
VWIC-1MFT-E1	One-port RJ-48 multiflex trunk—E1
VWIC-2MFT-E1	Two-port RJ-48 multiflex trunk—E1
VWIC_2MFT-E1-DI	Two-port RJ-48 multiflex trunk—E1 with drop and insert
VWIC-1MFT-G.703	One-port RJ-48 multiflex trunk—E1 G.703
VWIC-2MFT-G.703	Two-port RJ-48 multiflex trunk—E1 G.703

Pictured in Figure 4.15 is the rear view of the Cisco 1760 modular access router. As stated earlier, the 1760 has four slots for VICs, with Slots 2 and 3 used *only* for VICs. The slots are labeled Slot 0, Slot 1, Slot 2, and Slot 3. To install the VIC or WVIC, follow these steps:

1. Disconnect power to the router.

2. Use a Phillips screwdriver or flat-blade screwdriver to remove the filler panel from the VIC slot.

3. Align the card with the guides and slide it gently into the VIC slot.

4. Push the card until you feel it connect securely in the router chassis.

5. Connect cabling and power up.

6. Verify that the slot you placed the VIC in states "OK" on the LED at the back of the router.

Figure 4.15 Cisco 1760, Rear View

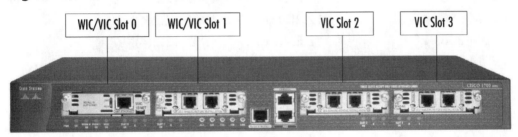

The Cisco 1760 includes one PVDM-256K-4 (one DSP) that supports one analog VIC. If two analog VICs or one or more digital ISDN VICs are used, additional DSPs are required. The Cisco 1760 has two DSP slots to support additional voice channels. See Table 4.9 for a complete list of DSP modules and Table 4.10 for minimum supported IOS releases.

WARNING

A PVDM is required to support VICs on the Cisco 1750 and 1760 routers. These two chassis require PVDMs to be placed on the motherboard, unlike the Cisco 2600, 3600, and 3700 routers, which have DSP support on the VNMs.

Table 4.9 Cisco 1760 DSP Modules

DSP Model	Description
PVDM-256K-4	A 4-channel packet voice/fax DSP module (one DSP)
PVDM-256K-8	An 8-channel packet voice/fax DSP module (two DSPs)
PVDM-256K-12	A 12-channel packet voice/fax DSP module (three DSPs)
PVDM-256K-16	A 16-channel packet voice/fax DSP module (four DSPs)
PVDM-256K-20	A 20-channel packet voice/fax DSP module (five DSPs)

Table 4.10 Cisco 1760 Minimum Supported Software Release

DSP and VIC Model	Minimum Supported Software Release
PVDM-256K-12	12.2(2)XK, 12.2(4)XL, 12.2(4)XW
PVDM-256K-16	12.2(2)XK, 12.2(4)XL, 12.2(4)XW
PVDM-256K-20	12.2(2)XK, 12.2(4)XL, 12.2(4)XW
PVDM-256K-4	12.2(2)XK, 12.2(4)XL, 12.2(4)XW
PVDM-256K-8	12.2(2)XK, 12.2(4)XL, 12.2(4)XW
VIC-2BRI-NT/TE	12.2(2)XK, 12.2(4)XL, 12.2(4)XW
VIC-2DID	12.2(2)XK, 12.2(4)XL, 12.2(4)XW
VIC-2E/M	12.2(2)XK, 12.2(4)XL, 12.2(4)XW
VIC-2FXO-EU	12.2(2)XK, 12.2(4)XL, 12.2(4)XW
VIC-2FXO-M1	12.2(2)XK, 12.2(4)XL, 12.2(4)XW
VIC-2FXO-M2	12.2(2)XK, 12.2(4)XL, 12.2(4)XW
VIC-2FXO-M3	12.2(2)XK, 12.2(4)XL, 12.2(4)XW
VIC-2FXO	12.2(2)XK, 12.2(4)XL, 12.2(4)XW
VIC-2FXS	12.2(2)XK, 12.2(4)XL, 12.2(4)XW
VWIC-1MFT-E1	12.2(4)YB
VWIC-1MFT-T1	12.2(4)YB
VWIC-2MFT-E1-D1	12.2(4)YB
VWIC-2MFT-E1	12.2(4)YB
VWIC-2MFT-T1-D1	12.2(4)YB
VWIC-2MFT-T1	12.2(4)YB

2600, 3600, and 3700 Series Router Configurations

Cisco's 2600, 3600, and 3700 series routers come in a variety of base configurations that differ in the amount and/or type of standard network interfaces (RJ-45 ports, serial ports, and ISDN ports) that are available. See Table 4.11 for a 2600 platform overview. Figure 4.16 shows a rear view of a 2600. The Cisco 2600, 3600, and 3700 are designed primarily for traditional and power branch office solutions.

Table 4.11 2600 Series Available Network Modules and WIC Slots

Platform	NMs	WICs	Fixed LAN Ports
CISCO2610/11	1	2	1 E/2E
CISCO2610XM/11XM	1	2	1 FE/2FE
CISCO2612	1	2	1TR/1E
CISCO2620/21	1	2	1 FE/2FE
CISCO2620XM/21XM	1	2	1 FE/2FE
CISCO2650/51	1	2	1 FE/2FE
CISCO2650XM/51XM	1	2	1 FE/2FE
CISCO2691	1	3	2 FE

Figure 4.16 Cisco 2611, Rear View

The 3600 series router comes in three varieties: the 3620, which has two network module slots; the 3640, which has four network module slots; and the 3660, which is equipped with six network module slots. Figure 4.17 shows a 3660 chassis.

The 3700 series router comes in two varieties: the 3725, which has three integrated WIC slots and two network module slots, and the 3745, which has three integrated WIC slots and four network module slots. (Currently, the built-in WICs do not support VICs.) Figure 4.18 shows a 3745 chassis.

Figure 4.17 Cisco 3660, Rear View

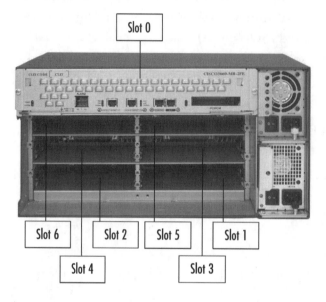

Figure 4.18 Cisco 3745, Rear View

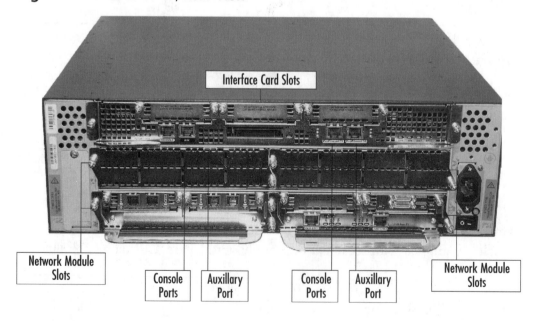

Most VICs used for the Cisco 1700 series routers are also used for the 2600, 3600, and 3700 series except that a VNM is required in these higher-end routers. Installation of these VNMs is covered later in this chapter.

Pictured in Figure 4.19 is the rear view of the Cisco 3640 modular access router. Figure 4.20 shows the VNM with VICs installed. To install the VNMs, complete the following steps:

1. Disconnect power to the router.

2. Use a Phillips screwdriver or flat-blade screwdriver to remove the filler panel from the slot.

3. Align the module with the guides and slide it gently into the chassis.

4. Push the module until you feel it connect securely.

5. Fasten the screws using the Phillips or flat-blade screwdriver.

6. Install VICs as described previously for the Cisco 1700 router.

7. Power up the system.

8. Ensure that the LED indicates that the module has passed its self-tests.

9. Verify that the slot you placed the VIC in has the "OK" LED lit on the back of the router.

Figure 4.19 Cisco 3640, Empty Chassis

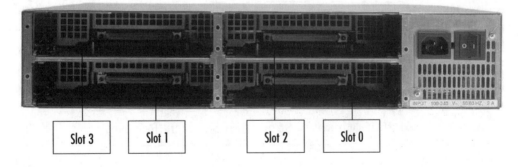

Slot 3   Slot 1   Slot 2   Slot 0

WARNING

To install VNMs and VICs, the 2600, 3620, and 3640 models must be offline. If an insertion or an upgrade has been performed on these models, the router must be powered down to complete the process. Therefore, data and voice traffic will be halted for the length of the upgrade.

Figure 4.20 Voice Network Module with Voice Interface Cards

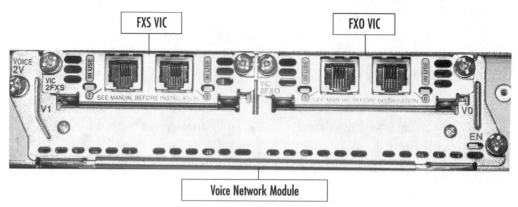

NOTE

Network modules can be replaced in a Cisco 3660 router and in Cisco 3700 series routers while the power is on without affecting operation. Although it is possible to complete online insertion and removal of the network modules, it might be a good idea to arrange outage windows whenever possible to allow a complete shutdown and restart of the router. This is good practice because in rare instances, completing this procedure could inadvertently cause a reboot or other traffic-affecting issues.

Table 4.12 shows the minimum supported software releases for the Cisco 2600 family of routers.

Table 4.12 Cisco 2600 Minimum Supported Software Releases

Compatible Hardware Product Number(s)	Minimum Supported Software Release
NM-1V	11.3(2)XA, 11.3(3)T, 12.0(1)T, 12.0(1), 12.0(3)T, 12.0(5)XK, 12.0(7)T, 12.1(1)T, 12.1(1), 12.1(5)YB, 12.1(5)YD, 12.2(1), 12.2(2)T, 12.2(2)XT
NM-2V	11.3(2)XA, 11.3(3)T, 12.0(1)T, 12.0(1), 12.0(3)T, 12.1(1)T, 12.1(1), 12.1(5)YB, 12.1(5)YD, 12.2(1), 12.2(2)T, 12.2(2)XT

Continued

Table 4.12 Continued

Compatible Hardware Product Number(s)	Minimum Supported Software Release
NM-HDV-1E1-12	12.0(7)XK, 12.1(2)T, 12.1(5)YB, 12.1(5)YD, 12.2(1), 12.2(2)T, 12.2(2)XT
NM-HDV	12.0(5)XK, 12.0(7)T, 12.0(7)XK, 12.1(1)T, 12.1(1), 12.1(5)YB, 12.1(5)YD, 12.2(1), 12.2(2)T, 12.2(2)XT
NM-HDV-1E1-30	12.0(7)XK, 12.1(2)T, 12.1(5)YB, 12.1(5)YD, 12.2(1), 12.2(2)T, 12.2(2)XT
NM-HDV-1E1-30E	12.0(7)XK, 12.1(2)T, 12.1(5)YB, 12.1(5)YD, 12.2(1), 12.2(2)T, 12.2(2)XT
NM-HDV-1T1-12	12.0(5)XK, 12.0(7)T, 12.0(7)XK, 12.1(1)T, 12.1(1), 12.1(5)YB, 12.1(5)YD, 12.2(1), 12.2(2)T, 12.2(2)XT
NM-HDV-1T1-24	12.0(5)XK, 12.0(7)T, 12.0(7)XK, 12.1(1)T, 12.1(1), 12.1(5)YB, 12.1(5)YD, 12.2(1), 12.2(2)T, 12.2(2)XT
NM-HDV-1T1-24E	12.0(5)XK, 12.0(7)T, 12.0(7)XK, 12.1(1)T, 12.1(1), 12.1(5)YB, 12.1(5)YD, 12.2(1), 12.2(2)T, 12.2(2)XT
NM-HDV-2E1-60	12.0(7)XK, 12.1(2)T, 12.1(5)YB, 12.1(5)YD, 12.2(1), 12.2(2)T, 12.2(2)XT
NM-HDV-2T1-48	12.0(5)XK, 12.0(7)T, 12.0(7)XK, 12.1(1)T, 12.1(1), 12.1(5)YB, 12.1(5)YD, 12.2(1), 12.2(2)T, 12.2(2)XT
PVDM-12	12.0(5)XK, 12.0(7)T, 12.0(7)XK, 12.1(1)T, 12.1(1), 12.1(5)YB, 12.1(5)YD, 12.2(1), 12.2(2)T, 12.2(2)XT
VIC-2BRI-S/T-TE	12.0(2)XD, 12.0(3)T, 12.0(5)XK, 12.0(7)T, 12.0(7)XK, 12.1(1)T, 12.1(1), 12.1(5)YB, 12.1(5)YD, 12.2(1), 12.2(2)T, 12.2(2)XT
VIC-2DID	12.1(5)XM1, 12.2(2)T, 12.2(2)XT
VIC-2E/M	11.3(2)XA, 11.3(3)T, 12.0(1)T, 12.0(1), 12.0(3)T, 12.0(5)XK, 12.0(7)T, 12.0(7)XK, 12.1(1)T, 12.1(1), 12.1(5)YB, 12.1(5)YD, 12.2(1), 12.2(2)T, 12.2(2)XT
VIC-2FXO	11.3(2)XA, 11.3(3)T, 12.0(1)T, 12.0(1), 12.0(3)T, 12.0(5)XK, 12.0(7)T, 12.0(7)XK, 12.1(1)T, 12.1(1), 12.1(5)YB, 12.1(5)YD, 12.2(1), 12.2(2)T, 12.2(2)XT
VIC-2FXS	11.3(2)XA, 11.3(3)T, 12.0(1)T, 12.0(1), 12.0(3)T, 12.0(5)XK, 12.0(7)T, 12.0(7)XK, 12.1(1)T, 12.1(1), 12.1(5)YB, 12.1(5)YD, 12.2(1), 12.2(2)T, 12.2(2)XT

Continued

Table 4.12 Continued

Compatible Hardware Product Number(s)	Minimum Supported Software Release
VWIC-1MFT-E1	12.0(5)XK, 12.0(7)T, 12.0(7)XK, 12.1(1)T, 12.1(1), 12.1(5)YB, 12.1(5)YD, 12.2(1), 12.2(2)T, 12.2(2)XT
VWIC-1MFT-G703	12.1(1)T, 12.1(5)YB, 12.1(5)YD, 12.2(1), 12.2(2)T, 12.2(2)XT
VWIC-1MFT-T1	12.0(5)XK, 12.0(7)T, 12.0(7)XK, 12.1(1)T, 12.1(1), 12.1(5)YB, 12.1(5)YD, 12.2(1), 12.2(2)T, 12.2(2)XT
VWIC-2MFT-E1-DI	12.0(5)XK, 12.0(7)T, 12.0(7)XK, 12.1(1)T, 12.1(1), 12.1(5)YB, 12.1(5)YD, 12.2(1), 12.2(2)T, 12.2(2)XT
VWIC-2MFT-E1	12.0(5)XK, 12.0(7)T, 12.0(7)XK, 12.1(1)T, 12.1(1), 12.1(5)YB, 12.1(5)YD, 12.2(1), 12.2(2)T, 12.2(2)XT
VWIC-2MFT-G703	12.1(1)T, 12.1(5)YB, 12.1(5)YD, 12.2(1), 12.2(2)T, 12.2(2)XT
VWIC-2MFT-T1-DI	12.0(5)XK, 12.0(7)T, 12.0(7)XK, 12.1(1)T, 12.1(1), 12.1(5)YB, 12.1(5)YD, 12.2(1), 12.2(2)T, 12.2(2)XT
VWIC-2MFT-T1	12.0(5)XK, 12.0(7)T, 12.0(7)XK, 12.1(1)T, 12.1(1), 12.1(5)YB, 12.1(5)YD, 12.2(1), 12.2(2)T, 12.2(2)XT

Table 4.13 shows the minimum supported software releases for the Cisco 3600 family of routers.

Table 4.13 Cisco 3600 Minimum Supported Software Releases

Compatible Hardware Product Number(s)	Minimum Supported Software Release
NM-1HDV	12.0(5)XK, 12.0(7)T, 12.0(7)XK, 12.1(1)T, 12.1(1), 12.1(5)YB, 12.1(5)YD, 12.2(1), 12.2(2)T, 12.2(2)XT, 12.2(8)T
NM-1V	11.3(1)T, 12.0(1)T, 12.0(1), 12.0(2)T, 12.0(2)XC, 12.0(2)XD, 12.0(3)T, 12.0(5)XK, 12.0(7)T, 12.0(7)XK, 12.1(1)T, 12.1(1), 12.1(5)YB, 12.1(5)YD, 12.2(1), 12.2(2)T, 12.2(2)XT, 12.2(8)T
NM-2V	11.3(1)T, 12.0(1)T, 12.0(1), 12.0(2)T, 12.0(2)XC, 12.0(2)XD, 12.0(3)T, 12.0(5)XK, 12.0(7)T, 12.0(7)XK, 12.1(1)T, 12.1(1), 12.1(5)YB, 12.1(5)YD, 12.2(1), 12.2(2)T, 12.2(2)XT, 12.2(8)T

Continued

Table 4.13 Continued

Compatible Hardware Product Number(s)	Minimum Supported Software Release
NM-HDV-1E1-12	12.0(7)XK, 12.1(2)T, 12.1(5)YB, 12.1(5)YD, 12.2(1), 12.2(2)T, 12.2(2)XT, 12.2(8)T
NM-HDV-1E1-30	12.0(7)XK, 12.1(2)T, 12.1(5)YB, 12.1(5)YD, 12.2(1), 12.2(2)T, 12.2(2)XT, 12.2(8)T
NM-HDV-1E1-30E	12.0(7)XK, 12.1(2)T, 12.1(5)YB, 12.1(5)YD, 12.2(1), 12.2(2)T, 12.2(2)XT, 12.2(8)T
NM-HDV-1J1-30	12.2(8)T
NM-HDV-1J1-30E	12.2(8)T
NM-HDV-1T1-12	12.0(5)XK, 12.0(7)T, 12.0(7)XK, 12.1(1)T, 12.1(1), 12.1(5)YB, 12.1(5)YD, 12.2(1), 12.2(2)T, 12.2(2)XT, 12.2(8)T
NM-HDV-1T1-24	12.0(5)XK, 12.0(7)T, 12.0(7)XK, 12.1(1)T, 12.1(1), 12.1(5)YB, 12.1(5)YD, 12.2(1), 12.2(2)T, 12.2(2)XT, 12.2(8)T
NM-HDV-1T1-24E	12.0(5)XK, 12.0(7)T, 12.0(7)XK, 12.1(1)T, 12.1(1), 12.1(5)YB, 12.1(5)YD, 12.2(1), 12.2(2)T, 12.2(2)XT, 12.2(8)T
NM-HDV-2E1-60	12.0(7)XK, 12.1(2)T, 12.1(5)YB, 12.1(5)YD, 12.2(1), 12.2(2)T, 12.2(2)XT, 12.2(8)T
NM-HDV-2T1-48	12.0(5)XK, 12.0(7)T, 12.0(7)XK, 12.1(1)T, 12.1(1), 12.1(5)YB, 12.1(5)YD, 12.2(1), 12.2(2)T, 12.2(2)XT, 12.2(8)T
NM-HDV	12.0(5)XK, 12.0(7)T, 12.0(7)XK, 12.1(1)T, 12.1(1), 12.1(5)YB, 12.1(5)YD, 12.2(1), 12.2(2)T, 12.2(2)XT, 12.2(8)T
PVDM-12	12.0(5)XK, 12.0(7)T, 12.0(7)XK, 12.1(1)T, 12.1(1), 12.1(5)YB, 12.1(5)YD, 12.2(1), 12.2(2)T, 12.2(2)XT, 12.2(8)T
VIC-1J1	12.2(8)T
VIC-2BRI-S/T-TE	12.0(2)XD, 12.0(3)T, 12.0(5)XK, 12.0(7)T, 12.0(7)XK, 12.1(1)T, 12.1(1), 12.1(5)YB, 12.1(5)YD, 12.2(1), 12.2(2)T, 12.2(2)XT, 12.2(8)T
VIC-2DID	12.1(5)XM1, 12.2(2)T, 12.2(2)XT, 12.2(8)T

Continued

Table 4.13 Continued

Compatible Hardware Product Number(s)	Minimum Supported Software Release
VIC-2E/M	11.3(1)T, 12.0(1)T, 12.0(1), 12.0(2)T, 12.0(2)XC, 12.0(2)XD, 12.0(3)T, 12.0(5)XK, 12.0(7)T, 12.0(7)XK, 12.1(1)T, 12.1(1), 12.1(5)YB, 12.1(5)YD, 12.2(1), 12.2(2)T, 12.2(2)XT, 12.2(8)T
VIC-2FXO	11.3(1)T, 12.0(1)T, 12.0(1), 12.0(2)T, 12.0(2)XC, 12.0(2)XD, 12.0(3)T, 12.0(5)XK, 12.0(7)T, 12.0(7)XK, 12.1(1)T, 12.1(1), 12.1(5)YB, 12.1(5)YD, 12.2(1), 12.2(2)T, 12.2(2)XT, 12.2(8)T
VIC-2FXS	11.3(1)T, 12.0(1)T, 12.0(1), 12.0(2)T, 12.0(2)XC, 12.0(2)XD, 12.0(3)T, 12.0(5)XK, 12.0(7)T, 12.0(7)XK, 12.1(1)T, 12.1(1), 12.1(5)YB, 12.1(5)YD, 12.2(1), 12.2(2)T, 12.2(2)XT, 12.2(8)T
VWIC-1MFT-E1	12.0(5)XK, 12.0(7)T, 12.0(7)XK, 12.1(1)T, 12.1(1), 12.1(5)YB, 12.1(5)YD, 12.2(1), 12.2(2)T, 12.2(2)XT, 12.2(8)T
VWIC-1MFT-G703	12.1(1)T, 12.1(5)YB, 12.1(5)YD, 12.2(1), 12.2(2)T, 12.2(2)XT, 12.2(8)T
VWIC-1MFT-T1	12.0(5)XK, 12.0(7)T, 12.0(7)XK, 12.1(1)T, 12.1(1), 12.1(5)YB, 12.1(5)YD, 12.2(1), 12.2(2)T, 12.2(2)XT, 12.2(8)T
VWIC-2MFT-E1	12.0(5)XK, 12.0(7)T, 12.0(7)XK, 12.1(1)T, 12.1(1), 12.1(5)YB, 12.1(5)YD, 12.2(1), 12.2(2)T, 12.2(2)XT, 12.2(8)T
VWIC-2MFT-E1-DI	12.0(5)XK, 12.0(7)T, 12.0(7)XK, 12.1(1)T, 12.1(1), 12.1(5)YB, 12.1(5)YD, 12.2(1), 12.2(2)T, 12.2(2)XT, 12.2(8)T
VWIC-2MFT-G703	12.1(1)T, 12.1(5)YB, 12.1(5)YD, 12.2(1), 12.2(2)T, 12.2(2)XT, 12.2(8)T
VWIC-2MFT-T1	12.0(5)XK, 12.0(7)T, 12.0(7)XK, 12.1(1)T, 12.1(1), 12.1(5)YB, 12.1(5)YD, 12.2(1), 12.2(2)T, 12.2(2)XT, 12.2(8)T
VWIC-2MFT-T1-DI	12.0(5)XK, 12.0(7)T, 12.0(7)XK, 12.1(1)T, 12.1(1), 12.1(5)YB, 12.1(5)YD, 12.2(1), 12.2(2)T, 12.2(2)XT, 12.2(8)T

NOTE

Note that for 3700 platforms, the minimum IOS release is IOS 12.2(8)T for all network modules and VICs.

7200 and 7500 Series Router Configurations

The 7200 and 7500 series modular access routers are Cisco high-end routers for voice, video, and data. The 7200 router family consists of the 7204, with a four-slot chassis, and the 7206, which has a six-slot chassis. The Cisco 7500 series includes the Cisco 7505, the Cisco 7507, and the Cisco 7513 with 5, 7, and 13 slots respectively. These chassis all use the T1 or E1 enhanced digital voice port adapters to support voice traffic over the IP network. These adapters include the two-port T1 and E1 high-capacity enhanced digital voice port adapter, the two-port T1 and E1 moderate-capacity enhanced digital voice port adapter, and the one-port T1 and E1 enhanced digital voice port adapters.

Pictured in Figures 4.21 and 4.22 is the rear view of the Cisco 7206 and 7507 routers.

Figure 4.21 Cisco 7200, Rear View

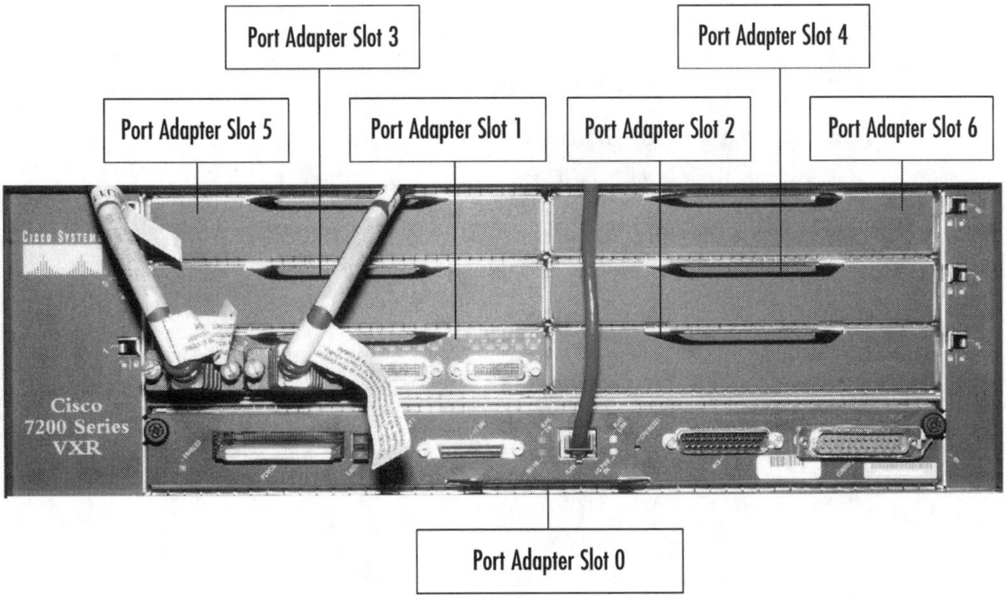

Port Adapter Slot 3

Port Adapter Slot 4

Port Adapter Slot 5

Port Adapter Slot 1

Port Adapter Slot 2

Port Adapter Slot 6

Port Adapter Slot 0

Figure 4.22 Cisco 7507, Rear View

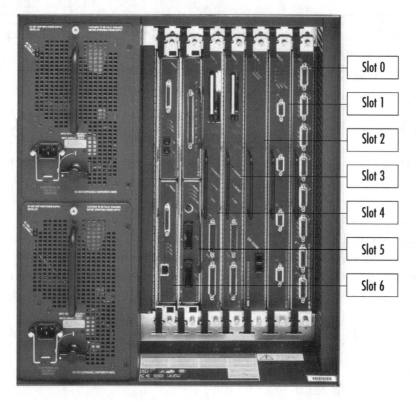

To install the enhanced T1 voice port adapter, follow these steps:

1. Align the port adapter carrier between the port adapter slot.

2. Slide the port adapter halfway into the slot.

3. Connect cable and finish sliding in the port adapter until seated.

4. After the port adapter is seated, lock the port adapter lever.

The preceding procedure can be completed online because the 7200 and 7500 support online insertion and removal.

Table 4.14 shows the minimum supported IOS releases for the 7200 and the 7500.

Table 4.14 Cisco 7200 and 7500 Minimum Supported IOS Releases

Chassis	Module	Minimum Supported Software Release
Cisco 7200	PA-VXA-1TE1-24+	12.2(4)T
Cisco 7200	PA-VXA-1TE1-30+	12.2(4)T
Cisco 7200	PA-VXB-2TE1+	12.1(2)T, 12.2(1), 12.2(2)T
Cisco 7200	PA-VXB-2TE1	12.0(5)XE, 12.0(7)XE, 12.0(7)XE1, 12.0(7)XK, 12.1(1)E
Cisco 7200	PA-VXC-2TE1+	12.1(2)T, 12.2(1), 12.2(2)T
Cisco 7200	PA-VXC-2TE1	12.0(5)XE, 12.0(7)XE, 12.0(7)XE1, 12.0(7)XK, 12.1(1)E
Cisco 7500	PA-VXA-1TE1-24+	12.2(4)T2
Cisco 7500	PA-VXA-1TE1-30+	12.2(4)T2
Cisco 7500	PA-VXB-2TE1+	12.1(2)T, 12.2(1), 12.2(2)T
Cisco 7500	PA-VXC-2TE1+	12.1(2)T, 12.2(1), 12.2(2)T

MC3810 Router Configurations

The Cisco MC3810 is a multiservice access concentrator used to integrate data, voice/fax, and video signals and connect them to an asynchronous transfer mode (ATM), Frame Relay, or leased-line network. The MC3810 consists of five basic hardware variations dependent on the choice of optional modules. All five chassis variations are equipped with two serial data ports, one Ethernet 10BaseT port, and two administrative ports. Through its various configuration options, the Cisco MC3810 can support a variety of network and user interfaces, including T1/E1 trunks, PBXs, telephone key systems, analog phones, and ISDN BRI services. Figure 4.23 shows the MC3810-V.

Figure 4.23 Cisco MC3810-V, Rear View

AS5350 and 5850 Universal Gateway Configuration

The Cisco AS5350 and AS5850 universal gateways can provide between 2 and 96 T1s or E1s that can be used to support data, voice, wireless, and fax services on any port. These two chassis have replaced the older versions of the AS5300 and the AS5800. The new AS5350 is only one rack unit high rather than two and supports 216 voice, dial, or universal ports, compared with the 120 voice ports supported by the AS5300. The AS5350 is mainly intended for ISPs and enterprises, whereas the Cisco AS5850 was designed for large service providers. The newer AS5850 is 14 rack units high versus 22 and supports 2688 voice or universal ports, compared with the 1344 voice ports supported by the AS5800. Both chassis include support for hot-swappable cards and fans in order to have little or no service interruption. The AS5350 supports two-, four-, or eight–T1/E1 configurations; the AS5850 supports up to four 24-port T1 cards for a total of 96 T1s.

Figure 4.24 shows the front view of the Cisco AS5350 router. Table 4.15 shows the minimum supported software releases to enable support of the T1 dial feature card (DFC). To install the T1 (DFC), complete the following steps:

1. Loosen the captive screws that secure the blank to the chassis until each screw is free of the chassis, and then remove the blank.

2. Slide the DFC into the slot until the connector pins make contact with the carrier card backplane connector.

3. Align the captive screws with their holes, and seat the card completely.

4. Tighten the screws to secure the DFC to the chassis.

Figure 4.24 Cisco AS5350, Front View

Table 4.15 Cisco AS5350 Minimum Supported Software Releases for the T1 DFC Cards

Chassis	T1 DFC Module	Minimum Supported Software Release
Cisco 5300	AS535-DFC-8CT1	12.1(3)XQ, 12.1(5)XM3, 12.2(2)XA, 12.2(2)XB
Cisco 5300	AS5X-DFC-2T1	12.1(3)XQ, 12.1(5)XM, 12.2(2)XA, 12.2(2)XB
Cisco 5300	AS5X-DFC-4T1	12.1(3)XQ, 12.1(5)XM, 12.2(2)XA, 12.2(2)XB

Pictured in Figure 4.25 is the rear view of the Cisco AS5850 router. To install the 24–channel T1 card, follow these steps:

1. Use a Phillips screwdriver and loosen the panel fasteners at the top and bottom of the card front panel.

2. Remove the blank in slot.

3. Align the card carrier guides with the grooves in the slot.

4. Open the ejector levers to their fully extended positions.

5. Start seating the card in the backplane by pushing the card until the ejector levers fold in toward the trunk card front panel and the front panel is flush with the chassis frame.

6. Finish seating the card by pushing the levers as far as you can toward the chassis.

7. Using a Phillips screwdriver, tighten the panel fasteners on the top and bottom of the card front panel.

Figure 4.25 Cisco AS5850, Rear View

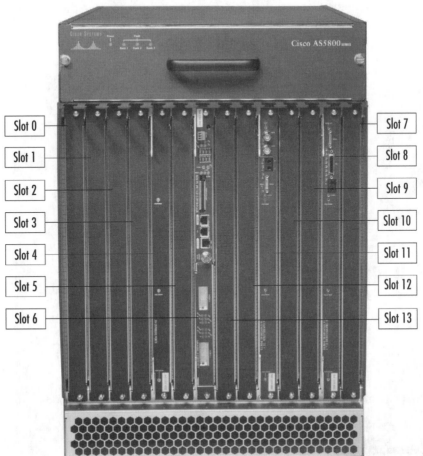

NOTE

Note that for the Cisco AS5850 platform, the minimum IOS release is IOS 12.2(1)XB for the 24-channel T1 card.

Cisco Catalyst 4000 and 6000 Series Switches

The Cisco Catalyst 4000 and 6000 series switches are modular chassis available in several configurations. They are designed primarily for enterprise offices, branch offices, and multisite campuses. Both chassis can provide inline power for end-user Cisco IP phones and thus can also centralize power management.

The 4000 series comes in a four- or six-slot chassis with redundant power. To enable voice capabilities, the Access Gateway Module is required. The Access Gateway Module is equipped with slots for DSP modules, high-density analog, Gigabit Ethernet, and three slots for VICs. Figure 4.26 shows the slot view of a Cisco 4006.

Figure 4.26 Cisco Catalyst 4006, Rear View

The Cisco 6000 series switch utilizes the eight-port T1 card for connectivity to the local PSTN or PBX as well as the 24-port FXS module for connecting legacy analog equipment. Figure 4.27 shows the slot view of a Cisco 6509.

Figure 4.27 Cisco Catalyst 6509, Rear View

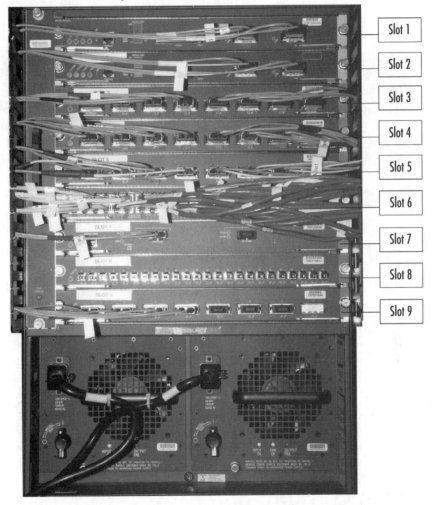

Cisco Catalyst 4200

The Cisco Catalyst 4200 is a small branch office device that can provide voice gateway capabilities, IP routing, and Ethernet switching in a single chassis. It comes equipped with a 24-port 10/100 switch that can provide inline power to Cisco IP phones and a built-in eight-port FXS module for support of legacy analog telephony equipment. It is capable of using the same voice/WAN interface cards as the 1700, 2600, and 3600 families of routers. Figure 4.28 shows the slot view of a Cisco Catalyst 4224 switch.

Figure 4.28 Cisco Catalyst 4224, Rear View

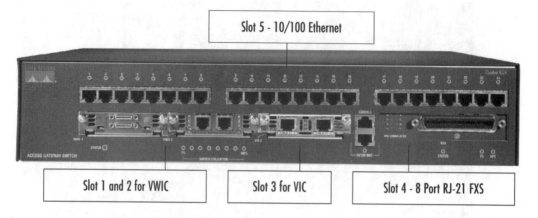

VoIP Terminology

The following is a list of terms and acronyms you'll commonly see in discussions of VoIP technology. This list is intended to be used as a general reference guide for VoIP terms but is in no way an attempt to cover all terminology currently used in voice networking.

ATM

Asynchronous transfer mode (ATM) is an OSI Layer 2, multidrop WAN technology that features a 53-byte cell as the transport mechanism. It also features rigid class-of-service (CoS) features and several transport modes. It is capable of closely simulating TDM services while still accommodating "bursty" data services.

Bandwidth Consumption

Bandwidth consumption is the characteristic bandwidth required between two points to transport traffic. Bandwidth consumption is moderated by several methods of call admission control.

CAC

Call admission control (CAC) is the tracking of bandwidth resources and traffic requests for the purpose of preventing oversubscription within the constraints of the existing bandwidth.

Call Legs

Call legs are the portions of the network defined by the selected dial plan and that form an extension.

Codec

A *codec*, or *coder/decoder*, is a means of sampling, then digitally representing voice, an analog waveform, with a given level of compression. Some common codecs include G.711 (64kbps), G.723 (5.5kbps), G.728 (24kbps), and G.729a (8kbps)

Delay

Delay is the latency, one-way or round-trip, incurred when packets are transmitted from one location to another. This includes the amount of processing time for intervening hops. For VoIP to maintain the expected voice quality, the round-trip delay should remain within approximately 120 milliseconds.

Dial Peers

Dial peers are a means of establishing a voice-over-*X* peer relationship between two voice-over-*X* speakers. They may use POTS, VoIP, VoFR, and VoATM. Dial peers may be prioritized for redundancy.

Dial Plans

Dial plans are the overall routing plans for telephony networks. In common use within the United States is the North American dial plan. It comprises a country code, an area code, and seven-digit phone number. A dial plan for a telephony network is analogous to an IP addressing structure for IP networks. A poorly conceived IP plan or dial plan can result in incorrectly routed IP packets or phone calls.

Echo

Echo is the reflection of sound caused by a mismatch in impedance. This phenomenon typically occurs in the hybrid section, where a two-wire system is converted to a four-wire system.

Frame Relay

Frame Relay is an OSI Layer 2, multidrop WAN technology that features a variable-size frame as the transport mechanism. It assumes reliability of the underlying network, forward and backward congestion notification, traffic shaping, and "bursting" above the committed information rate (CIR). Frame Relay is generally considered a replacement for X.25 networks. Frame Relay standards are defined by the Frame Relay Forum in FRF documents.

Gateways and Gatekeepers

Gateways and *gatekeepers* are the major components of an H.323 network. Gateways signal a gatekeeper for requests for call admission and overall process signaling.

H.323

H.323 is a standard protocol for establishing and transporting VoIP traffic. It features the concept of gateways and a gatekeeper. The standardized messages contain messages for the setup and teardown of connections and call admission control.

Jitter

Jitter is the variation in the delay incurred in a given voice or packet stream. Jitter is typically compensated for by the inclusion of de-jitter buffers to smooth out the variation in delay. The greater the size of the de-jitter buffer, the greater the level of jitter that can be compensated for. Conversely, the larger the de-jitter buffer, the greater the overall processing delay incurred as the packets are held in queue for reassembly.

MGCP

Media Gateway Control Protocol (MGCP) is a standard protocol for establishing and transporting VoIP traffic. The primary goal of MGCP is to coordinate and supervise different media gateways and the subsequent connection attempts made between these gateways. MGCP has been released by the IETF as RFC 2705.

Number Extension and Digit Translation

The *number extension* is analogous to a host IP address. *Digit translation* is the manipulation of dial number to specific route patterns. Such manipulation may include the stripping of a country code or area code where only seven- or four-digit dialing is required. Further digit translation can include routing calls to a dial peer accessible over the WAN instead of routing calls over the PSTN.

PSTN

Public switched telephony network (PSTN) is the familiar telephone network, comprising central offices and tie lines, which provide local and long distance calling.

POTS

Plain old telephone service (POTS) is traditional two-wire or four-wire telephone service. It brings standard dial tone to analog telephones and modems. Given the ubiquity of traditional telephony network, the new world paradigm must interoperate with traditional service to be accepted.

Serialization Delay

Serialization delay is incurred when encapsulating or segmenting a data stream into packets for egress from a given interface. The interface must service the packets one at a time—hence the delay.

SGCP

Skinny Gateway Control Protocol (SGCP) is a standard protocol for the establishment and transport of VoIP traffic. It is based on H.323 but is limited to a subset of control messages, including those for session initialization and session teardown.

TDM

Time-domain multiplexing (TDM) is a means of providing access to transmission media through the use of a time slot. Several signals may be interleaved on the transmission media through the use of multiple time slots. The greater the number of time slots, the shorter the duration of each. Inefficiencies are noticed when a given signal is allotted its time slot but has nothing to transmit.

VAD

Voice activity detection (VAD) is an algorithm that takes note of silence, characteristic in two-way phone conversations, and suppresses the transmission of packets with no information contained within them.

VoATM

Voice over ATM (VoATM) is the encoding and compressing of voice streams directly into the OSI Layer 2 ATM cells. The resulting data stream takes on the characteristics of the Layer 2 network.

VoFR

Voice over Frame Relay (VoFR) is the encoding and compressing of voice streams directly into the OSI Layer 2 frames. The resulting data stream takes on the characteristics of the Layer 2 network.

VoIP

Voice over Internet Protocol (VoIP) is a means of compressing voice using a standardized codec, then encapsulating the results within IP for transport over data networks.

Summary

In this chapter, we discussed the Cisco implementation of VoIP and a majority of the voice products currently offered. This was not meant to be an exhaustive list, since new products and services are always being developed. Therefore, it is important to check with a Cisco sales representative or www.cisco.com to get a current listing of voice products and services prior to designing or implementing any new or existing VoIP network.

The voice ports used to connect to the PSTN from your IP network are called *FXOs*. FXS ports are used to connect the router to standard telephony devices and end stations such as basic telephone equipment. E&M ports are commonly used to connect one PBX to another.

T1 connectivity is available throughout the Cisco product line via various interfaces. The Cisco 1700, 2600, 3600, and 3700 families, for example, all share one- and two-port T1 VICs and VWICs, thus allowing them to act as tandem switch points from T1 tie lines to PBXs and the PSTN to the IP internal network.

Network modules come in several types, including analog, high-density with slots for PVDMs, and even modules for the Catalyst 4000 line of switches. These modules are necessary in order to process telephony signaling for transport across the IP network.

The chassis available for voice services is extensive and covers a wide range of applications, from the Cisco 1751 that can be used in a small office environment to the AS5850, which can be used by the largest of service providers. A Cisco router or switch is available to cover just about any voice situation you face.

Solutions Fast Track

Exploring the Types of Voice Ports

☑ An FXS port is used to connect to basic telephone equipment, keysets, or fax machines.

☑ FXO ports are used to connect IP networks to PSTNs or CO.

☑ The E&M interface allows for connections to PBX trunk lines between PBXs.

☑ T1 connectivity allows T1 voice connectivity to PBXs or to a CO.

Voice Modules and Cards

- ☑ Routers and switches use voice network modules to transform voice signaling.

- ☑ There are three models of VNM for the 2600/3600 series routers:

  1. **NM-1V** One-port network module

  2. **NM-2V** Two-port network module

  3. **HD-VNM** High-density voice network module

- ☑ The Catalyst 4000 uses an access gateway module that acts as a VNM.

- ☑ The two-port E&M module is typically used to connect an IP network directly to a PBX system.

- ☑ The two-port FXS module is used to connect to endpoint equipment such as a telephone, keypad, or fax.

- ☑ The two-port FXO module is typically used to connect to a PBX or PSTN.

- ☑ The two-port voice MFT T1 card is used for voice, data, and integrated voice/data applications.

- ☑ The two-port ISDN BRI is used for terminating to an ISDN telephone network.

- ☑ The four-port DID/FXS card is used to provide DID service to extensions on a PBX.

Connecting VNMs and VICs to the Router

- ☑ The 1700 series routers are used for small to medium-sized businesses and small enterprise branch offices.

- ☑ The Cisco 2600, 3600, and 3700 are designed primarily for traditional and power branch office solutions.

- ☑ The 7200 and 7500 series modular access routers are Cisco high-end routers for voice, video, and data.

- ☑ The Cisco AS5350 and AS5850 universal gateways can provide between 2 and 96 T1s or E1s.

☑ The Cisco MC3810 is used to integrate data, voice/fax, and video signals to an ATM, Frame Relay, or leased-line network.

☑ The Cisco 4000 and 6000 switches are used for enterprise offices, branch offices, and multisite campuses.

☑ The Cisco 4200 is a small branch office device that provides voice gateway capabilities, IP routing, and Ethernet switching.

VoIP Terminology

☑ When you discuss VoIP, you should be familiar with the list of commonly used terms and acronyms because you will encounter these over and over in the field.

Frequently Asked Questions

The following Frequently Asked Questions, answered by the authors of this book, are designed to both measure your understanding of the concepts presented in this chapter and to assist you with real-life implementation of these concepts. To have your questions about this chapter answered by the author, browse to **www.syngress.com/solutions** and click on the **"Ask the Author"** form.

Q: What are the important criteria involved in trying to decide on a router that would be used in a branch office?

A: The important criteria to look for in a branch router or gateway are:

- Features such as QoS, traffic shaping, low latency queuing, link fragmentation and interleaving, and compressed RTP support

- Telephony interface support and adequate density to meet your requirements.

- The forwarding performance of the router itself and the required WAN bandwidth that you would like to utilize

Q: What features does the Cisco 3660 Series offer over the current Cisco 2600 and 3600 series products?

A: The 3660 has several new features:

- **Built-in ports** The 3660 has several built-in ports, including one- or two-port 10/100 Fast Ethernet ports built into the motherboard.

- **Hot-swap capabilities** The 3660 is able to hot-swap network modules. This allows a network module to be removed or installed while the power is on and passing traffic without impact to that traffic.

- **Redundant power supplies** The 3660 chassis supports up to two AC or DC power supplies. Power supplies must be powered down before being removed or inserted, but this does not affect traffic.

Q: When would I choose to use the Cisco 1760 over the Cisco 2610?

A: The Cisco 1760 is typically used for a small to medium-sized business or small branch office that required a rack-mountable router for analog and digital voice and data. The Cisco 2610 is used for enterprise-class functionality when a higher application density is required along with increased WAN ports and further voice/data options.

Q: When would I need to have the DSP option for the Catalyst 4000 Access Gateway Module?

A: The DSP option is required when voice functionality is enabled to include any voice gateway functions or voice network services.

Q: Is an MFT (Multi-Flex Trunk) module required to enable voice features on the MC3810 router?

A: The MFT is only required for enabling VoATM features on the MC3810. This module is needed to support the ATM encapsulation.

Q. What is the minimum Cisco IOS release for the Digital T1/E1 Voice Trunk Network Module?

A. Cisco IOS Plus Feature Set 12.0(5)XK1 or 12.0(7)T or later is required to support T1 CAS. Cisco IOS Plus Feature Set 12.0(07)XK or 12.1(02)T or later is required to support T1 QSIG and E1 QSIG. Furthermore, T1/E1 PRI is supported with Cisco IOS 12.1(02)XH or 12.1(03)T or later.

Chapter 5

VoIP Configurations

Solutions in this chapter:

- **Voice Port Cabling and Configuration**
- **Configuring Voice Ports**
- **Voice Port-Tuning Commands**
- **Configuring Dial Plans and Dial Peers**
- **Creating and Implementing Dial Plans**
- **Configuring Trunking**
- **Configuring ISDN for Voice**
- **Configuring Gateways and Gatekeepers**

☑ **Summary**

☑ **Solutions Fast Track**

☑ **Frequently Asked Questions**

Introduction

This chapter discusses the various voice-supported hardware modules, cabling, tuning, and gateway/gatekeeper configurations with respect to VoIP. This chapter also provides examples of some actual configurations for a VoIP network. The varying types of voice modules were discussed in Chapter 4, so the focus here is on their cabling and layout in the routers.

This chapter commences with a review of Cisco port- and module-numbering schemes that are essential for the reader to understand in order to effectively configure a router for VoIP. We also cover the various analog interface configurations, pulling them together with the remaining commands to complete a VoIP configuration such as dial peers. All this information is obtained through the process of completing the dial plan. For installations that require greater capacity, digital voice module options are covered, with an emphasis on ISDN and its configuration. We finish with the handling of multiple sites that have gateways and how they can communicate via a gatekeeper.

Voice Port Cabling and Configuration

We commence this chapter with a discussion of how *voice interface card (VIC)* modules are used in the various routers. Cisco has done a good job of giving us the flexibility of using the same modules in a number of different routers. This consistency improves on the ease of configuration from router to router, since the configuration is very similar in each case. The selection of analog or digital voice modules is based on the connectivity requirements to the router. (We discuss digital voice module configuration later in the chapter.) It is important to understand the various voice port modules and cabling before discussing the configuration of each of these ports. The analog VICs supported are foreign exchange station (FXS), foreign exchange office (FXO), ear and mouth (E&M), and direct inward dial (DID). Depending on the model of the router and switch, these cards are inserted directly into an open slot in the router or are submodules to a voice network module (VNM), such as the NM-1V and NM-2V. The NM-1V and NM-2V are supported in the Cisco 2600, 3600, and 3700 series routers.

It is important to understand that although some of the ports share physical characteristics, they cannot be connected to all remote devices. Connecting a remote device to the incorrect port type can result in undesired consequences such as lost software configuration or hardware failure. The FXS, FXO, and DID VIC use RJ-11 cabling, whereas the E&M module utilizes a two-wire/four-wire connection with RJ-1CX cabling. FXS ports are always color-coded gray. Do not connect an FXS port to the PSTN. The FXS ports are not designed to handle direct connectivity to the PSTN. The FXO ports are always color-coded pink. Connect only an FXO port approved for your country to the PSTN. Otherwise, connect an FXO port only to a PBX (connections from the PBX to the PSTN are permitted). E&M ports are always color-coded brown. Do not connect an E&M port to the PSTN. This can cause disruptions and unpredictable results back at the PSTN's CO.

As mentioned, there are one-port and two-port voice network modules. Figure 5.1 displays how the slot numbering is assigned. Any combination of the VIC cards can be inserted into these slots.

Figure 5.1 NM-2V Slot Numbers

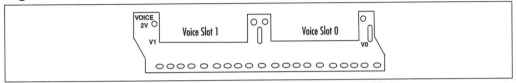

Each of the VIC modules has two ports. The ports are always numbered 0 and 1 from right to left, as shown in Figure 5.2.

Figure 5.2 VIC Module Port Layout

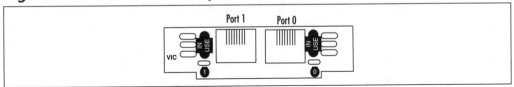

As you can see, the individual VIC ports and voice slots on the VNMs are numbered from right to left. This is not necessarily the case with the individual VICs regarding where these modules are installed in the various routers. Next we discuss the slot and port numbering for each router.

Port Numbering on the 1700 Series

Cisco 175X routers support up to three VIC modules. Slots 0 and 1 are WIC/VIC capable, and Slot 2 is a VIC-only slot. Slots 0 and 1 are on the left side, with Slot 0 on the bottom of the two. Slot 2 is located in the upper-right side of the router, as shown in Figure 5.3.

Figure 5.3 The Cisco 175X Chassis

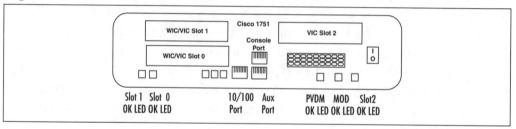

The Cisco 1760 layout is quite different from other 1700 series routers in that it is a 19-inch rack-mountable model. The 1760 router (see Figure 5.4) has four VIC-capable slots, which are numbered 0 to 3 from left to right. Two slots support VIC and WIC models, and the remaining two are VIC-only slots. Cisco 175x/1760 routers use the following command to configure voice ports: *Router(config)#**voice-port slot/port***.

Figure 5.4 Cisco 1760 Chassis

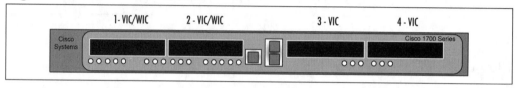

The following are the tag numbers and their corresponding descriptions in reference to voice-supported slots:

- **1** VIC/WIC Slot 0
- **2** VIC/WIC Slot 1
- **3** VIC Slot 2
- **4** VIC Slot 3

Port Numbering on the 2600 and 3600 Series

All 2600 and 3600 series routers support VNMs. The VNM is available as a one- and a two-port model. The VIC modules are inserted into the VNM. The 2600 series has one slot available for the VNM, which is located on the left side of the router, as shown in Figure 5.5.

Figure 5.5 Cisco 2600 Series Router

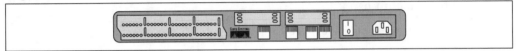

The Cisco 3600 series routers are configured the same as the 2600 series. The main difference is the greater slot capacity on the 3600 series. All VIC modules are configured on these models with the following command line:

router(config)#voice-port slot/subunit/port.

Port Numbering on the MC3810 Series

The hardware configuration of the MC3810 is a little different from most other Cisco VoX routers. The MC3810 router supports six analog personality modules (APMs), and the modules can be installed in any combination. Table 5.1 displays the supported voice modules and their valid slots and capacities.

Table 5.1 MC3810 Voice Modules and Slots

Type	Slot	Valid Port Numbers
Analog voice module (AVM)	1	1–6
Digital voice module (DVM)	1	Digital T1: 1–24; digital E1: 1–15 and 17–31
Multiflex trunk module (MFT)	0	Digital T1: 1-24; digital E1: 1–15 and 17–31

To determine the type of module, quantity, and default configuration, enter the following command:

```
router> show voice port
```

The analog voice ports are always configured as Slot 1 and the ports are numbered 1 to 6. So, the voice ports are designated as 1/1, 1/2, 1/3, 1/4,1/5,and 1/6, as shown in Figure 5.6.

Figure 5.6 MC3810 Analog Voice Module Port Numbers

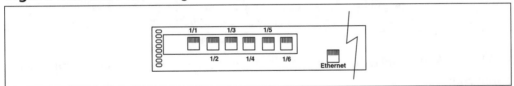

To enter the basic configuration of a voice port, from the configuration prompt enter the command:

```
router(config)#voice-port slot/port
```

Port Numbering on the 7200 Series

The Cisco 7200 Series router always has Slot 0 reserved for Fast Ethernet ports in the bottom slot. Slot 1 is located in the lower-left side of the router; Slot 2 is to the right of Slot 1. The 7206 router's Slots 3 through 6 continue this left-to-right pattern for the remaining port adapters, as shown in Figure 5.7. The 7200 series routers are also available in a four-slot configuration in the 7204 model.

Figure 5.7 Cisco 7200 Series Slot Numbering

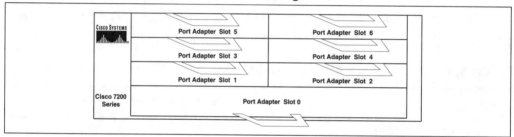

The Cisco 7200 and 7200 VXR series routers support the PA-VXA, PA-VXB, and PA-VXC port adapter interfaces. The interface address configuration format is *port adapter slot number/interface port number*. For example, a single T1 port adapter located in Slot 1 would be referenced as 1/0.

Port Numbering on the AS5x00 Series

The Cisco AS5300 series router supports VoIP cards and works in conjunction with T1/E1 ports to terminate calls from the PSTN or PBX. The slots are laid out similarly to the newer AS5350, which is shown in Figure 5.8.

Figure 5.8 Cisco AS5350 Chassis Slot Numbering

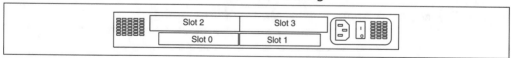

The AS5300 displays the status of the VoIP card when you enter the following command:

```
5300#show vfc slot_number board
```

A difference between the AS5300 and AS5350 routers is that the AS5350 works with the newer universal port card. The universal port card supports channelized T1, E1, and T3 interfaces. The AS5400 supports more slots than the AS5350. The AS5350 and AS5400 support eight and four slots, respectively. An AS5400's slot-numbering scheme is illustrated in Figure 5.9.

Figure 5.9 Cisco AS5400 Chassis Slot Numbering

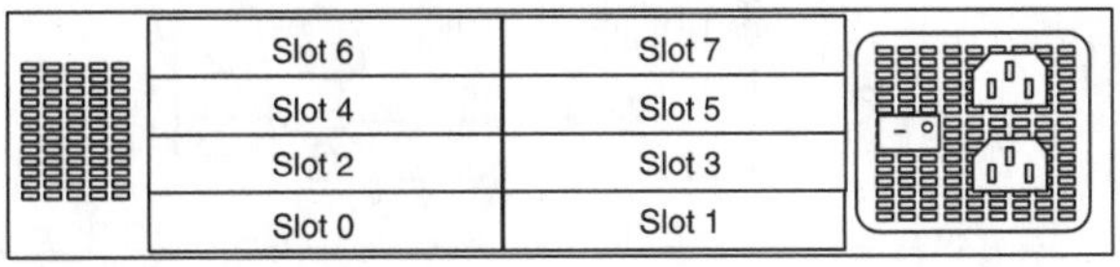

Slot 6
Slot 7
Slot 4
Slot 5
Slot 2
Slot 3
Slot 0
Slot 1

To configure universal ports on the AS5350 and AS5400, enter the following commands:

```
AS5400(config)#line slot/port slot/port
```

For example, if you want to configure 60 ports in Slot 1, enter **line 1/00 1/59**. If you want to configure 180 ports in Slots 3, 4, and 5, enter **line 3/00 5/179**.

NOTE

The Cisco AS5300 and AS5800 Access Servers will not be available for ordering after June 30, 2002.

LED Status

The VNMs come with LEDs to help you troubleshoot hardware responsiveness. There is only one LED per VNM, and it represents an active or dormant status. The LED is located in the lower right of the module, as shown in Figure 5.10. When the LED is green, it means that the module has passed the self-test and is active.

Figure 5.10 NM-2V LED

VOICE
2V
V1
Voice Slot 1
Voice Slot 0
V0
EN
Enable LED

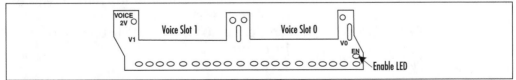

The VICs also come with LEDs to help troubleshoot hardware responsiveness. Figure 5.11 shows that they have one LED per port, representing an active or dormant status. When the LED is green, the port has an active signal on it. When the LED is off, the port is in a dormant state.

Figure 5.11 VIC LEDs

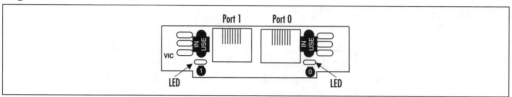

Since the Cisco 175*x* and 1760 series routers do not support the VNM modules, which act as carriers for the VICs, the LEDs are located on the router itself. This was previously illustrated in Figures 5.3 and 5.4. Table 5.2 describes the function of each relative slot. The functionality is the same on the 1750 and 1760 series. Table 5.3 describes the various LED states and their functions for the Cisco 7200 series routers with a port adapter module installed.

Table 5.2 Cisco 1750/1751 Rear LEDs

Type	Status	Color	Function
Slot 0	OK	Green	On; either a WIC or VIC installed properly
Slot 1	OK	Green	On; either a WIC or VIC installed properly
Slot 2	OK	Green	On; a VIC installed properly
PVDM	OK	Green	On; a packet voice data module (PVDM) installed properly

Table 5.3 Cisco 7200 PA-VXA, PA-VXB, and PA-VXC Port Adapter LEDs

LED Label	Color	State	Function
En	Green	On	Powered up
	N/A	Off	Not ready or disabled
AL	Amber	On	Alarm condition exists on the remote end of one of the T1/E1 ports
	Red	On	Alarm condition exists locally on one of the T1/E1 ports
	N/A	Off	No alarms

Continued

Table 5.3 Continued

LED Label	Color	State	Function
Unlabeled, 0, or 1	Green	On	Port is enabled
	Yellow	On	Port is in loopback
	N/A	Off	Port is not enabled, the received signal is bad, or an alarm condition exists

Configuring Voice Ports

We have now discussed the basic hardware installation for VNMs and VICs. The next step is to configure the cards on the Cisco router IOS. Voice card configuration is covered in the following sections. Some basic configuration parameters must be set in order for a voice port to operate. To configure a basic voice port on an MC3810, complete the following steps.

1. Enter Privileged Exec mode:

   ```
   router>enable
   ```

2. Check the DSP voice channel activity with the following command:

   ```
   router#show voice dsp
   ```

3. Enter Global Configuration mode:

   ```
   router#configure terminal
   ```

4. Enter Voice Card Configuration mode. On the MC3810, the slot must be 0:

   ```
   router(config)#voice-card slot
   ```

5. Enter the codec type for the voice card:

   ```
   router(config-voicecard)#codec {med | high}
   ```

   This series of steps sets the codec compression technique, which is either high or medium complexity. High complexity can handle fewer calls per DSP. This is due to the higher CPU utilization required for high codec complexity operation. Let's look at the difference between high and medium complexity:

- **High complexity**   Specifies two voice channels encoded in any of the following formats: G.711ulaw, G.711alaw, G.723.1 (r5.3), G.723.1 Annex A (r5.3), G.723.1 (r6.3), G.723.1 Annex A (r6.3), G.726 (r16), G.726 (r24), G.726 (r32), G.728, G.729, G.729 Annex B, and fax relay.
- **Medium (default) complexity**   Specifies four voice channels encoded in any of the following formats: G.711ulaw, G.711alaw, G.726 (r16), G.726 (r24), G.726 (r32), G.729 Annex A, G.729 Annex B with Annex A, and fax relay.

Configuring FXO or FXS Voice Ports

All these parameters have default settings, and FXS and FXO port default config-uration values are adequate for most situations. Therefore, user intervention is rarely needed. The following settings are mandatory to any FXS/FXO port configuration:

- Signal type
- Call progress tone
- Ring frequency
- Ring number
- Dial type (FXO only)
- PLAR connection mode
- Music threshold
- Description
- VAD
- Comfort noise

Follow these steps to complete a basic setup for all FXS/FXO voice ports:

1. Enter Privileged Exec mode:

    `router>`**`enable`**

2. Enter Global Configuration mode:

    `router#`**`configure terminal`**

3. Identify which port to configure on a 2600 and 3600 series router:

```
router(config)#voice-port nm-module/vic-module/port-number
router(config)#voice-port slot/port (Cisco 175x/1760 and MC3810)
```

4. Select the appropriate signaling for the start of a call:

```
router(config-voiceport)#signal [loop-start|ground-start]
```

5. Select the appropriate country codes for call progression signaling. The default is *northamerica*:

```
router(config-voiceport)#cptone country-code
```

6. Configure the voice port connection mode type. If the connection will be to a PBX, use the tie-line option. If the connection will be for private line automatic ringdown (PLAR), use the plar option. If the connection will be for PLAR off-premises extension (OPX), use the *plar-opx* option.

```
router(config-voiceport)#connection {tie-line | plar | plar-opx}
string
```

7. Assign the appropriate out-dialing dial type (FXO only):

```
router(config-voiceport#dial-type{dtmf | pulse}
```

8. Configure the frequency in Hertz of ringing for the system that is attached on a Cisco 1750, 2600, and 3600 series router (FXS only):

```
router(config-voiceport)#ring frequency [25| 50]
router(config-voiceport)#ring frequency [20| 30] (Cisco MC3810
router)
```

9. Configure the maximum number of rings allowed before answering a call (FXO only):

```
router(config-voiceport)#ring number number
```

10. Specify an existing pattern for ring tone or define a new one (FXS only). Each pattern specifies a ring-pulse time and a ring-interval time:

```
router(config-voiceport)#ring cadence {[pattern01 | pattern02 |
    pattern03 | pattern04 | pattern05 | pattern06 | pattern07 |
    pattern08 | pattern09 | pattern10 | pattern11 | pattern12]
    | [define pulse interval]}
```

11. Specify the termination impedance, which needs to match the specifications of the PBX it is attaching to:

```
router(config-voiceport)#impedance [600c|600r|900c|complex1|complex2]
```

12. Configure the threshold in decibels for hold music:

```
router(config-voiceport)#music-threshold number
```

13. Optional: Configure a text string to the configuration that describes the connection for this voice port:

```
router(config-voiceport)#description string
```

14. Configure background noise generation for the comfort of a user when there is no noise:

```
router(config-voiceport)#comfort-noise
```

15. Optional: Enable voice activity detection (VAD):

```
router(config-voiceport)#vad
```

Configuring E&M Ports

Contrary to FXS/FXO defaults, E&M default settings are usually *not* sufficient to enable voice transmissions over IP. This is because E&M ports are designed to connect directly to a PBX and therefore must match the particular PBX's specifications. The following settings are mandatory to implement an E&M port:

- Signal type
- Call progress tone
- Operation
- Type
- Impedance

The following commands complete a basic setup for all E&M voice ports:

1. Enter Privileged Exec mode:

```
router>enable
```

2. Enter Global Configuration mode:

```
router#configure terminal
```

3. Identify which port to configure on a 2600 and 3600 series router:

```
router(config)#voice-port nm-module/vic-module/port-number
router(config)#voice-port slot/port (Cisco 175x/1760 and MC3810)
```

4. Select the appropriate signaling for the interface:

```
router(config-voiceport)#signal [wink-start|immediate|delay-dial]
```

5. Select the appropriate country codes for call progression signaling. The default is *us*. The *northamerica* keyword is for the Cisco MC3810 multi-service concentrator for versions prior to Cisco IOS Release 12.0(4)T and for ISDN PRI:

```
router(config-voiceport)#cptone country code
```

6. Define cabling scheme operation:

```
router(config-voiceport)#operation [2-wire|4-wire]
```

7. Select the appropriate E&M interface type:

```
router(config-voiceport)#type [1|2|3|5]
```

8. Specify the termination impedance, which needs to match the specifications of the PBX the port is attaching to:

```
router(config-voiceport)#impedance [600c|600r|900c|complex1|complex2]
```

Some optional configurations for the E&M port are not required for operation. As with the FXS/FXO ports, the following configurations are used for optimization and usability:

■ Connection mode

■ Music threshold

■ Description

■ Comfort tone (VAD-activated only)

Use the following commands to adjust any of these optional configuration parameters for E&M ports:

1. Enter Privileged Exec mode:

```
router>enable
```

2. Enter Global Configuration mode:

```
router#configure terminal
```

3. Identify which port to configure on a 2600 and 3600 series router:

```
router(config)#voice-port nm-module/vic-module/port-number
router(config)#voice-port slot/port (Cisco 175x/1760 and MC3810)
```

4. Specify that the port configured for PLAR (which we discuss in more detail later in this chapter):

```
router(config-voiceport)#connection plar string
```

5. Define the threshold in decibels for hold music:

```
router(config-voiceport)#music-threshold number
```

6. Specify a description field for port:

```
router(config-voiceport)#description string
```

7. Set comfort noise to generate background noise for the user when there is no sound on the line:

```
router(config-voiceport)#comfort-noise
```

Configuring DID Ports

Configuring analog DID ports allows connections to the PSTN in which calls are routed to phones as if they all had direct lines to the PSTN. The following commands complete a basic setup for analog DID voice ports:

1. Enter Privileged Exec mode:

```
router>enable
```

2. Enter Global Configuration mode:

```
router#configure terminal
```

3. Identify the port to configure on a 2600 and 3600 series router:

```
router(config)#voice-port nm-module/vic-module/port-number
router(config)#voice-port slot/port (Cisco 175x/1760 and MC3810)
```

4. Select the appropriate signaling for the interface:

```
router(config-voiceport)#signal did [wink-start|immediate|delay-dial]
```

Now that you have individually configured all the voice ports on the router, you need to address the task of getting voice packets from one router to another. To accomplish this task, we need to look at voice-routing methods such as direct dial, trunking, and PLAR.

The Connection Command

The *connection* command in voice port configuration mode allows special modes to be set for specific voice ports. If the *connection* command is not configured, the session application assumes that there is a "standard" connection being initiated and it will output a dial tone when the interface senses an off-hook state. The dial tone will last until enough digits are collected to match a dial peer and complete the call or until the timeout for digit entry is met. The syntax for the *connection* command is as follows:

```
connection [plar | tie-line | trunk | plar-opx] string
```

- **string** Represents the destination telephone number.

- **plar** Short for *private line automatic ringdown*; used to automatically dial a destination pattern as soon as the receiver on the phone is lifted and the port is activated. No digits need to be entered to establish the connection. An example is if the user picks up the handset and the call is automatically placed to the far end.

- **tie-line** Specifies that the particular port is a tie-line connection to a PBX. It is used on the MC3810 when a dial plan requires that additional digits are added in front of any digits dialed by the PBX and the combined set of digits is used to route the call via the dial-peer settings and into the network.

- **trunk** Specifies that the particular port is a straight tie-line connection to a PBX. The "connection trunk" mode can be used for E&M-E&M trunks, FX0-FXS trunks, and FXS-FXS trunks. It should be noted that signaling will be transported for the E&M-E&M and FXO-FXS trunks but not for FXS-FXS trunks since they do not support signaling parameters between them.

- **plar-opx** Specifies a PLAR connection to an off-premises extension. Using this option, the local voice port provides a local response before the remote voice port receives an answer. This method ensures that the call is answered before the call flow is completed.

Voice Port-Tuning Commands

Depending on the special needs of your VoIP environment, you might first need to adjust some variables to allow fine-tuning of the voice transmissions. Voice port fine-tuning commands are instructions to the voice port that adjust timing, delay, impedance parameters, input gain, and output attenuation. Once these adjustments are made, you can fine-tune such aspects of your transmission as volume control, how the number pads are dialed, and how long a voice port will wait before hanging up a signal.

Concepts of Delay and Echo

The most challenging part of designing a VoIP network is that it involves the transmission of real-time traffic. Voice communication is sensitive to delays and echo. Each affects the quality of the conversation. This is even more prevalent in a VoIP versus traditional TDM voice communication with convergence of voice and data traffic over the same media. Speech patterns become awkward and indistinguishable if there is too much delay in the voice traffic. Delay is a natural phenomenon of data trafficking, and several factors inherent in any network will cause delay factors. The idea is to minimize delay as much as you can to get the voice traffic as close to real time as possible. In today's voice trafficking, two different kinds of delay must be handled: fixed delay and variable delay. The various delay points are illustrated in Figure 5.12.

Figure 5.12 Voice Packet Delay

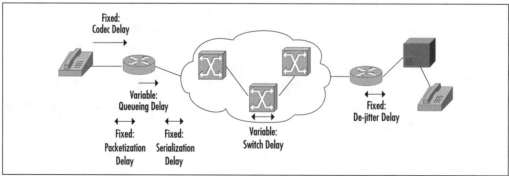

Fixed delay is the amount of time the signal needs to transverse whatever medium is being utilized to send the signal, such as copper, fiber, or microwave. This time is fixed because the laws of physics dictate how fast the data signals will go on particular media. Acceptable levels for most users are below 150ms one-way per ITU G.114. Fixed delays are composed of codec delays, packetization delays, and serialization.

- **Codec induced delay** This is the time it takes for the compression/decompression of a voice packet from analog to digital format and back to analog again. The delay amount ranges from 0.75ms to 30ms depending on the type of codec used.

- **Packetization delay** The time it takes the equipment to actually produce a data packet. The goal is to keep this time under 30ms.

- **Serialization** The time it takes to clock a voice or data frame onto a network interface. Serialization is affected by the frame size and line speed.

Variable delays are synonymous with jitter and are caused by queuing variances during the transmission of a packet through the network. Voice packets share the bandwidth with larger data packets so, as the packets are transferred out of the queue, there can be a delay between voice packets that sounds like stuttering speech. As we saw earlier in the book, this delay is called *jitter*. QoS features can be used to alleviate the effects of jitter by prioritizing the voice traffic. Therefore, the best place to reduce delay factors is in the variable delay in the following factors:

- **Queuing** The time it takes for a packet to exit the output queue of the device that is routing the data. This period is measured from the time the data is generated on the input queue to when it is released by the output queue.

- **Network switching** The delay across the public network such as a Frame Relay or ATM network.

- **De-jitter** Voice traffic works best if there is a constant flow of packets. Jitter must be minimized to improve the quality of the conversation. Jitter is the amount of time between the expected arrival of a voice packet and the actual arrival of a voice packet. Excessive jitter can cause a disruption in real-time speech patterns. De-jitter buffers are utilized on the receiving end to adjust the variable delays into a fixed delay.

The command that adjusts the Cisco de-jitter buffering is **playout-delay**. The **playout-delay** command was configured under the voice-port configuration mode before IOS release 12.1(5)T. Release 12.1(5)T and later implement the command under the dial-peer configuration mode. The following steps are used to configure playout delay:

1. Enter Privileged Exec mode:

   ```
   router>enable
   ```

2. Enter Global Configuration mode:

   ```
   router#configure terminal
   ```

3. Identify the port to configure on a 2600 and 3600 series router:

   ```
   router(config)#voice-port nm-module/vic-module/port-number
   router(config)#voice-port slot/port (Cisco 175x/1760 and MC3810)
   ```

4. Determine the mode in which the jitter buffer will operate for calls on this voice port. The keywords are as follows:

   - **Adaptive** Adjusts the jitter buffer size and amount of playout delay during a call based on current network conditions. This is the default setting.

   - **Fixed** Defines the jitter buffer size as fixed so that the playout delay does not adjust during a call. A constant playout delay is added.

   ```
   router(config-voiceport)#playout-delay mode {adaptive| fixed]
   ```

5. Tune the playout buffer to accommodate packet jitter caused by switches in the WAN:

   ```
   router(config-voiceport)#playout-delay {nominal value| maximum value
       | minimum {default | low | high}}
   ```

Echo is defined as hearing your own voice reflected back to you over the receiver of the telephony equipment. A certain amount of echo is acceptable and desirable because it helps assure the end user of his speech patterns. Too much echo causes a disruption because the speaker will not be able to discern between his speech and the echo signals. Some of the commands that minimize echo in conversations are listed as Steps 6–8 in the "Fine-Tuning FXS/FXO Ports" section, which follows. Steps 4 and 5 in the same section are used to adjust the voice levels, which will also improve the quality of the conversation.

Fine-Tuning FXS/FXO Ports

Special parameters can be adjusted to fine-tune the ports, minimizing some of the issues involved with delay and echo. In most cases, the default parameters for FXO/FXS ports will be sufficient, but special values can be set for the following parameters:

- Input gain
- Output attenuation
- Echo-cancel coverage
- Nonlinear processing
- Initial digit timeouts
- Interdigit timeouts
- Timing other than timeouts

To change any of these parameters, follow these steps:

1. Enter Privileged Exec mode:

   `router>`**`enable`**

2. Enter Global Configuration mode:

   `router#`**`configure terminal`**

3. Identify the port to configure:

   `router#`**`(config)voice-port`** `nm-module/vic-module/port-number`

4. Specify the amount of receiver gain on the interface in decibels. Value can be (−6) to 14:

   `router(config-voiceport)#`**`input gain`** `value`

5. Specify the amount of transmit attenuation on the interface in decibels. Value can be 0 to 14:

   `router(config-voiceport)#`**`output attenuation`** `value`

6. Enable echo-cancellation for voice signals sent out of the interface and received back on the same interface. Excessive echo can cause disruption

to normal conversation patterns. This is often a problem on cellular phone technology:

```
router(config-voiceport)#echo-cancel enable
```

7. Adjust the size of the echo-cancel coverage time in milliseconds. Values are 16, 24, or 32:

```
router(config-voiceport)#echo-cancel coverage value
```

8. Enable "non-linear" processing, which shuts off any signal if no speech is detected on the near end. This is used in conjunction with echo cancellation:

```
router(config-voiceport)#non-linear
```

9. Configure how long the system will wait for the first digit to be input by the user after an off-hook state is detected. This value can be anywhere between 0 and 120 seconds:

```
router(config-voiceport)#timeouts initial seconds
```

10. Configure how long the system will wait for subsequent digits after the initial digit is received. This value can be anywhere between 0 and 120 seconds:

```
router(config-voiceport)#timeouts interdigit seconds
```

11. Specify how long the digital signal lasts for DTMF digit signals. The range is from 50 to 100 milliseconds, with a default of 100 milliseconds:

```
router(config-voiceport)#timing digit milliseconds
```

12. Specify the delay between digit signals for DTMF digit signals. Range is from 50 to 100 milliseconds, the default being 100 milliseconds:

```
router(config-voiceport)#timing inter-digit milliseconds
```

13. Configure the length of pulse signal. This command is for FXO ports only using pulse signals. The range is 10 to 20 milliseconds and the default is 20 milliseconds:

```
router(config-voiceport)#timing pulse-digit milliseconds
```

14. Configure length of delay between digit signals. This command is for FXO ports only using pulse signals. The range is from 100 to 1000 milliseconds and the default is 500 milliseconds:

```
router(config-voiceport)# timing pulse-inter-digit milliseconds
```

Fine-Tuning E&M Ports

Some additional features always need to be adjusted for E&M ports. Contrary to the default settings of the FXO/FXS ports, E&M ports in most cases require fine-tuning adjustments. The following steps are used to fine-tune E&M ports:

1. Enter Privileged Exec mode:

```
router>enable
```

2. Enter Global Configuration mode:

```
router#configure terminal
```

3. Identify the port to configure:

```
router#(config)voice-port nm-module/vic-module/port-number
```

4. Specify the amount of receiver gain on the interface in decibels. Value can be (–6) to 14:

```
router#(config-voiceport)input gain value
```

5. Specify the amount of transmit attenuation on the interface in decibels. Value can be 0 to 14:

```
router#(config-voiceport)output attenuation value
```

6. Enable echo-cancellation for voice signals sent out of the interface and received back on the same interface. Excessive echo can cause disruption to normal conversation patterns. This is often a problem on cellular phone technology:

```
router#(config-voiceport)echo-cancel enable
```

7. Adjust the size of the echo-cancel coverage in milliseconds. Values are 16, 24, or 32:

```
router#(config-voiceport)echo-cancel coverage value
```

8. Enable "non-linear" processing, which shuts off any signal if no speech is detected on the near end. This is used in conjunction with echo cancellation:

```
router#(config-voiceport)non-linear
```

9. Configure how long the system will wait for the first digit to be input by the user after an off-hook state is detected. This value can be anywhere between 0 and 120 seconds:

```
router#(config-voiceport)timeouts initial seconds
```

10. Configure how long the system will wait for subsequent digits after the initial digit is received. This value can be anywhere between 0 and 120 seconds:

```
router#(config-voiceport)timeouts interdigit seconds
```

11. Specify how long the digit signal will last for DTMF digit signals. The range is from 50 to 100 milliseconds:

```
router#(config-voiceport)timing digit milliseconds
```

12. Specify the delay between digit signals for DTMF digit signals. The range is from 50 to 500 milliseconds:

```
router#(config-voiceport)timing inter-digit milliseconds
```

13. Specify the pulse-dialing rate. This is used for pulse dialing only. The range is from 10 to 20 pulses per second:

```
router#(config-voiceport)timing pulse pulse-per-second
```

14. Configure the delay between digit signals. This is used for pulse dialing only. The range is from 100 to 1000 milliseconds:

```
router#(config-voiceport)timing pulse-inter-digit milliseconds
```

15. Configure the delay signal time for delay dial signaling. The range is from 100 to 5000 milliseconds:

```
router#(config-voiceport)timing delay-duration milliseconds
```

16. Configure the minimum time for outgoing seizure to out-dial address. The range is from 20 to 2000 milliseconds:

```
router#(config-voiceport)timing delay-duration milliseconds
```

17. Specify the time between generation of "wink-like" pulses. The range is from 0 to 5000 milliseconds:

```
router#(config-voiceport)timing delay-pulse min-delay milliseconds
```

18. Specify the minimum amount of time between the off-hook signal and the call being completely cleared. The range is from 200 to 2000 milliseconds:

```
router#(config-voiceport)timing clear-wait milliseconds
```

19. Specify the delay signal time for delay dial signaling. The range is from 100 to 5000 milliseconds:

```
router#(config-voiceport)timing delay-duration milliseconds
```

20. Configure the maximum wink-wait duration. The range is from 100 to 400 milliseconds:

```
router#(config-voiceport)timing wink-duration milliseconds
```

21. Configure the maximum wink-wait duration for wink-start signal. The range is from 100 to 5000 milliseconds:

```
router#(config-voiceport)timing wink-wait milliseconds
```

Some added features always need to be adjusted for the DID ports. Contrary to the default settings of the FXO/FXS ports, in most cases DID ports require fine-tuning adjustments. Follow these steps to fine-tune DID ports:

1. Enter Privileged Exec mode:

```
router>enable
```

2. Enter Global Configuration mode:

```
router#configure terminal
```

3. Identify the port to configure:

```
router#(config)voice-port nm-module/vic-module/port-number
```

4. This command sets the maximum time to wait for wink signaling after an outgoing seizure is sent. This is optional for wink-start ports only:

```
router(config-voiceport)#timing wait-wink milliseconds
```

5. This command sets the maximum time to wait before sending wink sig-
    nals after an incoming seizure is detected. This is optional for wink-start
    ports only:

    ```
    router(config-voiceport)#timing wink-wait milliseconds
    ```

6. This command sets the duration of a wink-start signal. This is optional
    for wink-start ports only:

    ```
    router(config-voiceport)#timing wink-duration milliseconds
    ```

7. This command sets the duration of the delay signal. This is optional for
    delay dial ports only:

    ```
    router(config-voiceport)#timing delay-duration milliseconds
    ```

8. This command sets the delay interval after an incoming seizure is
    detected. This is optional for delay dial ports only:

    ```
    router(config-voiceport)#timing delay-start milliseconds
    ```

Configuring Dial Plans and Dial Peers

Now that we have discussed the steps necessary to configure the individual VIC
ports and fine-tuning commands, we need to set up the dial plans and dial peers.
The *dial plan* is the numbers and patterns that the user dials to reach the
receiving party. Another view of this concept is the routing plan for numbers that
are dialed. The North American PSTN uses a 10-digit dial plan, where the first
three digits signify the area code, the next three signify the local prefix, and the
remaining four digits specify telephone numbers within that prefix. Dial plans are
manually configured on Cisco routers. This section further discusses in detail dial
plans and dial peers. A collection of dial peers creates a dial plan.

Designing & Planning…

Dial Plans

A dial plan is a template from which your company can implement the VoIP routing structure. Each routed area of the business will be assigned a set of phone numbers, along with an area code and other shortcuts such as quick dialing features that allow calling parties to reach the calling area without dialing the entire number. Before a VoIP network can be implemented, all voice parameters, phone numbers, and dialing conveniences need to be identified and planned ahead of time. Such planning exponentially decreases the time needed for configuring and implementing the dial plan configuration commands. The following items should be documented before configuring any commands:

- **Router and dial peer** The router and dial peer tag identifier.
- **Number expansion** This number pattern is substituted for the called number.
- **Destination pattern** The pattern of the number that is being dialed.
- **Peer type** Plain old telephone service (POTS), VoIP, VoFR, and VoATM; the type of connection, whether to a POTS connection (PSTN, PBX, telephone, and fax) or private WAN using either VoIP, VoFR, or VoATM.
- **Voice port** The physical port for the voice connectivity, which could be an analog phone, PSTN connection, or PBX.
- **Session target** The remote target address across the IP, Frame Relay, or ATM network.
- **Codec** The voice compression algorithm implemented.

Table 5.4 is an example of a chart, which should be filled in prior to implementing the dial-plan configurations on the routers.

Continued

Table 5.4 Dial-Plan Information

Router/ Dial- Peer Tag Number	Number Expansion Extension	Destination Pattern	Type of Peer	Voice Port	Session Target	Codec

Call Legs: POTS versus Voice Network Dial Peers

Prior to creating the dial plans and peers, we need to discuss the various call legs. *Call legs* are individual segments between two voice termination points such as phone or PBX and a VoIP router. Another leg would be between two VoIP routers via a Frame Relay, IP, or ATM cloud. The call legs are configured in the routers as dial peer statements. There are two types of dial peer: POTS and voice network. The voice network dial peers can be VoIP, VoFR, or VoATM.

The POTS dial peers are analog or digital connections to a telephone, fax, PBX, and PSTN. Figure 5.13 illustrates the call legs involved to complete a call. These steps equate to four dial peer statements, with each router requiring two statements, since Call Leg 2 must be configured on both routers.

Figure 5.13 Dial-Peer Call Legs

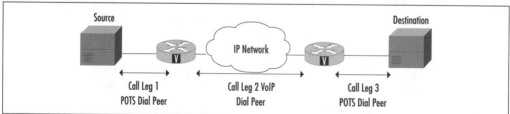

Call Legs 1 and 3 are considered inbound call legs, whereas Call Leg 2 is an outbound leg. An inbound leg is the POTS dial peer. An outbound leg n this example is the leg where the call transverses the voice network, which can be VoIP, VoATM, or VoFR. Note that the concepts of inbound and outbound are from the router's perspective.

Creating and Implementing Dial Plans

Let's discuss a basic dial plan scenario. We have a main/headquarter site and a branch/remote site, as shown in Figure 5.14. The scenario is simplified to help explain the items that need to be captured for the dial plan and then configured in the routers.

Figure 5.14 Basic Dial-Plan Architecture

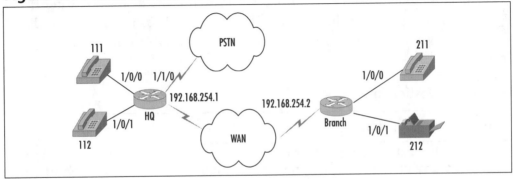

Let's complete the chart below based on the information in Table 5.5.

Table 5.5 Basic Dial Plan Information

Router/ Dial- Peer Tag Number	Number Expansion Extension	Destination Pattern	Type of Peer	Voice Port	Session Target	CODEC
HQ	1...	4046781...				
111		111	POTS	1/0/0		
112		112	POTS	1/0/1		
9		9T	POTS	1/1/0		
21		21.	VoIP		ipv4:192.168.254.2	G729r8

Continued

Table 5.5 Continued

Router/ Dial- Peer Tag Number	Number Expansion Extension	Destination Pattern	Type of Peer	Voice Port	Session Target	CODEC
Branch	1...	4046781...				
211		211	POTS	1/0/0		
212		212	POTS	1/0/1		
9		9T	VoIP		ipv4:192.168.254.1	G729r8
11		11.			Ipv4:192.168.254.1	G729r8

One of the fields that needs further explanation is the destination pattern. The destination pattern is the pattern of the string of digits that have been dialed. Table 5.6 gives a description of all the possible symbols that can be used in the pattern.

Table 5.6 Destination Pattern

Symbol	Description
.	Indicates a single-digit placeholder. For example, 555.... matches any dialed string beginning with 555, plus at least four additional digits.
[ ]	Indicates a range of digits. A consecutive range is indicated with a hyphen (-); for example, [5-7]. A nonconsecutive range is indicated with a comma (,); for example, [5,8]. Hyphens and commas can be used in combination; for example, [5-7,9]. Please note that only single-digit ranges are supported. For example, [98-102] is invalid.
( )	Indicates a pattern; for example, 408(555). It is used in conjunction with the symbols ?, %, or +.
?	Indicates that the preceding digit occurred zero times or one time. Enter **Ctrl-v** before entering **?** from your keyboard.
%	Indicates that the preceding digit occurred zero or more times. This functions the same as the * used in regular expressions.
+	Indicates that the preceding digit occurred one or more times.
T	Indicates the interdigit timeout. The router pauses to collect additional dialed digits.

With this information captured, we can begin configuring the dial-peer information on the routers. The basic LAN and WAN information should already be planned, designed, and configured prior to configuring the voice-specific commands.

Configuring Dial Peers

We can now discuss the commands to configure the POTS and voice network dial peers. The POTS dial peer requires the following variables for a basic setup:

- Tag number (we recommend using a tag number that relates to the destination pattern)
- Destination pattern
- Voice port

Only a few commands are necessary to set up a basic POTS dial-peer configuration. The steps are:

1. Enter Privileged Exec mode:

   `router>`**`enable`**

2. Enter Global Configuration mode:

   `router#`**`configure terminal`**

3. Enter dial-peer mode. Set the tag number to relate to the destination pattern. The dial-peer type is POTS:

   `router(config)#`**`dial-peer voice`** `tag-number` **`pots`**

4. Define the destination pattern that is to be reached by this router:

   `router(config-dial-peer)#`**`destination-pattern`** `string`

5. Specify the voice port number that this call will be routed through:

   `router(config-dial-peer)#`**`port`** `location`

The following is an example of the dial-peer commands for the POTS connections from the HQ site, which are also summarized in Table 5.7:

```
dial-peer voice 111 pots
 port 1/0/0
 destination-pattern 111
```

```
!
dial-peer voice 112 pots
  port 1/0/1
  destination-pattern 112
```

Table 5.7 Optional Dial-Peer Commands for POTS

Optional Related Command	Description
router(config-dial-peer) #**answer-address** *string*	Selects the inbound dial peer based on the calling number.
router(config-dial-peer) # **incoming called-number** *string*	Selects the inbound dial peer based on the called number to identify voice and modem calls.
router(config-dial-peer) # **direct-inward-dial** *string*	Enables the DID call treatment for the incoming called number.
router(config-dial-peer) # **forward-digits** {*num-digit* | *all* | *extra*}	Configures the digit-forwarding method used by the dial peer. The valid range for the number of digits forwarded (num-digit) is 0 through 32.
router(config-dial-peer) # **max-conn** *number*	Specifies the maximum number of allowed connections to and from the POTS dial peer. The valid range is 1 through 2147483647.
router(config-dial-peer) # **numbering-type** {*abbreviated* | *international* | *national* | *network* | *reserved* | *subscriber* | *unknown*}	Specifies the numbering type to match, as defined by the ITU Q.931 specification.
router(config-dial-peer) # **preference** *value*	Configures a preference for the POTS dial peer. The valid range is 0 through 10, where the lower the number, the higher the preference.
router(config-dial-peer) # **prefix** *string*	Includes a prefix that the system adds automatically to the front of the dial string before passing it to the telephony interface. Valid entries for the string argument are 0 through 9 and a comma (,). Use a comma to include a one-second pause between digits to allow for a secondary dial tone.

Continued

Table 5.7 Continued

Optional Related Command	Description
router(config-dial-peer) # **translate-outgoing** {*called* | *calling*} *name-tag*	Specifies the translation rule set to apply to the calling number or called number.

The voice network can be over IP, Frame Relay, or ATM. We start with VoIP. The VoIP dial-peer setup requires the following variable for a basic setup:

- Tag number (we recommend using a tag number that relates to the destination pattern)

- IP address for session target

- Destination telephone number pattern

The following are the basic dial-peer commands necessary for VoIP:

1. Enter the dial-peer mode for VoIP peer. *Tag-number* is a unique decimal number that identifies the peer. It is only held by the local router, so you can use the number on another router without affecting the current configuration:

   ```
   router(config)# dial-peer voice tag-number voip
   ```

2. Define the IP address of the router that is connected to the remote telephony device:

   ```
   router(config-dial-peer)#session target {ipv4:destination-address
       | dns:[$s$. | $d$. | $e$.| $u$.] host-name}
   ```

3. Define the codec for the dial peer:

   ```
   Router(config-dialpeer)#codec {g711alaw | g711ulaw | g723ar53 |
       g723ar63 | g723r53 | g723r63 | g726r16 | g726r24 | g726r32 |
       g728 | g729br8 | g729r8
       [pre-ietf]} [bytes]
   ```

4. Define the destination pattern that is to be reached by this router. Example: 11., which is a group of phone numbers that can be reached across the connection. Table 5.8 lists all the options available for the string:

   ```
   router(config-dial-peer)#destination-pattern string
   ```

The following is an example of the dial-peer commands for the VoIP connections from the HQ site:

```
dial-peer voice 11 voip
 codec g729r8
 ip precedence 5
 session target ipv4:192.168.1.1
 vad
 destination-pattern 11.
!
dial-peer voice 9 voip
 codec g729r8
 ip precedence 5
 session target ipv4:192.168.1.1
 vad
 destination-pattern 9T
```

Table 5.8 Optional Dial-Peer Commands for VoIP

Optional Command	Description
router(config-dial-peer) #answer-address *string*	Selects the inbound dial peer based on the calling number.
router(config-dial-peer) # incoming called-number *string*	Selects the inbound dial peer based on the called number to identify voice and modem calls.
router(config-dial-peer) # dtmf-relay *[cisco-rtp]* *[h245-signal]* *[h245-alphanumeric]*	Configures the tone that sounds in response to a key-press on a touch-tone telephone. DTMF tones are compressed at one end of a call and decompressed at the other end.
router(config-dial-peer) # fax rate *{2400	4800	7200	9600	12000	14400	disable	voice}*	Specifies the transmission speed of a fax to be sent to this dial peer. The disable keyword turns off fax transmission capability. The voice keyword, which is the default, specifies the highest possible transmission speed supported by the voice rate.

Continued

Table 5.8 Continued

Optional Command	Description
router(config-dial-peer) # **numbering-type** {*abbreviated* | *international* | *national* | *network* | *reserved* | *subscriber* | *unknown*}	Specifies the numbering type to match, as defined by the ITU Q.931 specification.
router(config-dial-peer) # **playout-delay mode** {*adaptive* | *fixed*}	Specifies the type of jitter buffer playout delay to use.
router(config-dial-peer) # **playout-delay** {*maximum value* | *nominal value* | *minimum* {*default* | *low* | *high*}}	Specifies the amount of time that a packet is held in the jitter buffer before it is played out on the audio.
router(config-dial-peer) # **preference** *value*	With multiple dial peers pointing to the same destination, the preference can be set for the preferred one.
router(config-dial-peer) # **tech-prefix** *number*	Specifies that a particular technology prefix be prepended to the destination pattern of this dial peer.
router(config-dial-peer) # **translate-outgoing** {*called* | *calling*} **name-tag**.	Specifies the translation rule set to apply to the calling number or called number
router(config-dial-peer)# **vad**	Enables voice activity detection, which suppress voice packets during periods of silence.

The VoFR dial-peer setup requires the following variables for a basic setup:

- Tag number (we recommend using a tag number that relates to the destination pattern)

- Frame Relay DLCI number for session target

- Destination telephone number pattern

Configuring & Implementing...

Fax over VoIP

Today, corporations send faxes as commonly as they use the telephone to communicate with customers and vendors. As the migration to VoIP continues, the need to incorporate faxing into VoIP networks will increase. T.38 is the standard for fax relay with VoIP. T.38 is supported on the Cisco 2600, 3600, and MC3810 routers with IOS 12.1.3T. The AS5350, AS5400, and AS5800 also support it T.38 12.1.5XM. The commands to configured T.38 fax relay can be configured at either the global or dial-peer command level. The following example lists both methods:

- Global commands:

```
router(config)#voice service voip
router(config-voice-service)#fax protocol {cisco | t38
    [ls_redundancy value] [hs_redundancy value]}
```

- Dial-peer commands:

```
router(config)#dial-peer voice {peer tag} voip
router(config-dial-peer)# fax protocol {cisco | t38 [ls_redundancy
    value] [hs_redundancy value]}
```

The following are the basic dial-peer commands necessary for VoFR:

1. Enter the dial-peer mode for VoFR peer. *Tag-number* is a unique decimal number that identifies the peer. It is only held by the local router, so you can use the number on another router without affecting the current configuration:

   ```
   router(config)#dial-peer voice tag-number vofr
   ```

2. Configure the Frame Relay session target for the previous dial-peer command. This should point to the router's DLCI number.

   ```
   router(config-dial-peer)#session target interface dlci [cid]
   ```

3. Define the codec for the dial peer:

```
router(config-dialpeer)#codec {g711alaw | g711ulaw | g723ar53 |
    g723ar63 | g723r53 | g723r63 | g726r16 | g726r24 | g726r32 |
    g728 | g729br8 | g729r8 [pre-ietf]} [bytes]
```

4. Define the destination pattern that is to be reached by this router. Example: 11., which is a group of phone numbers that can be reached across the connection. Table 5.9 lists all the options available for the string:

```
router(config-dial-peer)#destination-pattern string
```

VoFR dial peers can use most of the optional dial-peer commands from VoIP. The commands in Table 5.9 are optional commands specifically for VoFR dial peers.

Table 5.9 Optional Dial-Peer Commands for VoFR

Optional Command	Description
router(config-dial-peer) # session protocol {cisco-switched	frf11-trunk}	Configures the session protocol to support switched calls or FRF.11 trunk calls.
router(config-dial-peer) # signal-type {cas	cept	ext-signal	transparent}	If Cisco trunk permanent calls are being configured, the signal type is required.
router(config-dial-peer) # called-number termination-string	Required for the Cisco 2600/3600 series routers only. Configures the termination string for FRF.11 trunk calls. This command is required to enable the router to establish an incoming trunk connection. This command applies only when the session protocol command is set to **frf11-trunk**.

Other commands usually need to be configured for a proper VoFR configuration such as Frame Relay traffic shaping and other QoS commands. These topics are covered in later chapters that discuss QoS issues.

Finally, let's look at some of the commands necessary to set up VoATM. First, there are some restrictions with respect to VoATM. These restrictions are documented for IOS release 12.2 at the following link: www.cisco.com/univercd/cc/td/doc/product/software/ios122/122cgcr/fvvfax_c/vvfvoatm.htm#xtocid6.

The following are the basic commands to set up VoATM:

1. Define the dial peer and enters dial-peer configuration mode:

   ```
   router(config)#dial-peer voice number voatm
   ```

2. Configure the destination pattern:

   ```
   router(config-dial-peer)#destination-pattern string
   ```

3. Configure the ATM session target for the dial peer:

   ```
   router(config-dial-peer)#session target ATM x/y pvc {name | vpi/vci
   | vci}
   ```

Number Expansion

In most corporations, it is not necessary to dial the entire phone number to reach an individual within the company. Instead, a part of the number is used to signify a certain telephone set, also known as an *extension*.

To make the process easier and increase the usability of the network program, use the *num-exp* command on the dial-peer configuration as follows:

```
num-exp 66.. 55566..
```

Now, when someone dials the pattern **66..** the router expands that number into **55566....** For example, if the site has phone numbers 5556601 through 5556625, the router would only need to pass the last four digits to identify where the call is to be routed. When working out your dial plan, try to keep all number expansions unique on the VoIP network.

Direct Inward Dialing

Direct inward dialing (DID) is a system that allows voice customers to have many private voice numbers allocated to the business and at the same time lower costs by reducing the number of actual lines needed to service those numbers.

DID can be used on digital and analog circuits. The trick to using DID over VoIP is that the router is configured to pass the DID information directly over to the DID-enabled PBX for processing. The first scenario is where the router has a T1/E1 connection to the PSTN and you want DID capabilities on this circuit. Of course, the telco needs to be set up to support this functionality. Telcos use the Digital Number Identification Service (DNIS), which sends the called number (the number that is dialed). The configuration on the router is done by enabling DID on the dial peer, as shown in the following example:

```
router(config)#dial-peer voice number pots
router(config-dial-peer)#direct-inward-dial
```

In the situation with just an analog connection to the PSTN, the DID VIC can be configured to support DID, as mentioned earlier in the chapter. This capability was added in IOS release12.1(5)XM on the Cisco 2600 and 3600 series routers. It was integrated later into 12.2(2)T. It is a simple configuration with the following the only required command:

```
voice-port 1/1/0
  signal did wink-start
```

Several of the wink-timing commands might need to be entered to make the appropriate adjustments with the PSTN connection. To verify that the command was successfully enabled, execute the *show voice port 1/1/0* command:

```
Router#show voice port 1/1/0
Foreign Exchange Station with Direct Inward Dialing (FXS-DID) 1/1/0 Slot
        is 1, Sub-unit is 1, Port is 0
  Type of VoicePort is DID-IN
  Operation State is DORMANT
  Administrative State is UP
  No Interface Down Failure
  Description is not set
  Noise Regeneration is enabled
  Non Linear Processing is enabled
  Music On Hold Threshold is Set to -38 dBm
  In Gain is Set to 0 dB
  Out Attenuation is Set to 0 dB
  Echo Cancellation is enabled
  Echo Cancel Coverage is set to 8 ms
  Playout-delay Mode is set to default
  Playout-delay Nominal is set to 60 ms
  Playout-delay Maximum is set to 200 ms
  Playout-delay Minimum mode is set to default, value 4 ms
  Playout-delay Fax is set to 300 ms
  Connection Mode is normal
  Connection Number is not set
  Initial Time Out is set to 10 s
```

```
Interdigit Time Out is set to 10 s
Call Disconnect Time Out is set to 3 s
Ringing Time Out is set to 180 s
Wait Release Time Out is set to 3 s
Companding Type is u-law
Region Tone is set for US


Analog Info Follows:
Currently processing none
Maintenance Mode Set to None (not in mtc mode)
Number of signaling protocol errors are 0
Impedance is set to 600r Ohm
Station name Richard Flanagan, Station number 4326534


Voice card specific Info Follows:
Signal Type is wink-start
Dial Type is dtmf
In Seizure is inactive
Out Seizure is inactive
Digit Duration Timing is set to 100 ms
InterDigit Duration Timing is set to 100 ms
Pulse Rate Timing is set to 10 pulses/second
InterDigit Pulse Duration Timing is set to 750 ms
Clear Wait Duration Timing is set to 400 ms
Wink Wait Duration Timing is set to 200 ms
Wait Wink Duration Timing is set to 550 ms
Wink Duration Timing is set to 200 ms
Delay Start Timing is set to 300 ms
Delay Duration Timing is set to 2000 ms
Dial Pulse Min. Delay is set to 140 ms
Percent Break of Pulse is 60 percent
Auto Cut-through is disabled
Dialout Delay for immediate start is 300 ms
```

Configuring Trunking

In telephone systems, a *trunk* is a line that carries multiple voice or data channels between two telephone exchange switching systems. From the aspect of VoIP, the trunk is a virtual connection between two PBXs. The virtual connection can be either permanent or switched. These virtual connections are implemented with the *connection* command, which is described earlier in the chapter. We discuss the configuration and uses of the various *connection* command types in this section.

Trunks

Configure the command *connection trunk* to provide a permanent connection between two PBXs, as shown in Figure 5.15. This function is supported on the following routers:

- Cisco 2600 and 3600 series digital and analog interfaces
- Cisco 7200/7500 series digital interfaces.
- Cisco MC3810 (Cisco IOS Release 12.0(3)XG or later)
- Cisco 1750 (Cisco IOS Release 12.2. o r later)

The connections between the router and the PBX must be T1 CAS. T1 CAS to E1 CAS mapping does not work by default; bit-order manipulation must be performed. T1 CCS is not supported. Voice port combinations that are supported are E&M-E&M, FXS-FXO, and FXS-FXS.

Figure 5.15 Connection Trunk Example

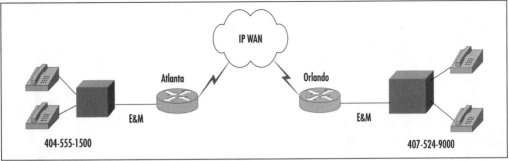

The partial configuration in the following list is from the Atlanta and Orlando routers, as illustrated in Figure 5.15. Here is the Atlanta configuration:

```
voice?card 1
!
controller T1 1/0
framing esf
linecode b8zs
ds0?group 1 timeslots 1-24 type e&m
clock source line
!
voice?port 1/0:1
connection trunk
!
dial-peer voice 404 pots
destination-pattern 4045551500
port 1/0:1
!
dial-peer voice 407 voip
session-target ipv4:192.168.254.2
destination-pattern 4075249000
```

Here is the Orlando configuration:

```
voice?card 1
!
controller T1 1/0
framing esf
linecode b8zs
ds0?group 1 timeslots 1-24 type e&m
clock source line
!
voice?port 1/0:1
connection trunk
!
dial-peer voice 407 pots
destination-pattern 4075249000
port 1/0:1
!
dial-peer voice 404 voip
session-target ipv4:192.168.254.1
destination-pattern 4045551500
```

Tie Lines

The *connection* command variable *tie-line* has a similar effect to the *trunk* variable, but the connection between the two PBXs emulates a temporary tie-line trunk. If you need to prepend additional digits to be sent to the PBX, use the *connection tie-line* command. The following is an example of the complete syntax:

```
voice-port 1/0/0
connection tie-line 4326534
```

PLAR

PLAR is configured to automatically call a remote phone without the user dialing any number from the handset. PLAR, also known as *bat phone*, dials a remote phone when the local telephone handset is taken off-hook. PLAR works with any of the signaling types—E&M, FXO, or FXS. A voice port can be configured to accept either digits dialed or a PLAR connection. The configuration is enabled by simply adding the command *connection plar string* to the voice port, where *string* is the number to automatically be dialed. To verify that the command is enabled correctly on the voice port, type *show voice port nm-module/ vic-module/port-number* at the Exec Privileged mode prompt. Note that the following output is from a 3600 router with *plar* configured to destination 1500 (part of the *show* command results):

```
branch#show voice port 1/0/0

Foreign Exchange Office
  Type of VoicePort is FXS
  Operation State is DORMANT
  Administrative State is UP
  The Last Interface Down Failure Cause is Administrative Shutdown
  Description is not set
  Noise Regeneration is enabled
  Non Linear Processing is enabled
  Music On Hold Threshold is Set to -38 dBm
  In Gain is Set to 0 dB
  Out Attenuation is Set to 0 dB
  Echo Cancellation is enabled
```

```
Echo Cancel Coverage is set to 8 ms
Connection Mode is plar
Connection Number is 1500
```

PLAR-OPX

The *connection plar-opx* command allows connectivity between FXS and FXO interfaces to provide an acknowledgment prior to the remote FXS device answering the call. For example, if a call comes in and the remote end device does not answer the call, the PBX could roll the call to voicemail if voicemail is installed.

Direct Voice Trunking versus Dial-Digit Interpretation

Trunking allows for semitransparent connections between two PBXs, a PBX and a local extension, or some other combination of telephony devices that will be permanently linked together. There is no need to analyze the dialed digits for a destination pattern, since the connections are set up to be permanently trunked together and data will automatically pass between the two interfaces. Therefore, route analysis is unnecessary when you use trunking, since the connection is up all the time.

The following are some advantages and disadvantages of using trunking technology:

- **Advantages** Less overhead on the routers that are passing the traffic. The destination patterns need not be interpreted or analyzed to determine the destination path. The packets are simply passed on to the PBX for analysis and interpretation.

- **Disadvantages** No control of the packets that are coming in. The external PBX handles all the end-station routing. Any fine-tuning of the voice ports or special configurations are not usable in this mode. Special attention must be placed on codec management. By passing information on trunk connections, all codecs need to match along the entire path of transmission. If the trunking is being performed with a centralized tandem switch, encoding/decoding needs to be consistent to ensure no data corruption occurs when analog:digital:analog encoding occurs. Proper codecs must be used for each FXO port connected to the tandem switch.

Standard Dialing Analysis: Digit Interpretation

If trunking is not being used, the router that receives an initiating call signal needs to access and analyze the incoming dialed digits (destination pattern) of the receiving entity. The router in turn uses its dial-peer configurations to determine where to route the call over the IP network.

There are advantages and disadvantages to using this method as well:

- **Advantages** Call routing is completely controlled by the routing architecture, which allows for greater control and fine-tuning of the VoIP system. There is more control over QoS levels, since routing can be fine-tuned down to a destination pattern and an IP port.

- **Disadvantages** More overhead is placed on the routers in the VoIP network, since the processors must interpret the dial peers rather than just pass on the data in a trunking format. Increased latency in passing packets through the system can also occur because the router must interpret all the calls.

Supervisory Disconnect

Supervisory disconnect is a command used when the router's FXO interface is connected to the PBX, PSTN, or a key system. The FXO interface closes the loop to specify that it is off-hook. Normally the phone controls the interaction between the switch and the phone to tell the switch to end the call by hanging up. Unfortunately, the router cannot perform this action, so some of the other options are E&M, ground-start signaling, power denial, battery reversal, and supervisory disconnect tone.

E&M provides better communication between the PBX and the router. *Ground-start signaling* is mainly used with FXO and PSTN, but it might not be available with the PBX. *Power denial* is the situation where the PBX or the PSTN CO has a 600ms interruption of power on the line. The router translates this interruption into a supervisor disconnect. *Battery reversal* is the configuration in which the switch changes the polarity on the line and router interprets this change as the supervisor disconnect. This is supported when the *battery-reversal* command is used. In the last method, the *supervisory disconnect tone*, a detectable tone is sent from the PSTN or PBX; the router senses this tone and disconnects the call. This method is supported only on analog FXO loop start configurations. The command to enable this functionality is *supervisory disconnect*. The steps to configure supervisory disconnect tone are:

1. Configure the voice class to specify the tones to be detected.

2. Assign the voice class to an FXO voice port.

The following are all the steps to set up a supervisory disconnect voice class:

1. Create a voice class for defining one tone detection pattern:

   ```
   router(config)#voice class dualtone tag
   ```

2. Specify the two frequencies, in Hz, for a tone to be detected (or one frequency if a nondual tone is to be detected):

   ```
   router(config-voice-class)#freq-pair tone-id frequency-1 frequency-2
   ```

3. Specify the maximum frequency deviation that will be detected, in Hz:

   ```
   router(config-voice-class)#freq-max-deviation frequency
   ```

4. Specify the maximum tone power that will be detected, in dBmO:

   ```
   router(config-voice-class)#freq-max-power dBmO
   ```

5. Specify the minimum tone power that will be detected, in dBmO:

   ```
   router(config-voice-class)#freq-min-power dBmO
   ```

6. Specify the power difference allowed between the two frequencies, in dBmO:

   ```
   router(config-voice-class)#freq-power-twist dBmO
   ```

7. Specify the timing difference allowed between the two frequencies, in 10ms increments:

   ```
   router(config-voice-class)#freq-max-delay time
   ```

8. Specify the minimum tone on-time that will be detected, in 10ms increments:

   ```
   router(config-voice-class)#cadence-min-on-time time
   ```

9. Specify the maximum tone off-time that will be detected, in 10ms increments:

   ```
   router(config-voice-class)#cadence-max-off-time time
   ```

10. Specify a tone cadence pattern to be detected. Specify an on–time and off–time for each cycle of the cadence pattern. This is an optional configuration:

```
router(config-voice-class)#cadence-list cadence-id cycle-1-on-time
    cycle-1-off-time cycle-2-on-time cycle-2-off-time cycle-3-on-time
    cycle-3-off-time cycle-4-on-time cycle-4-off-time
```

11. Specify the maximum time that the tone onset can vary from the specified onset time and still be detected, in 10ms increments. This is an optional configuration:

```
router(config-voice-class)#cadence-variation time
```

12. Specify a tone cadence pattern to be detected. Specify an on–time and off–time for each. This is an optional configuration:

```
router(config-voice-class)#exit
```

Once the voice class has been created, apply it to the voice port interface. The following steps enable the voice class and supervisory disconnect commands on a Cisco 2600 router with FXO port 1/0/0 and voice class number 100:

```
router#config terminal
router(config)#voice-port 1/0/0
router(config-voiceport)#supervisory disconnect dualtone voice-class 100
router(config-voiceport)#exit
```

Wink-Start Signaling versus Immediate-Start Signaling

Both wink start and immediate start are start–dial supervision signaling methods used for E&M trunks. Wink start is the most popular signaling protocol. The wink-start process is defined as the originating switch going off–hook and waiting for an off–hook pulse, a "wink" from the terminating switch, the terminating switch sending the "wink," and the originating switch sending the digits. With immediate start, the more basic protocol, the originating switch goes off–hook for a certain amount of time, usually less than 200ms, and starts sending digits.

The advantage of wink start versus immediate is that wink start offers an acknowledgment between the originating and terminating switches, which helps in situations where one side is too busy to answer or both are trying to seize the line at the same time.

The detailed wink-start commands are listed in the section, "Fine-Tuning E&M Ports," as Steps 20 and 21. An example of the configuration steps follows:

```
router#configure terminal
router(config)#voice-port 1/0/0
router(config-voiceport)#timing wink-duration 250
router(config-voiceport)#timing wink-wait 300
router(config-voiceport)#exit
```

To confirm that the commands are enabled on the voice port, enter the following *show* command: *show voice port nm-module/vic-module/port-number:*

```
router#show voice port 1/0/0

recEive And transMit 1/0/0 Slot is 1, Sub-unit is 0, Port is 0
 Type of VoicePort is E&M
 Operation State is DORMANT
 Administrative State is UP
 .
 .
 .
 Interdigit Time Out is set to 10 s
 Call-Disconnect Time Out is set to 60 s
 Region Tone is set for US

 Analog Info Follows:
 Currently processing none
 Maintenance Mode Set to None (not in mtc mode)
 Number of signaling protocol errors are 0
 Impedance is set to 600r Ohm

 Voice card specific Info Follows:
 Signal Type is wink-start
 Operation Type is 2-wire
 E&M Type is 2
 Dial Type is dtmf
 In Seizure is inactive
 Out Seizure is inactive
 Digit Duration Timing is set to 100 ms
```

```
InterDigit Duration Timing is set to 100 ms
Pulse Rate Timing is set to 10 pulses/second
InterDigit Pulse Duration Timing is set to 500 ms
Clear Wait Duration Timing is set to 400 ms
Wink Wait Duration Timing is set to 300 ms
Wink Duration Timing is set to 250 ms
Delay Start Timing is set to 300 ms
Delay Duration Timing is set to 2000 ms
Dial Pulse Min. Delay is set to 140 ms
```

Configuring ISDN for Voice

ISDN connectivity is a major part of the VoIP environment, with a large share of circuits used to connect to the PSTN and PBXs. Both ISDN PRI and BRI are supported on Cisco routers. Table 5.10 lists the supported interfaces and router platforms. Cisco supports Q.931 network and user-side, Q.SIG, and CCS ISDN configurations. Cisco plans to support BRI NT ISDN interfaces for the Cisco 2691 and 3700 series routers.

Table 5.10 Cisco Router Platform ISDN Support

Router Model	ISDN Interface
Cisco 1751	BRI: NT
Cisco 1760	BRI: NT
Cisco 2600	BRI: NT and S/T
Cisco 3620,3640	BRI: NT and S/T PRI
Cisco 3660	BRI: NT and S/T PRI
Cisco 2691, 3700	BRI: S/T
Cisco MC3810	BRI: NT PRI
Cisco 7200	PRI
Cisco AS5xxx	PRI

Configuring ISDN BRI Voice Ports

Cisco routers support the two voice interface cards VIC-2BRI-S/T-TE and VIC-2BRI-NT/TE, as shown in Figure 5.16. They support connectivity to a PBX or PSTN. A benefit of using the ISDN BRI VIC rather than the analog VIC modules is the additional calling information that is passed.

Figure 5.16 Cisco VIC-2BRI Voice Interface Card

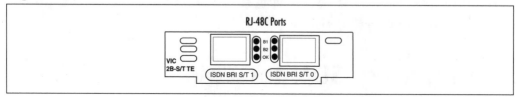

Up to four calls are supported when the VIC-2BRI is installed in the NM-2V module. The BRI VIC needs to be installed in Slot 0 of the NM-2V for both ports to be active. If an additional VIC is installed in the second slot of the NM-2V, the second port on the first VIC will be disabled. This is based on the two ports of the BRI VIC requiring four DSPs. The VIC interface modules support both ISDN network and user-side configurations. The following are the steps necessary to configure ISDN BRI to a PBX:

1. Enter Global Configuration mode:

   `router#`**`configure terminal`**

2. Set the global ISDN switch type. The only NT supported type is basic-net or basic-qsig:

   `router(config)#`**`isdn switch-type`** *`switch-type`*

3. Set the ISDN BRI interface slot and port:

   `router(config)#`**`interface bri`** *`slot/port`*

4. Ensure that no IP address is configured for the ISDN interface (voice only):

   `router(config-if)#`**`no ip address`**

5. Specify incoming voice calls over ISDN:

   `router(config-if)#`**`isdn incoming-voice voice`**

6. Shut down the interface. Configure physical layer type. Enable interface with no shutdown:

- Enter *user* to configure the port as TE and to function as a clock slave. This is the default.

- Enter *network* to configure the port as NT and to function as a clock master.

```
router(config-if)#shutdown
router(config-if)#isdn layer1-emulate {user | network}
router(config-if)#no shutdown
```

7. Turn on or off the power supplied from an NT-configured port to a TE device:

```
router(config-if)#[no] line-power
```

8. Configure the Layer 2 and Layer 3 port protocol:

```
router(config-if)#isdn protocol-emulate {user | network}
```

9. Exit global configuration mode:

```
router(config)#end
```

Figure 5.17 illustrates a scenario with ISDN BRI connectivity to a PBX and PSTN. A partial configuration lists the commands pertaining to the PSTN and PBX interfaces.

Figure 5.17 ISDN BRI PBX and PBX Scenario

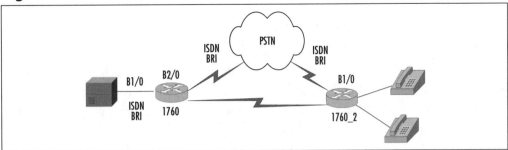

```
(Partial Cisco 1760 configuration)
!
hostname 1760
!
```

```
isdn switch-type basic-net3
!
interface BRI 1/0
 no shutdown
 description connected to PBX
 no ip address
 isdn switch-type basic-net3
 isdn incoming-voice voice
 shutdown
 isdn layer1-emulate user
 no shutdown
 isdn protocol-emulate user
!
interface BRI 2/0
 no shutdown
 description connected to PSTN
 no ip address
 isdn switch-type basic-net3
 isdn incoming-voice voice
 isdn overlap-receiving
 shutdown
 isdn layer1-emulate network
 no shutdown
 isdn protocol-emulate network
!
```

Configuring ISDN PRI Voice Ports

Earlier in the chapter, we discussed the analog VICs modules such as the E&M, FXO, and FXS, but larger organizations that need higher-density interfaces to the PSTN or PBX typically use digital T1/E1 modules. The following is a list of digital voice interfaces and supported platforms:

- **Digital T1/E1 Packet Voice Trunk Network Module, NM-HDV (VWIC–1MFT and VWIC–2MFT)** Cisco 2600 and 3600 series.

- **Digital voice interface card (DVM)** Cisco MC3810.

- **Octal or Quad T1/E1/PRI feature card** Cisco AS5300 universal access server.

- **Channelized trunk card and voice feature card** Cisco AS5800 universal access server.

- **T1/E1 high-capacity digital voice port adapter** Cisco 7200 and 7500 series.

A combination of Figures 5.18 and 5.19 creates the digital T1 voice module for the Cisco 2600 and 3600 series routers. The Cisco 1760 router can use the individual VWIC-2MFT-T1 card as an interface to a PBX or PSTN for digital connectivity. The card uses a RJ-48 crossover cable for connection to a PBX. The pinouts are listed below:

- **Pin 1** RX ring

- **Pin 2** RX tip

- **Pin 4** TX ring

- **Pin 5** TX tip

Figure 5.18 NM-HDV

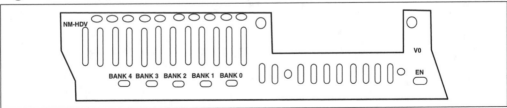

Figure 5.19 VWIC-2MFT-T1

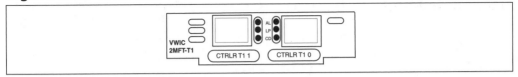

Let's focus on the digital interface cards for the Cisco 2600, 3600 and MC3810 series routers. The items needed for configuration of the controller settings are the following:

- **Line interface** T1 or E1

- **Signaling interface** FXO, FXS, or E&M and ISDN PRI or BRI—
  Q.SIG or CCS

- **Line coding** AMI or B8ZS for T1, and AMI or HDB3 for E1

- **Framing format** SF (D4) or ESF for T1, and CRC4 or no-CRC4
  for E1

- **Number of channels**

The controller configuration steps for an ISDN PRI connection to a PBX
are as follows:

```
router#config terminal
router(config)#isdn switch-type basic-ni1
router(config)#controller t1 1/0
router(config-controller)#framing esf
router(config-controller)#clock source internal
router(config-controller)#linecode b8zs
router(config-controller)#pri-group timeslots 1-24
```

This produces the following configuration:

```
(Partial Router configuration)
!
hostname router
!
!
memory-size iomem 15
voice-card 1
!
isdn switch-type ni1
!
controller t1 1/0
framing esf
clock source line
linecode b8zs
pri-group timeslots 1-24
!
.

.

interface Serial1/0:23
```

```
no ip address
no logging event link-status
isdn switch-type primary-ni1
isdn incoming-voice voice
isdn T310 60000
no cdp enable
!
voice-port 1/0:23
!
```

Configuring Q.931 Support

Q.931 is used for the setup and teardown of the connection in the ISDN circuit. This occurs at the network layer in the protocol stack. The basic steps to configure ISDN PRI with Q.931 are as follows:

1. Select the service provider ISDN PRI switch type:

    router(config)#**isdn switch-type primary-net5**

2. Configure the ISDN T1/E1 controller by setting the time slots, which are used for a T1. The range is 1–23:

    router(config)#**controller {T1 | E1}** *slot/port*
    router(config-controller)#**pri-group timeslots** *range*

3. Exit from the T1/E1 controller configuration mode:

    router(config-controller)#**exit**

4. Configure the ISDN D channel interface:

    router(config)#**interface serial0/0:***n*

5. Configure the ISDN protocol as primary slave or the primary master:

    router(config)#**isdn protocol-emulate** *{network | user}*

6. Enable or disable power supplied from an NT configured port:

    router(config-if)#**[no] line-power**

7. Allow incoming voice calls:

    router(config-if)#**isdn incoming-voice voice**

Configuring QSIG

The configuration of QSIG protocol with Cisco routers allows connectivity to PBXs, key systems, and the PSTN via the telco CO. QSIG is based on Q.921 and Q.931 standards and is enjoying increase acceptance in Europe and North America. With QSIG, a Cisco router can appear as the PSTN to the PBXs at each of the sites, as shown in Figure 5.20.

Figure 5.20 QSIG Protocol

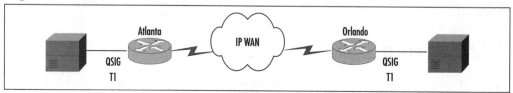

The two commands that are used for configuring QSIG with an ISDN PRI circuits are as follows. Configure the QSIG protocol at the global configuration prompt:

```
router(config)#isdn switch-type primary-qsig
```

Under the D channel interface such as interface serial0:23, enter the following command to configure QSIG master/network or slave/user type:

```
router(config-if)#isdn protocol-emulate {user | network}
```

Configuring CAS

Let's change the connection between the Atlanta router and PBX to a T1 with CAS signaling. Figure 5.21 shows a basic example of PBX to router with T1 CAS signaling.

Figure 5.21 T1 CAS Example

The configuration commands that pertain to the T1 CAS example are:

```
controller T1 0
   framing esf
```

```
clock source line primary
linecode b8zs
cas-group 0 timeslots 1-24 type e&m-fgb dtmf dnis
```

The remaining part of the configuration is very similar to the rest of the scenarios. The command *cas-group 0 timeslots 1-24 type e&m-fgb dtmf dnis* sets the T1 CAS group number and channels with the type of signaling. The other types of signaling are shown in Table 5.11.

Table 5.11 CAS Signaling Types

Signaling Type	Description
e&m-fgb	E&M Type II FGB
e&m-fgd	E&M Type II FGD
e&m-immediate-start	E&M immediate start
fxs-ground-start	FXS ground start
fxs-loop-start	FXS loop start
p7	P7 switch
r2-analog	R2 ITU Q411
r2-digital	R2 ITU Q421
r2-pulse	R2 ITU supplement 7
sas-ground-start	SAS ground start
sas-loop-start	SAS loop start

Configuring CCS

Now let's change the connection between the Atlanta router and PBX to ISDN PRI with CCS signaling. Figure 5.22 shows a basic example of PBX to router with ISDN PRI CCS signaling.

Figure 5.22 ISDN PRI CCS Example

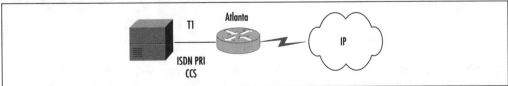

The partial configuration that follows lists the basic commands necessary for the Atlanta router with ISDN PRI connectivity to a PBX with CCS signaling.

```
isdn switch-type primary-dms100
!
!
controller T1 0
 framing esf
 clock source line primary
 linecode b8zs
 pri-group timeslots 1-24
!
dial-peer voice 5000 pots
  destination-pattern 5...
  direct-inward-dial
  port 0:D
```

Configuring T-CCS

If QSIG is not supported on the PBX system, *Transparent Common Channel Signaling (T-CCS)* is another option. Unlike CAS signaling, CCS uses a dedicated channel for signaling. There are three modes for configuring T-CCS: cross-connect, clear-channel codec, and frame forwarding. We discuss clear-channel codec T-CCS in detail.

T-CCS is supported with VoATM, VoFR, and VoIP. An example using T-CCS is illustrated in Figure 5.23, with two sites connected via IP and their respective telephone extensions per PBX.

Figure 5.23 T-CCS Example

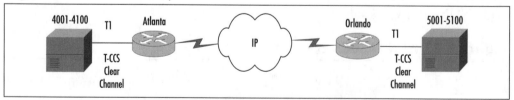

Based on the example in Figure 5.23, the following steps are needed to complete a basic T-CCS configuration to the router at the Atlanta location. The Orlando configuration would be very similar and have mirrored dial peer statements:

1. Configure the T1 controller:

   ```
   router(config)#controller T1 1/0
   ```

2. Set the T1 channels that are used and the signaling associated with each channel:

   ```
   router(config-controller)#ds0-group 0 timeslots 1-24 type ext-sig
   ```

3. Enable the T1 controller:

   ```
   router(config-controller)#no shutdown
   ```

4. Exit from Controller Configuration mode:

   ```
   router(config-controller)#exit
   ```

5. Set up the local dial peer for the connection to the PBX:

   ```
   router(config)#dial-peer voice 4000 pots
   ```

6. Set up the local destination pattern for the connection to the PBX:

   ```
   router(config-dialpeer)#destination-pattern 4…
   ```

7. Associate the T1 ds0-group to the dial peer:

   ```
   router(config-dialpeer)#port 1/0:0
   ```

8. Exit dial-peer configuration mode:

   ```
   router(config-dialpeer)#exit
   ```

9. Set up the dial peer for the connection to the remote PBX:

   ```
   router(config)#dial-peer voice 5000 voip
   ```

10. Set the codec complexity to clear channel:

    ```
    router(config-dialpeer)#codec clear-channel
    ```

11. Set up the destination-pattern for the connection the remote PBX:

    ```
    router(config-dialpeer)#destination-pattern 5…
    ```

12. Configure the IP session target for the dial peer pointing to the remote router:

    ```
    router(config-dialpeer)#session target ipv4:192.168.254.2
    ```

Configuring Gateways and Gatekeepers

The H.323 systems work primarily around two entities on the network: gateways and gatekeepers. Gateways perform the function of controlling access to resources on the network, and gatekeepers control the access to the gateways. In this section, we discuss the basic configuration steps for each entity.

Configuring H.323 Gateway

To configure a basic H.323 gateway, you need to enable VoIP gateway functionality. You do this using the *gateway* command. To enable H.323 gateway functionality, use the following commands:

1. Enter Global Configuration mode:

   ```
   router#configure terminal
   ```

2. Enable the VoIP gateway:

   ```
   router(config)#gateway
   ```

3. Exit Gateway Configuration mode:

   ```
   router(config-gateway)#exit
   ```

The next step in configuring an H.323 gateway is to configure the gateway interface parameters. You do this by first defining which interface will be presented to the VoIP network as this gateway's H.323 interface. Only one interface is allowed to be the gateway interface. You can select either the interface that is connected to the gatekeeper or a loopback interface.

After you define the gateway interface, you configure the gateway to discover the gatekeeper, either through multicasting or by directing it to a specific host. Finally, you configure the gateway's H.323 identification number and any technology prefixes that this gateway should register with the gatekeeper.

Use the next set of commands to define the Ethernet 1/0 interface to be used as the H.323 gateway interface and configure the H.323 gateway interface parameters, beginning in Global Configuration mode. For this example, let's assume that the gateway and gatekeeper's IP addresses are 192.168.1.1 and 192.168.1.254, respectively:

1. Enter Interface Configuration mode:

   ```
   router(config)#interface ethernet 1/0
   ```

2. Configure an IP address for this interface with a subnet mask:

```
router(config-if)#ip address 192.168.1.1 255.255.255.0
```

3. Designate this interface as being the H.323 gateway interface:

```
router(config-if)#h323-gateway voip interface
```

4. Specify an H.323 name (ID) for the gateway associated with this interface. The gateway uses this ID when it communicates with the gatekeeper. Usually, the H.323 ID is the name given to the gateway, with the gatekeeper domain name appended to the end:

```
router(config-if)#h323-gateway voip h323-id interface-id
```

5. Specify the name (ID) of the gatekeeper associated with this gateway and how the gateway finds it. The gatekeeper ID configured here must exactly match the gatekeeper ID in the gatekeeper configuration. The gateway determines the location of the gateway in one of three ways: by a defined IP address, through multicast, or via RAS.

```
router(config-if)#h323-gateway voip id atl2600gk 192.168.1.254 1719
```

6. Define the H.323 name of the gateway, identifying this gateway to its associated gatekeeper:

```
router(config-if)#h323-gateway voip h323-id atl2600gw1@cisco.com
```

7. Specify a technology prefix. A technology prefix is used to identify a type of service that this gateway is capable of providing. This is an optional configuration.

```
router(config-if)#h323-gateway voip tech-prefix 9#
```

Configuring H.323 Gatekeeper

Setting up a Cisco router for gatekeeper functionality involves registering the zone of influence, stating where the other gatekeepers are for other zones, and registering any zone prefixes, technology prefixes, and E.164 addresses with the gatekeeper.

H.323 ID Addresses

Interzone communications are handled via the registration of domain names. As an example, when you're using DNS servers to access resources on the Internet, there needs to be a DNS server for each domain registered with InterNIC, the overall recognized Internet authority that controls domain name registrations. That server is responsible for its domain of influence and in turn is registered with a DNS server in whose domain it happens to reside on the Internet.

H.323 interzone communications work very much the same way. Every gatekeeper is responsible for its own zone. The zone is registered as an H.323 domain, and each domain has a domain name. For example, to resolve an address *gateway1@zone1.com*, the end station's gatekeeper will find a gatekeeper that has the *zone1.com* domain registered. It will then send a request for an IP address resolution to that gatekeeper in the form of an LRQ request to resolve the *gateway1* entity.

Zone Prefixes

Zone prefixes perform the same functionality as domain names but handle it in a different numeric fashion. A good example of zone prefixes is an area code on the PSTN. When placing a local call, you do not have to include the area code with the telephone number you're dialing if the destination you're calling is within the same area, or zone. To get to a number outside your area code, you need to dial the destination area code first so that the telephone company can route the call properly. Zone prefixes are the internal functions that handle this problem.

Consider this example: The local gatekeeper knows that if it receives a telephone call with a zone prefix of 404*xxxxxxx* (the area code of 404 followed by seven arbitrary digits), the call is to be forwarded to the gatekeeper registered with that zone: atlgk. This command is issued on the local gatekeeper using the following syntax:

```
Atlanta(config-gk)#zone prefix atlgk 404. . . . . . .
```

In this case, the zone remote command will also be specified to indicate that the zone is not handled by the local gatekeeper. This helps the gateway determine how to handle the transmission more efficiently and immediately tells the gateway to send an LRQ to the remote gatekeeper for resolution. If this command is not used, the local gatekeeper is queried first. It will have to perform general broadcasts for resolution to other gatekeepers. With the *zone remote* command, this process is streamlined and performance is improved. In conjunction with the *zone remote* command, the *zone local* command identifies a zone as belonging to the local gatekeeper. The resolution process is again streamlined by prequalifying the zone as local.

The *zone remote* command sends the call from the Atlanta gatekeeper to the gatekeeper in Orlando. At this point, the call is received by the Orlando York gatekeeper and is routed out to its final destination zone. If the E.164 address for the destination is registered with the gatekeeper, it will be able to immediately route the call to the H.323-enabled device. Usually, the device is not an H.323-enabled device and is not registered with the gatekeeper. The call is most likely going to a standard telephone that is not registered directly with the gatekeeper and needs to be forwarded to a gateway for processing. At this point, the gatekeeper needs to look at zone prefixes or technology prefixes to determine the proper gateway. Figure 5.24 illustrates the local and remote zone concepts.

Figure 5.24 Gatekeeper Zone Prefix

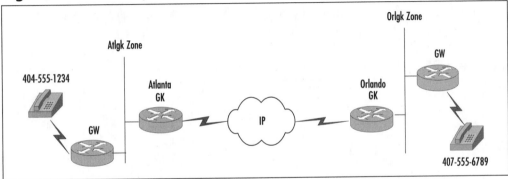

Technology Prefixes

When setting up gateways, network administrators need to determine the type or class of gateway they are initializing—in other words, the services the gateway is providing. When administrators assign technology prefixes to the gateway, the gateway then registers itself with its local gatekeeper with the prefix information. The prefixes are determined by functionality; for example, voice gateways can be registered with a prefix of 1*xxx*, and voicemail gateways can be registered with 2*xxx*. Multiple gateways can register the same tech prefix number, but they all have to have the same functionality. When multiple gateways are configured, the gatekeeper needs to determine which to use.

Multiple gateways within a zone can advertise the technology prefix, allowing the gatekeeper to distribute workload and handle bandwidth management processes. They have autonomy from the zone selection process, so calls can be routed within and between zones and only apply to the local zone selection. This requires that the technology prefixes be ignored during the zone selection process and that zone prefixes be used so that version 2 features can be utilized to determine gateway selection.

Consider this example: Once the local gatekeeper has located the remote gatekeeper to handle the processing of a call, it then requests the location, via an LRQ request, of the remote end station. The remote gatekeeper then decides to which gateway within its zone to send the call for processing based on zone prefixes, bandwidth availability, preferences, and then, finally, technology prefixes if nothing else is able to settle the selection.

With the advent of zone prefixes and the precedence abilities now incorporated into H.323 version 2, technology prefixes are maintained for backward compatibility to H.323 version 1 networks. With the proper programming of version 2 enabled devices, an entire network can potentially be configured without the use of technology prefixes. Figure 5.25 illustrates the use of tech prefix for gateways and gatekeepers in the same area or zone.

Figure 5.25 Gatekeeper Tech-Prefix Example

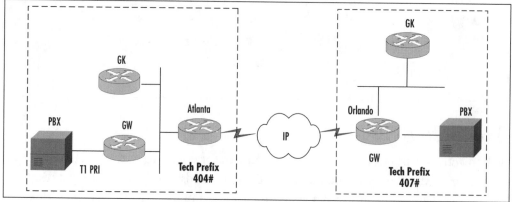

To assign a technology prefix, use the following command in Gatekeeper Configuration mode:

```
router(config-gk)#gw-type-prefix
```

To verify that the technology prefixes programmed into the gatekeeper are functional, use the following command to list the gateway functions:

```
router#show gatekeeper gw-type-prefix
```

```
GATEWAY TYPE PREFIX TABLE
============================
Prefix:12#*      (Default gateway-technology)
  Zone atlgk master gateway list:
    192.168.1.1:1720 atlgw1
  Zone atlgk prefix 404....... priority gateway list(s):
    Priority 10:
    192.168.1.1:1720 atlgw1
Prefix:7#*       (Hopoff zone orlgk)
  Statically-configured gateways (not necessarily currently registered):
    192.168.2.1:1720
  Zone orlgk master gateway list:
    192.168.2.1:1720 orlgw1
```

Let's discuss the steps to configure a gatekeeper based on the example scenario in Figure 5.26.

Figure 5.26 Basic Gatekeeper Example

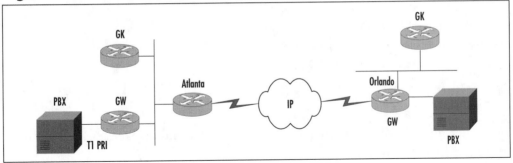

The steps to take to configure a Cisco router to act as an H.323 gatekeeper are:

1. Enter Global Configuration mode:

   ```
   router#configure terminal
   ```

2. Activate the gatekeeper functionality on the router:

   ```
   router(config)#gatekeeper
   ```

3. Specify a zone controlled by a gatekeeper:

   ```
   router(config-gk)#zone local gatekeeper-name domain-name [ ras-IP-
       address]
   ```

4. Set a static entry for another zone's gatekeeper address so that information for that zone can be forwarded:

```
router(config-gk)#zone remote other-gatekeeper-name other-domain-
    name other-gatekeeper-ipaddress [port number]
```

5. Configures the gatekeeper to acknowledge its own or remote prefixes:

```
router(config-gk)#zone prefix gatekeeper-name e.164-prefix
```

6. Configure a technology prefix for the various types of service in the zone. The *hopoff* command tells to which gatekeeper to pass off the tech prefix, if appropriate. Configure the gatekeeper to acknowledge its own or remote prefixes:

```
router(config-gk)#gw-type-prefix type-prefix [hopoff gkid]
    [default-technology] [[gw ipaddr ipaddr [port]]…]
```

The following is a partial configuration clip from the Atlanta gatekeeper router:

```
gatekeeper
    zone local Atlgk1 cisco.com
    zone remote Orlgk1 cisco.com 192.168.2.1 1719
    zone prefix Atlgk1 404.......
    gw?type?prefix 404#*
    no shutdown
```

Enter the following command to verify gateway and gatekeeper configuration from the Atlanta gateway:

```
Atlgw1#sh gate
Gateway Atlgw1@cisco.com is registered to Gatekeeper Atlgk1
Alias list (CLI configured)
    H323-ID Atlgw1@cisco.com
Alias list (last RCF)
    H323-ID Atlgw1@cisco.com
```

Summary

As you complete this chapter, we hope you come away with a basic understanding of configuration commands for a VoIP network. Starting from the hardware level, you now understand the router slot and module-numbering system as well as the importance of the types of cables used for the various modules. The hardware and its configuration needs are determined based on the current PBX hardware and PSTN connections in place. Other aspects that affect the hardware requirements are planning and design, which determine where you require different analog and digital voice modules. With regard to use, a particular signaling type with either module is based on the features that you are trying to achieve, such as caller ID.

The next step is to design the dial plan for the VoIP network. This plan helps chart destination patterns, dial peers, and session targets. Once you have the basic configuration is place, you can focus on fine-tuning your configurations. At this point, you will be able to successfully make VoIP calls.

We discussed the various voice interface cards, or VICs: FXS, FXO, E&M, and DID; which ones are appropriate for connectivity to the PSTN, PBXs, or phones; and the consequences of connecting an incorrect type of port to an end device. Fine-tuning can be accomplished on each type of interface, which can help to eliminate echo and improve the quality of the call.

When installations are performed in larger organizations, the use of ISDN and T1/E1 digital connectivity are the most common approaches. The two types of signaling are CAS and CCS. H.323 systems, however, are based primarily on two components: gateways and gatekeepers. Gateways allow contact with the resources and applications for the VoIP network. They are able to interact with the PSTN, PBXs, and other regions of the VoIP network incorporating messaging and faxing.

Gatekeepers are the regulators and directory servers on the H.323 systems. There must be one gatekeeper for each zone of the network, and all the H.323 registered units must register with the gatekeeper in order to have use of the resources and applications. They also have the responsibility of translation among the zones to keep track of the route that H.323 packets should filter through the network. Gatekeepers are also accountable for bandwidth management on the network, thus finding the best possible gateway based on technological ability, bandwidth available, and the preferred settings.

Solutions Fast Track

Voice Port Cabling and Configuration

☑ NM-1V and NM-2V modules are carrier modules for E&M, FXO, and FXS VICs. NM-1V and NM-2V are required in Cisco 2600 and 3600 series routers.

☑ E&M VIC are color-coded brown and have PBX connections with RJ-1CX cables.

☑ FXO VIC are color-coded pink and have PBX and PSTN connectivity with RJ-11C cables.

☑ FXS ports are always color-coded gray. Do not connect an FXS port to the PSTN. The FXS ports are not designed to handle direct connectivity to the PSTN.

☑ DID VICs have analog PSTN DID connections with RJ-11C cables.

Configuring Voice Ports

☑ Configure the codec for the voice card slot or module. Configure as medium or high complexity, depending on the type of codec you want to support.

☑ Configure FXS and FXO for connections to analog phones and PBX or PSTN, respectively. An FXS or FXO port usually functions without adding any commands. The following are some of the interface command variables that can be configured: signal type, call progress tone, ring frequency, ring number, dial type (FXO only), PLAR connection mode, music threshold, description, VAD, and comfort noise.

☑ PBX connectivity can be established E&M interfaces. Similarly to FXS and FXO, E&M supports the following command variables: signal type, call progress tone, operation, type, and impedance.

☑ Configure DID to allow analog direct inward dialing to phones as if they all had individual trunk lines to the PSTN. The main command required is *signal did [wink|immediate|delay-dial]*.

Voice Port-Tuning Commands

☑ Tuning commands to correct delay and echo are available for each of VIC types. The *playout-delay* command is used to adjust buffers to accommodate packet jitter.

☑ FXS, FXO, and E&M tuning commands deal with adjusting the gain and attenuation parameters for their respective circuits. Interdigit timeout variables are also used on FXO and E&M interfaces.

☑ Analog DID tuning commands focus on modifying the duration for wink- and delay-start signaling.

☑ *VAD* is an additional tuning command commonly used to suppress packets during periods of silence in the conversation.

Configuring Dial Plans and Dial Peers

☑ To configure a dial plan, you need the following information: dial-peer number, number expansion, destination pattern, peer type, voice port, session target, and codec.

☑ Voice network segments can be over IP, Frame Relay, or ATM.

☑ VoFR dial peers use most of the optional dial-peer commands from VoIP.

Creating and Implementing Dial Plans

☑ Make a template from which you can implement a VoIP routing structure.

☑ Identify all voice parameters, phone numbers, and dialing conveniences needed.

☑ Define items that need to be captured for the dial plan, then configured into the router.

Configuring Trunking

☑ In telephone systems, a trunk is a line that carries multiple voice or data channel between two telephone exchange switching systems.

☑ Trunks are a virtual connection between PBXs.

☑ Virtual connections are implemented with the *connection* command.

Configuring ISDN for Voice

☑ ISDN connectivity is a large part of VoIP environment, with a large share of circuits used to connect PSTN and PBXs.

☑ Using the ISDN BRI VIC rather than analog VIC modules allows for additional calling information to be passed.

Configuring Gateways and Gatekeepers

☑ Gateways translate analog and digits calls to packets to be sent over the VoIP, VoFR, or VoATM network. Gateways register with the gatekeeper.

☑ Gatekeepers control access between the zones.

☑ Interzone communications are handled with domain names by the gatekeeper.

☑ Zone prefixes perform the same functionality as a domain name.

Frequently Asked Questions

The following Frequently Asked Questions, answered by the authors of this book, are designed to both measure your understanding of the concepts presented in this chapter and to assist you with real-life implementation of these concepts. To have your questions about this chapter answered by the author, browse to **www.syngress.com/solutions** and click on the **"Ask the Author"** form.

Q: What is a high-density analog telephony network module?

A: The High Density Analog Voice Network Module (NM-HDA) is a new voice module that fits into a regular network module slot on Cisco 2600, 3640, and 3660 series routers. The base card supports four FXS ports and can be expanded to support any of the following configurations: 12 FXS, 8 FXO + 4FXS, or 12 FXS and 4 FXO ports. The NM-HDA uses a standard telco RJ-21 amphenol connector.

Q: How can I send incoming calls directly to a particular phone extension with only analog connectivity to the PSTN?

A: Install the VIC-2DID module and configure it for DID support, which allows calls to be routed to a specific phone extension.

Q: I have a Cisco 1760 router with three VIC modules, but it supports only two voice calls. What is the problem?

A: The problem could be a defective VIC module, or the router might not have enough packet voice data modules (PVDMs) installed. The PVDM houses the digital signal processors (DSPs). The 175x and 1760 needs a four-channel PVDM per two calls. Install additional PVDMs on the motherboard.

Q: How do I calculate accurate voice bandwidth requirements?

A: You need to first calculate the voice packet size by bytes. The voice packet size is the (Layer 2 MLPPP or FRF.12 header) + (IP/UDP/RTP header) + (voice payload). Multiply the voice packet size in bytes by 8, which gives you voice packet size in bits. Calculate the voice packets per second (pps), which is the codec bit rate/voice payload size. Divide the voice packet size in bits by the pps. This gives you the bandwidth requirement per call.

Q: Can I use FXO interfaces for connectivity of two PBXs and routers?

A: For the best results, use a combination of FXO and FXS interfaces or E&M on both routers. E&M is the preferred method.

Q: I have a H.323 gateway and want to configure the H.323 bind source address command. Can I use subinterfaces?

A: No. H.323does support virtual interfaces such as tunnels and loopbacks in addition to physical interfaces but not subinterfaces.

Chapter 6

Configuring QoS for VoIP

Solutions in this chapter:

- **QoS Overview**

- **Available QoS Options**

- **VoIP QoS Configuration Examples**

- ☑ **Summary**

- ☑ **Solutions Fast Track**

- ☑ **Frequently Asked Questions**

Introduction

It is much less expensive to own and operate one network than it is to own and operate two networks. For this reason, converging voice and data on one single network has enormous financial benefits. Migrating to VoIP allows us to better utilize the network as a whole because unused voice bandwidth can be used for data, and vice versa. Furthermore, with convergence we require just one group to administer and manage the network. However, putting voice and data on the same network brings other issues. If a file transfer is slow, people could get somewhat irritated, but they have come to expect that from time to time. Voice communications, on the other hand, become virtually impossible when they experience excessive delay or packet loss.

To address the unique problem of making voice and data traffic get along, we use Quality of Service (QoS), the term used to define the ability of a network to provide different levels of service assurances to the various forms of traffic. QoS gives network administrators the ability to give priority to their voice traffic or alter the flow of their data traffic to prevent it from choking out voice. A host of options are available for configuring a network to enable voice and data to share the resources without sacrificing quality for either service.

The QoS puzzle has many different pieces. We must take into account the type of network, number of users, and bandwidth available. We must also think about the kind of quality that is acceptable; some people are willing to accept somewhat lower voice quality, and some aren't. Furthermore, we might need to consider the other core business applications that will be sharing the network with the voice traffic as well as their relative priorities. These are just a few things to consider when you're implementing a QoS plan.

This chapter is divided into two sections. The first provides an overview of QoS and a description of several different options for implementation. The second section goes into detail on how to configure the network for each QoS solution.

QoS Overview

QoS is simply a set of tools available to network administrators to enforce certain assurances that a minimum level of service will be provided to certain classes of traffic. By prioritizing certain classes of traffic, congestion management techniques enable business-critical or delay-sensitive applications to operate properly in a congested network environment.

There are three levels of QoS:

- **Best effort** Best-effort service occurs when the network makes every possible attempt to deliver a packet to its destination. This service type carries no guarantees a packet will reach the destination.

- **Integrated services** The integrated service model provides applications with a guaranteed level of service by negotiating network parameters end to end. Applications request the level of service necessary for them to operate properly and rely on the QoS mechanism to reserve the necessary network resources before the application begins its transmission.

- **Differentiated service** Differentiated service includes a set of classification tools and queuing mechanisms to provide certain protocols or applications with a certain priority over other network traffic. Differentiated services rely on the edge routers to perform the classification of the various types of packets traversing a network.

QoS can be implemented in any number of ways via one or more of these methods. Many of the options discussed in this chapter can be used either on their own or in conjunction with other QoS techniques. For that reason, the process of deploying QoS on a network can be very complex. The aim of this chapter is to cast some light on the methods of QoS available in order to help make the decision process and implementation easier. Because each network is different, it is impossible to provide a single scheme for QoS. Instead, each network needs to be evaluated individually and have a solution custom-tailored to address its specific needs. In the following sections we discuss individual techniques, describing the purpose, basics of operation, advantages and disadvantages, and configuration information for each.

Available QoS Options

A great many options for implementing QoS are available on today's networks. For the purposes of this chapter, we focus on measures available on Cisco routers. These measures include several methods of bandwidth maximization via various queuing techniques as well as packet classification and bandwidth reservation. We also discuss available methods of congestion avoidance and management as well as packet fragmentation.

Maximizing Bandwidth

The demand for more bandwidth and faster response times is due to the result of today's networks' ever-increasing traffic and applications that require more bandwidth and faster response times. As we start connecting these networks together and allow remote users to dial in and access them, cost constraints mean that we are unlikely to have unlimited bandwidth available. It is the network designer's job to ensure that the applications running across these links can maintain a satisfactory level of performance and responsiveness as well as make efficient use of the available bandwidth.

Congestion management is a generic term that encompasses various types of queuing strategies used to manage situations in which network applications' bandwidth demands exceed the total bandwidth that the network can provide. Congestion management does not control congestion before it occurs. It controls the injection of traffic into the network so that certain network flows have priority over others. In this section, the most basic of the congestion management queuing techniques is discussed at a high level. A more detailed explanation follows in this chapter. Here we examine the following QoS techniques:

- cRTP
- Queuing
  - Priority queuing
  - Custom queuing
  - Weighted fair queuing (WFQ)
  - Class-based WFQ (CBWFQ)
  - Priority queuing with WFQ
- Packet classification
- IP precedence
- Policy routing
- Resource Reservation Protocol (RSVP)
- Call Admission Control (CAC)

Implementing and configuring priority and custom queuing on the router require the network administrator to put in some basic planning and forethought.

The network administrator must have a good understanding of the traffic flows and how the traffic should be prioritized to engineer an efficient queuing strategy. Poorly planned prioritization can lead to situations worse than the congestive state itself. First in, first out (FIFO) and WFQ, on the other hand, require very little configuration in order to work properly. In the Cisco IOS, WFQ is enabled by default on links of E1 speed (2.048Mbps) or slower. Conversely, FIFO is enabled by default on links faster than E1 speeds. We cover these default behaviors in greater detail later in this chapter.

Compressed Real-Time Transport Protocol

Compressed Real-Time Transport Protocol (cRTP) provides a mechanism by which we can reduce the header overhead for RTP traffic by eliminating redundant information between packets. For instance, imagine a data stream consisting of 100 packets, where the first 99 have identical headers and the last one signals the end of the transmission. Why would the router need to continue to use up valuable bandwidth to send the exact same information 99 times? It wouldn't. Therefore, it simply sends the first packet, then tags each packet after that to let the far end know where to look for the header info—in this case, to packet number 1—thereby greatly reducing overhead.

Understanding Real-Time Transport Protocol

RTP, which is described in RFC1889, is used on IP networks to handle audio compression for IP packets. RTP manages the audio path transport for VoIP. RTP provides such services as sequencing to identify lost packets and 32-bit values to identify and distinguish between multiple senders in a multicast stream. VoIP packets are composed of one or more speech codec samples or frames encapsulated in 40 bytes of IP/UDP/RTP headers. 40 bytes is a large amount of overhead for VoIP payloads, considering that the voice payload is usually about 20 bytes. This is especially true when voice is traveling over low-speed links. For this reason, RTP header compression (cRTP) detailed in RFC 2508 was created to reduce the header size that RTP must add.

RTP Header Compression

RFC 2508 specifies two formats of cRTP:

- **Compressed RTP (CR)** Used when the IP, UDP, and RTP headers remain consistent. All three headers are compressed.

■ **Compressed UDP (CU)** Used when there is a large change in the RTP timestamp or when the RTP payload type changes. The IP and UDP headers are compressed, but the RTP header is not.

In the section "Maximizing Bandwidth," we saw that there are two basic types of traffic optimization; cRTP falls under header compression. Compressing the IP/UDP/RTP header in an RTP packet can effectively reduce the amount of bandwidth required in a VoIP network. Results from compression can be great, taking the header size from 40 bytes down to about 2 bytes where no checksums are being sent and 4 bytes with checksums (see Figure 6.1).

Figure 6.1 RTP/UDP/IP Packet Headers

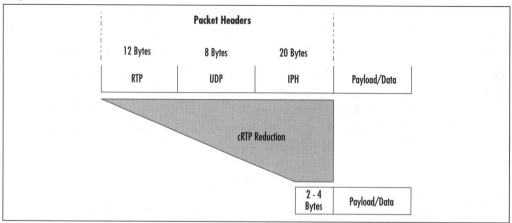

In Figure 6.2 we see the RTP header compression process. Queuing occurs before the compression process. The engine then determines RTP traffic, and only RTP packets are compressed. All packets, non–RTP and cRTP, are then passed on to the interface.

Figure 6.2 RTP Header Compression

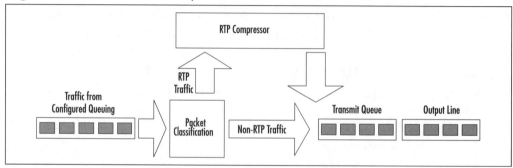

cRTP Implementation

You should configure cRTP if the following conditions exist in your network:

- Slow links
- The need to save bandwidth

Enabling compression on both ends of a low-bandwidth serial link can greatly reduce the network overhead if the network carries a lot of RTP traffic. cRTP is supported on serial lines using Frame Relay, HDLC, or PPP encapsulation. It is also supported over ISDN interfaces.

It's important to mention that the available router resources (CPU) should be taken into consideration when you're implementing cRTP—or in fact any QoS technique. CRTP is performed via the main processor, and it could cause utilization to rise, depending on your traffic patterns and considerations.

> **NOTE**
>
> cRTP should not be used on links greater than 2Mbps.

Queuing

It is important to understand the basics of the queuing process. In a router, queues act as a *holding area*. Queues hold packets until enough resources are available to forward the packets out the egress port. The packets will be forwarded immediately, provided there is no congestion in the router. Network queues are used to handle traffic bursts arriving faster than the egress interface can handle. For example, a router connecting a Fast Ethernet LAN interface to a T1 WAN circuit often sees chunks of traffic arriving on the LAN interface faster than it can send it out to the WAN. In this case, the queue places the traffic in a "holding area" so that the T1 circuit can process the packets at its own pace. This is a normal network operation necessary to handle traffic going in and out of an interface and does not necessarily indicate a congestion problem.

Several queuing types could be beneficial in a VoIP network. The following queuing strategies are addressed in this section:

- Custom queuing
- Priority queuing

- WFQ
- CBWFQ

Custom Queuing

Custom queuing (CQ) works by allowing a *custom* configuration of a specified number of bytes to be forwarded from a queue each time that queue has been serviced. A maximum number of packets per queue can also be specified. CQ handles traffic by specifying the number of bytes to be serviced for each class of traffic. It services the queues by cycling through them, sending the portion of allocated data for each queue before moving to the next queue. When the router comes upon an empty queue, it sends packets from the next queue that has packets ready to send. When a particular queue is being processed, packets are sent until the number of bytes sent exceeds the queue byte count or the queue is empty. Bandwidth used by a particular queue can be specified only in terms of byte count and queue length. Figure 6.3 shows how CQ works.

Figure 6.3 Custom Queuing

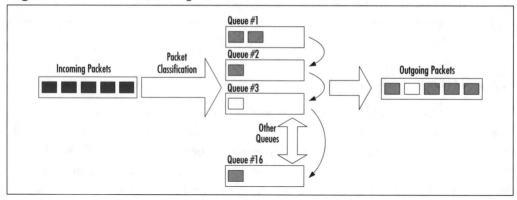

Configuring CQ allows the user to specify that no application or specified group of applications is permitted more than the allocated amount of overall capacity when the link is congested. The configuration of CQ is not dynamic, so it will not alter existing network conditions.

Priority Queuing

PQ allows you to define how traffic is prioritized in the network. The router places traffic in these queues, based on filters that are predefined. The queue with the highest priority is serviced first until it is empty, then the lower queues are serviced in sequence. As its name suggests, traffic is processed based on priority. Traffic with the highest priority is given precedence over low-priority queues. Four output queues exist, and traffic is placed in these queues based on user-configured criteria. The four output queues are:

- High
- Medium
- Normal
- Low

Packets that are not classified by priority fall into the normal queue. Figure 6.4 shows how PQ works.

Figure 6.4 Priority Queuing

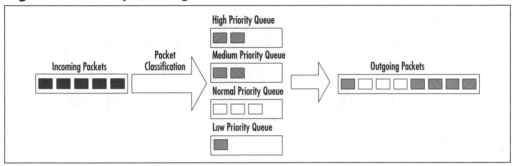

Priority queues on an interface are scanned for packets in descending order of priority, starting with the high-priority queue, then the medium priority queue, and so forth. The packet at the head of the highest queue is then chosen for transmission. Every time a packet is to be sent, the procedure repeats itself. It should be noted that priority queuing can lead to situations in which lower-priority queues are *starved*; this is a situation that occurs when there is always data that needs to be serviced in higher-priority queues.

Weighted Fair Queuing

WFQ is a dynamic scheduling method that provides fair bandwidth allocation to all network traffic. WFQ applies weights to packets to determine how much bandwidth each conversation is allowed relative to other conversations.

WFQ provides traffic priority management that dynamically sorts traffic into messages that make up a conversation. WFQ breaks up the train of packets within a conversation to ensure that bandwidth is shared fairly between individual conversations and that low-volume traffic is transferred in a timely fashion.

WFQ classifies traffic into different flows based on packet header addressing, including such characteristics as source and destination network address, source and destination port numbers, and type of service (ToS) value. There are two categories of flow:

- High-bandwidth sessions
- Low-bandwidth sessions

Low-bandwidth traffic has effective priority over high-bandwidth traffic, and high-bandwidth traffic shares the transmission service proportionally according to assigned weights. Low-bandwidth traffic streams, which make up the majority of traffic, receive preferential service, allowing their entire offered loads to be sent in a timely fashion. High-volume traffic streams share the remaining capacity proportionally among themselves.

WFQ places packets of the various conversations in the fair queues before transmission. The order of removal from the fair queues is determined by the virtual time of delivery of the last bit of each arriving packet.

New messages for high-bandwidth flows are discarded after the congestive-messages threshold has been met. However, low-bandwidth flows, which include control-message conversations, continue to enqueue data. As a result, the fair queue can occasionally contain more messages than are specified by the threshold number.

Flow-based WFQ is used as the default queuing mode on most serial interfaces configured to run at or below E1 speeds (2.048Mbps).

WFQ provides the solution for situations in which it is desirable to provide consistent response time to heavy and light network users alike without adding excessive bandwidth. WFQ automatically adapts to changing network traffic conditions.

CBWFQ

CBWFQ extends the standard WFQ functionality to provide support for user-defined traffic classes. For CBWFQ, you define traffic classes based on match criteria including protocols, access control lists (ACLs), and input interfaces. Packets satisfying the match criteria for a class constitute the traffic for that class. A queue is reserved for each class, and traffic belonging to a class is directed to the queue for that class.

Once a class has been defined according to its match criteria, you can assign it characteristics. To characterize a class, you assign it bandwidth, weight, and maximum packet limit. The bandwidth assigned to a class is the guaranteed bandwidth delivered to the class during congestion.

To characterize a class, you also specify the queue limit for that class, which is the maximum number of packets allowed to accumulate in the queue for the class. Packets belonging to a class are subject to the bandwidth and queue limits that characterize the class.

After a queue has reached its configured queue limit, enqueuing of additional packets to the class causes tail drop or packet drop to take effect, depending on how class policy is configured. Tail drop is used for CBWFQ classes unless you explicitly configure policy for a class to use weighted random early detect (WRED) to drop packets as a means of avoiding congestion. Note that if you use WRED packet drop instead of tail drop for one or more classes comprising a policy map, you must ensure that WRED is not configured for the interface to which you attach that service policy.

If a default class is configured with the *bandwidth policy-map* class configuration command, all unclassified traffic is put into a single queue and treated according to the configured bandwidth. If a default class is configured with the *fair-queue* command, all unclassified traffic is flow classified and given best-effort treatment. Once a packet is classified, all the standard mechanisms that can be used to differentiate service among the classes apply.

Flow classification is standard WFQ treatment. That is, packets with the same source IP address, destination IP address, source TCP or UDP port, or destination TCP or UDP port are classified as belonging to the same flow. WFQ allocates an equal share of bandwidth to each flow.

For CBWFQ, which extends the standard WFQ concept of fair queuing, the weight specified for the class becomes the weight of each packet that meets the match criteria of the class. Packets that arrive at the output interface are classified according to the match criteria filters you define, and then each one is assigned the appropriate weight. The weight for a packet belonging to a specific class is derived from the bandwidth you assigned to the class when you configured it; in this sense the weight for a class is user-configurable.

After the weight for a packet is assigned, the packet is enqueued in the appropriate class queue. CBWFQ uses the weights assigned to the queued packets to ensure that the class queue is serviced fairly.

Priority Queuing with WFQ

IP RTP Priority (which is commonly known as *priority queuing with WFQ*) is an enhancement within Cisco IOS to identify and expedite RTP/UDP traffic because this traffic is usually time sensitive. This is a priority-based queuing algorithm. This queuing strategy features a priority queue, reserved bandwidth queues, and an unreserved queue. It is optimized for RTP and all other traffic treated with a WFQ algorithm. The strict priority applied here means that if datagrams exit a port in the priority queue, they are dequeued first, ahead of any other traffic.

IP RTP Priority gives absolute priority to voice traffic, when implemented along with CBWFQ. This also allows the user to set up additional classes within CBWFQ for other traffic types requiring something better than best-effort service but not a strict priority. All nonvoice traffic will be serviced fairly by WFQ according to its assigned weights.

Packet Classification

Sometimes, in a network, you need to classify traffic. The reasons for classifying traffic vary from network to network but can range from marking packets with a "flag" to make them relatively more or less important than other packets on the network to identifying packets to drop. This chapter introduces you to several different theories of traffic classification and discusses the mechanics of how these "flags" are set in a packet.

You can set these flags in several ways, and the levels of classification depend on which method is used. Classification can be viewed as infusing data packets with a directive intelligence with regard to network devices. The use of prioritization schemes such as random early detection (RED) and adaptive bit rate (ABR) force the router to analyze data streams and congestion characteristics and then apply congestion controls to the data streams. These applications can involve the utilization of the TCP sliding window or backoff algorithms, the utilization of leaky or token bucket queuing mechanisms, or a number of other strategies. The use of traffic classification flags within the packet removes decision functionality from the router and establishes the service levels that are required for the packet's particular traffic flow. The router then attempts to provide the packet with the requested QoS.

IP Precedence

IP precedence is a definable parameter on dial peers that gives a priority value on the network. It is manually assigned to the particular dial peer in VoIP configuration mode as follows:

```
dial-peer voice 10 VoIP
ip precedence 5
```

This command should be used to give voice IP packets more priority than standard data packets when they share the same available bandwidth. In the following sections, you will see how IP precedence settings affect the CBWFQ algorithms and how they help achieve greater performance for voice data transmissions.

There are advantages and disadvantages to using either method of QoS for VoIP. One of the most important factors to take into account is the kind of QoS features your network can use. It is important to understand the types of traffic that the network is passing for data as well as voice so that you do not cut out any vital data traffic in lieu of voice traffic. Keep in mind the following points when you're deciding which algorithms to use:

- IP precedence is more controllable for the network administrator. You can choose the level of precedence that is available to the traffic that you want to use QoS on. It cannot be controlled dynamically; it is set manually on each individual dial peer. Therefore, QoS will have a higher administration overhead should the network need to be fine-tuned.

- RSVP is harder to set up initially, since traffic levels need to be analyzed and adjusted on each physical port. RSVP is extremely powerful on highly congested links and slow WAN links. It also has the extra benefit of being a dynamically control system. RSVP pipes are built and torn down as needed, so there is no wasteful use of bandwidth.

- At this time, we recommend use of the IP precedence methods instead of RSVP due to streamlining efforts of the RSVP technologies. IP precedence is a more stable method of control. RSVP is discussed in more detail later in this chapter.

Policy Routing

Policy-based routing (PBR) is a method by which a packet can be directed, based on a given set of criteria (a policy), to take a route other than that which would be taken using the standard routing protocols. PBR classifies traffic based on configured ACLs and then applies the configured policy accordingly. Classification and policy application is performed by a packet filter called a *route map*. Route maps consist of two types of statements: Match and Set. The Match statement compares a packet to either a standard or extended access list and/or matches packet length. The Set statement determines the action that is performed on matching packets and can include setting IP precedence, IP next-hop, interface, IP default next-hop, or default interface. With Cisco IOS release 12.0 and later, PBR can be fast-switched rather than only process-switched. With fast switching, the *set IP default next-hop* and *set default interface* commands are not available, and the *set interface* command is available only on point-to-point links unless there is a route-cache entry for the specified interface. In addition, when fast-switched PBR is used, a matching packet is forwarded blindly, without checking the routing table to ensure that it is a valid route.

Resource Reservation Protocol

Resource Reservation Protocol (RSVP) is used to provide reserved bandwidth end to end on an IP flow for either unicast or multicast traffic. A major difference between RSVP and routing protocols is that RSVP works on the entire flow, rather than routing individual datagrams. The reservation is actually made from the receiving node back to the sending node, and the connection is a simplex session, so two-way traffic requires two individual RSVP sessions. A session consists of a flow of data to a particular destination and protocol, identified by the destination address, protocol ID (PID), and destination port. There are three types of RSVP traffic:

- Best effort

- Rate sensitive

- Delay sensitive
    - Controlled delay
    - Predictive service

Best-effort traffic is standard IP connectionless traffic, where upper-level protocols are responsible for error checking and flow control. *Rate-sensitive* traffic, sometimes referred to as *guaranteed bit-rate service*, is a class in which the flow requires a constant rate (such as 128kbs or 384kbps) and is able to withstand queuing delays as a tradeoff for the guaranteed bandwidth. *Delay-sensitive* traffic is split into two classifications. *Controlled-delay* traffic is for nonreal-time applications, whereas *predictive service* traffic is used for voice, video, and other real-time applications.

Call Admission Control

CAC is a generic term to describe a method by which a node can prevent oversubscription of network resources, thus preserving the quality of existing transmissions. Often used with voice applications or videoconferencing, CAC rejects a request for network resources if the requesting application requires more bandwidth than is currently available. For example, if an interface is configured for 128k, and five VoIP calls requiring 24k each are in progress, CAC will prevent a sixth call from being completed, because adding that call would degrade the quality of *all six* calls. This system ensures that all existing connections maintain the bandwidth they need. When a connection is rejected, the originating node will, depending on the network configuration, either look for an alternate path or provide a reorder tone or fast busy signal to the calling party.

In the following three figures, assume that each call requires 24k of bandwidth. In Figure 6.5, two calls exist between Router1 and Router3 (labeled 1 and 2).

In Figure 6.6, a third call is placed (labeled 3), and Router1 sends the call to the next hop, Router2. However, there is not enough bandwidth to support the new call, so CAC rejects it.

Figure 6.5 Rerouting a Call Due to CAC Rejection: Two Calls Exist

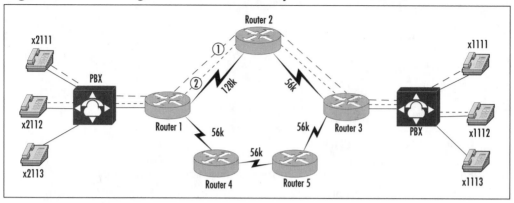

Figure 6.6 Rerouting a Call Due to CAC Rejection: Third Call Is Rejected

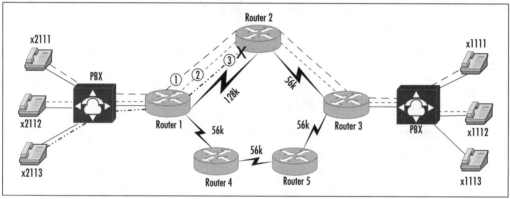

In Figure 6.7, after the rejection, Router1 is able to reroute the call via Router4 to complete the call.

Figure 6.7 Rerouting a Call Due to CAC Rejection: Third Call Is Rerouted

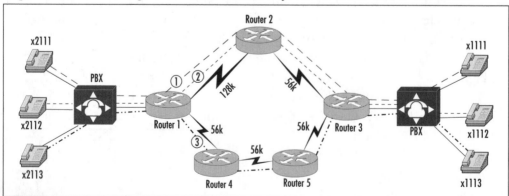

There are several different methods for implementing CAC, but for the purposes of VoIP, the most commonly used are RSVP and H.323 gateway zone bandwidth. The H.323 gatekeeper, in that case, monitors the network and makes decisions on call admission based on static calculations to either accept or reject a call, similar to the illustration in Figure 6.7. The gatekeeper is not aware of how much bandwidth is currently in use and makes no bandwidth reservations. Instead, it relies on configured bandwidth for WAN links and preset values for per-call bandwidth use. The gatekeeper then merely subtracts that rate from the total bandwidth for each active call and rejects a call request that would drop the bandwidth below zero.

Designing & Planning…

Networkwide or Just One Interface?

When developing your QoS design, keep in mind that some techniques require implementation across the entire network; some only require each end of a connection to be configured, and others can be implemented on a single interface. Take into account that implementing several methods on a small router could cause utilization issues, which could jeopardize the network.

Furthermore, pay particular attention to bandwidth and link type throughout your network, because a method that is designed for slow-speed serial links is not going to be an optimal solution for a 10/100 LAN, and vice versa.

RTP Priority

Real-Time Transport Protocol (RTP) priority provides absolute priority to delay-sensitive UDP data transmissions. Via the *ip rtp priority* command, users are able to specify particular RTP ports that will have priority over other queues on the same interface. Once configured, packets that are identified with the RTP port number are given priority over all other packets on the interface. The RTP priority queue polices based on total bandwidth, not the number of individual connections. Therefore, if the queue is configured for 128Kbps, it simply reserves that amount of bandwidth but does not prevent excess calls from being admitted.

The result , given the previous example, is that if five calls requiring 24Kbps each were in progress, a sixth could be admitted, reducing the actual per-call bandwidth to 21Kbps and jeopardizing call quality. For this reason, it is up to the user to ensure that the reserved bandwidth is not exceeded.

Traffic Shaping

Traffic shaping is a means to smooth out data transmissions by restricting outbound traffic to a particular speed while buffering bursts in the traffic that are in excess of that speed. There are two basic traffic-shaping features: Frame Relay traffic shaping (FRTS) and generic traffic shaping (GTS).

FRTS uses a variety of parameters to manage traffic flows in order to avoid or reduce congestion in the network. Parameters include committed information rate (CIR), forward explicit congestion notification (FECN), backward explicit congestion notification (BECN) and excess information rate (EIR). For example, rate enforcement, in which traffic is limited to a particular bit rate, can be configured on a per-VC basis for CIR, EIR, or some other value. Traffic can also be throttled dynamically using BECN tagged packets, also on a per-VC basis. When throttling in this manner, packets are held in queue and transmitted at a reduced rate until the congestion condition has cleared. Additionally, Cisco's implementation of FRTS can be integrated with the Foresight feature available on Cisco's StrataCom line of ATM switches.

GTS is an interface-specific flow control mechanism. Outbound traffic is constrained to a particular bit rate (using a token bucket system), and periodic bursts are queued to limit the flow. In this way, traffic that meets a certain profile can be shaped to eliminate congestion due to downstream rate mismatches. GTS can be used on a Frame Relay interface and configured to respond to BECN signals, or to simply smooth traffic to a specified rate. GTS can also be configured to respond to RSVP signaling on ATM permanent virtual circuits (PVCs). General traffic shaping may also be combined with CBWFQ to accomplish class-based shaping.

Weighted Random Early Detection

WRED is a method by which routers are able to manage their queues, thereby avoiding congestion before it occurs. WRED builds on the RED algorithm, which monitors traffic in a specific class/interface and drops packets as congestion begins to increase. When the source detects the dropped packet, it slows transmission. Because a queue has a limited depth, once it fills up, packets will be dropped simply because there are no more resources available to buffer them. This phenomenon is referred to as *tail dropping*. Tail dropping is undesirable because it is indiscriminate; the router does not have a chance to identify the priority. WRED addressed this problem by setting thresholds for dropping packets of varying precedence levels. Take, for instance, a network in which the following thresholds are set:

- Minimum threshold for IP precedence of 0 = 20
- Minimum threshold for IP precedence of 1 = 22
- Minimum threshold for IP precedence of 2 = 24

If the queue depth is 21, packets with a precedence of 0 can be dropped, but those with 1 or 2 will not. If the queue depth increases to 22, the packets with a 0 or 1 can be dropped, whereas those with a precedence of 2 will not be.

WRED works best with TCP traffic because when packets are dropped, TCP throttles back, reducing congestion. For this reason, WRED can cause problems in networks with large amounts of UDP traffic. Because UDP does not respond to drops it will not throttle back its transmission rate. The result is that as congestion continues, TCP continues to be dropped, causing more and more reduction in transmission rate, while UDP packets continue to be transmitted at their original rate.

Link Fragmentation and Interleaving

Link fragmentation and interleaving (LFI) is a method used to reduce serialization delay for time-sensitive applications, such as VoIP. Consider a 1500-byte FTP packet traversing a 128k serial link. The packet would take 94ms to be serialized. A VoIP packet that arrived after the FTP packet could then be forced to wait in the queue for up to 94ms. Considering that overall end-to end delay for a VoIP packet should not exceed 150ms (G.114), you can see that the delay induced by waiting for the larger packet can have a significant impact on voice quality. LFI resolves this issue by fragmenting large packets so that smaller time-sensitive packets can be interleaved with the large ones, reducing delay. The packets are then reassembled at the far end. LFI requires that the interface be configured to use multilink PPP and have interleaving enabled. LFI is generally configured on serial interfaces slower than 768kbps. Figure 6.8 shows traffic flow without LFI enabled, and Figure 6.9 shows how the flow is changed with LFI. The large FTP packet is labeled *FTP*, VoIP packets are labeled *V*, and the fragmented FTP packet is labeled *F*.

Figure 6.8 Serialization Without LFI

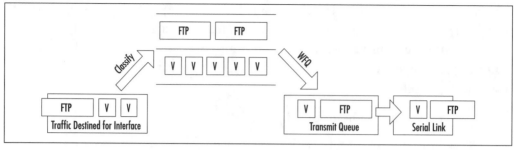

Figure 6.9 Serialization with LFI Enabled

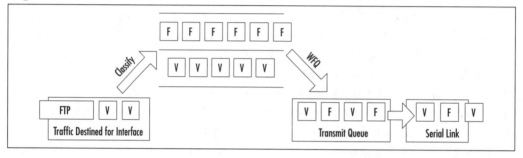

VoIP QoS Configuration Examples

Now that you are familiar with some of the QoS mechanisms available, it's time to implement them on the network. The following sections provide configuration information for each of the QoS techniques described previously. Keep in mind that the examples provided are just that, and that optional parameters need to be tailored to your particular network and business needs.

Maximizing Bandwidth

As noted earlier, it is important to examine your network closely prior to implementing any QoS procedures. Take into account the speed of your WAN links, where traffic will be going, and so on. Many bandwidth-maximizing techniques can actually impede VoIP traffic if implemented incorrectly or on a link that does not require it. For instance, configuring LFI or cRTP over a LAN segment just adds delay while the packet is fragmented or compressed, whereas it would have otherwise just been forwarded on a link where there is less danger of it being dropped due to bandwidth limitations.

Configuring cRTP

Before you can enable RTP header compression, you must have configured a serial line that uses Frame Relay, HDLC, or PPP encapsulation, or an ISDN interface. The following sections describe how to enable RTP header compression for these interface types.

Enable cRTP on a Serial Interface

To enable cRTP headers for serial encapsulation on HDLC or PPP, use the command in Table 6.1 while in Interface Configuration mode. (You must enable compression on both ends of a serial connection.)

Table 6.1 Serial cRTP

Command	Purpose
ip rtp header-compression [passive]	Enables RTP header compression.

If you include the *passive* keyword, the software compresses outgoing RTP packets only if incoming RTP packets on the same interface are compressed. If you use the command without the *passive* keyword, the software compresses all RTP traffic.

Enable cRTP with Frame Relay Encapsulation

To enable cRTP headers with Frame Relay encapsulation, use one of the commands in Table 6.2 while in Interface Configuration mode.

Table 6.2 Frame Relay cRTP

Command	Purpose
frame-relay ip rtp header-compression [passive]	Enables RTP header compression on the physical interface and all the interface maps will inherit it. Subsequently, all maps will perform RTP/IP header compression.
frame-relay map ip *ip-address* *dlci* [broadcast] rtp header-compression [active | passive]	Enables RTP header compression only on the particular map specified.
frame-relay map ip *ip-address* *dlci* [broadcast] compress	Enables both RTP and TCP header compression on this link.

Change the Number of Header Compression Connections

By default, the Cisco IOS supports a total of 16 RTP header compression connections on an interface. To change that number, use the command in Table 6.3 while in Interface Configuration mode.

Table 6.3 Header Compression

Command	Purpose
ip rtp compression connections *number*	Specifies the total number of RTP header compression connections supported on an interface.

Displaying Statistics

You can display specific statistics such as the contents of IP routing tables, caches, and databases. Information provided can be used to determine resource utilization and solve network problems. You can also display information about node reachability and discover the routing path your packets are taking through the network.

To display compressed RTP statistics, use the commands from Table 6.4 while in EXEC mode.

Table 6.4 Routing Statistics

Command	Purpose
show frame-relay ip rtp header-compression [interface *type number*]	Displays Frame Relay RTP header compression statistics.
show ip rtp header-compression [*type number*] [detail]	Displays RTP header compression statistics.

CRTP Configuration Examples

The following example enables RTP header compression for a serial, ISDN, or asynchronous interface. For ISDN, you also need a broadcast dialer map:

```
interface serial 0 :or interface bri 0
ip rtp header-compression
encapsulation ppp
ip rtp compression-connections 25
```

The following example for Frame Relay encapsulation enables RTP header compression on the specified map:

```
interface serial 0
ip address 1.0.0.2 255.0.0.0
encapsulation frame-relay
no keepalive
frame-relay map ip 1.0.0.1 17 broadcast rtp header-compression
```

Configuring & Implementing…

cRTP Scalability

In Cisco IOS Software releases 12.0.5T and earlier, cRTP is process-switched, severely limiting the scalability of cRTP solutions due to CPU performance. Most of these issues have been resolved through various cRTP performance improvements introduced in IOS software releases 12.0.7T through 12.1.2T.

In summary, the history of performance parameters for cRTP is:

- Up to versions 12.0.5T, cRTP is process-switched.

- In 12.0.7T and continuing in 12.1.1T, fast- and Cisco Express Forwarding (CEF)-switching support for cRTP was introduced.

- In 12.1.2T, algorithmic performance improvements were introduced.

Moving cRTP into the fast-switching path significantly increases the number of RTP sessions (VoIP calls) that VoIP gateways and intermediate routers can process.

Configuring Queuing

Now that you have an understanding of the basic queuing and congestion avoidance mechanisms, it is time to become familiar with how these mechanisms are configured. WFQ requires very little configuration, but CBWFQ, custom, and priority queuing configurations can range from extremely simple to quite complex. The level of complexity is almost entirely related to the access lists that control the functions of the queuing mechanisms, so it is important that you review access lists in detail before configuring these mechanisms. The configurations shown in this chapter do not represent every possible configuration scenario or configuration option.

Configuring Custom Queuing

The tasks involved in configuring custom queuing are as follows:

- Define a custom queue list.
- Assign the custom queue list to an interface.

Of the two tasks, defining the priority list is the most important because it is at this point that the packet classification is determined for the entire custom queuing process. This section examines several examples of custom queuing and explains the potential pitfalls to be avoided when preparing a custom queue list.

Enabling Custom Queuing

The first task in configuring custom queuing is to declare a valid custom queue list. This is accomplished using the global configuration command, *queue-list*. As with priority queuing, custom queue lists are identified using a list number:

```
Router1(config)#queue-list 1 ?
default Set custom queue for unspecified datagrams
interface Establish priority for packets from an interface
lowest-custom Set lowest number of queue to be treated as
custom
protocol Priority queueing by protocol
queue Configure parameters for a particular queue
stun Establish priorities for stun packets
```

This code output shows the various parameters used to configure priorities. As with priority queuing, custom queuing can prioritize by inbound interface or by protocols. The default keyword is used to define the queue that will handle all unclassified traffic.

Let's now configure a custom queue list to meet the following requirements. All default traffic will be assigned to Queue 1. All AppleTalk and IPX traffic will be assigned to Queue 2. All Telnet traffic will be assigned to Queue 3. All traffic from IPX Host 3C.ABCD.ABCD.ABCD is to be assigned to Queue 4. All traffic coming from interface Ethernet 0/0 is to be assigned to Queue 5. Finally, all remaining IP traffic will be assigned to Queue 6. Unlike priority queuing, the queue numbers used by custom queuing do not represent assigned priority levels. The following custom queue list configuration meets these requirements:

```
Router1#configure terminal
      \\Enter configuration commands, one per line. End with CNTL/Z.
Router1(config)#access-list 801 permit 3c.abcd.abcd.abcd -1
Router1(config)#access-list 801 deny -1
Router1(config)#
Router1(config)#queue-list 1 default ?
<0-16> queue number
Router1(config)#queue-list 1 protocol appletalk 2
Router1(config)#queue-list 1 protocol ipx 2
Router1(config)#queue-list 1 protocol ip 3 tcp telnet
Router1(config)#queue-list 1 protocol ipx 4 list 801
Router1(config)#queue-list 1 interface serial 0/0 5
Router1(config)#queue-list 1 protocol ip 6
Router1(config)#queue-list 1 default 1
Router1(config)#end
Router1#
```

The first part of the configuration identifies IPX host 3C.ABCD.ABCD.ABCD with the definition of an access list. This access list is later applied in the custom queue list to place IPX traffic from that host into custom Queue 4. As shown in this example, the classification of custom queuing traffic can use the same level of granularity as priority queuing. So far, we have classified various protocols and interfaces into six different queues. Each of these queues has a default byte count of 1500 bytes and a default queue depth of 20 packets. This means that the custom queuing process should service an equal number of bytes among each queue. However, this does not always remain true when larger packets reach the custom queuing process.

Adjusting Byte Counts and Queue Sizes

In order to modify the byte count and queue size of each queue, the *queue* key-word of the *queue-list* command is used. Each queue is individually configured. In the following example, we change the byte count of Queues 1, 2, and 3 to 3000 bytes and the queue depth of Queues 4, 5, and 6 to 60 packets:

```
Router1#configure terminal
```

```
                    \\Enter configuration commands, one per line. End with CNTL/Z.
Router1(config)#queue-list 1 queue 1 ?
                    \\byte-count Specify size in bytes of a particular queue
                    \\limit Set queue entry limit of a particular queue
Router1(config)#queue-list 1 queue 1 byte-count ?
                    \\<0-16777215> size in bytes
Router1(config)#queue-list 1 queue 1 byte-count 3000
Router1(config)#queue-list 1 queue 2 byte-count 3000
Router1(config)#queue-list 1 queue 3 byte-count 3000
Router1(config)#queue-list 1 queue 3 limit ?
                    \\<0-32767> number of queue entries
Router1(config)#queue-list 1 queue 4 limit 60
Router1(config)#queue-list 1 queue 5 limit 60
Router1(config)#queue-list 1 queue 6 limit 60
Router1(config)#end
Router1#
```

Applying Your Configuration to an Interface

Once you have successfully configured your custom queue list, the second step is to apply the list against an interface. The interface command *custom-queue-list* is used to perform this function. In the following code, we apply the custom queue configuration defined previously to interface serial 0/0.

```
Router1#configure terminal
        \\Enter configuration commands, one per line. End with CNTL/Z.
Router1(config)#interface serial 0/0
Router1(config-if)#custom-queue-list 1
Router1(config-if)#end
Router1#
```

At this point, you should have a valid, operational custom queuing configuration.

Verifying Custom Queuing

The first step in verifying custom queuing is to verify that your configuration is properly applied to the interface. This is accomplished using the *show interface* command:

```
Router1#show interface serial 0/0
Serial0/0 is up, line protocol is up
```

```
Hardware is PowerQUICC Serial
Internet address is 192.168.10.1/24
MTU 1500 bytes, BW 1544 Kbit, DLY 20000 usec,
reliability 255/255, txload 1/255, rxload 1/255
Encapsulation HDLC, loopback not set, keepalive set (10 sec)
Last input 00:00:07, output 00:00:08, output hang never
Last clearing of "show interface" counters never
Input queue: 0/75/0 (size/max/drops); Total output drops: 0
Queueing strategy: custom-list 1
Output queues: (queue #: size/max/drops)
0: 0/20/0 1: 0/20/0 2: 0/20/0 3: 0/20/0 4: 0/60/0
5: 0/60/0 6: 0/60/0 7: 0/20/0 8: 0/20/0 9: 0/20/0
10: 0/20/0 11: 0/20/0 12: 0/20/0 13: 0/20/0 14: 0/20/0
15: 0/20/0 16: 0/20/0
5 minute input rate 0 bits/sec, 0 packets/sec
5 minute output rate 0 bits/sec, 0 packets/sec
17212 packets input, 1533621 bytes, 0 no buffer
Received 16828 broadcasts, 0 runts, 0 giants, 0 throttles
2 input errors, 0 CRC, 2 frame, 0 overrun, 0 ignored, 0 abor
15098 packets output, 940003 bytes, 0 underruns
0 output errors, 0 collisions, 15 interface resets
0 output buffer failures, 0 output buffers swapped out
0 carrier transitions
DCD=up DSR=up DTR=up RTS=up CTS=up
Router1#
```

This output shows that custom queue list 1 was successfully applied to interface serial 0/0. The command also shows the state of each queue at the time the command was issued. We can see that the queue depths for Queues 4, 5, and 6 were successfully adjusted to 60 packets. Notice that all 16 custom queues are displayed. This means that the IOS allocated memory space for all possible configurable queues, even though we have used only six of them. We can also use the command *show queuing* to show the actual configuration of the custom queues:

```
Router1#show queuing ?
custom custom queuing list configuration
fair fair queuing configuration
priority priority queuing list configuration
```

```
red random early detection configuration
<cr>
Router1#show queuing custom
Current custom queue configuration:
List Queue Args
1 2 protocol appletalk
1 2 protocol ipx
1 3 protocol ip tcp port telnet
1 4 protocol ipx list 801
1 5 interface Ethernet0/0
1 6 protocol ip
1 1 byte-count 3000
1 2 byte-count 3000
1 3 byte-count 3000
1 4 limit 60
1 5 limit 60
1 6 limit 60
Router1#
```

Configuring Priority Queuing

The tasks involved in configuring priority queuing are as follows:

- Define a priority list.
- Assign the priority list to an interface.

As with custom queuing, the definition of the priority list is vital to the proper operation of priority queuing. The following discussion includes multiple ways to classify network traffic, which will help you apply the principles of priority queuing in your network.

Enabling Priority Queuing

The first step in configuring priority queuing is to define the priority list. The following code depicts the *priority-list* command and its parameters:

```
Router1(config)#priority-list ?
    \\<1-16> Priority list number
Router1(config)#priority-list 1 ?
```

```
default        Set priority queue for unspecified datagrams
interface      Establish priorities for packets from an interface
protocol       Priority queuing by protocol
queue-limit    Set queue limits for priority queues
```

The command first requires us to select a priority list number between 1 and 16. This is necessary because multiple priority lists can be configured on a single router to control different interfaces using different priority queuing policies. Next, the command requires us to select what we want to prioritize. We can prioritize by inbound interface or by protocol type. The command also allows us to select the default priority of unclassified traffic and to set the queue limits in packets.

Consider the following sample requirements. All packets that enter the router from interface Ethernet 0/0 should be classified as medium priority. The default priority of all unclassified packets should be low. AppleTalk traffic should have priority over all other traffic, so we should assign it to the high-priority queue. TCP/IP traffic should be placed in the normal queue. The code to set up this configuration is as follows:

```
Router1#configure terminal
        \\Enter configuration commands, one per line. End with CNTL/Z.
Router1(config)#priority-list 1 protocol appletalk high
Router1(config)#priority-list 1 interface ethernet 0/0 medium
Router1(config)#priority-list 1 protocol ip normal
Router1(config)#priority-list 1 default low
Router1(config)#end
Router1#
```

Configuring the Queue Limits

The default queue size values are 20, 40, 60, and 80 packets for the high, medium, normal, and low priority queues, respectively. To modify these default values, the *queue-limit* parameter is used at the global configuration level. In the following code output, the high, medium, normal, and low priority queues are adjusted to values of 200, 400, 600, and 800 packets, respectively:

```
Router1#configure terminal
        \\Enter configuration commands, one per line. End with CNTL/Z.
Router1(config)#priority-list 4 queue-limit ?
        \\<0-32767> High limit
```

```
Router1(config)#priority-list 4 queue-limit 200 ?
    \\<0-32767> Medium limit
Router1(config)#priority-list 4 queue-limit 200 400 ?
    \\<0-32767> Normal limit
Router1(config)#priority-list 4 queue-limit 200 400 600 ?
    \\<0-32767> Lower limit
Router1(config)#priority-list 4 queue-limit 200 400 600 800
Router1(config)#end
Router1#
```

Be careful when changing these default values. Setting the queue sizes to
larger values could have a negative impact on router operations because of the
amount of memory used by the queuing process. In addition, having larger high-
priority queues and funneling more traffic to them can cause the queuing process
to spend too much time emptying those queues. The lower-priority queues will
thus not get serviced in time, and the upper-layer protocols will start timing out.
Conversely, reducing the queue sizes to values that are too small will result in
unnecessary tail drops. This in turn will negatively impact the operation of the
protocols flowing through the queues.

Applying Your Priority List to an Interface

The process of configuring priority queuing is similar to the process of defining
and applying an access list using the *access-list* and *access-group* commands. First, the
priority list is defined, and then the priority group is applied to the interface. This
second step, applying the priority list to an interface, is accomplished using the
interface command *priority-group*. In this example, we apply priority lists 1 and 2,
defined earlier, to interfaces serial 0/0 and 0/1, respectively:

```
Router1#configure terminal
    \\Enter configuration commands, one per line. End with CNTL/Z.
Router1(config)#interface serial 0/0
Router1(config-if)#priority-group 1
Router1(config-if)#exit
Router1(config)#interface serial 0/1
Router1(config-if)#priority-group 2
Router1(config-if)#end
Router1#
```

Verifying Priority Queuing

As with custom queuing, the first step in verifying the priority queuing configuration is to determine if the queuing process runs properly on the interface. The command *show interface* is used for this purpose:

```
Router1#show interface serial 0/0
Serial0/0 is up, line protocol is up
Hardware is PowerQUICC Serial
Internet address is 192.168.10.1/24
MTU 1500 bytes, BW 1544 Kbit, DLY 20000 usec,
reliability 255/255, txload 1/255, rxload 1/255
Encapsulation HDLC, loopback not set, keepalive set (10 sec)
Last input 00:00:04, output 00:00:00, output hang never
Last clearing of "show interface" counters never
Input queue: 0/75/0 (size/max/drops); Total output drops: 0
Queuing strategy: priority-list 1
Output queue (queue priority: size/max/drops):
high: 0/20/0, medium: 0/40/0, normal 0/60/0, low 0/80/0
5 minute input rate 0 bits/sec, 0 packets/sec
5 minute output rate 0 bits/sec, 0 packets/sec
937 packets input, 84028 bytes, 0 no buffer
Received 937 broadcasts, 0 runts, 0 giants, 0 throttles
1 input errors, 0 CRC, 1 frame, 0 overrun, 0 ignored, 0 abor
820 packets output, 51295 bytes, 0 underruns
0 output errors, 0 collisions, 15 interface resets
0 output buffer failures, 0 output buffers swapped out
0 carrier transitions
DCD=up DSR=up DTR=up RTS=up CTS=up
Router1#
```

This command also shows the present state of the queues as well as the maximum size and tail drops for each queue. Next, you can verify the configuration of the priority lists using the command *show queuing priority*:

```
Router1#show queuing priority
Current priority queue configuration:
List Queue Args
1 low default
1 medium interface Serial0/0
```

```
1 high protocol appletalk
1 normal protocol ip
2 low default
2 normal interface Ethernet0/0
2 high protocol ip tcp port telnet
2 medium protocol ip gt 1000
2 high protocol ip list 101
Router1#
```

This command shows the queuing process alphanumerically, then it shows the unique characteristics of the queuing policy alphanumerically, not the way it will be processed. To see how it will be processed, you have to look at the configuration file.

Configuring Weighted Fair Queuing

Configuring WFQ is fairly simple. It involves applying the WFQ configuration commands at the interface level. Keep in mind that WFQ is enabled by default on links of E1 speeds (2.048Mbps) or less. These configurations will not show up in the router's configuration when the *show running-config* command is issued, but they are visible through the *show interface* command. You might want to modify these default configurations.

Enabling Weighted Fair Queuing

The interface command *fair-queue* is used to configure the WFQ process on an interface. The optional parameters are congestive discard threshold, the maximum number of dynamic conversation queues, and the maximum number of RSVP reservable queues. The number of conversation queues must be a power of 2 (16, 32, 64, 128, 256, 512, 1024); otherwise, the IOS will refuse the command. The following code configures serial interface 0/0 with a congestive discard threshold of 512 bytes, a maximum of 1024 dynamic conversation queues, and 10 reservable queues for RSVP:

```
Router1#configure terminal
    \\Enter configuration commands, one per line.  End with CNTL/Z.
Router1(config)#interface serial 0/0
Router1(config-if)#fair-queue 512 1048 10
    \\Number of dynamic queues must be a power of 2 (16, 32, 64, 128,
        256, 512, 1024)
Router1(config-if)#fair-queue 512 1024 10
```

```
Router1(config-if)#end
Router1#
```

Verifying Weighted Fair Queuing

As with the other queuing processes discussed, the first step in verifying the operation of WFQ is to use the *show interface* command to see if the queuing process is in operation on that interface:

```
Router1#show interface serial 0/0
Serial0/0 is up, line protocol is up
Hardware is PowerQUICC Serial
Internet address is 192.168.10.1/24
MTU 1500 bytes, BW 1544 Kbit, DLY 20000 usec,
reliability 255/255, txload 1/255, rxload 1/255
Encapsulation HDLC, loopback not set, keepalive set (10 sec)
Last input 00:00:01, output 00:00:00, output hang never
Last clearing of "show interface" counters never
Input queue: 0/75/0 (size/max/drops); Total output drops: 0
Queuing strategy: weighted fair
Output queue: 0/1000/512/0 (size/max total/threshold/drops)
Conversations 0/1/1024 (active/max active/max total)
Reserved Conversations 0/0 (allocated/max allocated)
5 minute input rate 0 bits/sec, 0 packets/sec
5 minute output rate 0 bits/sec, 0 packets/sec
341 packets input, 30537 bytes, 0 no buffer
Received 341 broadcasts, 0 runts, 0 giants, 0 throttles
4 input errors, 0 CRC, 4 frame, 0 overrun, 0 ignored, 0 abor
298 packets output, 18667 bytes, 0 underruns
0 output errors, 0 collisions, 16 interface resets
0 output buffer failures, 0 output buffers swapped out
2 carrier transitions
DCD=up DSR=up DTR=up RTS=up CTS=up
Router1#
```

The command indicates that WFQ is in operation on this interface. It also shows the status of the WFQ process when the command was issued. In this example, 0 packets were in the output queue. The queue itself has a maximum size of 1000 packets, and WFQ starts the congestive discard process as the queue reaches a depth of 512 packets. There have been 0 tail drops so far. We can also see the state of the conversations. Of a total maximum of 1024 conversations, 0 conversations are currently active. In addition, 0 of 10 RSVP reservable queues are in operation. The *show interface* command properly reflects the configuration we applied to the interface. We can also use the command *show queuing fair* to display the configuration of the WFQ process:

```
Router1#show queuing fair
Current fair queue configuration:
Interface Discard Dynamic Reserved
threshold queue count queue count
BRI0/0 64 256 0
BRI0/0:1 64 256 0
BRI0/0:2 64 256 0
Serial0/0 512 1024 10
Serial0/1 64 256 0
Router1#
```

We can see that the router has properly configured the WFQ process on interface serial 0/0 with the nondefault values we entered.

Configuring Class-Based Weighted Fair Queuing

Before attempting to configure CBWFQ, you first have to determine how many classes you need in order to categorize all your traffic. You also need to know the criteria you are going to use to map traffic into those classes and the bandwidth guarantees you will give to each class. If you have already classified your traffic at the edge of the network, IP precedence might be the only criterion you need. If you are configuring a more modest, point-to-point implementation of CBWFQ, you will probably use extended ACLs to categorize incoming traffic into classes. There are three major steps in configuring CBWFQ:

1. Define class maps.
2. Create policy maps.
3. Attach policies to interfaces.

Class maps determine the traffic that goes into each class and can be used in one or more policy maps. Policy maps determine the way that traffic is handled. But no QoS is delivered until the policy map is applied to the interfaces. Let's see how this is done.

Defining Class Maps

The use of the *class-map* configuration command allows you to determine how traffic should be classified. The configured class must have a name that you can reference later. Within the class map, you set your match criteria. Consider this example:

```
router1#config t
     \\Enter configuration commands, one per line. End with CNTL/Z.
router1(config)#class-map Gold
router1(config-cmap)#match access-group name Gold
```

In this example, we created a class map with the name Gold. This could be a premium service offered to applications that guarantees a certain bandwidth. Furthermore, while in the *class-map (config-cmap)* command mode, we entered a match criterion—namely, the ACL named Gold. Thus, all traffic that matches the ACL will be part of the Gold class map. We have used the same name, Gold, for both the class map and the ACL name for consistency. It is necessary to configure the ACLs if you want the class maps to use them. In this case, the ACL might be configured like this:

```
router1(config)#ip access-list extended Gold
router1(config-ext-nacl)#permit ip any any precedence flash-override
```

An extended ACL is used so we can specify a match for any IP packet with a precedence of 4 (the fourth level of precedence is traditionally given the name *flash-override*). Table 6.5 lists the available IP precedence levels and their associated names.

Table 6.5 IP Precedence Levels

IP Precedence	Name
0	Routine
1	Priority
2	Immediate
3	Flash
4	Flash-Override
5	Critical
6	Internet
7	Network

If you have a topology where packets are not marked at the edge of the network with IP precedence, you would use an ACL that classifies traffic based on criteria like protocol and port number. If you are not already familiar with ACLs, you should take some time to learn more about them. They are used frequently in many Cisco router features and are essential if you want fine control over the kinds of traffic that end up in your QoS classes. Now that the Gold class has been configured, we can configure more class maps the same way:

```
router1(config)#class-map Silver
router1(config-cmap)#match access-group name Silver
router1(config-cmap)#class-map Bronze
router1(config-cmap)#match access-group name Bronze
```

The extended access lists would be defined as follows:

```
router1(config-ext-nacl)#ip access-list extended Silver
router1(config-ext-nacl)#permit ip any any precedence flash
router1(config)#ip access-list extended Bronze
router1(config-ext-nacl)#permit ip any any precedence immediate
```

This gives us three classes, Gold, Bronze, and Silver, mapped to the IP precedence levels 4, 3, and 2, respectively.

Creating Policies

Now that we have defined class maps, we can continue to the second step to create the policy maps that specify the QoS the classes will ultimately have. Let's configure the policy for the Gold class we configured in the previous example:

```
router1(config)#policy-map PPP-T1
router1(config-pmap)#class Gold
router1(config-pmap-c)#bandwidth 216
```

We have given the name PPP-T1 to the policy map. You should use a descriptive name, such as one that describes the kind of circuit bandwidth it was meant to run on. This leads us into the policy map command context (*config-pmap*). We now enter the class that we want to specify parameters for, in this case, Gold. Under this new context (*config-pmap-c*), we specify the bandwidth reserved for this class in Kbps. You can enter the following commands to configure the QoS the class will be given:

- **bandwidth** Bandwidth (in Kbps, in percent or remaining percent)
- **queue-limit** Maximum queue threshold for tail drop
- **random-detect** Enable WRED as drop policy

The bandwidth is the rate guaranteed to this class in Kbps. By default, the sum of all bandwidth rates for a policy cannot exceed 75 percent of the interface's total bandwidth. This leaves room for Layer 2 keepalives, routing updates, and so on. You should carefully decide the amount of bandwidth required for each class, based on your needs and the needs of the traffic being assigned. Remember that since the bandwidth you give to a class is measured at the interface, it must be large enough to accommodate Layer 2 overhead. The last two configurable parameters, *queue-limit* and *random-detect*, specify the drop policy for the class. By default, the drop policy is tail drop with a queue limit of 64 for that class. You may use the *queue-limit* command to change it to a value between 1 and 64. A shorter queue drops packets more quickly in times of congestion. WRED can be configured with the *random-detect* command. Additionally, the *random-detect exponential-weighting-constant* command can be used to adjust how adaptive WRED is to bursts of traffic. See the discussion on WRED in a later section in this chapter for configuration specifics.

Unclassified traffic—that is, traffic that is not matched into any of the user-defined classes—is put into a special class called *class-default*. This class does not appear explicitly in the router configuration unless you configure it. By default, unclassified traffic will be flow-classified and queued by WFQ. However, if you configure this class specifically, you can give it a bandwidth guarantee, too. Let's configure the default class:

```
router1(config)#policy-map PPP-T1
router1(config-pmap)#class class-default
router1(config-pmap-c)#bandwidth 31
```

Instead of being fair-queued, the default class, consisting of unclassified traffic, will now be guaranteed at least 31Kbps of bandwidth. We can thus configure the policy map (PPP-T1) with the other classes we are interested in so that the entire policy looks as follows in the router's configuration:

```
class-map Gold
match access-group Gold
class-map Bronze
match access-group Bronze
class-map Silver
match access-group Silver
!
policy-map PPP-T1
```

```
class Gold
bandwidth 216
class Silver
bandwidth 169
class Bronze
bandwidth 108
class class-default
bandwidth 31
!
. . .
!
ip access-list extended Gold
permit ip any any precedence flash-override
ip access-list extended Bronze
permit ip any any precedence immediate
ip access-list extended Silver
permit ip any any precedence flash
```

Attaching Policies to Interfaces

The final step required to enable CBWFQ is to attach the service policy to an interface:

router1(config)#**interface serial 0/0**

router1(config-if)#**service-policy output PPP-T1**

After a service policy is defined, it can be enabled on multiple interfaces, assuming that the interface has enough bandwidth to support all the guarantees. In contrast, only one policy can be attached to a single interface in a given direction (input/output). The preceding three-step approach to enabling CBWFQ is a demonstration of Cisco's Modular QoS Command Line Interface. It is this modular approach that allows you not only to modify policies without disturbing interfaces and to attach policies to multiple interfaces but also to copy a policy to like routers, thereby making networkwide configuration of QoS easier.

Verifying CBWFQ

The first step in ensuring that your policies are configured correctly is to look at the configuration with the *show running-config* command. After that, you can view a particular policy with the *show policy-map* command:

```
router1#show policy-map
Policy Map PPP-T1
Weighted Fair Queuing
Class Gold
Bandwidth 216 (kbps) Max Thresh 64 (packets)
Class Silver
Bandwidth 169 (kbps) Max Thresh 64 (packets)
Class Bronze
Bandwidth 108 (kbps) Max Thresh 64 (packets)
Class class-default
Bandwidth 31 (kbps) Max Thresh 64 (packets)
```

This shows the configured bandwidth for each class within the policy and the maximum threshold for the queue before tail drop is enacted. If you have multiple policies configured, you can specify the name of the policy with the same command *show policy-map policy-map-name* and even the specific class within the policy:

```
router1#show policy-map PPP-T1 class Gold
Class Gold
Bandwidth 216 (kbps) Max Thresh 64 (packets)
```

To view the statistics of how the policy has been functioning on the interface, use the *show policy-map interface* command:

```
router1#show policy-map interface serial 0/0
Serial0/0 output : PPP-T1
Weighted Fair Queuing
Class Gold
Output Queue: Conversation 265
Bandwidth 216 (kbps) Packets Matched 248318 Max Threshold 64
(packets)
(discards/tail drops) 95418/84680
Class Silver
Output Queue: Conversation 266
```

```
Bandwidth 169 (kbps) Packets Matched 248305 Max Threshold 64
(packets)
(discards/tail drops) 119558/109829
Class Bronze
Output Queue: Conversation 267
Bandwidth 108 (kbps) Packets Matched 248292 Max Threshold 64
(packets)
(discards/tail drops) 156598/148956
Class class-default
Output Queue: Conversation 268
Bandwidth 31 (kbps) Packets Matched 428362 Max Threshold 64
(packets)
(discards/tail drops) 234720/222514
```

You can use this command to see your class composition with respect to the number of packets matched into the classes and the effect of tail drop (or WRED) on each class. You can always see the overall performance of the interface to which the policy is applied by using the *show interface* or *show queue* command:

```
router1#show queue serial 0/0
Input queue: 0/75/0 (size/max/drops); Total output drops: 778978
Queuing strategy: weighted fair
Output queue: 0/1000/64/778978 (size/max total/threshold/drops)
Conversations 0/4/256 (active/max active/max total)
Reserved Conversations 4/4 (allocated/max allocated)
```

This shows the current state of the input and output queues, including current size, maximum size, and number of drops. It also shows the specifics of WFQ. As usual, the total number of conversations is 256. However, note that four reserved conversations correspond to the four classes (including the default class) configured on the interface by the policy.

Configuring Packet Classification

Packet classification can be performed in a variety of manners. The two methods that we focus on here are IP precedence and policy-based routing (PBR). Each of these methods can be implemented individually, but they can also be mixed such that your policy can set the IP precedence for a packet.

IP Precedence

IP precedence in a VoIP implementation is often configured on individual dial peers. When performing this configuration, you can either set the precedence bits for all dial peers to be high priority—a six or seven—and leave all other traffic at zero or one, or you can choose to specify a different precedence for each dial peer based on the importance of the communications on that port. Valid values for IP precedence are from zero (best effort) to seven (highest priority). See the section "Defining Class Maps" under CBWFQ for a complete list of IP precedence values. Actual configuration of IP precedence is very simple and can be done either from a dial peer, a Frame Relay port, or as part of a policy map:

```
Router1(config-dial-peer)#ip precedence precedence
```

For instance, to configure a dial peer to assign a precedence of six, enter the following in Global Configuration mode:

```
Router1(config)#dial-peer voice 1 voip
Router1(config-dial-peer)#ip precedence 6
```

Verifying IP Precedence

Use *show* commands to verify IP precedence configuration. Sample output is shown here:

```
!
dial-peer voice 1 voip
  destination pattern 1234
  ip precedence 4
  session target ras
!
dial-peer voice 2 pots
  destination pattern 1001
  ip precedence 3
  port 0/0/0
!
dial-peer voice 3 pots
  destination pattern 1002
  ip precedence 2
  port 0/0/1
!
```

Policy Routing

PBR is fairly simple to configure. Begin by creating an ACL for the traffic that is to be classified. Next, create *route-map* statements that act on the ACLs. A route map that specifies *permit* applies the policy to any packet that matches the ACL, and all others will be routed normally. A *deny* route map does just the opposite, routing the packets that match and applying the policy to those that do not. Each *route-map* statement must also have a sequence number, and the router will apply the statements in order to each packet and classify the packet based on the first statement it matches. Following the *match* statements are *set* statements, which tell the router what policy to apply to the packet. *Set* statements can be used in conjunction with each other, so it is possible to send a matching packet to a particular interface and also set the precedence. After the *route-map* statements are complete, apply the route map to an interface with the *ip policy route-map* command.

Command context:

```
route-map map-name [permit | deny] sequence-number
match length min max
match ip address [access-list-number | name]
set ip precedence [number | name]
set ip next-hop ip-address
set interface interface-type interface-number
set ip default next-hop ip-address
set default interface interface-type interface-number
interface interface-type interface-number
ip policy route-map map-name
```

Verifying Policy Routing

Use *show* commands to verify your configuration. For instance, the following configuration assigns an IP precedence of 5 to all H.323 packets and sends them out interface Serial 0/1:

```
!
interface vlan 1
    ip address 10.10.10.1 255.255.255.0
    ip policy route-map voip
```

```
!
route-map voip permit 10
match ip address 101
set ip precedence 5
set interface s0/1
!
access list 101 permit tcp any any eq 1300
!
```

Configuring RSVP

RSVP is enabled on individual interfaces within the network with the *ip rsvp bandwidth* command. While in Interface Configuration mode, specify the bandwidth of the link. Then enter the *ip rsvp bandwidth* command to specify the total amount of bandwidth available to RSVP and the maximum speed of any individual reservation.

For instance:

```
Router1 (config)#interface s1/0
Router1 (config-if)#bandwidth 1536
Router1 (config-if)#ip rsvp bandwidth 1152 128
```

In this example, interface Serial 1/0 is configured for 1536kbps. RSVP is then configured to reserve a maximum of 1152kbps, and no individual connection will be allocated more than 128kbps. Remember that only 75 percent of the total link speed can be used for RSVP:

```
interface interface-type interface-number
bandwidth bandwidth
ip rsvp bandwidth available-bandwidth max-bandwidth
```

Verifying RSVP

You can confirm that your RSVP configuration is entered properly with the *show run* command, but there are other commands that you will find useful to monitor the status of RSVP. With the *show ip rsvp installed* command, all the current reservations can be displayed for each interface:

```
Router1#show ip rsvp installed
RSVP: Ethernet2/0 has no installed reservations
RSVP: Serial5/0:0
```

```
BPS To From Protoc DPort Sport Weight Conversation
128K 10.0.1.2 10.0.6.2 TCP 0 0 6 271
64K 10.0.1.3 10.0.6.3 TCP 0 0 12 272
```

In this example, two reservations are going out Serial5/0:0 from the senders 10.0.1.2 and 10.0.1.3 to the receivers 10.0.6.2 and 10.0.6.3. The first reservation is for 128Kbps, and the second is for 64Kbps. The weight listed is the weighting factor used by WFQ. The conversation is the number assigned to that flow. Since the session flow is toward Client B from Client A, and because WFQ and WRED work on output interfaces, there is no reservation on the Ethernet 2/0, even though the session is flowing *into* the router through this interface. To see interface-specific information, such as how much total bandwidth has been set aside for RSVP (i/f max) and the amount currently being used (allocated), issue the *show ip rsvp interface* command:

```
Router1#show ip rsvp interface
interface allocated i/f max flow max pct UDP IP UDP_IP UDP M/C
Et2/0 0M 7500K 7500K 0 0 2 0 0
Se5/0:0 192K 1152K 1152K 16 0 1 0 0
```

Sometimes it is helpful to see all neighboring nodes that are participating in RSVP. To do this, use the *show ip rsvp neighbor* command:

```
Router1#show ip rsvp neighbor
Interface Neighbor Encapsulation
Et2/0 10.0.6.3 RSVP
Et2/0 10.0.6.2 RSVP
Se5/0:0 10.0.101.5 RSVP
```

This tells us that there are two RSVP neighbors out the Ethernet 2/0 interface and another one out the Se5/0:0 interface. These neighbors can be any nodes that are currently using RSVP. They could be end stations (10.0.6.3 and 10.0.6.2) or RSVP-participating router interfaces (10.0.101.5). To display RSVP information such as requests flowing upstream and receiver and sender information currently in the database, use the following commands, respectively:

```
Router1#show ip rsvp request
To From Pro DPort Sport Next Hop I/F Fi Serv BPS Bytes
10.0.1.2 10.0.6.2 TCP 0 0 10.0.6.2 Et2/0 FF LOAD 128K 64K
10.0.1.3 10.0.6.3 TCP 0 0 10.0.6.3 Et2/0 FF RATE 64K 1K
Router1#show ip rsvp reservation
```

```
To From Pro DPort Sport Next Hop I/F Fi Serv BPS Bytes
10.0.1.2 10.0.6.2 TCP 0 0 10.0.101.5 Se5/0 FF LOAD 128K 64K
10.0.1.3 10.0.6.3 TCP 0 0 10.0.101.5 Se5/0 FF RATE 64K 1K
Router1#show ip rsvp sender
To From Pro DPort Sport Prev Hop I/F BPS Bytes
10.0.1.2 10.0.6.2 TCP 0 0 10.0.6.2 Et2/0 128K 1K
10.0.1.3 10.0.6.3 TCP 0 0 10.0.6.3 Et2/0 64K 1K
```

The *request* and *reservation show* commands also indicate the type of service desired, either controlled-load (LOAD) or guaranteed-rate (RATE).

Call Admission Control

RSVP was covered in the previous section, so this section focuses on the configuration of H.323 gateway zone bandwidth for CAC. From Gatekeeper Configuration mode, enter the *bandwidth* command. To configure a specific bandwidth from the current zone to another zone, use the *interzone* parameter. The *total* parameter is used to specify the total bandwidth available within the current zone, and the *session* parameter specifies a maximum bandwidth for an individual call. Bandwidth is entered in Kbps, and valid values are 1 to 10,000,000Kbps for interzone or total configurations and 1 to 5000Kbps for session configurations.

In Figure 6.10, there are three routers, each with two POTS lines, arranged into two zones, plus a gatekeeper.

Figure 6.10 Call Admission Control

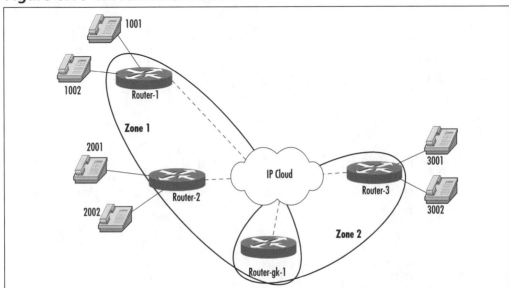

The necessary configuration commands are highlighted in the following output:

```
hostname Router-1
!
interface ethernet 1/0
   ip address 10.10.10.101 255.25.255.0
   h323-gateway voip interface
   h323-gateway voip id zone1 ipaddr 10.10.10.104
   h323-gateway voip h323-id gw_1
   h323-gateway voip bind srcarrd 10.10.10.101
!
voice-port 0/0/0
!
voice-port 0/0/1
!
!
dial-peer voice 1 voip
   destination pattern ….
   session target ras
!
dial-peer voice 2 pots
   destination pattern 1001
   port 0/0/0
!
dial-peer voice 3 pots
   destination pattern 1002
   port 0/0/1
!
gateway
```

Verifying Call Admission Control

Verification of your CAC configuration can be done with simple *show* commands, as shown here:

```
hostname Router-2
!
interface ethernet 1/0
```

```
  ip address 10.10.10.102 255.25.255.0
  h323-gateway voip interface
  h323-gateway voip id zone1 ipaddr 10.10.10.104
  h323-gateway voip h323-id gw_2
  h323-gateway voip bind srcarrd 10.10.10.102
!
voice-port 0/0/0
!
voice-port 0/0/1
!
!
dial-peer voice 1 voip
  destination pattern ….
  session target ras
!
dial-peer voice 2 pots
  destination pattern 2001
  port 0/0/0
!
dial-peer voice 3 pots
  destination pattern 2002
  port 0/0/1
!
gateway


!
hostname Router-3
!
!
interface ethernet 1/0
  ip address 10.10.10.103 255.25.255.0
  h323-gateway voip interface
  h323-gateway voip id zone2 ipaddr 10.10.10.104
  h323-gateway voip h323-id gw_3
  h323-gateway voip bind srcarrd 10.10.10.103
!
```

```
voice-port 0/0/0
!
voice-port 0/0/1
!
!
dial-peer voice 1 voip
  destination pattern ….
  session target ras
!
dial-peer voice 2 pots
  destination pattern 3001
  port 0/0/0
!
dial-peer voice 3 pots
  destination pattern 3002
  port 0/0/1
!
gateway

!
hostname Router-gk-1
!
interface Ethernet 1/0
  ip address 10.10.10.104 255.255.255.0
!
gatekeeper
  zone local zone1
  zone local zone2
  zone prefix zone1 1… gw-priority 10 gw_1
  zone prefix zone1 2… gw-priority 10 gw_2
  zone prefix zone2 3… gw-priority 10 gw_3
  bandwidth interzone zone1 64
  bandwidth total zone zone1 128
!
```

Notice that bandwidth is limited to 64Kbps for Zone 1 for interzone calls and 128Kbps total bandwidth. Because the gatekeeper assumes 64Kbps per call, this limits Zone 1 to a maximum of one call from outside the zone and two calls total. So, assuming that no calls are currently in progress, if a call is placed from 3001 to 1001, it will be connected. If a call is then attempted from 3002 to 2002, it will be rejected because there is already one interzone call taking place. However, a call from 1002 to 2001 would be allowed because there can be up to two simultaneous calls within Zone 1. For a graphical representation of this scenario, see Figure 6.11.

Figure 6.11 H.323 Gateway Call Flow

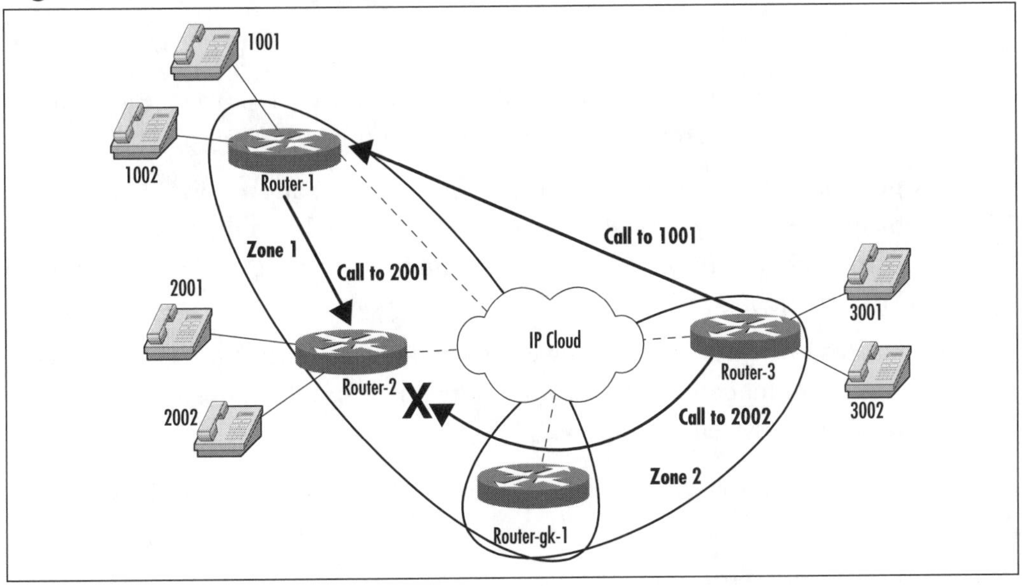

Command context:

```
bandwidth {interzone | total | session} {default | zone zone-name}
max-bandwidth
```

Configuring Priority Queuing with WFQ (IP RTP Priority)

Configure RTP on an interface by issuing the *ip rtp priority* command while in Interface Configuration mode. This command specifies a starting port number, port number range (number of ports that qualify), and total queue bandwidth. For instance, if you want to configure RTP on interface Serial 1/0 for ports 16384 through 17000, with a total bandwidth of 128kbps, the commands would be as follows:

```
!
Router1(config)#interface s1/0
Router1(config-if)#ip rtp priority 16384 616 128
```

Note that the second parameter is the range—that is, a number that, when added to the starting number, results in the highest port number that is to be used. In the preceding example, 16384 + 616 = 17000.

Context:

```
ip rtp priority starting-rtp-port-number port-number-range bandwidth
```

When configuring IP RTP priority for voice, use the following guidelines:

- **starting-rtp-port** Lower bound of UDP port. The lowest port number to which the packets are sent. For VoIP, set this value to **16384**.

- **port-number-range** The range of UDP destination ports. A number that, added to the *starting-rtp-port-number*, yields the highest UDP port number. For VoIP, set this value to **16383** because the upper port for VoIP traffic is 32767 (32767 − 16384 = 16383).

- **bandwidth** Maximum allowed bandwidth (kbps) in the priority queue. Set this number according to the number of simultaneous calls you require the system to support.

The following sample configuration enables IP RTP priority to 720Kbps for VoIP on a serial interface:

```
Router1(config)#interface Serial0/0
Router1(config-if)#ip rtp priority 16384 16383 720
```

Note that if the interface being configured for IP RTP priority is greater than 2Mbps, you need to enable WFQ with the *fair-queue* Interface Configuration command.

Verifying Priority Queuing with WFQ

Verify your IP RTP priority configuration by displaying the interface with the *show* command. Sample output for a serial interface configured as described previously is as follows:

```
!
interface Serial0/1
 bandwidth 64
 ip address 10.10.10.101 255.255.255.252
```

```
no ip directed-broadcast
ip rtp priority 16384 16383 720
!
```

Configuring Traffic Shaping

FRTS and GTS use similar methods for maintaining traffic rates while buffering bursty traffic. The parameters for each function in the same way, but they use different terminology. See Table 6.6 for a description of parameters.

Table 6.6 Traffic-Shaping Terminology

FRTS Term	GTS Term	Definition
CIR	Bit rate	Committed information rate; the average rate of traffic to be sent out the interface.
Bc	Burst size	Committed burst; number of bits to be transmitted over a specific time period (Tc).
Be	Excess burst size	Excess burst; number of bits that can be transmitted during the first interval of transmission after a period of no transmission.
Mincir	N/A	Minimum transmission rate during periods of congestion.
Tc	Tc	Time interval that is equal to Bc/CIR.

Traffic shaping is configured from Interface Configuration mode with the *traffic-shape rate* command for GTS or the *frame-relay traffic-shaping* command for Frame Relay interfaces. When traffic shaping is applied to an interface, it reverts to fast switching. All parameters are input in bits per second. Tc cannot be configured but rather is calculated internally and can be no larger than 125ms. Therefore, Bc can be no more than one-eighth of CIR. The smaller the value for Tc, the less tolerant the interface will be of bursts in traffic and the closer the service will become to a CBR-type offering. If Be is not entered, it defaults to the same value as was entered for Bc. For Frame Relay interfaces, adaptive traffic shaping can also be configured. In Adaptive mode, the interface will respond to BECN signals by reducing its transmission rate.

For instance, to configure interface Serial 1/0 with a CIR of 128kbps with a committed burst of 16kbps and ensure that the transmission rate never drops below 32kbps:

```
!
Router1 (config)# interface s1/0
Router1 (config-if)# traffic-shape rate 128000 16000
Router1 (config-if)# traffic-shape adaptive 32000
```

Context:

```
traffic-shape rate CIR [Bc [Be]]
traffic-shape adaptive mincir
```

Configuration of a Frame Relay interface is very similar to the previous example, with a few differences. Using the same parameters as described earlier, use the following commands to configure Frame Relay traffic shaping:

```
!
Router1 (config)#interface s1/0
Router1 (config-if)#encapsulation frame-relay
Router1 (config-if)#frame-relay traffic-shaping
Router1 (config)#interface s1/0.100 point-to-point
Router1 (config-if)#ip address 10.10.10.101 255.255.255.252
Router1 (config-if)#frame-relay traffic-rate 128000 144000
Router1 (config-if)#frame-relay adaptive-shaping becn
Router1 (config-if)#frame-relay mincir 32000
Router1 (config-if)#frame-relay interface-dlci 100
```

Context:

```
frame-relay traffic-rate CIR [peak]
frame-relay adaptive-shaping {becn | foresight}
frame-relay mincir mincir
```

It is important to note that the optional peak value in the *frame-relay traffic-rate* command is the highest possible rate and is equal to Cir + Bc. So, for our example, the CIR is 128k, and the Bc is 16k, so the *peak* is 128 + 16, or 144k. Adaptive shaping can be configured to respond to either BECN or to foresight, if the interface will be connected to a Cisco StrataCom device using foresight traffic shaping.

Verifying Traffic Shaping

You can use basic *show* commands to verify the configuration of FRTS on an interface. The following is a fragment of a FRTS configuration for a serial port with a CIR of 128Kbps and a committed burst of 32Kbps:

```
interface Serial1/0
no ip address
no ip directed-broadcast
encapsulation frame-relay
no ip mroute-cache
no fair-queue
service-module t1 timeslots 1-4
frame-relay traffic-shaping
!
interface Serial1/0.100 point-to-point
ip address 10.10.10.100 255.255.255.252
no ip directed-broadcast
frame-relay traffic-rate 128000 144000
frame-relay adaptive-shaping becn
frame-relay mincir 32000
frame-relay interface-dlci 100
!
```

Configuring Congestion Avoidance with WRED

To configure WRED, issue the *random-detect* command in Interface Configuration mode. This command enables WRED with its default configuration, which is normally sufficient. However, the parameters used by WRED can be altered if necessary. The WRED algorithm uses the average queue depth to determine the probability of packet drops. The weighting factor of this average can be reconfigured from its default of 9, although Cisco does not recommend doing so. A higher number makes the queue less sensitive to changes in speed, whereas a lower number makes it more sensitive. Note that a too-high number can make the algorithm react too slowly to congestion situations, whereas a too-low number can cause unnecessary packet drops.

Another configurable aspect is the weighting of each IP precedence level. Minimum threshold, maximum threshold, and the mark probability denominator for each precedence level can be reconfigured with the *random-detect precedence* command. Table 6.7 shows the default configuration. As described earlier in this chapter, packets begin to be dropped at the minimum threshold, and above the maximum threshold all packets are dropped. The mark probability denominator (MPD) is the fraction of packets that will be dropped below the maximum threshold (1/MPD).

Table 6.7 Default Values for WRED Parameters

IP Precedence	Minimum Threshold	Maximum Threshold	MPD
0	20	40	10
1	22	40	10
2	24	40	10
3	26	40	10
4	28	40	10
5	31	40	10
6	33	40	10
7	35	40	10
RSVP	37	40	10

All WRED configuration commands are performed in Interface Configuration mode. The context of the commands is as follows:

```
random-detect
random-detect precedence precedence min-threshold max-threshold
    mark-prob-denominator
random-detect exponential-weighting-constant weighting-factor
```

Verifying WRED

After enabling WRED, check the configured parameters and the number of drops per class (IP precedence) using the *show queuing random-detect* command:

```
router1#show queuing random-detect
Current random-detect configuration:
Serial5/0:0
Queuing strategy: random early detection (WRED)
Exp-weight-constant: 9 (1/512)
```

```
Mean queue depth: 0
Class Random drop Tail drop Minimum Maximum Mark
pkts/bytes pkts/bytes threshold threshold probability
0  4914/560382  18964/2161896  20  40  1/10
1  4786/545604  18834/2147076  22  40  1/10
2  4705/536370  18853/2149242  24  40  1/10
3  4700/535800  18938/2158932  26  40  1/10
4  4612/525768  18830/2146620  28  40  1/10
5  4543/517902  18857/2149698  31  40  1/10
6  4494/512282  18928/2157622  33  40  1/10
7  4380/499320  18851/2149014  35  40  1/10
rsvp 0/0 0/0 37 40 1/10
```

This provides good information on the kind of traffic, with respect to IP precedence (or *class*), is flowing through the router and the kind of drop treatment it is getting—random drop or tail drop. We can see from this output that each IP precedence level (0 to 7) dropped approximately the same number of packets. For congestion notification responsive flows such as TCP traffic, you should not see a lot of tail drop. Tail drop occurs when the upper threshold has been exceeded. When this occurs, packets are dropped wholesale. In this example, there is a high amount of tail drop because the traffic was created with a packet generator that did not throttle down when packets were dropped.

Configuring Link Fragmentation and Interleaving

In order to apply LFI to an interface, multilink PPP must first be configured on that interface. This protocol is usually used to bundle multiple PPP-encapsulated circuits, but it can also be used on a single link in order to facilitate LFI. In order to accomplish this goal, a multilink interface must be created, then attached to a parent serial interface. To configure multilink PPP, create a multilink interface from Global Configuration mode. Next, apply an IP address to the new interface, activate interleaving, and turn on WFQ. For example, to create a multilink interface named Multilink 1:

```
router1(config)#interface Multilink 1
router1(config-if)#ip address 10.10.10.101 255.255.255.252
router1(config-if)#ppp multilink interleave
router1(config-if)#fair-queue
```

Keep in mind that when the multilink interface is bound to the serial interface, the assigned IP address becomes the address of the serial link. Therefore, in order to avoid an addressing conflict, the IP address of the serial link should be removed prior to configuring the multilink interface. Activation of the interleaving feature with the *ppp multilink interleave* and *fair-queue* commands is crucial; otherwise, the fragmented packets would not be interleaved with other packets, and there would be no benefit to the fragmentation process.

Additionally, fragmentation delay can be configured in order to specify a maximum serialization delay, which defaults to 30ms. A delay of 10 to 20ms is desirable for VoIP implementations. The command for this configuration is performed in Interface Configuration mode:

```
router1(config-if)#ppp multilink fragment-delay 20
```

The final step is to attach the multilink interface to the parent serial interface:

```
router1(config)#interface s1/0
router1(config-if)#ppp multilink
router1(config-if)#multilink-group 1
```

Verifying Link Fragmentation and Interleaving

After configuring PPP multilink, view the status using the *show ppp multilink* command:

```
router1#show ppp multilink
Multilink1, bundle name is router2
0 lost fragments, 0 reordered, 0 unassigned, sequence 0x2BF/0x524
rcvd/sent
0 discarded, 0 lost received, 1/255 load
Member links: 1 active, 0 inactive (max not set, min not set)
Serial0/0 1920 weight
```

Even though we are using only one serial interface, multilink still shows as a bundle, with the bundle name being the host name of the far router. If there are any problems with multilink encapsulation, you will see it manifested here as fragments or reordered, unassigned, discarded, or lost packets. In addition, since we now have the multilink interface as a virtual interface, we can display the interface statistics with the *show interfaces* command:

```
router1#show interfaces multilink 1
Multilink1 is up, line protocol is up
```

```
Hardware is multilink group interface
Internet address is 10.0.101.10/30
MTU 1500 bytes, BW 1536 Kbit, DLY 100000 usec,
reliability 255/255, txload 43/255, rxload 1/255
Encapsulation PPP, loopback not set
Keepalive set (10 sec)
DTR is pulsed for 2 seconds on reset
LCP Open, multilink Open
Open: IPCP, CDPCP
Last input 00:00:00, output never, output hang never
Last clearing of "show interface" counters 5d21h
Input queue: 2/75/0 (size/max/drops); Total output drops: 0
Queuing strategy: weighted fair
Output queue: 6/1000/64/0 (size/max total/threshold/drops)
Conversations 1/3/256 (active/max active/max total)
Reserved Conversations 0/0 (allocated/max allocated)
5 minute input rate 3000 bits/sec, 10 packets/sec
5 minute output rate 264000 bits/sec, 35 packets/sec
1003558 packets input, 128454537 bytes, 0 no buffer
Received 0 broadcasts, 0 runts, 0 giants, 0 throttles
0 input errors, 0 CRC, 0 frame, 0 overrun, 0 ignored, 0 abort
35573 packets output, 24346968 bytes, 0 underruns
0 output errors, 0 collisions, 0 interface resets
0 output buffer failures, 0 output buffers swapped out
0 carrier transitions
```

Summary

As we have discussed, QoS is an integral part of deploying a VoIP solution. Unfortunately, there is no silver bullet as far as deciding which method is best. Each QoS solution has its advantages and disadvantages and needs to be evaluated for each network. Every network scenario is different, so there really can't be a one-size-fits-all solution to deploying QoS. A network with lots of available bandwidth utilizing low-bandwidth codecs has very different requirements from an implementation with lower-bandwidth WAN links and PCM voice. In order to successfully implement a solution, you must address several key factors:

- What call quality do you expect, and what quality are you willing to accept?

- How much bandwidth is required per call?

- How many calls can be expected?

- How big are the WAN links?

- What other applications are running, and what are their priorities within your business?

Once you have answered these questions, you can decide on the types of QoS practices that can best benefit your particular situation and develop an overall QoS solution. Keep in mind that many different methods can be used within a network or on an individual interface. It is not at all uncommon to see an interface configured with PBR, CBWFQ, and IP precedence.

The key to a successful QoS implementation to improve or enable VoIP lies both in initial planning and on continual monitoring. You now know the steps necessary to activate many different QoS techniques on your network. In order to make the most of that knowledge, invest the time up front to identify your needs, then assess all the possibilities that Cisco QoS offers. Once you have implemented the solution, keep watching, and keep testing the network. Make adjustments to your policies, queue depths, precedences, and the like in order to optimize your network to fill your particular business need.

Solutions Fast Track

QoS Overview

☑ QoS is a set of tools available on Cisco routers to allow administrators to guarantee service levels to various traffic types.

☑ QoS has three levels: best effort (no guarantees), integrated services (end-to-end service level guarantee), and differentiated service (packet classification and priority).

☑ Multiple QoS techniques can be implemented within a network, within a router, or even on a single interface; they are not mutually exclusive.

Available QoS Options

☑ Several queuing strategies are available for QoS, including WFQ, CBWFQ, LLQ, priority queuing, and custom queuing.

☑ Packet classification can be implemented easily throughout the network to provide priority to voice traffic. Examples of packet classification include policy-based routing and IP precedence.

☑ CAC and RSVP are useful for both providing guaranteed bandwidth to individual voice connections as well as protecting other data from being crushed by voice traffic.

☑ Techniques such as cRTP and LFI can be useful in managing low-bandwidth WAN links to reduce overhead and improve serialization delay on time-sensitive traffic.

VoIP QoS Configuration Examples

☑ RSVP is an end-to-end bandwidth reservation mechanism, so make sure that it has been configured all the way through the network. In addition, keep in mind that only 75 percent of a link's bandwidth can be reserved by RSVP.

☑ Don't make your QoS implementation any more difficult than it needs to be. Unless you have circumstances that require a change, try to stick with default values wherever possible.

☑ When configuring QoS on Frame Relay connections, be sure that your service provider supports your configuration and that its CIR, burst rates, and the like match yours. Otherwise, you might not be able to get the service level you are trying to achieve.

Frequently Asked Questions

The following Frequently Asked Questions, answered by the authors of this book, are designed to both measure your understanding of the concepts presented in this chapter and to assist you with real-life implementation of these concepts. To have your questions about this chapter answered by the author, browse to **www.syngress.com/solutions** and click on the **"Ask the Author"** form.

Q: Is QoS really necessary for VoIP?

A: Only if you want your voice connections across the network to be usable. In most networks, QoS provides reduced delay and fewer dropped packets to voice traffic, making it a viable alternative to a traditional voice implementation. Electing not to configure QoS could allow your voice traffic to be impacted by other applications, rendering it useless.

Q: Do I need to pick a single QoS strategy?

A: No. Each QoS technique has certain advantages and disadvantages in each situation. The best design will likely mix various methods throughout the network to maximize the efficiency of your VoIP services.

Q: I planned my QoS strategy, but when I implemented it, VoIP didn't work. What did I do wrong?

A: This tends to be a normal phenomenon because it is extremely rare that anyone gets a QoS implementation perfect the first time out. Once you have implemented your strategy, verify how it is operating and then go back and make adjustments. Initial planning goes a long way toward getting it close on the initial implementation, but every network still needs to be fine-tuned.

Q: Which method is right for me?

A: No networking text would be complete without this answer: It depends. Because each network, business, and VoIP implementation is unique, each case must be examined individually. A solution that works wonderfully on one system could make voice communications impossible on another. Each implementation of QoS for VoIP must be evaluated on its own to establish the optimal solution for any given situation.

Chapter 7

Testing and Troubleshooting VoIP

Solutions in this chapter:

- **A Basic Troubleshooting Methodology**

- **Layer 1 Troubleshooting**

- **Layer 2 Troubleshooting**

- **Layer 3 Troubleshooting**

- **Troubleshooting Dial Plans**

- **Troubleshooting Voice Ports**

- **Troubleshooting Dial Peers**

- **Troubleshooting Signaling Errors**

☑ **Summary**

☑ **Solutions Fast Track**

☑ **Frequently Asked Questions**

Introduction

Troubleshooting VoIP can be challenging, especially if you do not structure your efforts. This chapter presents a logical and methodological approach to testing, troubleshooting, and supporting VoIP. Before you can successfully troubleshoot, you need to have a thorough understanding of the steps and commands necessary to configure VoIP. The testing and troubleshooting information contained in this chapter is by no means exhaustive; rather, it provides a framework that you can expand to fit your own VoIP troubleshooting situations.

We use the Open Systems Interconnection (OSI) model to guide our VoIP troubleshooting. We cover the OSI model in this chapter as it pertains to troubleshooting, but suffice it to say, the OSI approach starts at Layer 1 (the physical layer) and works its way up. This structured approach enables you to troubleshoot layer by layer with confidence, knowing that the previous layer is not the problem.

One of the most important tasks in any VoIP deployment is not the technology or the VoIP commands, but the planning of all aspects of VoIP: dial plans, dial peers, bandwidth reservations, and so on. Before you even log onto your first VoIP router, your configuration should more or less be built. The commands you enter should do nothing more than execute your design. You will see how this concept pertains to troubleshooting and how it can make the difference between a smooth-running, easy-to-troubleshoot VoIP configuration or a caller's nightmare.

This chapter also discusses signaling and highlights signaling issues of which you need to be aware. Entire libraries have been written on telephone signaling, ranging from simple tomes on how telephones work to massive texts on the physics of voice communications. This chapter is not as exhaustive in its coverage as the latter, but it provides a practical review of the most relevant telephony topics.

Cisco provides many tools that can be used in VoIP troubleshooting. Numerous VoIP commands can aid you in determining where the problem lies. As we'll discuss, some troubleshooting commands are not VoIP specific but can have an indirect impact on VoIP.

By the time you reach the end of this chapter, you should have the tools and techniques you need to begin troubleshooting and supporting your VoIP configuration. More important, you will have a methodology that will guide your efforts. If and when you encounter a problem in the real world, you will be prepared. The approach advocated in this chapter is logical and methodical, providing structured steps to unstructured problems. It will help you stay focused and attack the problem in such a way that no step is overlooked. This chapter can also serve as a reference for the various troubleshooting commands available.

Much of the information contained in this chapter is a review of information presented in earlier chapters. However, this chapter's material is reintroduced to reinforce and facilitate the troubleshooting information provided in other chapters.

A Basic Troubleshooting Methodology

One of the biggest pitfalls in troubleshooting any network problem, let alone VoIP, is the lack of methodology. Such a lack can cause problem isolation and resolution to take longer than they should as you sidetrack, backtrack, and repeat steps in your quest to find the solution. This does not have to be the case, as you will see.

To begin, let's review the OSI reference model, shown in Figure 7.1. This model provides a framework for developing and deploying network protocols, layer by layer. We want to stress that the OSI model itself is not a network protocol or stack such as TCP/IP or AppleTalk. It is a model for developing network protocols. Its primary mission is to guide these development efforts by providing a logical structure. Each of the seven layers governs a particular aspect of networking. For example, the network layer governs the development of routing protocols.

Figure 7.1 The OSI Reference Model

Application	Provides the user/application an interface into the network.
Presentation	Converts and restores data in a format that can be transported between network devices. Example protocols include ASCII or EBCDIC.
Session	Manages and synchronizes the sessions between devices.
Transport	Segments and reassembles data for the Session and Network layers. Establishes connections and provides flow control.
Network	Addresses and routes data on a network. IP and IPX are examples of network protocols. OSPF, EIGRP, and other routing protocols operate at this layer.
Data Link	Assembles raw data into acceptable formats for the Physical and the Network layers. 802.3 and HDLC are example protocols.
Physical	Addresses details of connecting to physical media such as 10BaseT cable or V.35 interface.

Figure 7.1 provides a succinct description of each layer of the OSI model; this description is sufficient for our purposes. For more information on the OSI model, you can visit the official ISO site: www.iso.org.

When you begin troubleshooting, you should start at Layer 1, the physical layer. Often you will find your problem cause here in the form of faulty hardware or miswired cable. Once you have ascertained to your satisfaction that Layer 1 components are not at fault, move on to the next layer, Layer 2.

Layer 2, the data link layer, is responsible for formatting and getting data to the physical layer for transport on the network and for passing data received from the physical layer to Layer 3. Layer 2 is perhaps most famous for housing the MAC (also known as hardware) address. Devices at this layer are typically bridges, switches, hubs, and so on. We discuss Layer 2 troubleshooting in greater detail later in this chapter.

Layer 3, the network layer, is concerned with addressing and routing traffic from Point A to Point B. Here you will find IP addresses and IP routing protocols, both critical to the operation of VoIP. Your primary focus at this layer is to ensure that IP addressing and routing are correct.

Once you have satisfied yourself that Layer 3 is operating as it should, you are then ready to look at your VoIP configuration and start troubleshooting it. In the scheme of things, VoIP uses all layers of the OSI model; VoIP-specific configuration resides above Layer 3 but does not neatly break out into specific layers.

Layer 1 Troubleshooting

Layer 1 is the physical layer of the OSI model. It is concerned with the transmission and reception of bits on the physical media. By that definition, all hardware in and attached to a router operates at the physical layer. This means testing and verifying physical components such as the router, its modules, cards, interfaces, and cables. Your goal in troubleshooting this layer is to eliminate physical components as the chief suspects in causing the problem.

Troubleshooting Equipment, from Powerup to Operating State

In VoIP, your primary piece of equipment is your voice router. At Layer 1, the bare minimum that your router should be able to do is power up and enable you to inventory its hardware. When you power on your router, be sure you watch its power-on self-tests (POSTs) and note any errors. After a successful powerup, log on to the router and execute the *show version* command to obtain an inventory of your router's hardware and software. The output of this command is:

```
Cisco Internetwork Operating System Software
IOS (tm) 3600 Software (C3640-IS-M), Version 12.1(2)T,   RELEASE
    SOFTWARE (fc1)

Copyright (c) 1986-2000 by cisco Systems, Inc.
Compiled Tue 16-May-00 12:47 by ccai
Image text-base: 0x600088F0, data-base: 0x6101A000

ROM: System Bootstrap, Version 11.1(20)AA2, EARLY DEPLOYMENT RELEASE
    SOFTWARE (fc1)

usa3640 uptime is 26 minutes
System returned to ROM by reload
System image file is "flash:c3640-is-mz.121-2.t.bin"

cisco 3640 (R4700) processor (revision 0x00) with 60416K/5120K bytes
    of memory.
Processor board ID 19592029
R4700 CPU at 100Mhz, Implementation 33, Rev 1.0
Bridging software.
X.25 software, Version 3.0.0.
SuperLAT software (copyright 1990 by Meridian Technology Corp).
Primary Rate ISDN software, Version 1.1.
2 Ethernet/IEEE 802.3 interface(s)
2 Serial network interface(s)
2 Channelized T1/PRI port(s)
2 Voice FXS interface(s)
2 Voice E & M interface(s)
DRAM configuration is 64 bits wide with parity disabled.
125K bytes of non-volatile configuration memory.
32768K bytes of processor board System flash (Read/Write)

Configuration register is 0x2102
```

For example, if you installed what you thought were FXO interfaces and it shows up in this listing as FXS interfaces, then either you need an IOS upgrade or your router hardware is faulty, *or* you actually installed FXS voice ports. Possible fixes include powering down the router and reseating the module, moving the module to a different slot, or considering the possibility that your version of IOS does not support the module.

Refer to Chapter 4 or check www.cisco.com for feature support and minimum feature sets required to support voice hardware on a particular router platform. As a rule of thumb, your IOS generally should be at least version 12.1 or later; this will vary by router platform and voice hardware. Some newer hardware requires at least version 12.2 or 12.2T; again, check the voice hardware compatibility matrix on the Cisco Web site because it changes regularly to accommodate new hardware or new features.

Several other commands that can give useful hardware information are *show controllers* (to list the various controllers installed in your router) and *show diagnostic* (to list information about your router's components).

Troubleshooting Cabling

Cabling used in VoIP configurations is fairly straightforward and probably one of the easiest components to troubleshoot, given the standard cables used and the wide variety of cable-testing equipment available to you. Cisco routers can support a large variety of cable types, ranging from simple RS232 and V.35 to ATM DS3 cables—far too many to cover in a single troubleshooting chapter. We have opted to provide you a structured checklist of cable troubleshooting steps, shown in Table 7.1.

Table 7.1 Checklist of Troubleshooting Steps

Problem	First Thing to Check
Right cable connected to right interface?	Check cable and verify slot and port number
Right end of cable connected to right interface?	DCE versus DTE: verify with *show controllers*
Right cable type connected to communications equipment?	RS232, V.35, etc.
Cable pinouts correct?	Visually inspect and check with cable tester?
Cable verified as good?	Test with cable tester or swap to known good equipment and test

You'll use specific telephony cables to build your VoIP network. These are the registered jack (RJ) standards such as RJ11, RJ45, and RJ48. The most common problem with these types of cables occurs with their pinouts: It must be correct or will not work or, even worse, it will work intermittently. Figure 7.2 shows the wire diagram for the RJ11, RJ45, and RJ48 cables.

Figure 7.2 RJ11, RJ45, and RJ48 Wire Pinouts

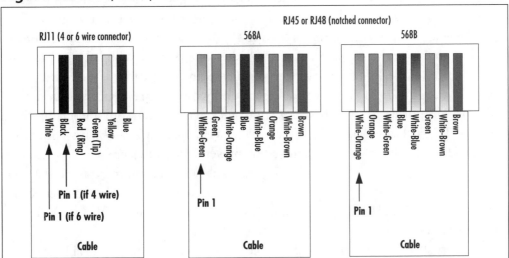

The RJ11 standard is typically used for most analog telephone communications. RJ11 cables are used in VoIP to connect the router's FXS and FXO interfaces to various communications devices such as telephones and PBXs. Later in this chapter, we cover FXS and FXO ports more fully. For now, just remember that FXS and FXO voice ports connect using RJ11 cables and jacks.

As shown in Figure 7.2, the RJ11 standard uses two wires for analog telephone communications: one for receive (ring) and one for transmit (tip), corresponding in our figure to the red and green wires, respectively. The RJ11 connector can be either a four-pin or a six-pin connector, but only two wires are used for analog telephone communications. VoIP networks use RJ45 and RJ48 connectors if E&M voice ports are involved. Again, we cover E&M ports in greater detail later in this chapter. The RJ45 and the RJ48 standards are similar in that they both have eight wires (four pairs). The RJ45 standard was developed for high-speed LANs such as 100BaseT, whereas the RJ48 standard is geared more toward data communications such as T1 circuits. Both standards can handle the same load requirements; they were merely designed for different purposes.

One difference is that the RJ48 has a connector that is keyed to a slotted jack; the RJ45 standard does not. Interestingly enough, the RJ45 can be substituted for an RJ48 cable since its lack of a slot does not prevent it from fitting into a RJ48 jack. The converse is not true: A RJ48 connector cannot fit into a RJ45 jack, because the notch on the RJ48 prevents it from fitting into the RJ45 jack. Nowadays, the RJ48 cable is still around, but you don't see it very much anymore. The RJ45 cable can serve quite adequately in place of an RJ48 cable. Keep this fact in mind as you select cable to support your VoIP network.

There are two wiring schemes for the RJ45 standard: TA568A and TA568B. It is important that your cable adhere to either one of these standards to prevent interference (crosstalk). If you were to dismantle an RJ45 cable, you would see that it has four pairs of wires. In each pair, the two wires are twisted around each other to minimize crosstalk. If you were to pick wires at random and crimp them into the RJ45 connector, chances are you would experience problems with your cables. TA568A/B cables are optimized to prevent such interference.

Troubleshooting cabling is relatively easy thanks to the numerous cable testers on the market, ranging from simple pin-checking devices (like the one you can find at www.copperandfibertools.com/testers.asp) to expensive full-featured testers such as those offered by Fluke (www.fluke.com).

Your first step in verifying RJ*xx* cable is to visually inspect the cable for breaks. Check the wiring pinouts against Figure 7.2. If they match and appear to be in good physical shape, your next step is to test the cable using a cable tester. Most cable testers allow you to map the wiring to ensure that Pin 1 goes to Pin 1, Pin 2 to Pin 2, and so on; pin mismatches are a very common problem. If you still have problems with the cable after it passes the cable tester (it shouldn't, if you got a good tester), throw the cable away and get a new one. Chances are, you have a rare bad mix of plastic and metal composition that went into the making of that cable, and it is interfering with the cable's ability to transport electrons. If you do not have a cable tester and are not sure of the cable, replace it.

Figure 7.3 shows the "standard" deployment of these cables in a VoIP network. Remember that an RJ45 cable can stand in for an RJ48 cable. Keep this figure close at hand as you cable up your voice ports, and always ensure that you double-check your work. For example, an RJ11 cable can also fit into RJ45 and RJ48 ports. You could easily insert an RJ11 cable where you really need to use an RJ45 cable.

Figure 7.3 RJ11 and RJ45 Use

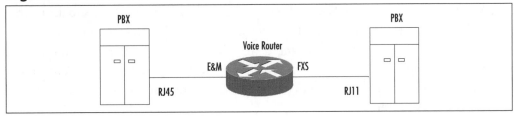

Troubleshooting Ports

Cisco routers (such as the 2600 or 3600 series) or the multifunction chassis (MC3810) have voice ports used to provide telephony services. These voice ports can be classified as FXS, FXO, or E&M. What does this mean to troubleshooting efforts? This section reviews the meaning of these terms and briefly touch on the purpose of each. Review Chapter 4 for more information relating to these port types.

An FXS voice port is typically used to connect end-user telephony devices such as analog telephones, fax machines, and modems. FXS voice ports have standard RJ11 jacks. As with a "normal" telephone line, FXS voice ports supply the necessary dial tone, ring, and voltage to the end device, enabling the telephone to ring on incoming calls and dial tone to sound for outgoing calls. As far as the telephony device is concerned, it is plugged into the telephone network. Figure 7.4 shows some typical uses of FXS ports on Cisco routers.

Figure 7.4 FXS Port Uses

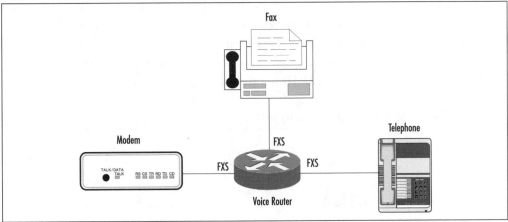

An FXO voice port is typically used for trunk support, such as connecting the VoIP network to a PSTN CO. FXO voice ports can be used in situations in which you want to connect a VoIP network to a PSTN. FXO ports do not provide dial tone, ring, or voltage, meaning that they cannot be used with the analog devices supported by the FXS interface. FXO interfaces use the same RJ11 connectors and jacks as any analog device. Figure 7.5 shows some typical uses of FXS ports on Cisco routers.

Figure 7.5 FXO Port Use

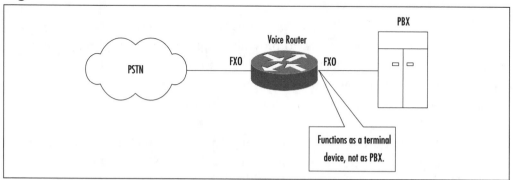

The expansion of the E&M acronym is quite diverse. Depending on whom you ask for a definition, it stands for rEceive and transMit, ear and mouth, or earth and magnet. E&M ports provide an analog trunk to connect two or more PBXs over a network (IP, Frame Relay, or ATM). This can be useful in situations in which you have multiple remote locations with numerous telephone lines and a PBX at each location. A router with an E&M port can tie these PBXs together and route calls between them, as shown in Figure 7.6. Contrast this scenario with the alternative, which is purchasing a trunk from the telco to each site. The cost savings can be significant if you use VoIP for tie-line replacement instead. We look into the configuration of VoIP for tie-line replacement in Chapter 8.

Figure 7.6 E&M Ports Connecting PBXs

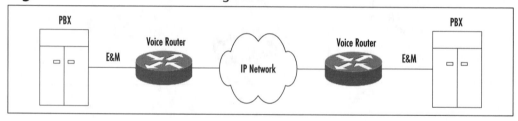

The E&M standard uses RJ48, which, you will recall is more or less a keyed (notched) RJ45 connector and jack. The trunk line provided by E&M can be either two-wire or four-wire, although there might actually be six or eight physical wires.

At Layer 1, troubleshooting voice ports is relatively simple. A common problem is misidentifying the ports and attempting to use them for other than their designed purpose. For example, plugging an analog telephone into an FXO port is a common mistake. Another problem could involve plugging a crossover cable with RJ45 connectors into the E&M port (which is RJ48): The cable used must be straight-through cable.

Each port type (FXS, FXO, and E&M) must be used for its intended purpose, as described in the previous section. Avoid problems by plugging in the correct equipment with the correct cable. Once each port has been configured in the software, you can perform simple tests such as lifting the telephone handset and listening for dial tone (in case of FXS ports) or placing a call from one PBX to another connected over a WAN via E&M ports.

In case of E&M configuration, you can eliminate the local PBX as a source of problems by dialing another telephone connected to that PBX. If that is successful, the problem lies with the E&M port and/or the VoIP configuration.

Problems with E&M ports can occur due to the way E&M operates. E&M configuration can be relatively complex, so its Layer 1 troubleshooting must be logical and thorough. At Layer 1, the singular cause of problems for E&M ports is the physical cable. You need to ensure that the cable you are using can support whatever E&M type you have configured. (We discuss E&M types more fully later.) Basically, each type of E&M has a different way of handling the E and M wires as well as signaling. The local device signals its off-hook condition via the E wire, whereas off-hook conditions on a remote device are indicated on the M wire.

Types I and V E&M use two wires for signaling and for E and M and have six physical wires. Types II, III, and IV use four wires for E, M, signal grounding, and signal battery and have eight physical wires. If the cable you are using lacks the necessary wires or a critical wire in the cable is bad, you will experience problems. Ensure that your cable is verified well before you use it.

Troubleshooting Other Physical Layer Issues

Problems can occur in other Layer 1 aspects of voice communications. Components such as PBX, CO, and circuits can have a significant impact on your VoIP network. This is not an exhaustive list; you might have other unique components in your network. You should have a complete inventory of the devices that are used to support your VoIP network.

Troubleshooting Private Branch Exchange Problems

Unless you are a telephony specialist, you might not be familiar with PBXs and what they do. In simplest terms, a PBX is a hub for telephone lines. PBXs reduce the number of physical wires that a telephone company has to install to support a location that needs multiple telephone lines. If you have a building with hundreds or thousands of telephone numbers, it would be impractical and cost prohibitive for the telephone company to install such large quantities of individual telephone wires lines from its nearest CO.

Enter PBXs. Individual lines in a building or campus are run to an on-site PBX, which in turn has a trunk to the telephone company PSTN, typically to a CO. Calls are made through the PBX. Calls to any lines not on the immediate PBX traverse the PBX's trunk to reach other PBXs or the PSTN. Most PBXs are privately owned (hence the word *private* in its name) and maintained by the organization that needs these multiple telephone lines.

Generally speaking, the PBX is an install-and-forget device. You will not often have much to do with a PBX. However, if you want to connect the PBXs of different locations to each other or connect the PBX to a PSTN over a VoIP network, you need to know how to configure and troubleshoot the E&M ports on Cisco routers. By developing your dial plan, dial peers, and so on and then connecting each location PBX to an E&M port on the voice router, you can use your existing WAN links to transports your calls, as opposed to paying expensive trunk costs. In addition, you have much tighter control over your telephony network with this design.

Problems that occur with this arrangement will most likely be mismatch or misconfiguration issues between the PBX and the E&M port. In addition to configuring the Cisco E&M port, you also need to configure the PBX, using its native operating system commands. The following is an excerpt from a Nortel configuration example; the PBX is being configured for two-wire operation. The example shows that these commands are radically different from the familiar Cisco IOS commands. This is merely one command to perform one task; if you are not familiar with the PBX's commands, you need to consult with a PBX technician before proceeding any further. At the very least, you need to obtain information about your PBX before you can configure your E&M port to interoperate with it:

```
SIGL<EAM>
```

The make of PBX determines whether the Cisco E&M port supports it. Currently, at this writing, Cisco supports Lucent, Nortel, and select NEC PBXs on its E&M ports. Check for an updated list at www.cisco.com/univercd/cc/td/ doc/product/access/acs_mod/cis3600/sw_conf/pbx_int/index.htm. If this link does not work for you, do a search on www.cisco.com for *PBX interoperability*. Check this list before you attempt to connect a Cisco voice router to your PBX; if your device is not on this list, the device will not work.

Troubleshooting Central Office Problems

The CO is usually an unmanned building where trunk lines from the PBXs or telephone-line junction boxes terminate to connect to the PSTN. In context of VoIP networks, the trunk line from the PBX over which all the telephone lines ride connects to the CO, and from there, the CO is connected to the PSTN. Figure 7.7 shows a common CO arrangement.

Figure 7.7 Central Office Residential Line to PBX Line

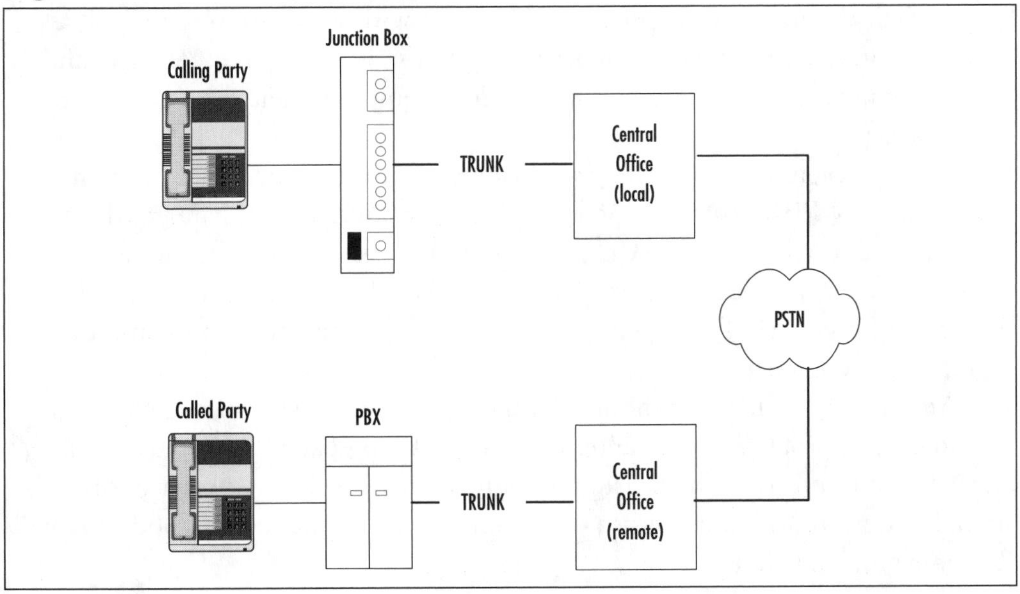

For most problems with a CO, there is little you as an end user can do to resolve them. What you can do is call your local telco provider *after* you have performed in-house troubleshooting and have confidently proven that the problem does not lie with your network, your wiring, or your configuration. Last-mile providers are notorious for their skepticism regarding the part of the telephone network in which the problem lies.

To prove your hypothesis that there is a problem with the CO or with the connection to the CO, try a few simple tests. If you can call another number internal to the same PBX, you can generally be sure that your PBX is operating normally. If you have several PBXs connected to each other via an E&M port on your voice router and each location can call the other, your VoIP configuration is working. If you cannot reach nonorganizational numbers (which normally traverse outside your PBX and VoIP network), the problem is definitely between your PBX and the CO, between the CO and its PSTN connection, or with your dial plan.

To test the connection between your PBX and the CO, try calling another number not on your PBX that terminates at the CO. If you can call successfully, the connection between your PBX and your CO is fine. However, this test requires that you know another number that terminates at the same CO. If that test is successful, try calling a number that terminates somewhere in the PSTN. If you are unable to make that call, the problem lies between that CO and the PSTN, in which case, it becomes a problem for the provider to resolve. Finally, ensure that your dial plan is perfect and is functioning as you want. If your dial plan is faulty, there is a possibility your VoIP network is not routing the call as you think it is. Ensure that the number destination is configured correctly and that it does indeed pass through the provider's equipment and network before you call them.

If the problem occurred after you made changes to your PBX to accommodate your new PBX-to-voice-router E&M connection, chances are good that you made an error in the PBX configuration. Check your PBX configuration, and if possible, consult an expert who knows the PBX inside and out. If you do not know how to verify or configure your PBX, it is best that you consult a company or engineer.

After doing all this, you should call the telco and inform your representative that there is a problem with the telco network. Be prepared to provide details such as trunk information, any support agreements you have, contact information, location information, and so on. At this point, the value of a good SLA will become quite apparent.

Troubleshooting Underlying Circuit and Network Problems

At some point, your VoIP network is going to have its calls transported over various network media, whether point to point T1 circuits, ATM DS3, Ethernet, ISDN, or the like. There are a large number of circuit types—too many to cover individually in this chapter. Instead, we present a simple methodology for troubleshooting suspect circuit problems.

At Layer 1, your concerns about any circuit or network are physical. Physical problems that can occur include problems with circuit equipment, cable problems, and interface failure. The following sections detail steps you can take to troubleshoot your suspected circuit and network problems.

Testing and Verifying Cable

We covered cable testing and verification in the Layer 1 troubleshooting section; here we revisit this topic with an eye toward circuits and networks. Cable verification can be either simple or an exercise in futility if you do not have cable testers or a known good cable to replace faulty cable. When you're verifying cable, start with a visual inspection. Check to ensure that no pins are bent, broken, or missing. With RJ45, RJ11, and RJ48 cables, ensure that their wiring (pinouts) are what you expect (that is, not configured in some unique, nonstandard configuration). If the cables are in a nonstandard pinout, either rewrite them to be standard or replace the cable with one that is standard.

These cables should be in a straight-through configuration, except in cases of certain Ethernet cables for which the Ethernet interface of one router is connected directly to the Ethernet interface of another router. If that is your requirement (which is unlikely), use a crossover cable wired as shown in Figure 7.8. Notice that a crossover cable for Ethernet is simply one end of the cable wired as TA568A and the other end as TA568B.

Figure 7.8 Crossover Cable Pinouts

568B		Cable	Cable		568A
	Brown			Brown	
	White-Brown			White-Brown	
	Green			Orange	
	White-Blue			White-Blue	
	Blue			Blue	
	White-Green			White-Orange	
	Orange			Green	
	White-Orange ◀— Pin 1		Pin 1 —▶ White-Green	

Cables that connect to a serial interface on Cisco routers can be a little trickier to troubleshoot. This is due to the fact Cisco cables typically have a proprietary high-density DB60 connector on the end that connects to the router serial interface, and they autoconfigure to adapt to the other end. The other end is typically an industry-standard connector such as RS232, V.35, RS535, and so on. Most commercial cable testers cannot easily (if at all) test such cables. The easiest and most economical test is to swap your existing cable with a known good one.

Cisco does provide an excellent command to verify that your cable is correctly seen. The *show controllers* command provides the following display and can confirm whether or not the router correctly sees your cable. A simple test you can do is to remove the cable, execute *show controllers* to verify you are connecting to the port you think you are, and the cable should disappear from the listing. This command tells you if the cable connected to the router interface is a DTE or a DCE, which can be useful in determining if you have the right cable for your communications equipment:

```
RR1# show controllers
   Interface 1 is Serial0, electrical interface is V.35 DCE
      10 total RX buffers, 11 buffer TX queue limit, buffer size 1520
      Transmitter delay is 0 microseconds
      High speed synchronous serial interface
```

Notice that *show controllers* tells us that there is a V.35 cable attached to our Serial 0 interface and that it is DCE, not DTE. This is a useful bit of information for troubleshooting.

Testing and Verifying Communications Equipment

Your VoIP network might use many different types of communications equipment. By communications equipment, we mean devices such as CSU/DSUs, hubs (LAN), and switches (LAN). For ease of discussion, we use the term *switch* to mean both hubs and switches.

A channel service unit/data service unit (CSU/DSU) is nothing more than a "modem" for connecting to digital lines. We use the shorthand *CSU* to refer to a CSU/DSU. Unlike a modem, which converts digital to analog, all CSU communication is digital. CSUs connect circuits with bandwidths ranging from 56k to T1/E1 speeds. Your make and model of CSU/DSU determines the features you have.

At a minimum, most CSUs support loopback testing, arguably one of the most important features of any CSU. Loopback testing is the capability to wrap a circuit so that test traffic is returned to the CSU of origin rather than the remote

CSU. This function enables you to verify that a circuit is good, regardless of the state of the CSU at the distant end. Figure 7.9 shows local and remote loopbacks and their reach.

Figure 7.9 Local and Remote Loopbacks

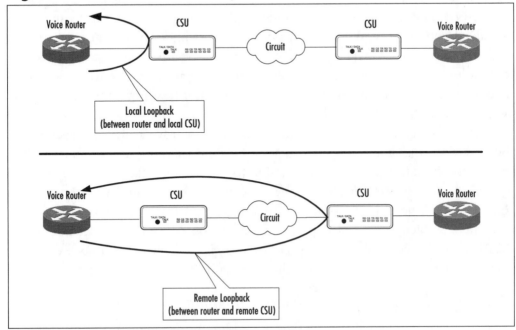

Your first loopback test should be local to verify good connectivity between the CSU and the router. Start by putting the CSU into a local loopback; the way you do this varies by make and model of CSU, but for the most part, you execute a series of menu steps on the CSU. Log onto the router, and execute a *show interface*; you should see a looped state as shown in the following code. Have the router ping its own interface. If the ping is successful, and you see the loop on the router, connectivity is good. When you do a *show interface serial x/x*, if communications are good between your router and your CSU, your display should look like the following:

```
Serial x/x is up, line protocol is up (looped)
(output abbreviated)
```

This output confirms that the cable between the router and the CSU is good, and it confirms that the CSU is operating correctly. Next, replace the local loopback with a remote loopback, and repeat the steps you did with the local loopback. If the loop is visible, there is good connectivity all the way back to the distant-end telco location, up to where the circuit connects to the distant end CSU. If you do not see the loop, there is a problem with the circuit between your CSU and the distant end. You will need to work with your telco provider to have its staff troubleshoot the circuit.

LAN switch troubleshooting can be simple: It either works or it doesn't. Troubleshooting can start with viewing switch port lights. If the lights are green and transmitting keepalives regularly, you have a good LAN connection. This is true at least at the physical layer. Be aware that just because you have good connectivity between the router and the switch does not mean that the switch (or its VLANs) is configured correctly.

If you suspect a problem with your switch, temporarily connect the router and other devices to a simple and verified good hub and run ping tests of other devices on the network. If these tests are successful, your router interface and cable are good. Your next step in troubleshooting is to check the switch configuration. Ensure that the ports are enabled and are in the right VLAN. Some router interfaces have problems with full-duplex communication, so try turning the interface off. You can also manually set the speed to 10Mbps or 100Mbps, as opposed to using autonegotiation, which is notorious for causing connectivity issues.

Testing and Verifying Cisco Router Interfaces

After we have ascertained that neither the cabling nor the circuit nor the communications equipment is the problem, we are ready to turn our attention to the Cisco router. Two of your best troubleshooting tools are *show* and *debug*. Both can provide useful Layer 1 information to aid your troubleshooting efforts. Here we highlight a few of those commands. The *show* command provides a quick snapshot of the current state of your hardware; *debug* affords a real-time display of events as they occur. The *debug* command can be quite resource intensive and can generate copious amounts of data, so it should be used sparingly and very specifically.

Let's start with a discussion of several *show* commands that can be useful in troubleshooting your VoIP router. The commands we present here are by no means complete; rather, they form the basics of your *show* toolbox.

The *show version* command can give you a quick snapshot of the version of IOS you are running on your router, how much memory and flash it has, how it is booting (from ROM or flash), the interfaces and ports that are installed, and so on. Sample output from this command is as follows:

```
----------------- show version -----------------
Cisco Internetwork Operating System Software
IOS (tm) 3600 Software (C3640-IS-M), Version 12.1(2)T, RELEASE
    SOFTWARE (fc1)
Copyright (c) 1986-2000 by cisco Systems, Inc.
Compiled Tue 16-May-00 12:47 by ccai
Image text-base: 0x600088F0, data-base: 0x6101A000


ROM: System Bootstrap, Version 11.1(20)AA2, EARLY DEPLOYMENT RELEASE
    SOFTWARE (fc1)


usa3640 uptime is 26 minutes
System returned to ROM by reload
System image file is "flash:c3640-is-mz.121-2.t.bin"


cisco 3640 (R4700) processor (revision 0x00) with 60416K/5120K bytes
    of memory.
Processor board ID 19592029
R4700 CPU at 100Mhz, Implementation 33, Rev 1.0
Bridging software.
X.25 software, Version 3.0.0.
SuperLAT software (copyright 1990 by Meridian Technology Corp).
Primary Rate ISDN software, Version 1.1.
2 Ethernet/IEEE 802.3 interface(s)
2 Serial network interface(s)
2 Channelized T1/PRI port(s)
2 Voice FXS interface(s)
2 Voice E & M interface(s)
DRAM configuration is 64 bits wide with parity disabled.
125K bytes of non-volatile configuration memory.
32768K bytes of processor
```

The *show diagnostic* command is a wonderful command that provides great detail on the cards and modules that are installed in your router. In the following display, we see that Slot 2 has a four-port voice module installed and that module has an E&M and an FXS voice port installed. Notice that you can also get the serial number of your hardware with this command:

```
Slot 2:
 4 PORT Voice PM for MARs Port adapter
 Port adapter is analyzed
 Port adapter insertion time unknown
 EEPROM contents at hardware discovery:
 Hardware revision 1.1              Board revision C0
 Serial number       10260117   Part number      800-02491-02
 Test history        0x0          RMA number       00-00-00
 EEPROM format version 1
 EEPROM contents (hex):
   0x20: 01 65 01 01 00 9C 8E 95 50 09 BB 02 00 00 00 00
   0x30: 60 00 00 00 98 10 08 17 FF FF FF FF FF FF FF FF


 WIC Slot 0:
 E&M Voice daughter card (2 port)
 Hardware revision 1.1              Board revision C0
 Serial number       10259431   Part number      800-02497-01
 Test history        0x0          RMA number       00-00-00
 Connector type      Wan Module
 EEPROM format version 1
 EEPROM contents (hex):
   0x20: 01 0F 01 01 00 9C 8B E7 50 09 C1 01 00 00 00 00
   0x30: 60 00 00 00 98 10 07 01 FF FF FF FF FF FF FF FF


 WIC Slot 1:
 FXS Voice daughter card (2 port)
 Hardware revision 1.1              Board revision C0
 Serial number       11242899   Part number      800-02493-01
 Test history        0x0          RMA number       00-00-00
 Connector type      Wan Module
 EEPROM format version 1
 EEPROM contents (hex):
   0x20: 01 0E 01 01 00 AB 8D 93 50 09 BD 01 00 00 00 0
```

The *show controllers* command is able to give you detailed information about your interfaces, as shown here. In this case, we see that a V.35 DTE cable is connected to serial 0/0. You can also check your buffers to see if they are being overwhelmed, which could indicate that you need to control your traffic or upgrade to a high-speed connection:

```
Interface Serial0/0
Hardware is Quicc 68360
DTE V.35 TX and RX clocks detected.
Comment:  Is the correct type of cable connected to your router?

(output omited)

buffer size 1524
QUICC SCC specific errors:
0 input aborts on receiving flag sequence
0 throttles, 0 enables
0 overruns
0 transmitter underruns
0 transmitter CTS losts
0 aborted short frames

Comment:  Are you experiencing conditions here which indicate that
     your buffers are being overwhelmed?
```

The *show interface* command is one of Cisco's workhorse commands. It is arguably one of the most used commands because it enables you to check the current status and configuration of your interfaces, as shown in the following output. Information you can verify includes the Layer 1 and Layer 2 state of your interface, IP addressing, buffers, and so on. We return to this command later; at this point, you should know to use this command to verify your interface is operational and that is able to handle the load placed on it:

```
Serial0/0 is up, line protocol is up
  Hardware is QUICC Serial
  Internet address is 10.99.99.101/24
  MTU 1500 bytes, BW 2048 Kbit, DLY 20000 usec,
     reliability 255/255, txload 1/255, rxload 1/255
  Encapsulation FRAME-RELAY, loopback not set
  Keepalive set (10 sec)
  LMI enq sent  158, LMI stat recvd 158, LMI upd recvd 0, DTE LMI up
  LMI enq recvd 0, LMI stat sent  0, LMI upd sent  0
```

```
LMI DLCI 1023   LMI type is CISCO   Frame Relay DTE
Broadcast queue 0/64, broadcasts sent/dropped 700/7, interface
    broadcasts 63
Last input 00:00:00, output 00:00:03, output hang never
Last clearing of "show interface" counters 00:26:23
Input queue: 0/75/0/0 (size/max/drops/flushes); Total output drops: 0
Queueing strategy: weighted fair
Output queue: 0/1000/64/0 (size/max total/threshold/drops)
   Conversations  0/2/256 (active/max active/max total)
   Reserved Conversations 0/0 (allocated/max allocated)
5 minute input rate 1000 bits/sec, 1 packets/sec
5 minute output rate 0 bits/sec, 0 packets/sec
   940 packets input, 196639 bytes, 0 no buffer
   Received 0 broadcasts, 0 runts, 0 giants, 0 throttles
   0 input errors, 0 CRC, 0 frame, 0 overrun, 0 ignored, 0 abort
   920 packets output, 182938 bytes, 0 underruns
   0 output errors, 0 collisions, 0 interface resets
   0 output buffer failures, 0 output buffers swapped out
   0 carrier transitions
   DCD=up  DSR=up  DTR=up  RTS=up  CTS=up
```

The *debug* commands can be useful in monitoring and capturing information as they occur. These commands enable you to track the consequences of a specific event at a specific point in time. Several *debug* commands can be useful, but use them with caution on a production system. The *debug* commands we describe in the following section cover interface-specific events. Since they generate copious amounts of information, we do not provide examples of output. Instead, we call your attention to specific *debug* commands that can aid you in troubleshooting your interfaces.

Several *debug* commands are specific for troubleshooting ATM. The command syntax is self explanatory with regards to the purpose of each command. The *debug atm errors* command enables you to view time errors as they occur on an ATM interface and specific virtual circuits. The information provided by this command is not necessarily critical, but it can indicate an underlying network or hardware problem if the errors are consistent and accumulative. The command *debug atm events* provides a snapshot of an ATM interface's general health. If the ATM interface is able to communicate successfully with the ATM service provider's network, modem state will be 0x0; otherwise, 0x8 indicates a communication problem. The *debug atm pvcd* command enables you to monitor the process ATM goes through to establish a VC, including catching any errors or mismatches that prevent such establishment from occurring. It can also be used to catch flapping VCs and aid you in isolating the cause.

Cisco also provides several beneficial commands for troubleshooting serial interfaces. The *debug serial interface* command captures serial interface events such as keepalive activity, outages, and buffer overflows. If you want information on packets as they flow through a serial interface, use *debug serial packet*. Be warned: This command tracks every single packet that flows through that interface. At the very least, it will enable you to confirm that your voice packets are being passed.

Layer 2 Troubleshooting

Once we have confirmed that Layer 1 has no problems, we are ready to start our Layer 2 (data link) troubleshooting. Layer 2 is not called the data link layer for nothing; it is the linkage between Layer 1 and Layer 3. Layer 2 packages data it receives from Layer 3 in a format that can be handed off to Layer 1. From there, Layer 1 puts the data on the wire as strings of 0s and 1s (binary data). It does the reverse upon receiving frames from Layer 1: It repackages them in the appropriate format for Layer 3 (IP packets, etc.).

Layer 2 has two sublayers that it uses to accomplish its job: the Media Access Control (MAC) sublayer and the Logical Link Control (LLC) sublayer. The MAC sublayer formats the data and provides addresses (called MAC addresses, hardware addresses, and so on) that are used to get the data from one physical device on the network to the other. The LLC sublayer manages traffic that transits Layer 2. It handles flow and error control for whatever physical media it is connected to. LLC provides identifying information about the network protocol being transported, such as IP or IPX.

You can accomplish several troubleshooting tasks at Layer 2. Many more troubleshooting options are available than we present here. Serial interfaces, Frame Relay, and ATM happen to be among the most common used to support VoIP networks.

Troubleshooting Serial Interfaces

When troubleshooting serial interfaces at Layer 2, you can look at several key items. Start with the *show interface serial x* command, where *x* is the interface number. Here is a sample display:

RR1#**show interfaces serial 0/0**

Serial0/0 is up, line protocol is up

Comment: Is the interface operating at Layer 2 (line protocol is up?)

   Hardware is QUICC Serial

   Internet address is 10.99.99.101/24

   MTU 1500 bytes, BW 2048 Kbit, DLY 20000 usec,

Comment: Is this the correct MTU for this network?

     reliability 255/255, txload 1/255, rxload 1/255

   Encapsulation FRAME-RELAY, loopback not set

Comment: Is the encapsulation correct?

   Keepalive set (10 sec)

   LMI enq sent 158, LMI stat recvd 158, LMI upd recvd 0, DTE LMI up

   LMI enq recvd 0, LMI stat sent 0, LMI upd sent 0

   LMI DLCI 1023 LMI type is CISCO Frame Relay DTE

Comment: In case of Frame Relay, are LMI messages being sent and

     received? Is the LMI type correct?

   Broadcast queue 0/64, broadcasts sent/dropped 700/7, interface

       broadcasts 63

   Last input 00:00:00, output 00:00:03, output hang never

   Last clearing of "show interface" counters 00:26:23

   Input queue: 0/75/0/0 (size/max/drops/flushes); Total output drops: 0

   Queueing strategy: weighted fair

   Output queue: 0/1000/64/0 (size/max total/threshold/drops)

     Conversations 0/2/256 (active/max active/max total)

     Reserved Conversations 0/0 (allocated/max allocated)

   5 minute input rate 1000 bits/sec, 1 packets/sec

   5 minute output rate 0 bits/sec, 0 packets/sec

     940 packets input, 196639 bytes, 0 no buffer

     Received 0 broadcasts, 0 runts, 0 giants, 0 throttles

     0 input errors, 0 CRC, 0 frame, 0 overrun, 0 ignored, 0 abort

     920 packets output, 182938 bytes, 0 underruns

     0 output errors, 0 collisions, 0 interface resets

     0 output buffer failures, 0 output buffers swapped out

```
0 carrier transitions

DCD=up   DSR=up   DTR=up   RTS=up   CTS=up
```

The first line, *Serial0/0 is up, line protocol is up,* is key to troubleshooting serial interface problems. It indicates whether the problem is at Layer 1, Layer 2, or both. Table 7.2 explains the possible states you can see with this command and their meanings.

Table 7.2 Interface States and Explanations

Serial Is ...	Line Protocol Is ...	Cause Is ...
Up	Up	Interface is up with no problems.
Up	Up (looped)	There is a loop on communications equipment.
Up	Up (disabled)	High error rates (due to circuit or communications problems) causes disabled state.
Administratively down	Down	Interface is shut down.
Down	Down	Nothing is connected to the interface, or communications equipment is off.

You can also look at the input and output queues. Keepalive intervals should match at both sides, and traffic counters should increment to show them being sent. Interface resets are another indication of problems; if it increments, it means that the circuit, communications equipment, or interface has toggled between up and down that number of times. Excessive carrier transitions can indicate a problem with the circuit (cable or communications equipment) attached to this interface. Increasing input or output errors can indicate that the interface cannot handle the amount of traffic passing through it. If that's the case, you should investigate the traffic being passed and ways to curb it (perhaps allow only certain traffic). CRC errors indicate line noise or problems with clocking.

Troubleshooting Frame Relay

Frame Relay is a packet-switching network technology that uses data link circuit identifiers (DLCIs) to build permanent and switched virtual circuits. The same issues that impact serial interfaces affect Frame Relay connections. This section focuses on several Frame Relay problems that you could encounter. In troubleshooting Frame Relay problems, ensure that you troubleshoot both sides of the connection.

Your Frame Relay troubleshooting needs to be logical and sequential; focus your labors on one aspect of Frame Relay at a time (good counsel for all troubleshooting, not just Frame Relay troubleshooting). Ensure that you have completed all Layer 1 troubleshooting and that all interfaces, cables, equipment, and so on have been verified as good. Perform a *show interface serial x/x* to confirm that the interface is not administratively shut down; if it is, do a *no shutdown* to bring it up.

DLCIs, which are Layer 2 addresses, identify a virtual circuit and are presented to the router by the Frame Relay switch. Typically, when you purchase Frame Relay service from your provider, the provider gives you the DLCI. Check and then double-check with the provider to ensure that you have the correct DLCI information, because a common problem is using incorrect DLCIs.

DLCIs (Layer 2) are mapped to Layer 3 addresses (IP, for example) to enable connectivity via Frame Relay. The *local* DLCI of the PVC connected to your router is mapped to the *remote* IP address of the distant router. In Figure 7.10, RR2 maps its DLCI to RR1's IP address, and vice versa. Regardless of the topology you use, the DLCI-to-IP address mapping must be valid in order for the routers connected via Frame Relay to communicate with each other. The concept shown in Figure 7.10 is fundamental for IP operation over Frame Relay.

Figure 7.10 Frame Relay DLCI and IP Address Mapping

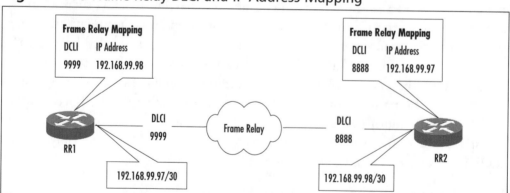

This mapping can be done automatically via inverse ARP or manual mappings that you engineer yourself. Unless you have a partial mesh topology or multiple DLCIs on a single circuit, it is best to let inverse ARP handle the mappings. Be aware that using map statements for IP on a particular DLCI automatically disables all inverse ARP for that DLCI for IP; in other words, you might need other map statements to all other IP addresses reachable via that DLCI.

Your use of physical interfaces or logical subinterfaces determines your mapping method. If your PVC is on a physical interface on either a point-to-point or a full mesh network, let inverse ARP work out the mappings. You do not need to use the *frame-relay interface-dlci* command to lock the DLCI to this interface. However, if this physical interface has more than PVC associated with it (a multipoint interface), you need to manually map remote IP addresses to local DLCIs with *frame-relay map x.x.x.x yyyy*. This can become unmanageable as your Frame Relay network grows.

Subinterfaces provide a workaround for this mapping requirement. Each subinterface is a separate network segment, and therefore, mapping is automatic. If you break your physical interfaces into point-to-point subinterfaces, you only need to execute the *frame-relay interface-dlci* command to ensure each point-to-point interface gets the right DLCI associated with it, and mapping is accomplished automatically by inverse ARP.

Point-to-multipoint interfaces are slightly trickier. Figure 7.11 shows a common spoke-and-hub configuration (a type of partial mesh topology). In this case, we would configure the hubs (RR2 and RR3) as point to point and the spoke (RR1) as point to multipoint. The complete configuration is shown in Figure 7.11.

Figure 7.11 Frame Relay Hub and Spoke

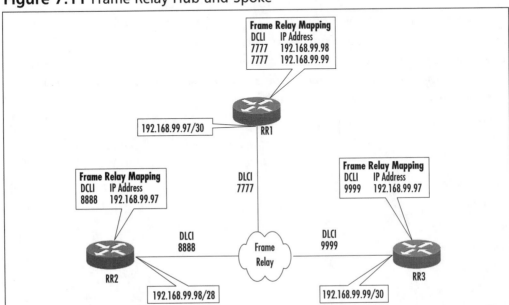

However, there is a problem: Although each hub can ping the spoke, and the spoke can ping each hub, neither hub can ping the other. This is due to the default nature of Frame Relay mapping on Cisco routers: Inverse ARP on RR1 creates mappings to RR2 and RR3, whereas RR2 and RR3 have their endpoints (RR1) mapped. Since neither RR2 nor RR3 is an endpoint to the other, no mapping occurs.

This is a problem if the VoIP peering needs to be from RR2 to RR3. If they cannot reach each other at the network layer, they will not be able to pass calls to each other. There are several solutions to fix this problem. You can set up a separate PVC between the spokes, which will change your topology from a hub and spoke to a full mesh.(This solution might not be possible if you are on a budget.) Alternatively, you can configure a Frame Relay map and make the hub the next hop for each spoke. Or you can configure a Frame Relay map on each spoke to the other spoke. You can even execute static routes on each spoke to point to the hub as the next hop for the other spoke. Regardless of the solution you implement, the spokes must be able to reach each other in order to become VoIP peers.

Encapsulation types are easier to troubleshoot. They either match or they don't. They are set with the *encapsulation frame-relay [ietf]* command. The key thing is that they must match on all routers on the same circuit. You can check the encapsulation type that is set on each router using either *show running* or *show interface*.

Cisco provides several commands that can be useful in troubleshooting Frame Relay. We discuss these commands in the following sections.

The *show frame-relay pvc* command lists the PVCs that have been configured and whether they are operational or not. In the following example, DCLI 102 is configured and currently active, whereas the PVC attached to DCLI 103 is not used and is not active, indicating a problem with either the configuration or between this router and the Frame Relay network:

```
RR1#show frame-relay pvc
```

	Active	Inactive	Deleted	Static
Local	0	0	0	0
Switched	0	0	0	0
Unused	8	3	0	0

```
DLCI = 102, DLCI USAGE = UNUSED, PVC STATUS = ACTIVE, INTERFACE = Serial0

    input pkts 0            output pkts 1            in bytes 0
    out bytes 34           dropped pkts 0           in FECN pkts 0
    in BECN pkts 0          out FECN pkts 0          out BECN pkts 0
    in DE pkts 0            out DE pkts 0
    out bcast pkts 1       out bcast bytes 34          num pkts switched 0
    pvc create time 00:00:08, last time pvc status changed 00:00:08


DLCI = 103, DLCI USAGE = UNUSED, PVC STATUS = INACTIVE, INTERFACE = Serial0

    input pkts 0            output pkts 0            in bytes 0
    out bytes 0            dropped pkts 0           in FECN pkts 0
    in BECN pkts 0          out FECN pkts 0          out BECN pkts 0
    in DE pkts 0            out DE pkts 0
    out bcast pkts 0        out bcast bytes 0          num pkts switched 0
    pvc create time 00:00:11, last time pvc status changed 00:00:11
```

Another useful command as far as VoIP is concerned is *show frame-relay map*. This command displays the DLCI-to-IP address mappings. As discussed previously, these mappings are vital in order to get VoIP functioning from one router to another. When troubleshooting, you should use this command to verify that the mappings are correct, regardless of whether they were dynamic or static.

As always, Cisco provides several *debug* commands to catch errors and events as they occur. The d*ebug frame-relay packet* command can be useful to catch DCLI-to-IP mapping errors. If there is no mapping to a particular IP address that you attempt to access while this command is running, you will get an error similar to the following:

```
debug frame packet
Serial0 : Encaps failed--no map entry link 7 (IP).
```

If you made changes and your INARP mappings are no longer valid, you can clear the mapping cache with the *clear frame-relay —inarp* command. The *debug frame-relay lmi* command is very important because it checks communications between the router and the Frame Relay switch. This command can determine whether they are communicating properly and whether you are using the correct DLCI (the command enables you to see what DLCI the switch is sending the router).

www.syngress.com

Troubleshooting Asynchronous Transfer Mode

ATM is similar in concept to Frame Relay in that it shares some of its genetic composition. ATM is probably one of the best, if not *the* best, network technologies for transporting VoIP traffic. Its support for constant and time-sensitive traffic such as voice and video and its ability to guarantee a set quality of service make it a superior choice over Frame Relay—or pretty much any other network technology.

Another facet of ATM that makes it a superior transport for voice traffic is that it uses fixed-length 53-byte cells (a 5-byte header preceding a 48-byte payload), as shown in Figure 7.12. Like Frame Relay, it builds and transports these cells over permanent and switched virtual circuits. Its negotiation process is borrowed from Broadband ISDN (B-ISDN). ATM also supports a wide range of bandwidth, from 2Mbps up to OC-192, making it ideal for the support and expansion of your voice networks.

Figure 7.12 ATM Cell

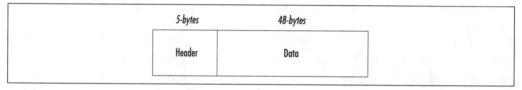

IP packets are segmented by the ATM module into cells and then transported to their destinations through the ATM network. At their destinations, these cells are reassembled into IP packets. The small and uniform size, as opposed to the large and differing sizes of other network technologies, enables ATM to easily and quickly transport the cells.

ATM can be configured in many ways to support many different needs and topologies. However, for ease of learning an ATM troubleshooting methodology, we focus on ATM PVC troubleshooting, probably the most common ATM implementation.

Two widespread problems that can occur with an ATM PVC configuration involve cells being dropped in the ATM provider's network or PVCs not being established all the way through. You can do several things to determine if cells are being dropped or if the PVC is broken in the ATM provider's network.

You can determine if the ATM network is dropping cells by sending pings. Responses that are less than 100 percent successful could indicate that cells are being dropped. If possible, do the ping test from both sides of the PVC. Once you determine that cells are consistently dropped, you need to check several possible causes.

The *show controller* command, as previously discussed, can be used to check for physical errors in either the router or the ATM module. In addition, two loop-back test options are available with ATM. You can physically loop the RX port to the TX port of the ATM interface, thus creating a hard local loopback; this option verifies that your interface is good. Cisco also provides a command to accomplish the same thing: *loopback diagnostic*. If the interface has no hardware problems, it will achieve an "up/up" state that you can view with the *show inter-face* command. Either way, once the loop is up, you should be able to ping the local interface, which essentially confirms that it is operational from Layers 1 to 3.

You can check the status of your ATM interface with the *show interface atm (module/port)* command. As with serial interfaces, this output can indicate the status of your ATM interface and show immediately if it is operating at Layer 1 and 2. An example of this command follows. Additionally, you can use the output from this command to determine if the amount of data being transferred is exceeding the bandwidth of the ATM circuit (which can result in dropped cells):

```
RR1#show interface atm 1/0
ATM1/0 is up, line protocol is up
  Hardware is ENHANCED ATM PA
  MTU 4470 bytes, sub MTU 4470, BW 149760 Kbit, DLY 80 usec,
     reliability 255/255, txload 1/255, rxload 1/255
  Encapsulation ATM, loopback not set
  Keepalive not supported
  Encapsulation(s): AAL5
  4096 maximum active VCs, 4 current VCCs
  VC idle disconnect time: 300 seconds  Signalling vc = 1, vpi = 0,
     vci = 5
  UNI Version = 4.0, Link Side = user
  0 carrier transitions
  Last input 00:05:16, output 00:08:23, output hang never
  Last clearing of "show interface" counters never
  Input queue: 0/75/0 (size/max/drops); Total output drops: 0
  Queueing strategy: Per VC Queueing
  5 minute input rate 0 bits/sec, 0 packets/sec
  5 minute output rate 0 bits/sec, 0 packets/sec
     345 packets input, 6544 bytes, 0 no buffer
```

```
    Received 0 broadcasts, 0 runts, 0 giants, 0 throttles
     2 input errors, 2 CRC, 0 frame, 0 overrun, 0 ignored, 0 abort
    345 packets output, 4278 bytes, 0 underruns
    0 output errors, 0 collisions, 1 interface resets
    0 output buffer failures, 0 output buffers swapped out
```

You can also check on the status of a PVC with the *show atm pvc module/port* command that follows. For voice traffic, it should be CBT (for *constant bit rate*) because voice demands a constant available bandwidth to be understood. The peak rate is the highest-speed bandwidth available on this PVC; if it is below the level voice requires, your voice quality will suffer:

```
RR1#show atm pvc 1/23
ATM1/0.23: VCD: 7, VPI: 1, VCI: 23
VBR-NRT, PeakRate: 2000, Average Rate: 1000, Burst Cells: 32
AAL5-LLC/SNAP, etype:0x0, Flags: 0x20, VCmode: 0x0
OAM frequency: 0 second(s), OAM retry frequency: 1 second(s), OAM retry
        frequen)
OAM up retry count: 3, OAM down retry count: 5
OAM Loopback status: OAM Disabled
OAM VC state: Not Managed
ILMI VC state: Not Managed
InARP frequency: 15 minutes(s)
Transmit priority 2
InPkts: 57634, OutPkts: 589623, InBytes: 6778670, OutBytes: 6751812
InPRoc: 64351, OutPRoc: 62986, Broadcasts: 0
InFast: 0, OutFast: 0, InAS: 0, OutAS: 0
InPktDrops: 0, OutPktDrops: 0
CrcErrors: 0, SarTimeOuts: 0, OverSizedSDUs: 0
OAM cells received: 0
F5 InEndloop: 0, F5 InSegloop: 0, F5 InAIS: 0, F5 InRDI: 0
F4 InEndloop: 0, F4 InSegloop: 0, F4 InAIS: 0, F4 InRDI: 0
OAM cells sent: 0
F5 OutEndloop: 0, F5 OutSegloop: 0, F5 OutRDI: 0
F4 OutEndloop: 0, F4 OutSegloop: 0, F4 OutRDI: 0
OAM cell drops: 0
Status: UP
```

As with Frame Relay, IP-address-to-ATM-address mappings can be either static (you create the map) or dynamic (inverse ARP [INVARP] creates the map). INVARP is enabled with the *pvc [name] vpi/vci* command, which is executed on a per-interface basis. Once that command is entered, ATM creates its mappings via the exchange of INVARP messages. You can create mappings statically using the *protocol ip x.x.x.x [[no] broadcast]* command; however, this command disables INVARP on whatever interface you execute it. The issues we discussed previously in the Frame Relay mapping section also apply to ATM. The technique you use to obtain your mappings depends on your particular network situation. The *show atm map* command can be used to check your mapping, as shown in this example:

```
RR1#show atm map
Map list test : PERMANENT
ip 192.168.99.99 maps to VC 999
```

As with any other WAN technology, your voice routers must be able to reach each other before voice peering can take place. With ATM, communications between your ATM interface and the ATM network must be operational, and IP addresses must be mapped to ATM addresses, either dynamically or statically. Ensure that IP is working over ATM before you attempt to start troubleshooting your voice configuration.

Layer 3 Troubleshooting

VoIP uses IP as its network protocol for transporting its calls. Unlike VoATM and VoFR, which directly use the Layer 2 protocols, VoIP configuration adds another layer to the mix (IP), meaning there's another layer to configure and troubleshoot. Problems with IP are problems for VoIP; VoIP cannot be separated from IP. Before you start troubleshooting your VoIP configuration, verify that your IP network is functioning correctly. You might also want to address additional Layer 3 issues such as QoS, queuing, and choosing the right bandwidth reservation schemes.

Troubleshooting IP

Common IP troubleshooting tasks include identifying and correcting addressing and routing problems. Issues with QoS, queuing, and other IP-based features will also crop up. Understanding these features used to support VoIP operation and troubleshooting them is important to VoIP. In this section, we discuss testing and verification measures you can take to ensure that your VoIP configuration is healthy.

IP Addressing and Routing

Entire books have been writing on IP, covering every aspect of it from subnetting to extensive troubleshooting. There is almost no end to the list of things that can go wrong with IP. Here we provide you with the fundamental tools and commands you can use to perform the testing and verification necessary to make VoIP function.

One of the first things you should do is check to ensure that the IP address and mask on each router is correct and consistent with the addressing and routing plan you developed and implemented. Sometimes the smallest mistake in addressing your interfaces can result in massive problems, as detailed in Figure 7.13, in which RR1 and RR2 are connected by a point-to-point circuit. As your first troubleshooting step, do a *show ip interface serial 0* on both to ensure that the addresses and mask are correct.

Figure 7.13 VoIP Network with Address and Routing Issues

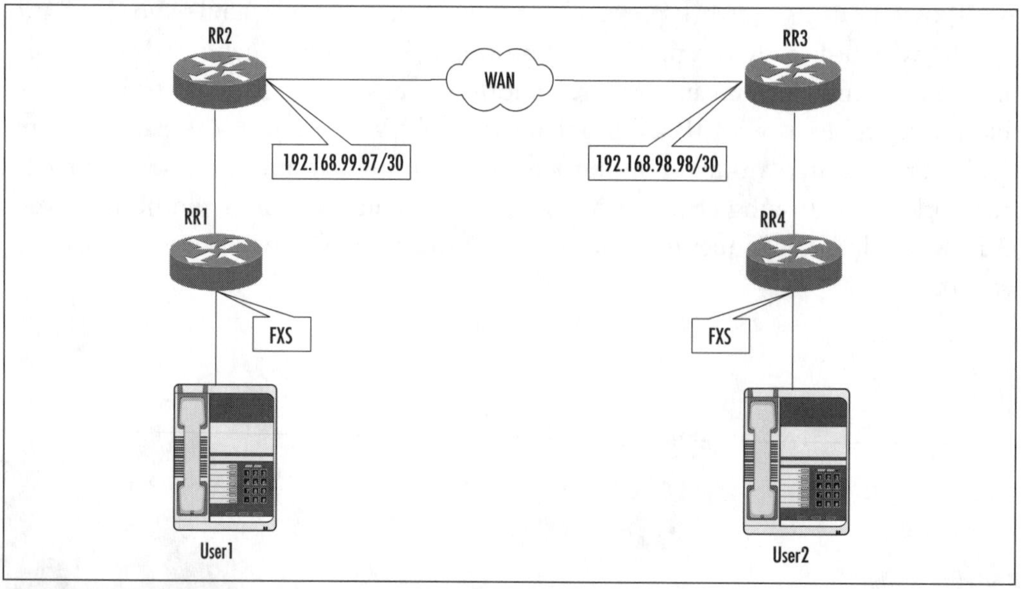
RR2
RR3
WAN
192.168.99.97/30
192.168.98.98/30
RR1
RR4
FXS
FXS
User1
User2

The IP network addresses of RR2 and RR3 are such that they are not on the same network. The third octet on RR3's side of the link should be 99, not 98. As result, if this problem is left unresolved, neither router will be able to communicate with each other or form the necessary routing relationships. This leads us to our next troubleshooting step: routing. Since RR2 and RR3 are not communicating or routing correctly, RR1 and RR4—which depend on RR2 and RR3 for connectivity to each other—will not be able to reach each other nor to form their dial peer relationships. No matter how accurate or correct your VoIP configuration on RR1 and RR4, it will not work because IP is not working between RR2 and RR3. The lessons of Figure 7.13 are tremendous to the understanding of the effects of IP on VoIP.

We can verify this reachability with a simple ping test. Neither RR1 nor RR4 can ping the other because RR2 does not have a route to RR4, and RR3 does not have a route to RR1. If you did a *show ip route* on RR2 and RR3, you would see that neither router has become a neighbor of the other. It does not matter what routing protocol you use—routers must share a common network between themselves in order to exchange routing information.

If we correct the third octet on RR3 from 98 to 99, the routers will converge and exchange updates. If you then repeat the ping test between RR1 and RR4, it will be successful, thanks to all routers now having complete routing tables.

With Cisco, we could have resolved our problem in a variety of ways, depending on what the actual problem was. For example, we could have put static routes on all routers or used a mix of dynamic routing protocols, default routes, and so on. Regardless of the solution you use, the point is that your VoIP routers that will peer with each other must be able to reach other. If you aren't able to accomplish that simple task, a more complex task such as VoIP is impossible.

You can use several commands to troubleshoot various IP addressing and routing problems. The *show ip interface* command can provide detailed information about a router's interfaces. You can obtain a snapshot of the routing protocols that are configured on a router with *show ip protocols*. The *show ip route* command enables you to view the contents of your routing table to confirm that the correct routes are being advertised and learned.

IP Quality of Service

IP QoS is the feature that enables the use of the IP precedence fields to provide faster service to selected (marked) traffic. This section discusses QoS and the ways it can be used to enhance VoIP performance. Simply enabling QoS is not enough; you also need to configure your queuing methods and bandwidth reservation protocols. Understanding of the configuration process is necessary to effective troubleshooting.

QoS enables you to ensure that VoIP is given the bandwidth it needs, that it bypasses congested links, and that it suffers no intolerable delays. Failure to do so means that your VoIP quality will suffer, meaning that VoIP users will have difficulty making calls and understanding each other.

The starting point for QoS is the IP header. Figure 7.14 shows the IP header; for purposes of QoS, we are most interested in the Type of Service, or ToS (precedence) field. It is in this field that you manipulate the settings to grant priority to VoIP traffic.

Figure 7.14 IP Packet

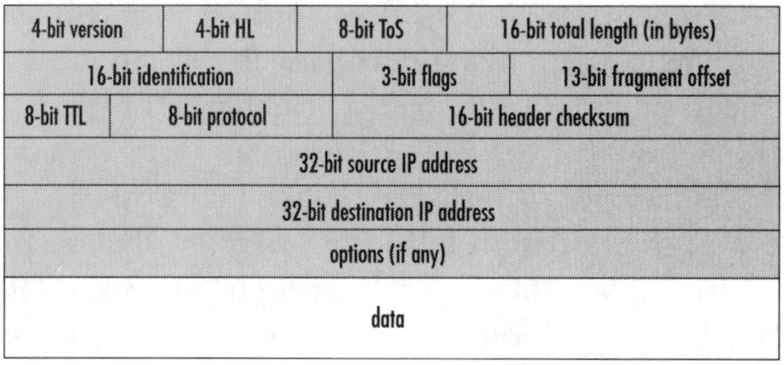

4-bit version	4-bit HL	8-bit ToS	16-bit total length (in bytes)	
16-bit identification		3-bit flags	13-bit fragment offset	
8-bit TTL	8-bit protocol	16-bit header checksum		
32-bit source IP address				
32-bit destination IP address				
options (if any)				
data				

The 8-bit ToS field in the IP header is where the precedence is set. Several values can be set to indicate the QoS desired. The 8-bit ToS field is broken down as shown in Table 7.3.

Table 7.3 Type of Service Bits and Meanings

Bits	Meaning
0–2	Precedence
3	Delay (0-normal, 1-low)
4	Throughput (0-normal, 1-high)
5	Reliability (0-normal, 1-high)
6–7	Reserved

The first three bits are used to set the precedence of an IP packet. They are set per the values shown in Table 7.4. Precedence values for VoIP should at least be priority (001); normal (nonprioritized) IP packets have their ToS set to 000 (routine). You set this value using Cisco IOS commands on the router interfaces.

Table 7.4 Precedence Bit Settings and Meanings

Bit Value	Meaning
111	Network Control
110	Internetwork Control
101	CRITIC/ECP
100	Flash Override
011	Flash
010	Immediate
001	Priority
000	Routine

When you want VoIP traffic to have precedence over other traffic, you need to mark it using the Cisco IOS commands that follow—specifically, the *ip precedence* command. In our example, we are setting the precedence to 5 (which is written in binary as 101), meaning that VoIP traffic will have marked as critical, giving it a very high priority:

```
dial-peer voice 999 voip
destination-pattern 999
session target ipv4:192.168.99.99
ip precedence 5
```

This setting ensures that VoIP traffic is given priority over many other traffic types.

Queuing

In addition to marking your VoIP packets via the IP header ToS precedence fields, you must configure a prioritization method that will support the precedence of VoIP packets. This capability is provided by the numerous priority queuing schemes Cisco supports. Of all the schemes available, Cisco recommends that low latency queuing (LLQ) be used for VoIP traffic. LLQ offers the flexibility to support multiple queues, enabling you to prioritize VoIP traffic. LLQ can ensure that VoIP gets the amount of bandwidth it needs for its calls yet still sets aside minimum bandwidth needed for other traffic. Such queuing is on a hop-by-hop basis and is effective only if enabled on each hop that the voice traffic must transit.

In this example, LLQ segregates traffic into four classes: a high priority class, two guaranteed bandwidth classes, and a default class. The priority class is guaranteed a priority over all other classes, regardless of how much bandwidth the other classes need. The two guaranteed bandwidth classes ensure that a certain minimum of bandwidth is obtainable for traffic placed in these queues. The default class is for any traffic not specifically allocated to either the priority or guaranteed classes.

To enable LLQ for VoIP, define an access list that permits voice traffic. Next, build class and policy maps that specify the bandwidth to be guaranteed VoIP traffic. Finally, apply this queuing policy to transit interface. An example of this configuration is shown here:

```
! Permit range of UDP ports used by VoIP traffic.
access-list 199 permit udp any any range 16384 37276
! TCP port used H.323 control channels.
access-list 199 permit tcp any any eq 1720
!
class-map voip
match access-group 199
!
policy-map PRIORITY
class voip
priority 32
!
interface Serial1/0
bandwidth 256
service-policy output PRIORITY
```

Cisco provides several commands to verify and troubleshoot LLQ. The *debug priority* command is used to monitor LLQ activity in real time. The *show queue* command shows priority queuing statistics such as packets passed or dropped through the priority queue. You can use the *show policy interface* command to check your interface to determine the policy that is running on it.

Bandwidth Reservation Schemes

As either an alternative or a complement to LLQ, you can use bandwidth reservation protocols to ensure available bandwidth for VoIP traffic. Cisco advocates two such schemes: Real-Time Protocol (RTP) and Resource Reservation Protocol (RSVP). This section covers each and provides troubleshooting guidance.

Real-Time Protocol

RTP can reserve a portion of your available bandwidth for UDP traffic. UDP is used to transport voice traffic in VoIP. RTP was not developed solely for VoIP traffic; rather, it was developed to support ensuring bandwidth for UDP traffic. When configuring it for VoIP traffic, ensure that you specify only the range of ports that VoIP uses. Otherwise, it will make reservations for ports not used by VoIP, which can steal bandwidth rightfully needed by VoIP. RTP marks voice traffic as priority over everything else, as shown in Figure 7.15. All other traffic is placed in queues are that prioritized and queued by either weighted fair queuing (WFQ) or class-based WFQ (CBWFQ).

Figure 7.15 Real-Time Protocol in Action

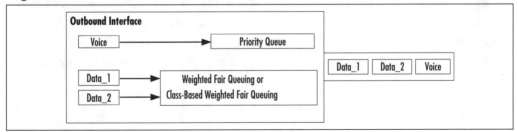

RTP is configured in interface configuration mode. Bandwidth is expressed in kilobits per second. RTP is enabled with a single command string, the generic syntax of which follows. In our example, we are reserving 64k for any traffic for 16,000 UDP ports starting with UDP port number 14,000. This means that UDP ports from 14,000 to 30,000 receive prioritized service on this interface:

```
ip rtp priority starting-UDP-port number-of-UDP-ports b/w-reserved-for-VOIP
ip rtp priority 14000 16000 64
```

Be aware that RTP makes a hard reservation. This bandwidth is locked and reserved, regardless of whether traffic is flowing over the selected ports or not. As far as VoIP is concerned, our configuration example was bad because it starts with 14,000. This means that our VoIP traffic could be dropped due to other protocols that use UDP ports specified in this range. Additionally, if we make a reservation for 16,000 ports and starting with port number 14,000, traffic could overwhelm the 64k reservation we created and steal bandwidth from VoIP traffic. We are giving precedence to non-VoIP ports: 14000 to 16383. Since voice ports typically use UDP ports in the range of 16384 to 37276, we should adjust our numbers accordingly to grant priority only to ports in this range.

The key to successful RTP use is identifying which and how many UDP ports are used by voice traffic and lock in the bandwidth for that range. When specifying the bandwidth, understand that this is the maximum amount of bandwidth that will be reserved for your VoIP traffic. Your calculations should factor the amount of bandwidth needed per call, the number of simultaneous calls, and a small burst budget. In addition to doing these calculations, you must be sure that you have enough bandwidth available on the circuit to support your requirements.

RTP offers an opportunity to increase bandwidth availability with its header compression. This feature can reduce the IP header from 40 bytes to 2 or 4 bytes, as shown in Figure 7.16. This is a per-packet reduction and is very significant when you consider that a typical voice call can send hundreds of packets per minute. Only a single command executed on the interface is needed to enable this compression:

```
ip rtp header-compression [passive]
```

The *passive* keyword needs to be entered on only one end. *Passive* turns on compression for outgoing packets if incoming packets have already been compressed.

Figure 7.16 RTP Header Compression

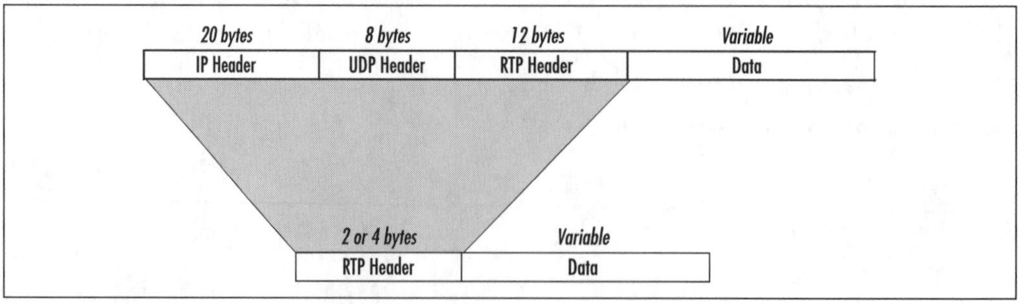

Verifying IP RTP Priority

Cisco provides several commands to check and monitor RTP. You can view the queuing operations on an interface with *show queue serial 0* to view queuing on interface serial 0, for example:

```
RR1#show queue serial 1/0
  Input queue: 0/128/0/0 (size/max/drops/flushes); Total output drops: 0
  Queueing strategy: weighted fair
  Output queue: 0/1000/128/0 (size/max total/threshold/drops)
    Conversations  0/1/16 (active/max active/max total)
    Reserved Conversations 0/0 (allocated/max allocated)
    Available Bandwidth 112 kilobits/sec
```

Several *debug* commands enable you to monitor RTP operations as they occur. The *debug priority* command is not RTP specific; rather, it shows the operation and errors with any priority queuing feature. This allows you to see if any packets are being dropped from your queue, which indicates that the maximum bandwidth you specified is enough or that you need to increase or decrease your range of UDP ports. You can also focus on specific RTP operations with *debug ip rtp header-compression* and *debug ip rtp packets*.

Resource Reservation Protocol

RTP reservations have to be specified on a hop-by-hop basis, repeating the same configuration on each router, but RSVP takes several steps toward automating the process. The originating RSVP host requests a path through the network that can support its bandwidth requirements. RSVP then queries each RSVP-enabled router to find the path that can support the bandwidth needed for the call. Once that path is built from source to destination, the call is switched along that path.

RSVP is enabled on an interface basis using a single command, as shown in the following syntax. You can specify that up to 75 percent of the interface bandwidth be reserved for RSVP traffic. In the command syntax, the *bandwidth* keyword specifies how much of the interface bandwidth is to be reserved for RSVP traffic. RSVP reservations are expressed in kilobits per second, so calculate accordingly:

```
ip rsvp bandwidth [interface-kbps] [single-flow-kbps]
ip rsvp bandwidth 64 64
```

Our example reserves 64k for our RSVP marked traffic, and of that, a single flow can use all 64k if necessary.

You request RSVP support for your VoIP traffic when you define the dial peer statements by including the following command. This syntax basically enables VoIP to mark traffic with a precedence in the ToS field that it is marked and prioritized for service by RSVP:

```
! Request RSVP
 req-qos controlled-load
```

Cisco provides several commands that you can use to troubleshoot and verify RSVP operation. The *show ip rsvp* command enables you to verify several aspects of RSVP, as described here. The *debug ip rsvp* command allows you to capture detail on RSVP activity as it occurs, either high level or detailed, depending on the amount of information you need:

```
show ip rsvp { atm-peak-rate-limit |  installed |  interface |  neighbor }
```

- *atm-peak-rate-limit* Maximum rate this ATM interface will handle (peak cell rate)

- *installed* Queues configured on this interface.

- *interface* Detailed RSVP information on this information.

- *neighbor* RSVP neighbors of this router.

```
debug ip rsvp { detail | detail sbm }
```

Troubleshooting Dial Plans

Dial plans are the number and digit patterns that you design and deploy in your network. They are defined in your dial peer configuration. Whatever dial plan you develop must be compatible with any existing PSTN network you are connecting to. Your telephone numbers (area codes, city codes, and so on) must interoperate with the digit scheme of your PSTN. If your VoIP is private and has no connection to any other network, PSTN or otherwise, you are free to deploy any number scheme you want.

The single most important thing you can do for your dial plan is to plan it. Before you begin to design your VoIP network, the first thing you should do is inventory your current network and your current telephone arrangements. After you audit and obtain this information, develop your dial plan and VoIP to be compatible with this existing arrangement and with any future growth needs you might have. The point of this activity is to avoid developing your VoIP in a vacuum. Figure 7.17 shows a simple VoIP network we will use to guide our discussion of dial plan planning.

Figure 7.17 Planning Your Dial Plan

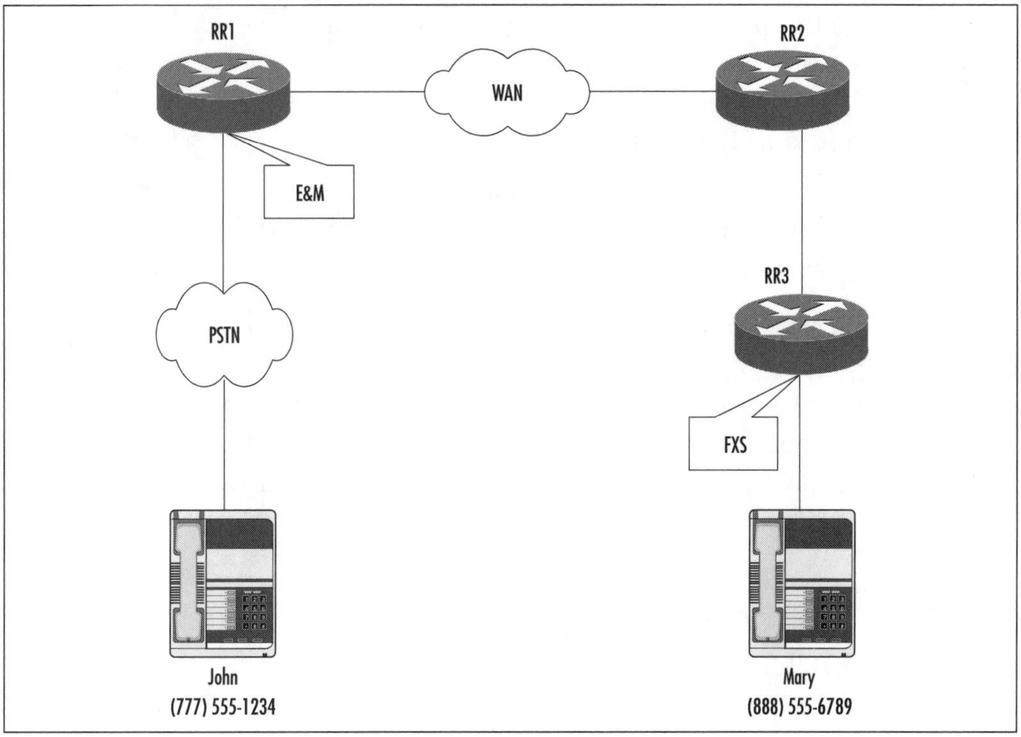

John is on a PSTN at telephone number (777) 555-1234 and wants to call Mary, who is reachable on a private VoIP network at (888) 555-6789. A number of things can go wrong if planning is overlooked:

1. The PSTN will have no idea how to reach Mary (that is, her number was developed without planning, or worse still, an actual number belonging to another entity was assigned to Mary, in which case, John will reach someone else).

2. Mary's number could be restricted to accepting calls only from other VoIP users, not outside users such as John.

3. John might need to dial a central number, then an extension number to reach Mary, rather than dialing directly. Although this is not necessarily a problem, this manual extra step can be an inconvenience.

4. Configuration on RR3 does not support 888 as a number: As far as it is concerned, Mary is at 6789 or 555-6789, not (888) 555-6789, and it will not know what to do with the number when it arrives.

An almost endless list of things can go wrong with a VoIP design. To avoid problems such as these, plan your design and decisions:

1. Use a dial plan that makes sense and can be easily routed through your network. For example, it could be that all calls that go to 888-555-*xxxx* should be routed to RR3, and from there, RR3 should be configured to send it to its final destination.

2. Arrange with your PSTN provider to route calls inward by getting telephone numbers that outside users can call. (You may opt to allow this only on selected phones.)

3. Consider all the dial situation possibilities (VoIP to PSTN, PSTN to VoIP, etc.) and address them.

4. Deploy your numbers so that switching is optimized, perhaps organizing the numbers along geographical and corporate organizational lines. One geographical area could contain all numbers starting with 888-555-*xxxx*, another could have all numbers starting with 888-556-*xxxx*, and so on.

Your dial plan should be utterly complete before you execute your first Cisco command. Before you deploy your plan, subject it to review within your organization so that you can be assured of addressing all angles.

Designing & Planning...

Dial Plans and You

When creating your dial plan, emphasis plan over everything else. Your planning needs to start with a requirements analysis to determine your needs for VoIP. This analysis should address potential VoIP locations, the number and types of users at each location, and the types of telephonic communications needed. For example, do all users need to call all other users? Does your network need to tie into a PSTN? Do PSTN callers need to be able to reach your users? What are your future expansion needs? Your plans could include replacing "expensive" telephone

Continued

company-provided lines with VoIP-based lines while retaining the same level of reachability.

After that requirements analysis is complete and has been structured into some semblance of logic and structure, you need to consider your dial plan. One of the biggest questions you need to address first is whether you want PSTN callers to be able to call users on your VoIP network. If the answer is yes, the other question you must address is whether you want them to be dialed directly (that is, the PSTN network calls a number and is immediately patched to your user). Or do you want the PSTN users call a central number, then dial an extension number to reach your VoIP user?

If you want PSTN users to be able to directly call your VoIP users, you need to acquire license numbers from your telephone company to cover them. Basically, you buy digits and install them on your VoIP network (telephone numbers without the telephone lines). If you opt to have outside callers dial a central number, then an extension to reach their desired caller, you can acquire a single number for each location to allow PSTN callers to reach your users. However, callers must take the extra step of dialing an extension to reach your user. Neither option is better than the other; your choice depends on your budget and needs.

Once you have settled your PSTN-to-VoIP calling issues, you are ready to assign numbers. Ideally, sites should have to have only a short string to reach other sites. In other words, instead of 500 dial strings to reach Site A, there should be a single dial string. For example, if the numbers at Site A start with 888-*xxx-xxxx*, all other sites should be able to reach Site A with a string of 888 and allow Cisco's number expansion features at the destination to do the rest.

Creating dial plans is a balance of costs, convenience, and efficiency. Follow the simple advice provided here to create elegant dial plans, and you will achieve these goals. Keep it simple, keep it cheap, and keep it easy.

The *show dialplan number xxxx* can match telephone numbers to dial peers. It can also provide useful statistics about your dial plan peers, such as how many calls have been made, destination patterns to be matched, and so on. The following sample output has been truncated to focus on the number expansion. In this case, we can see that a dial peer (Peer 1) has been configured to match and route anything starting with 99. Therefore, if we were having problems using any numbers starting with 99, we would check the configuration of this peer:

```
RR3#show dialplan number 9999
Macro Exp.: 9999

VoiceEncapPeer1
        information type = voice,
        tag = 1, destination-pattern = `99..',
        answer-address = `', preference=0,
        group = 1, Admin state is up, Operation state is up,
        incoming called-number = `', connections/maximum = 0/unlimited,
        application associated:
        type = pots, prefix = `',
        session-target = `', voice-port = `1/2/1',
        direct-inward-dial = disabled,
        register E.164 number with GK = TRUE
        Connect Time = 557, Charged Units = 0,
        Successful Calls = 40, Failed Calls = 8,
        Accepted Calls = 45, Refused Calls = 0,
        Last Disconnect Cause is "10",
        Last Disconnect Text is "normal call clearing.",
        Last Setup Time = 76528.
Matched: 9999    Digits: 2
Target:
```

For more information on dial plans, please refer to Chapter 5 of this book.

Troubleshooting Voice Ports

In our Layer 1 troubleshooting section, we discussed the physical characteristics of FXO, FXS, and E&M ports. In this section, we discuss the configuration troubleshooting of these ports. Troubleshooting processes for FXS and FXO type ports are similar, whereas E&M ports have their own checklist of troubleshooting steps. We cover some problems that you could encounter and provide tools with Cisco commands that you can use to isolate and resolve your problems.

Troubleshooting FXS and FXO Voice Ports

FXS ports are used to connect end devices such as telephones, fax machines, analog modems, and so on. FXO ports are used to connect to telco equipment such as PBXs. This is an important distinction to keep at the forefront of your mind as you configure VoIP on your equipment. We addressed the Layer 1 troubleshooting steps in the "Troubleshooting Voice Ports" section, so we do not rehash them here. Instead we delve into various Cisco commands that you can use to troubleshoot.

We use the simple VoIP network in Figure 7.18 to guide our voice port troubleshooting discussion. RR1 and RR2 are dial peers to each other, servicing VOIP Users 1 and 2, respectively.

Figure 7.18 VoIP Network Port Troubleshooting

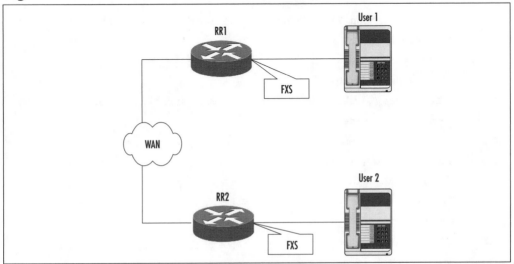

Start by ascertaining that everything is operational and healthy at Layer 1 by doing a *show version* to ensure that the router correctly recognizes the VoIP ports. You should get a display like the following:

```
R1#show version
Cisco Internetwork Operating System Software
(omitted content)
2 Voice FXS interface(s)
2 Voice E & M interface(s)
DRAM configuration is 64 bits wide with parity disabled.
125K bytes of non-volatile configuration memory.
32768K bytes of processor boar
```

Each router should recognize the ports as FXS voice ports, as shown in the preceding display. At this point, you can rest assured that your FXS card is installed and seated firmly, thus eliminating many physical Layer 1 problems.

If your telephones are plugged in, lift up a handset. You should get a dial tone. If you do not get a dial tone, ensure that your telephone is plugged into an FXS port and not an FXO port (which does not generate dial tone). This is a common mistake on routers that have both voice port types, since they look very similar. If the telephone is plugged into the FXS port and you still don't have dial tone, do a *show voice-port*:

```
Foreign Exchange Station 2/1/0 Slot is 2, Sub-unit is 1, Port is 0
 Type of VoicePort is FXS
 Operation State is DORMANT
 Administrative State is UP
 The Last Interface Down Failure Cause is Administrative Shutdown
 Description is Left Side Phone
 Noise Regeneration is enabled
 Non Linear Processing is enabled
 Music On Hold Threshold is Set to -38 dBm
 In Gain is Set to 0 dB
 Out Attenuation is Set to 0 dB
 Echo Cancellation is enabled
Echo Cancel Coverage is set to 8 ms
 Connection Mode is normal
 Connection Number is not set
 Initial Time Out is set to 10 s
 Interdigit Time Out is set to 10 s
 Call-Disconnect Time Out is set to 60 s
 Ringing Time Out is set to 180 s
 Companding Type is u-law
 Region Tone is set for US

 Analog Info Follows:
 Currently processing none
 Maintenance Mode Set to None (not in mtc mode)
 Number of signaling protocol errors are 0
 Impedance is set to 600r Ohm
 Wait Release Time Out is 30 s
```

```
Voice card specific Info Follows:
Signal Type is loopStart
Ring Frequency is 50 Hz
Hook Status is On Hook
Ring Active Status is inactive
Ring Ground Status is inactive
Tip Ground Status is inactive
Digit Duration Timing is set to 100 ms
InterDigit Duration Timing is set to 100 ms
Ring Cadence is defined by Cadence Pattern03
Ring Cadence are [15 35] * 100 mse
```

Check to see if your voice port is administratively shut down. Enable it with the *no shutdown* command. Lift the handset again, and you should have a dial tone. Ensure that the telephone you use for this test is a known good telephone and that it is not a digital telephone, which can have its own special requirements. Lift the handset and dial a number, any number; dial tone should cease.

Check your reachability: Have RR1 and RR2 ping each other. Are the response times acceptable for voice purposes? In our case, they are (less than 150ms):

```
R1#ping 192.168.99.99
Type escape sequence to abort.
Sending 5, 100-byte ICMP Echos to 192.168.99.99, timeout is 2 seconds:
Success rate is 100 percent (5/5), round-trip min/avg/max = 52/53/56
```

You can monitor voice port activity in real time with the *debug* commands. The *debug voice cp [slot/port]* command shows call activity on a particular interface. Here is an example:

1. Voice call processing state machine debugging is on:

   ```
   R1#debug voice cp 3/3
   ```

2. Handset is taken off-hook:

   ```
   3/3: CPD( ), idle gets event seize_ind
   3/3: CPD( ), idle gets event dsp_ready
   ```

3. Telephone number digit is entered:

```
3/3: CPD(in), collect gets event digit
3/3: CPD(in), collect gets event addr_done
```

4. Digits are completely entered and the call is initiated:

```
3/3: CPD(in), collect ==> request
3/3: CPD(in), request gets event call_proceeding
```

5. Waiting for response at called end (in this case, the telephone was answered):

```
3/3: CPD(in), request ==> in_wait_answer
3/3: CPD(in), in_wait_answer gets event call_accept
3/3: CPD(in), in_wait_answer gets event call_answered
```

6. Call has been completed, and the two peers are connected to each other:

```
3/3: CPD(in), in_wait_answer ==> connected
3/3: CPD(in), connected gets event peer_onhook
```

7. Call is disconnected (hang up):

```
3/3: CPD(in), connected ==> disconnect_wait
3/3: CPD(in), disconnect_wait gets event idle_ind
3/3: CPD(in), disconnect_wait ==> idle
```

Troubleshooting E&M Voice Ports

E&M troubleshooting is more complex than FXS/FXO troubleshooting. E&M ports are used for trunk or PBX-to-PBX communications. If a router has an E&M interface, it is performing PBX functions or communicating directly with a PBX as a PBX, complete with standard PBX functions and features.

Initial troubleshooting is similar to the troubleshooting of FXS and FXO ports. We use Figure 7.19 to guide our E&M voice port troubleshooting discussion. Figure 7.19 shows a simple configuration in which two PBXs are tied together via VoIP routers (R1 and R3). Note that RR2 has no voice capabilities of any kind; it is merely routing traffic between RR1 and RR3. RR1 and RR3 have their E&M ports connected to their respective PBXs.

Figure 7.19 E&M Configuration

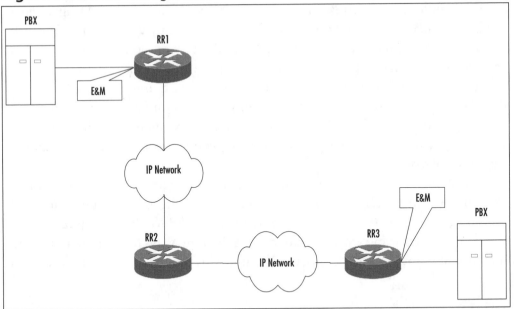

The initial troubleshooting process is similar to what you did for FXS and FXO ports, so you'll execute the same commands, such as *show version, show voice port*, and *ping* tests. Once successful, you can then focus specifically on E&M port issues.

If at this point the router does not recognize the E&M interface, power down the router and reinsert the voice modules. If the router still does not recognize the presence of the voice ports, you might need to upgrade your IOS to obtain VoIP support and to support the E&M cards. If, after doing all this, it the router does not recognize the cards, you might have faulty hardware, either with the router or with the E&M cards themselves.

If you have completed all the previous steps and detected no problems, you are ready to start troubleshooting the configuration of your E&M cards. PBXs have their own operating system and their own features that you need to configure the router to support. Currently, Cisco supports only a limited number of makes and models of PBX. Before you start extensive troubleshooting on your router, go to www.cisco.com and do a search for *PBX interoperability application notes* to obtain information on the PBXs Cisco supports. Any special configuration options you need to enable on either the router, the PBX, or both will be provided on this Web page.

Before configuring the router to interoperate with your PBX, you need to have in hand certain information about your PBX. What is the E&M signaling used by the PBX? Cisco supports I, II, III, and V, and only V (written as 5 in IOS configuration) is supported for U.S. configurations. Does the PBX use a two-wire or four-wire configuration for calls? How does the PBX signal call initiation—that is, the start of the dialing? PBXs can use wink-start, immediate, and delay-dial. You'll need to configure support for this function on your voice router. Is dial tone or dial pulse used? Nowadays, almost all new implementations are dial tone. Once you have this information in hand, you are ready to configure and troubleshoot your router configuration.

Check the configuration of the E&M interface by viewing the router's configuration file with the *show running* command. You can check the current status of the E&M voice port using the *show voice-port* command to obtain output, as shown in the following example. Notice that the type is E&M, and the port is up but currently not in use (*DORMANT*). Numerous timer values are also displayed:

```
R1#show voice port
recEive And transMit 1/1/0 Slot is 2, Sub-unit is 1, Port is 0
 Type of VoicePort is E&M
 Operation State is DORMANT
 Administrative State is UP
 No Interface Down Failure
 Description is not set
 Noise Regeneration is enabled
 Non Linear Processing is enabled
 Music On Hold Threshold is Set to -38 dBm
 In Gain is Set to 0 dB
 Out Attenuation is Set to 0 dB
 Echo Cancellation is enabled
 Echo Cancel Coverage is set to 8 ms
 Connection Mode is normal
 Connection Number is not set
 Initial Time Out is set to 10 s
 Interdigit Time Out is set to 10 s
 Call-Disconnect Time Out is set to 60 s
 Ringing Time Out is set to 180 s
 Companding Type is u-law
 Region Tone is set for US
```

PBX communications can be monitored in real time with several *debug* commands. The *debug vtsp dsp* command enables you to confirm whether telephone digits are exchanged between the E&M port and the PBX. In the following example (shortened for brevity), the E&M interface has sent the digits 20 to the PBX:

```
Jun 9 05:35:19.100: vtsp_process_dsp_message: MSG_TX_DTMF_DIGIT_OFF:
    digit=2, duration=110
Jun 9 05:35:19.500:: vtsp_process_dsp_message: MSG_TX_DTMF_DIGIT_BEGIN:
    digit=0, rtp_timestamp
```

Troubleshooting Dial Peers

Cisco defines four types of dial peer. One is the POTS dial peer, which is the simple mapping of a dial string to a voice port. The remaining three dial peers are VoFR, VoATM, and VoIP. The voice peer configuration starts with the command shown in the following example. The thrust of this chapter is VoIP, so we focus on troubleshooting VoIP dial peers.

At a minimum, in order for a VoIP peer configuration to be valid, it must have a destination pattern and a session target. The destination pattern is the digits or digits and wildcards of your telephonic destination; this would be a telephone number. It is entered with the dial peer subcommand, *destination-pattern*. The session target in the case of VoIP is an IP address of the remote VoIP peer. The session target is entered with *session target ipv4:x.x.x.x,* where *x.x.x.x* is the IP address of the remote peer. The answer address parameters are not required for calling but can make it easier to identify any calls from this peer. If this is not used, then incoming voice port identification information is used. It is entered with *answer-address xxx,* where *xxx* is the telephone number you want presented to the remote peer.

The following configuration shows the bare minimum you need configured to make a VoIP peer work:

```
dial-peer voice 11 voip
destination-pattern 9999.
session target ipv4:192.168.99.99
answer-address 3601
```

A large number of problems can occur with a VoIP configuration. Rather than attempting to address each scenario here, we discuss commands you have at your disposal to verify and support your configuration. We assume that you have already performed your troubleshooting at Layer 1 and 2 and that routing itself is not a problem. If you are at this point and have not done the troubleshooting as outlined previously in our methodology, go back and do so before diving into VoIP-specific troubleshooting commands.

Table 7.5 describes the commands you have at your disposal to check your dial peer configuration.

Table 7.5 Troubleshooting Commands

Command	Description
show call active voice	Displays a list of active calls (calls in progress).
show call history voice	Displays a history of calls made.
show controllers voice	Displays hardware information about voice modules and ports.
show diag	Displays information about the router hardware.
show dial-peer voice	Displays dial peers configured on the router.
show dialplan number *xxxx*	Shows how the digits you enter will be expanded and switched (the designation they are switched to).
debug vpm all	Debugs the voice-processing module (VPM) on the router.
debug cpm dsp	Debugs communications between VPM and DSP.
debug vpm port	Caution! Much output! Captures real-time port activity as the call progresses.
debug vpm signal	Captures signaling information.

Table 7.6 summarizes common VoIP problems, how to detect them, and how to resolve them. This is not an all-inclusive list, but it does cover several issues that you are likely to encounter.

Table 7.6 Common VoIP Issues

VoIP Issue	Resolution
Poor quality of calls	cptone might not be configured correctly.
Excessive echo	Adjust output of originating voice port with *output attention* command or try enabling *scho-cancel enable*. Try adjusting the echo-cancel coverage command.
Telephone does not ring	Use the *show voice port* command and ensure that the ring tone is configured correctly.
Slow or dropped voice traffic	Voice tolerates a maximum of 150ms one-way trip time; use a ping test to determine if the network is the problem and check your network for congestion.
Unable to make or receive calls	Ensure that peer statements are correct (*show running*).

Configuring & Implementing…

Compression and Consequences

Compression, of which there are several schemes that Cisco supports, can conserve bandwidth or enable more voice calls to be made with less bandwidth. As with anything in life, compression carries tradeoffs: You sacrifice voice quality for bandwidth savings. In addition, some troubleshooting issues could arise from using compression.

Uncompressed voice requires 64k to be clear and natural sounding (as natural as you can get with voice communications transmitted electronically). That is for one call. With the compression schemes shown in Table 7.7, you can transport your voice call using less bandwidth. This frees up bandwidth for other calls and/or data.

Continued

Table 7.7 Compression Techniques

Compression Scheme	Voice Bandwidth Required After Compression (kb)	Savings versus Quality
G.711 PCM	64	No bandwidth savings
G.726 adaptive PCM	32	50% savings, little voice degradation
G.729 Conjugate Structure Algebraic Code Excited Linear Prediction (CS-ACELP)	8	87.5% savings, acceptable voice degradation
G.723 MP-MLQ	6.3	Unacceptable voice quality
G.723 Algebraic Code Excited Linear Prediction (MP-ACELP)	5.2	Unacceptable voice quality

As a general rule, Cisco advocates and supports G.711 and G.729. Assuming a 64k bandwidth, G.726 offers only a 50-percent savings, which is just enough for one more call. G.729 allows you to cram eight calls in bandwidth that normally would be able to handle only one. You will notice a slight degradation in voice quality, though not an unacceptable quality. The G.723 standard is deemed pretty much unacceptable and offers little more savings over G.729. As a result, it is not often used.

Although you will acquire bandwidth savings, be aware that this compression is obtained by sampling voice at set intervals. This sampling can consume CPU cycles, and on an underpowered router (processor and buffers), this can cause delays, which can further degrade voice quality. If you are going to use compression, ensure that your router can handle it, that it has the most current and stable IOS, that there is ample memory to support sampling, and that your processor is powerful enough to handle the demands placed on it.

During the course of troubleshooting voice-quality problems, you need to eliminate or finger compression as a suspect. Use the layer-by-layer approach advocated in this chapter to ensure that all other pieces of VoIP are operational and working. If they are in good health, turn your attention to compression. Start by turning compression off for a particular call, and if the voice-quality issue disappears, compression is obviously the culprit.

Your next step is to determine *why* compression is the problem. Use the troubleshooting tools that Cisco provides to check buffers, processor

Continued

utilization, and so on. Chances are, you will find that you do not have adequate buffers available or a powerful enough processor to support compression. Your only recourse is to upgrade your hardware. If your hardware is not the problem, check your IOS support of compression; you might be able to solve your problem with a simple software upgrade.

Compression can be a wonderful bandwidth saver. Being able to troubleshoot and resolve voice-quality problems can aid your compression use.

Troubleshooting Signaling Errors

In this section, we discuss telephony signaling and trunking in detail as well as ways to resolve signaling issues. Signaling is not necessarily a VoIP-specific topic, because it applies to any sort of telephony. However, it is vital to have a good understanding of signaling so that you ensure that your troubleshooting is thorough. Probably one of the most common issues with signaling is mismatches that occur when a Cisco router is configured with the wrong signaling parameters.

FXS/FXO signaling

FXS and FXO interfaces share the same signaling types, of which there are two. Loop start and ground start are used to "seize" a line in preparation for making a call. This line seizure is also called *starting*, since it completes the circuit, enabling voltage to flow and thus "starting" the line.

Both loop start and ground start have three states. In the *idle state,* the handset is on-hook and no ring voltage is being applied to indicate an incoming call. The *seizure state* occurs when you take the handset off-hook, thus completing the loop and allowing current to flow. In the *ring state*, voltage is passed to the ring generator to indicate an incoming call. The same wires that carry voice are used by loop start and ground start to supply signaling. Doing so enables telephone companies to reduce the number of wires that they need to bring into a location.

Loop Start

Loop-start signaling is used on local loops to initiate a call, as shown in Figure 7.20. When a call comes in, the CO or PBX supplies AC current to the ring line, causing the ring generator to activate and thus ringing the phone. When you pick up the telephone, you complete the loop, and voltage ceases to flows to the ring generator.

Figure 7.20 Loop-Start Signaling

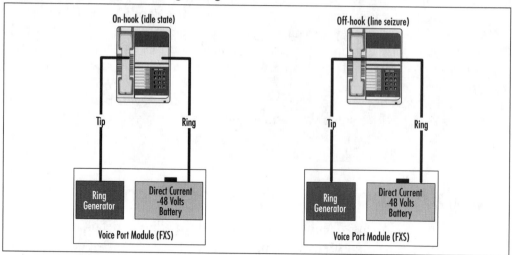

If you were initiate a call instead of responding to one, the mere act of lifting the handset would complete the loop, and the CO or PBX would generate your dial tone. When you dial your digits, the tones are sent back to the PBX or CO, and the call is completed.

Loop start works well for simple, single-line locations such as homes. However, it is prone to *glare*, a condition that happens when two parties want to speak to each other and call each other simultaneously, thus getting a busy signal and preventing the call from being completed. It is for this reason that ground-start signaling was developed.

Ground Start

Ground-start signaling works similarly to loop start, without the inherent glare weaknesses. Ground-start signaling can detect when loops have been seized at both ends. Figure 7.21 shows ground start in action.

When the line is idle, no voltage is supplied, as shown in the left side of the figure. When the line goes off-hook in preparation for making a call, voltage is supplied to tip and ring, and digits can then be passed to initiate the call, shown by the middle section of Figure 7.21. As with loop start, should a call come in, AC voltage flows over the ring wire, causing the ring generator to produce a ring tone. Should you lift the handset to make a call, you will complete the loop and get a dial tone.

Figure 7. 21 Ground-Start Signaling

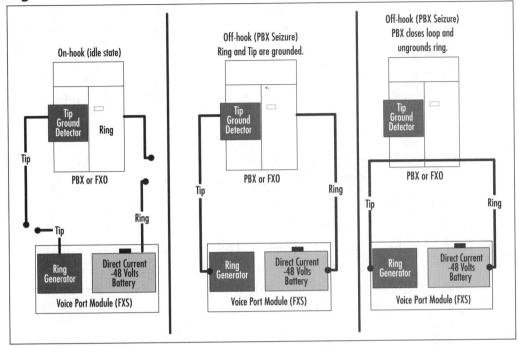

E&M Signaling

E&M signaling is more complicated to deal with because it is used on trunks as opposed to loops (lines). E&M is responsible for processing multiple calls simultaneously, rather than one like loop or ground start. Recall that one of the accepted definitions for the E&M acronym is *ear and mouth*. During its signaling processes, the M (mouth) wire sends the signal, which is received by the E (ear) wire. Let's discuss a few particulars of E&M.

Wiring Schemes

E&M has five wiring standards that dictate the purpose of individual wires. All except number 4 are supported by Cisco, as of this writing. Understanding each can be important to troubleshooting; they are overviewed in the following sections. Knowing the signaling types and where they are used can help with the configuration of E&M voice ports:

- **E&M Type I** According to Cisco, Type I is used in 75 percent of North American PBXs. This can be a key point to remember when configuring your router's E&M interface to support your PBX. Type I is a two-wire signaling scheme. It uses a separate wire for the E and a separate wire for the M; signaling information comes in on the E and goes out on the M.

- **E&M Type II** Type II is a four-wire signaling scheme. It has a wire for the E, a wire for the M, a wire for signal ground (SG), and a wire for signaling battery (SB). There is no common ground for the signaling; it is created on an ad hoc basis by the E and M return paths riding on the SG and SB wires, respectively.

- **E&M Type III** Type III is similar to Type II, with the exception that it provides a common ground. Type III is very uncommon.

- **E&M Type IV** Cisco does not support Type IV, a symmetric signaling scheme that uses a common ground.

- **E&M Type V** Type V is similar to Type I in that it is a two-wire signaling scheme. It is the most common signaling scheme outside North America, so if you are configuring your router to work with a PBX outside North America, knowing this can speed your configuration process. Type V has a common ground on its SG wire.

Trunk Seizure

In order to pass calls, E&M voice ports must seize the trunk. As with FXO and FXS using loop- and ground-start signaling to bring up the line and make the call, so must E&M interfaces initiate and use the trunk. E&M uses three techniques to seize the trunk and pass calls. We briefly cover them in this section. The figures in this section show PBX-to-PBX communications; the PBX icon in each figure can be an actual PBX or an E&M port performing PBX functions. Regardless, the signaling issues are applicable to both.

Wink-Start Signaling

Wink-start signaling derives its name from the fact that it technique has a certain wink appearance, as shown in Figure 7.22, from initiation to termination. In wink-start signaling, when the trunk goes off-hook, the remote PBX transmits an off-hook pulse at a set interval (measured in milliseconds). The originating switch waits a set interval (also in milliseconds) and then sends the telephone digits to the PBX. Wink-start signaling is very common.

Figure 7.22 Wink-Start Signaling

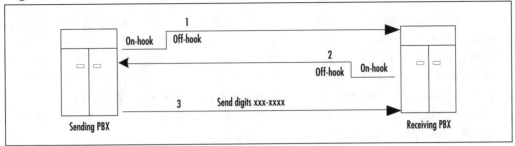

As shown in Figure 7.22, the sending PBX goes off-hook (1), and this condition is noted at the receiving PBX. The receiving PBX responds by also going off-hook (2). Upon receiving the "wink" (off-hook) condition from the receiving PBX, the send PBX then starts transmitting the digits (3).

Immediate-Start Signaling

With immediate-start signaling, the originating switch places the trunk in an off-hook condition, waits a set interval, and then starts the transmission of telephone digits to the PBX. Figure 7.23 shows a graphical representation of this behavior. This is different from wink-start signaling, in which the digit transmission does not start until the off-hook pulse is received from the remote switch.

Figure 7.23 Immediate Start Signaling

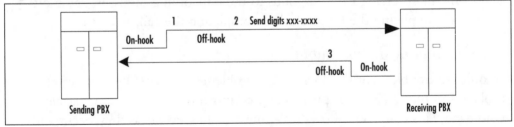

As shown in Figure 7.23, in immediate-start signaling, the sending PBX goes off-hook and waits approximately 200 milliseconds (1). Once that interval has lapsed, the sending PBX starts transmitting the digits to the destination PBX (2). The receiving PBX goes off-hook upon detecting the off-hook state of the sending PBX (3); this can be during the wait interval or upon receiving digits from the sending PBX.

Delay-Start Signaling

Delay-start signaling was developed to address a problem with wink-start signaling, wherein the remote switch might not be ready to receive the digits, even though it sent the off-hook pulse. With delay start signaling, when the originating side goes off-hook at the start, so does the remote side. The remote side remains off-hook until it can receive the digits, at which point it goes back on-hook. When the digits arrive, the remote side goes off-hook, and the call proceeds as normal. This behavior is illustrated in Figure 7.24.

Figure 7.24 Delay-Start Signaling

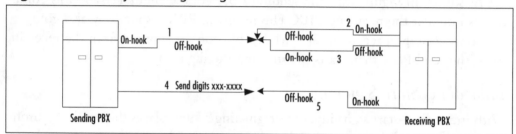

In Figure 7.24, the sending PBX starts by going off-hook (1). The receiving PBX then responds by also going off-hook (2). No digits are transmitted until the receiving PBX signals its readiness for reception by going back on-hook (3). When this on-hook state is detected by the sending PBX, it starts transmitting digits (4). The receiving PBX responds to these incoming digits by going off-hook and completing the loop (5), thus completing the call.

Troubleshooting Trunk Signaling

In order to troubleshoot trunk-signaling problems, your best bet is to catch the problems in the act. For this purpose, Cisco provided the *debug voice signaling* command. This command shows real-time signaling events as they occur and enables you to determine whether your E&M interface is communicating with the remote switches or local PBX properly. Optionally, you can specify a slot/port number combination to focus your troubleshooting on a particular E&M voice port. The output you see from this command is similar to that shown here. Notice that it provides information such as ring occurrences, hook states, and so on:

```
RR1#debug voice signaling 2/2
```

```
2/2: TIU, report_local_hook=1
2/2: TIU, set ring cadence=2
2/2: TIU, ringer on
2/2: TIU, ringer off
```

The *show voice port* command can also display information about the signaling method being used. *Show voice port summary* can provide a quick snapshot of your voice interfaces, as shown in the following. This quickly highlights your signaling on each port and can quicken your troubleshooting:

```
RR1#show voice port summary

                                IN       OUT
PORT    CH  SIG-TYPE   ADMIN OPER STATUS   STATUS   EC
======  ==  ========== ===== ==== ======== ======== ==
1/2     --  fxs-ls     up    dorm on-hook  idle     y
1/3     --  e&m-wnk    up    dorm idle     idle     y
1/5     --  fxo-ls     up    dorm idle     on-hook  y
```

Troubleshooting Gateways and Gatekeepers

Gateways and gatekeepers automate the translation of names (such as gatekeeper@ voip.com) and telephone numbers to IP addresses. They map and route traffic destined for a particular VoIP user to its destination. Gateways are edge devices such as routers configured for VoIP that connect the VoIP network to an H.323 device such as a gatekeeper. Gatekeepers are more concerned with routing calls through the network. To implement these functions requires IOS version 12.1(1), and hardware can be either AS53*xx* or 3640 and up.

Gatekeepers use and support the H.323 protocol to perform functions such as such as admission control and bandwidth control. It is to the gatekeeper device that VoIP devices register and request call support. This reduces the number of dial peer statements needed and automates call switching. Once configured correctly, gatekeepers provide dynamic switching of calls coming from a VoIP network.

Using a gatekeeper is useful in reducing your voice router configuration requirements (fewer dial peer statements are needed) and automates the call-switching process. You essentially reduce the amount of troubleshooting you need to do (less to troubleshoot on each router and a single point to check for call switching). As with all its other products, Cisco provides a wealth of trouble-shooting tools.

Use the *show gatekeeper zone status* command to determine the current status of your zones. You can also view information such as the maximum total bandwidth available for each zone you have defined. You can use this command to determine whether the bandwidth you have for a zone is sufficient or how much is currently available. This information can be useful if you need to determine whether your calls are being dropped due to insufficient bandwidth.

Another command you can use is *show gateway call* to view the current active calls. This command can be useful if you want to see if a particular gatekeeper is processing a call properly. It can also help you determine if the mappings are being done properly. Sample output of this command follows (abbreviated for ease of understanding). This is a call from 555-9999 to 555-6767; note the IP addresses used to make the call. You can use this command to ensure that your calls are being made as you expect them to be:

```
RR1#show gateway call

Total number of active calls = 3

                        GATEKEEPER CALL INFO

                        ====================

LocalCallID              Age(secs)       BW
12-9999                    60            64(Kbps)
  Endpt(s): Alias      E.164Addr    CallSignalAddr   Port   RASSignalAddr     Port
    src EP:              8885559999
    dst EP: RR2         8885556767   192.168.99.99    1720   192.168.99.100    52521
```

You can view the H.323 information of your gatekeeper with the *show gate* command. This command enables you to verify your gatekeeper configuration. Using *show gateway gw* displays information about the gateway function configured on this router:

```
RR1#show gateway gw
GATEWAY TYPE PREFIX TABLE

=========================
Prefix: 888#*


Prefix: 800#*
Zone ZONE800 master gateway list:
192.168.99.100: 1720 RR2
```

This output indicates that RR1 is an endpoint for calls starting with 888 and that calls to 800 numbers should go to RR2 in ZONE800.

The *show log* command reports on call history, both current and outstanding. It enables you to view the history of calls that were made from and to this gatekeeper.

In addition to these *show* commands, several *debug* commands can be used to track gatekeeper and VoIP events as they occur. As with all *debug* command, use them cautiously to solve a specific problem. Minimize use on a production device if you can. The *debug gatekeeper gup { asn1 | events}* command enables you to capture real-time data on gatekeeper events, which can aid in tracing and resolving gatekeeper problems.

Summary

Using a layered approached to your VoIP troubleshooting can greatly reduce your troubleshooting time. By starting at Layer 1 (physical) and working your way up the OSI model, you can logically attack your problems. By now, you should be familiar with at least the bottom three layers of the OSI model (physical, data link, and network) and how they pertain to VoIP troubleshooting.

Layer 1 is concerned with physical component problems. Typical physical components include the router, cabling, communications equipment, hubs, and so on. You must ensure that your physical components are healthy before tackling problems at the next-higher layer.

Layer 2 is concerned with access to the physical medium. It addresses issues such as packaging data for transport over some physical medium and reversing the process for incoming data. It has its own addressing schemes, such as Ethernet MAC addresses, that you need to know.

Layer 3, the network layer, is IP as far as VoIP is concerned. Addressing and routing needs to be operational and reliable before VoIP will work. Your routing protocols must be convergent. At the layers, your dial peers must be able to reach each other (verify with a simple ping test).

Start your troubleshooting at Layer 1 by checking your equipment (routers, CSU, and so on). At the bare minimum, your router should load and enable you to inventory its hardware. You can also verify the type of cables (if any) that are connected to your interfaces (such as V.35 DTE to Serial 0, for example). You must ensure that you have the right cable for the right job; sometimes, cable troubleshooting can be as simple as ensuring that the right cable is connected to the right port. The RJ11 and RJ45 standards have exacting requirements for the wiring; it is to your advantage to comply because doing so reduces problems due to crosstalk. As a rule of thumb, RJ11 cable should be plugged into FXS and FXO voice ports, whereas RJ45 or RJ48 cables can be used for E&M ports.

Knowing your voice ports and your signaling types is critical to dial peer configuration. Your voice port type (FXS, FXO, or E&M) determines the signaling (loop start, ground start, wink start, immediate start, or delay start) you configure.

FXS voice ports are used to connect end devices such as analog telephones, modems, and fax machines. FXO ports connect the voice router to a PSTN and do not supply dial tone. Either ground-start or loop-start signaling can be used with FXS and FXO ports. In the course of troubleshooting these ports, ensure that you have known good cable and that you are using the cables for their intended purpose. Because of the similarity in appearance of both ports, it's possible to misuse them (for example, plugging a telephone into an FXO port).

E&M voice ports are primarily for PBX interoperability and have three types of signaling: wink start, immediate start, and delay start. With E&M voice port configuration, you need information about your PBX configuration. E&M voice ports use either RJ45 or RJ48 cables; the former can substitute for the latter.

You need to be familiar with several areas to effectively troubleshoot your VoIP network. PBXs are used to consolidate telephone lines at location and transport them over a trunk to the nearest CO and from there, connect to the PSTN. You must be able to troubleshoot from your PBX to the CO and work with your provider to resolve common problems. Before you contact your provider, ensure that your VoIP and PBX are operating as they should. Circuits used in the transport of VoIP traffic must be healthy before VoIP will work; you should be able to perform loopback tests to isolate and resolve circuit problems.

In this chapter, we discussed Cisco routers and ways to verify them. Inventory the hardware and ensure that the router is recognizing the voice ports as well as ensuring that it has enough processor power and memory to support VoIP. At some point, VoIP traffic will traverse the router interfaces, so you need to ensure that they are configured and operating.

At Layer 2, you need to ensure that your interfaces are operating as they should. It is vital that they be configured and in an up state before VoIP troubleshooting is started. Frame Relay and ATM operate at Layer 2 and have some common issues such as network addressing mapping. Mapping is a very common problem, so you must ensure that IP addresses are mapped to Frame Relay DLCIs or ATM addresses before VoIP will work.

At Layer 3, IP addressing and routing need to be working cleanly, with correct addresses on all interfaces, and routing established such that each router in the VoIP network can reach the others. Without either of these configured and working, VoIP will fail to function. If you have limited bandwidth or want to ensure that VoIP calls are not degraded, you can implement various prioritization and queuing schemes. Liberal use of the ToS field in the IP header, along with a queuing scheme such as LLQ, can ensure that your voice calls do not suffer degradation of service, even during peak traffic times. With compression, you can get more calls into limited bandwidth, but be warned that compression can have a negative impact on voice quality.

Your first step in establishing your dial peering is planning, planning, and planning! Start with an analysis of your current dial situation to determine your requirements. By the time you touch your first voice router, your dial plan should be complete.

Gateways and gatekeepers can automate much of your call routing. If these are planned and deployed properly, you can configure the bare minimum on each voice router and use these products to route calls between sites. This can be a huge time saver as well as an aid to troubleshooting. You should know how to verify your gateway and gatekeeper configurations.

Once you have mastered all these areas, you are not only ready to configure your VoIP network, but to test, troubleshoot, and support it successfully.

Solutions Fast Track

A Basic Troubleshooting Methodology

- ☑ The OSI model, a seven-layer model for design and development, can be used to guide your VoIP troubleshooting.

- ☑ The OSI layers are physical, data link, network, transport, session, presentation, and application.

- ☑ When troubleshooting, start at the physical layer and work your way up.

- ☑ Structuring your troubleshooting layer by layer improves the efficiency and effectiveness of your efforts.

Layer 1 Troubleshooting

- ☑ Layer 1 troubleshooting is concerned with physical components such as routers, cables, CSUs, PBXs, and so on.

- ☑ Your troubleshooting should start at the physical layer so that you can be assured that your physical components are operational.

- ☑ FXS ports are used to directly connect end-user equipment such as modems, telephones, and faxes and provide dial tone.

- ☑ FXO ports are used to connect to a PSTN network and do not provide dial tone.

- ☑ E&M ports are used to connect PBXs.

☑ Cisco provides several commands for checking your router hardware, including *show diag* and *show controllers*.

Layer 2 Troubleshooting

☑ Layer 2 troubleshooting deals with data link issues such as getting data from Layer 3 to Layer 1.

☑ HDLC serial, Frame Relay, ATM, Ethernet, and so on operate at Layer 2, so you must be knowledgeable in troubleshooting them.

☑ Mapping issues are probably the most common issues in Frame Relay.

☑ ATM is one of the best network technologies for transporting voice due to its great support of QoS.

Layer 3 Troubleshooting

☑ Be sure that your IP addressing is correct (*show ip interface*).

☑ You can check your routing tables with *show ip route*.

☑ RTP creates a hard reservation priority queue for UDP traffic in a specified range (VoIP).

☑ LLQ is the Cisco-advocated queuing technique for VoIP traffic.

Troubleshooting Dial Plans

☑ The best thing you can do for dial plans is to completely plan them before execution.

☑ Your number scheme should seek to optimize call switching.

☑ Address PSTN-to-VoIP network issues in advance, and determine intercommunications that need to occur between the two.

Troubleshooting Voice Ports

☑ Ensure that you use your voice ports for their intended purposes; for example, do not plug a telephone into an E&M voice port.

☑ E&M voice ports have the potential to affect greater numbers of calls and require greater configuration.

☑ You need to have your PBX information available to successfully configure your E&M-to-PBX connection.

Troubleshooting Dial Peers

☑ The POTS dial peer is configured on a voice port that connects to the actual telephony device.

☑ The VoATM dial peer has its calls transported directly over ATM.

☑ The VoFR dial peer uses Frame Relay to transports its calls.

☑ The VoIP peer requires IP to operate and is sensitive to underlying IP problems.

Troubleshooting Signaling Errors

☑ FXS and FXO use loop-start and ground-start signaling.

☑ E&M voice ports use wink-start, immediate-start, and delay-start signaling.

☑ Your PBX determines the signaling technique you configure on your E&M interface.

Frequently Asked Questions

The following Frequently Asked Questions, answered by the authors of this book, are designed to both measure your understanding of the concepts presented in this chapter and to assist you with real-life implementation of these concepts. To have your questions about this chapter answered by the author, browse to **www.syngress.com/solutions** and click on the **"Ask the Author"** form.

Q: Can I use any signaling with any port?

A: No. FXS and FXO voice ports use loop-start and ground-start signaling. E&M ports use wink start, immediate start, and delay start.

Q: Does compression improve voice quality?

A: No. The goal of compression is to transport more voice traffic over limited bandwidth.

Q: Can I run VoIP over ATM and FR?

A: Yes, just as you do any other IP-based traffic. VoIP traffic is encapsulated in UDP packets, with IP addresses, and transported over ATM and FR. VoFR and VoATM are different in that they do not use IP addresses; instead, voice traffic is encapsulated directly into the Frame Relay packets and ATM cells.

Q: What is your first step in creating your dial plan?

A: Planning, which starts with an analysis of your current network and requirements.

Q: What are the issues with a PSTN-to-VoIP connection?

A: You need to ensure that PSTN users can call your VoIP users (either directly or via an extension system), and vice versa. This involves creating a dial plan and acquiring "legitimate" digits from telephone company.

Q: What is the difference between a gateway and a gatekeeper?

A: Gateways are edge devices such as voice routers that connect a VoIP network into an H.323 network, where gatekeepers route the call through to its final destination. Another way to look at it is that gateways bridge the VoIP network to the gatekeeper, which in turn routes the call to another gatekeeper or gateway until the final destination is reached.

Chapter 8

Connecting PABXs with VoIP Scenarios

Solutions in this chapter:

Introduction

Connecting private automatic branch exchanges (PABXs) with a VoIP solution is a simple method for introducing VoIP to an organization. Many corporations currently use tie lines, leased lines connecting PABXs, to connection offices that are in different geographic locations. This method of toll bypass is used to escape long distance charges that would be applied had the calls between the offices crossed the PSTN.

In this chapter we develop a case study with a sample corporation to test VoIP as a replacement for that company's current voice connections between PABXs. We follow this progression from information gathering to acceptance testing. We look at some of the techniques for collecting information and ways to assemble that information into a logical presentation for company officers or key decision makers. We also follow the steps involved in the design process and use the design to create configurations for a VoIP tie-line replacement. We add some advanced trunking scenarios and then integrate the voice and data networks; we conclude the chapter with a brief discussion of basic testing and verification of the VoIP solution.

Chapter 9 continues with the sample corporation moving into more complex VoIP solutions. Chapter 9 focuses on creating an intraoffice VoIP solution with one router, multiple routers, and connections to remote sites. Chapter 9 also covers basic Quality of Service (QoS) and traffic shaping for integrated networks.

Collecting the Information

In today's economy, many businesses are looking for ways to reduce costs in places they have never looked before. The telephone network is now a target for cost savings. VoIP has matured to a point that it is now deployed in conservative businesses that have traditionally avoided new technologies. VoIP includes the introduction of toll bypass, soft phones, PC-to-phone conversations, and desktop conferencing. The companies deploying these technologies are seeing an ROI within the first year of deployment.

Once the decision has been made to move to a VoIP solution, the planning process begins. The first step is collecting accurate information. This information will be used to decide on equipment that must be purchased, if new circuits must be ordered, what new options users anticipate, and any future plans that could impact the design.

Gathering Information for Design Purposes

A network analysis should be performed before any decisions have been made on design and before any equipment purchases have been made. You must understand the business drivers behind the change. What are the officers of the company hoping to gain with the move to VoIP? Which new features are the user groups going to expect? How will this design impact the current infrastructure? A company risks capital investment with no return on investment (ROI), or worse, destroying the current infrastructure with no viable alternative if current and future requirements are not identified.

Gathering information is done in several ways. In a business that has very detailed processes and detailed design documents, reviewing the existing documents could provide most of the information that's needed. In most instances, you will be required to interview key stakeholders and research their infrastructure. This process includes interviewing company officers to identify strategic initiatives, company mission, and long-term goals. Local administrators should be interviewed to assess current applications and platforms running on the network. Contractors or local support for voice systems can provide details on call volumes, inter- and intraoffice voice traffic, long distance calls, and available circuits. Information must be retrieved for any location that will be affected. The interviews can be conducted in formal meetings, informal one-on-one sessions, or by e-mail. If network documentation is current, it can be used; otherwise, a network assessment must be performed. That said, it always pays to verify the accuracy of existing documentation, even if is believed to be current. This can be accomplished using the network-monitoring system (if one is available) or manual network discovery if needed. Table 8.1 shows a sample checklist that can be used as a guide for gathering pertinent information.

Table 8.1 A Sample Checklist for Gathering Information

Key Components	Defined Areas	Sample Questions
Business Drivers	Scalability of existing system	Can the current system support the required change?
	Integration of current systems	Can any of the current systems be reused?

Continued

Table 8.1 Continued

Key Components	Defined Areas	Sample Questions
	Cost savings	What is the return on investment?
	Enhanced services	What new services can be offered?
Key Stakeholders	Company officers	What are the company's strategic goals? What projects are currently planned that can impact the deployment?
	Administrators	Which applications traverse the network? What applications require priority?
	Sample user groups	Which services do you want to gain? Which services would you like to see go away? What service can you not live without?
Hardware	PABX	Who services the PABX—staff or service contract? What ports are available? Will new hardware need to be purchased? Who provides moves, adds, and changes—staff or service contract?
	Network equipment	What new equipment must be ordered? Can the current equipment be reused or exchanged? Is HVAC available for an interim solution with both old and new hardware deployed?
	Servers	Do new servers need to be ordered?
	Wiring	Is current Ethernet wiring sufficient to deploy the new solution?
	Circuits	Will new circuits have to be ordered for voice service? Will new circuits have to be ordered for data service?

Continued

Table 8.1 Continued

Key Components	Defined Areas	Sample Questions
Software	Applications	Will new software need to be implemented for the solution?
	Network equipment	Will the OS need to be upgraded to support the new solution?
	VoIP	What codec will be used? What QoS will be deployed? Can the existing dial plan be migrated or will a new dial plan need to be developed?
Documentation	Network	Are current network diagrams available? Are all network element current configurations available?
	Servers	Are all servers and applications documented?
Security	Firewall	Will traffic traverse the firewall? Does the firewall support H.323?
	Servers	Is the OS on new systems hardened? Does the new system compromise any security policies?
	Network	Will any changes need to be made on the network to allow for H.323 traffic?

Designing & Planning...

Managing Your Network

In many small businesses, there is no active monitoring of any network elements. All problem management is reactive; when a remote site can no longer be reached or when the connection gets extremely slow, someone performs troubleshooting. In the past, it might have been acceptable to have the data network down for a couple of hours, but with the convergence of voice and data, most business are brought to a

Continued

stop in the event of a failure. As businesses move to integrated voice and data solutions, it becomes imperative that they begin actively monitoring their networks. This requires new equipment and new software and could require new personnel or training for existing IT staff. Many network solutions exist, from free and inexpensive solutions to feature-rich, expensive solutions. The cost associated with these solutions can be easily justified compared with the cost of having just 50 employees non-productive for hours or even days. Managing integrated solutions is not detailed in this book but should always be a consideration in any integrated voice and data design.

Compiling the Information

Once the information has been gathered, it should be consolidated and presented to the interviewees to verify content accuracy and overall intent. The intention here to ensure that everyone is on the same sheet of paper. Often your interpretation might not exactly match others' expectations. Once the information has been checked for accuracy, we need to place this information into a logical format for presentation to company officers and decision makers. This can be as simple as a small project—a one-sheet report summarizing findings with an attached invoice for equipment needs—to a large project with a detailed business case that has extensive voice and data traffic analysis and certified ROI detailing capital expenditures versus total savings for the projected life of the project. The end result is the same: to relay to the key stakeholders how this project will meet the company's goals. A typical business case for a project the size of this case study should include the following:

- Definition of business drivers and reasons to go to a new solution

- Explanation of any foreign technical terms; keep the explanations simple

- Summarized findings of the gathered information

- High-level drawings of current and proposed design

- Definitions of equipment, people, and process needs for the deployment of the new solution

- Definition of acceptance criteria

- Project plan with high-level tasks and associated time line

Once the business case has been presented and accepted, it is time to move into the design phase. It's worth noting that often during the design phase, we discover gaps in the gathered information. Although these project steps are presented sequentially here, they are quite often performed in parallel. As the designer is gathering information, he or she is refining the design. As the design is refined, he or she needs to revisit some of the information gathered or conduct additional surveys. Once this task is completed, the results are presented as an addendum to the business case and must again be reviewed for acceptance.

VoIP Corporation's Tie-Line Replacement

VoIP Corporation is headquartered in Atlanta, Georgia, with sales offices in various cities across the United States. VoIP Corporation currently has tie lines between its headquarters and each of its sales offices. The tie lines consist of fractional T1 leased lines connecting the PABX in Atlanta to the PABX at each office and utilize traditional voice signaling between these sites. The data network is a hub-and-spoke network using Frame Relay to each site. The company's corporate officers have decided to test VoIP in three of their offices as a replacement for their tie lines. They cannot tolerate an outage, so they prefer a slow migration. This migration will include deploying the VoIP trial in a separate network, and once it is proven, they will migrate the data traffic. They have used the sample checklist from Table 8.1 to help determine how to approach this trial. They came up with the following findings.

Business Drivers

- The current PABX does not support VoIP. A compatible solution will have to be deployed.

- The current PABX will still be used for all but interoffice calls.

- Immediate cost savings are realized by canceling the tie-line circuits.

- New 64Kbps circuit can be added to the tie-line replacement connecting to the PABX as long as bandwidth is available on the WAN with no intervention from the long distance provider.

Key Stakeholders

- The company is looking to be able to deploy enhanced services such as unified messaging, auto attendant, and videoconferencing in the future.

- The company has plans to move to a new Frame Relay carrier and move away from its current Cisco 2610 to the more robust Cisco 3640.

- The Washington, D.C., office is scheduled to move to a new location. This move will occur in the same time period as the VoIP trial. The test cities now include New York, Chicago, and Atlanta.

- All remote sites get e-mail and Internet service via the Atlanta office.

- Backups of local servers at each site are done over the WAN to tape drives at the Atlanta office. These backups are done after business hours.

- The VoIP trial should not adversely affect any users. No enhanced services will be deployed with this trial.

Hardware

- The VoIP Corporation maintains a service contract on its Nortel Meridian PABX. A service request will have to be opened to have a technician make required changes for the VoIP trial.

- The current tie-line port on the PABX will be utilized for the trial.

- New cards will have to be ordered for the Cisco 3640. A high-density voice network module with a two-port T1 multiflex voice/WAN interface card has been selected. Cisco part number is NM-HDV-2T1-48.

- It has been determined that all sites meet the space and environmental requirements of the new equipment to be installed.

- No servers are required for the VoIP trial.

- Only one new Ethernet connection will be needed to connect each new router to its existing LAN.

- New Frame Relay circuits have already been ordered and will be in place for the VoIP trial.

- The old Frame Relay circuits will be canceled once the VoIP trial is complete and VoIP and data traffic have been integrated.

Software

- The Cisco routers will be shipped running IOS version 12.2(6c) Enterprise Edition.

- The VoIP trial will initially be deployed using the G.729 codec. This might not be the final codec agreed upon.

- QoS issues will be addressed at a later date.

- The current dial plan can be ported to the VoIP trial using the following extensions:

  - **Atlanta** 4*xxxx*

  - **Chicago** 5*xxxx*

  - **New York** 6*xxxx*

Documentation

- Network diagrams have been updated with the latest changes.

- All configuration files are stored weekly on the TFTP server.

- No servers or applications need to be documented for this trial.

Security

- The VoIP trial will include only trusted entities and the remote sites and will not need to traverse the firewall.

- The new routers will employ the current security configuration template.

Compiling the Information

The planners have made the serendipitous discovery that a separate network is already in the implementation stage. This project is aimed at moving to higher-bandwidth circuits on a different Frame Relay provider. The project will complement the VoIP trial, allowing the VoIP traffic to be deployed first on the new Frame Relay network without the interference of data traffic. This trial, if successful, will give the company the confidence to move forward with a total VoIP deployment. Washington, D.C., was to be one of three cities to trial VoIP. This choice has now been changed to Chicago.

The VoIP deployment should be invisible to the user community. The remote office server backups are done after hours and will not affect VoIP traffic. The two-stage deployment will ensure that no outages occur during business hours. If problems are discovered during the trial period, interoffice traffic can be rerouted over the PSTN. This data has been compiled and placed in the following business case.

Business Case: VoIP Tie-Line Replacement

VoIP Corporation is a medium-sized sales organization headquartered in Atlanta, with regional sales offices across the United States. After enjoying remarkable sales over the last two fiscal years, the company has seen its sales slip over the current year, and the VoIP Corporation is looking to cut cost in any area not directly connected to sales. Combining voice and data networks appears to be a promising option. In an effort to assess the viability of a converged network, the company will perform a trial of VoIP by first removing its tie lines between headquarters and two of the high-volume sales offices and instead moving the calls over a converged network.

Key Terms

Here is a brief listing of the key terms used in this case study:

- **Public switched telephone network (PSTN)** The phone network created by the networking of various telephone companies' networks for public use.

- **Private automatic branch exchange (PABX)** A PABX provides switching for internal calls between extensions and switching for internal calls destined for the PSTN.

- **Tie line** A tie line or trunk is a leased-line connection between two PABXs, often deployed to bypass long distance toll charges.

- **Voice over Internet Protocol (VoIP)** Literally sampling voice streams and placing them in packets to be sent across an IP network.

Data Summary

Here is the data summary for this case study:

- **Business Drivers**
  - Immediate cost saving is realized by canceling current tie-line circuits.

- Voice capacity can be readily upgraded, given adequate bandwidth on the network.

- **Key Stakeholders**

  - The VoIP trial validates future plans to deploy a fully interacted VoIP solution with enhanced services such as unified messaging, auto attendant, and videoconferencing.

  - Integrating data with voice traffic should not affect voice quality. Peak utilization of the data network will occur after hours.

  - The VoIP trial will require no new training for end users, and the deployment should be invisible to them.

  - The VoIP trial will coincide with the planned upgrade to the Frame Relay network.

- **Hardware**

  - The VoIP Corporation maintains a service contract on its Nortel Meridian PABX. A service request will have to be opened to have a technician make required changes for the VoIP trial.

  - The current tie-line port on the PABX will be utilized for the trial.

  - New cards will have to be ordered for the Cisco 3640. A high-density voice network module with a two-port T1 multiplex voice/WAN interface card has been selected. The Cisco part number is NM-HDV-2T1-48.

  - Current space and environmental controls meet the new equipment's requirements.

  - No new servers will need to be purchased.

- **Software**

  - The Cisco routers will be shipped running IOS version 12.2.6c Enterprise Edition.

  - No new applications need to be purchased for the VoIP trial.

  - The current dial plan can be ported to the VoIP trial.

- **Network**

  - Network diagrams have been updated with the latest changes.

■ All configuration files are stored weekly on the TFTP server for backup recovery if needed.

■ **Security**

■ The VoIP trial will include only trusted entities, the remote sites, and will not need to traverse the firewall.

■ The new routers will employ the current security configuration template.

Network Design

The current data network is a hub-and-spoke Frame Relay network between headquarters and the sales offices. Each office has its own PABX, with tie lines connecting them back to the headquarters PABX. The tie lines are fractional T1 leased lines. The large sites have 10 channels going to headquarters, and smaller sites have fewer than 10 channels, according to voice traffic and staff size. Figure 8.1 shows the connections between headquarters and two sites.

Figure 8.1 A High-Level View of the Current Network

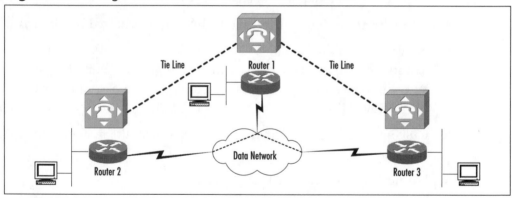

The planned network design removes the tie lines and pushes interoffice traffic between headquarters and two sales offices over the data network. The PABXs will connect to voice trunk cards on the voice-enabled Cisco WAN routers. The routers will encode the voice traffic and route it across the data network. The traffic will then be decoded at the far end and switched to the far-end PABX. Figure 8.2 depicts this configuration.

Figure 8.2 The Planned Network Design

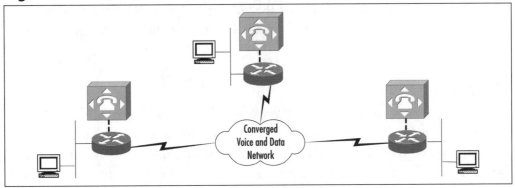

Deployment Requirements

Here is a listing of the deployment requirements:

- **Equipment**
  - Three new cards will have to be ordered for the Cisco 3640s. The Cisco part number is NM-HDV-2T1-48. These are high-density voice network modules with a two-port T1 multiplex voice/WAN interface. These cards will provide a port to connect the PABX with the router.
  - Three T1 crossover cables will provide a connection between the PABX and the router in each location. Extra crossover T1 cables should be purchased for spares.

- **People**
  - The staff will have to be trained on VoIP and QoS basics. The following are some recommended courses: Cisco Voice Over Frame Relay, ATM, and IP (CVOICE) v3.1 and Deploying QoS for Enterprise Networks (DQOS) v1.0. Check Cisco's Web site for the latest information.
  - The IT staff will have to coordinate with the PABX support contractor for both testing and turnup of the trunks between the routers and the PABX.

- **Processes**
  - The staff at each location will need to be informed that the IT staff will now be the point of contact for any voice/PABX issues.

- The IT staff will be in charge of troubleshooting any interoffice problems that are part of the VoIP trial. The staff will also be the point of contact with the PABX support contractor for any other voice/PABX issues.

Acceptance Criteria

The tie-line replacement trial will be considered a success after two weeks of normal business traffic with no reports of trouble. This situation will take place only after both voice and data have been combined on one network and normal business transactions, such as voice calls, e-mail, and file transfers, have been completed. After the two-week period, the PABX support contractor and the IT staff will check for errors in the router logs and in the call detail records (CDRs) from the PABX. When no new issues have surfaced, the trial will be deemed successful.

Project Time Line

The project plan in Figure 8.3 provides a high-level schedule of tasks that are to be completed for the successful implementation of the VoIP tie-line replacement trial.

Figure 8.3 The Project Plan for VoIP Tie-Line Replacement

	❶	Task Name	Duration	Start	Finish	Predecessors
1		⊟ VoIP Tie Line Replacement	35 days?	Tue 6/4/02	Mon 7/22/02	
2		⊟ Collecting the Information	6 days?	Tue 6/4/02	Tue 6/11/02	
3		Business Drivers	1 day?	Tue 6/4/02	Tue 6/4/02	
4		Key Stakeholders	1 day?	Wed 6/5/02	Wed 6/5/02	3
5		Hardware	1 day?	Thu 6/6/02	Thu 6/6/02	4
6		Software	1 day?	Fri 6/7/02	Fri 6/7/02	5
7		Documentation	1 day?	Mon 6/10/02	Mon 6/10/02	6
8		Security	1 day?	Tue 6/11/02	Tue 6/11/02	7
9		⊟ Compiling the information	3 days?	Wed 6/12/02	Fri 6/14/02	2
10	📆	Summarize the Findings	1 day?	Wed 6/12/02	Wed 6/12/02	
11		Verify the Findings	1 day?	Thu 6/13/02	Thu 6/13/02	10
12		Build a Business Case	1 day?	Fri 6/14/02	Fri 6/14/02	11
13		⊟ Designing a Basic Tie Line Replacement with VoIP	5 days?	Mon 6/17/02	Fri 6/21/02	9
14	📆	Create Basic Network Design	1 day?	Mon 6/17/02	Mon 6/17/02	
15		⊟ Create Detailed Network Design	4 days?	Tue 6/18/02	Fri 6/21/02	14
16	📆	Circuit Types	1 day?	Tue 6/18/02	Tue 6/18/02	
17	📆	Port Assignments	1 day?	Tue 6/18/02	Tue 6/18/02	
18	📆	IP addressing	1 day?	Wed 6/19/02	Wed 6/19/02	
19	📆	VoIP CODEC	1 day?	Wed 6/19/02	Wed 6/19/02	
20	📆	Bandwidth Requirements	1 day?	Thu 6/20/02	Thu 6/20/02	
21	📆	Cisco IOS Version	1 day?	Fri 6/21/02	Fri 6/21/02	
22	📆	Dial Plan	1 day?	Fri 6/21/02	Fri 6/21/02	
23		⊟ Configuring a Basic Tie Line Replacement with VoIP	3 days?	Tue 6/25/02	Thu 6/27/02	13
24	📆	Create Configurations	1 day?	Tue 6/25/02	Tue 6/25/02	
25	📆	Test Configurations	2 days?	Wed 6/26/02	Thu 6/27/02	24
26		⊟ Integrating Voice and Data	6 days?	Fri 6/28/02	Fri 7/5/02	23
27		Create VoIP Isolated Network	1 day?	Fri 6/28/02	Fri 6/28/02	
28	📆	Move old Frame Relay Network to new router.	1 day?	Wed 7/3/02	Wed 7/3/02	
29	📆	Combine VoIP and Data on New Frame Relay Network	1 day?	Fri 7/5/02	Fri 7/5/02	
30		⊟ Testing the Deployed Solutions	17 days?	Fri 6/28/02	Mon 7/22/02	
31	📆	Testing VoIP Isolated Network	4 days?	Fri 6/28/02	Wed 7/3/02	
32	📆	Testing Common Router/Diverse Frame Relay Networks	3 days?	Wed 7/3/02	Fri 7/5/02	
33	📆	Testing Converged Network	11 days?	Mon 7/8/02	Mon 7/22/02	

Designing a Basic Tie-Line Replacement with VoIP

The process of designing VoIP networks can go from the very simple tie-line or toll bypass deployments to very complicated multisite deployments integrating video, voice, and data. Complex VoIP network designs are covered in Chapters 9 and 10, but the following are some basic VoIP design guidelines:

- Design using the K.I.S.S rule: Keep-It-Simple Solutions. Do not over-complicate solutions.

- Mitigate risk. Understand the expertise of people who will support the network, and design accordingly.

- Know how much risk or downtime the corporation can endure when deploying leading-edge technologies.

- Provide for redundancy in both the server and the network equipment.

- Ensure that the solution is scalable. The solution should be able to grow with new technologies and business growth.

Basic Design Principles for Tie-Line Replacement

A VoIP tie-line replacement, although simple, should still follow basic design principles. At this point in our case study, data has been collected and compiled, and we will use this information to guide our design. First we create a basic network diagram detailing the planned network layout. The diagram should include any relevant systems such as routers, switches, PABXs, and servers. We want to ensure that the current router can support VoIP, has a port density to allow for additional growth, and has sufficient throughput to handle the addition of voice traffic. We assume that each voice stream will produce 50 packets per second (pps). Now, based on the number of voice streams and the number of trunks required, we can determine whether the current routers meet the requirements or need to be upgraded. Table 8.2 provides some example routers with their attributes.

Table 8.2 Router Attributes

Router	Processor	Port Density	Throughput	Voice Capable?
Cisco 2610	40MHz CPU	4 T1/E1	15Kpps	Yes
Cisco 2620	50MHz CPU	4 T1/E1	25Kpps	Yes
Cisco 3620	80MHz CPU	4 T1/E1	40Kpps	Yes
Cisco 3640	100MHz CPU	8 T1/E1	70Kpps	Yes
Cisco 7204	263MHz CPU	32 T1/E1	300Kpps	Yes

We must also ensure that sufficient ports are available on the LAN switch and that an adequate number of trunks are vacant on the PABX for the deployment. A solution that involves VoIP-enabled phones could also require that the switch provide power over Ethernet.

Next we want to populate the network design with circuit types that include PABX-to-router circuits and router-to-router WAN circuits and router port assignments with IP addresses. In the information-gathering phase, we determined the type of circuit that is currently used for the PABX tie line. This is either an analog or digital connection, which determines the type of trunk card needed for the router. Digital connections may use channel-associated signaling (CAS) or common channel signaling (CCS). ISDN is a familiar type of CCS, and robbed-bit signaling is a common type of CAS. Analog connections for tie lines are typically E&M interfaces. The interface can use E&M wink-start, E&M immediate-start, or delay-start supervisory signaling. You should check Cisco's Web site for the latest compatibility details between your PABX and your router. The network drawing currently includes circuit detail per router port and IP addresses for the LAN and WAN ports.

At this time we must choose a VoIP codec and router IOS to suit the company's needs. What is most important—voice quality or bandwidth conservation? Voice quality has been quantified using the *mean opinion score (MOS)*. MOS is derived from test groups listening to speech samples and grading them from bad to excellent (see Table 8.3). Each codec uses a different voice compression technique and different sampling sizes to encode voice traffic (see Table 8.4). The G.729 codec is often chosen for its compromise between high-quality voice and low bandwidth usage, but each company must choose the VoIP codec that most closely matches its needs.

Table 8.3 Mean Opinion Scores

Rating	Speech Quality	Level of Distortion
5	Excellent	Imperceptible
4	Good	Just perceptible; not annoying
3	Fair	Perceptible; slightly annoying
2	Poor	Annoying but not objectionable
1	Unsatisfactory	Very annoying; objectionable

Table 8.4 Codec Qualities

Encoding Compression	Mean Opinion Score (MSO)	Bit Rate (Kbps)	Voice Quality
G.711	4.1	64	A
G.729	3.92	8	A
G.723.1	3.65	5.3	C

We calculate the required bandwidth using VoIP codec and current voice traffic plus the data traffic, taking into account any new applications that could be deployed. Here are the calculations for G.729 over Frame Relay links:

- **Packet size** 6 bytes link layer + 40 bytes header + 20 bytes payload = 66 bytes per packet

- **Bandwidth per call** 66 bytes × 8 bits/byte × 50pps = 26.4kbps

- **Minimum VoIP bandwidth requirements (assuming a full T1 of traffic)** 24 calls × 26.4kbps = 0.634Mbps

- **Total bandwidth requirements** If we are currently using a maximum of 0.560Mbps for data traffic, the total bandwidth requirements will be 0.560Mbps + 0.634 Mbps = 1.20Mbps

Our total bandwidth requirements are 1.20Mbps for both voice and data. This figure needs to be calculated for each VoIP path. This is demonstrated in our case study with Atlanta, which has two paths for voice and data traffic, and the sales offices have only one path for voice and data. When you're purchasing bandwidth, always round up when calculating these figures to provide for growth. Once you have chosen a codec, you must select an IOS version for the routers. The same IOS will be deployed on the routers to ensure that no interoperability issues are created. In the case study, we have selected IOS version 12.2(6c) Enterprise Edition. With the rapid adoption of VoIP solutions, you should always refer to the Cisco Web site for the version of software that meet your needs, and always review the bug reports before electing an IOS version.

Finally, we add the dial plan and destination IP addresses to the network diagram. These additions help us visualize VoIP flow through the network. We can use this information to create a dial plan spreadsheet detailing voice port, dial peers, destination pattern, prefix, and type for each router (see Table 8.5).

Table 8.5 A Dial Plan Spreadsheet

Router	Dial Peer	Type	Destination Pattern	Target
Router1	10000	POTS	1....	Port1/0:1
	20000	VoIP	2....	10.10.1.2
	30000	VoIP	3....	10.10.1.3
Router2	10000	VoIP	1....	10.10.1.1
	20000	POTS	2....	Port1/0:1
Router3	10000	VoIP	1....	10.10.1.1
	30000	POTS	3....	Port1/0:1

We now have enough information to begin writing the router configurations. The configurations should be proven in a lab environment before being implemented in production network. Creating a lab environment for the VoIP tie-line replacement can be trying, given that few organizations have spare PABXs as test equipment, but you can employ some creative alternatives. To test call routing, FXS ports can be installed in the routers and analog phones can be attached to each. If a port is available on the PABX, it can be set up with a special extension for test purposes. Testing can be done after hours, when no calls are being processed. The tie-line can be temporarily removed from the PABX and replaced before traffic picks up in the morning. Try to make testing as close to the production network as possible, but improvise if needed. Finally, always test the solution before placing it into production.

Designing the Basic Tie-Line Replacement

VoIP Corporation has decided to take a conservative approach to deploying VoIP. Currently, the PABXs in each location are networked via fractional T1 connections, and the data network is a completely separate Frame Relay network (see Figure 8.4). The design entails replacing the current tie lines with VoIP connections across a Frame Relay WAN. The VoIP design is running in conjunction with a move to replace current 2600 routers with 3600 routers and to move to new Frame Relay provider for more bandwidth at a lower cost. The data network is designed as a hub-and-spoke rather than a full-mesh or partial-mesh topology. Most data flows are from headquarters to a remote office or from a remote office to headquarters. Very little data flows from sales office to sales office. Although this setup does provide a single point of failure for the network, the cost savings still outweigh the cost of redundant connections. With the integration of voice on the data network, redundant links can eventually be justified.

Figure 8.4 VoIP Corporation's Current Network

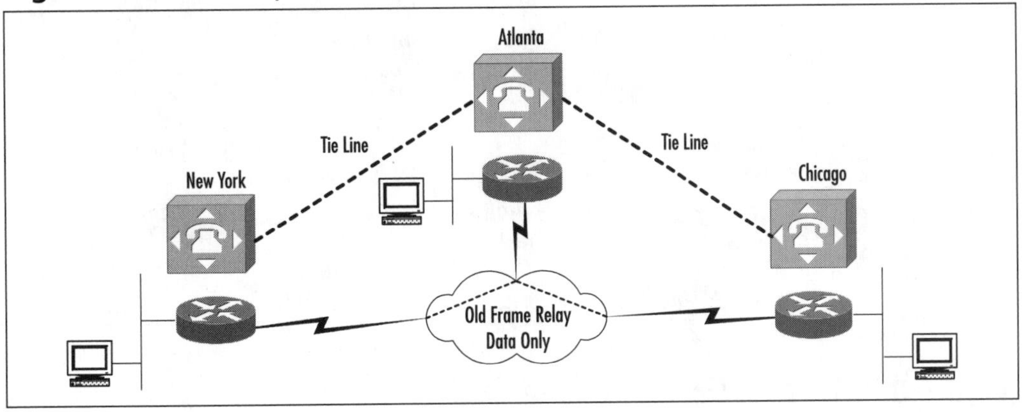

In the first stage, the voice and data networks will remain separate. The VoIP network will run over the new 3600 routers and the new Frame Relay network (see Figure 8.5). This will allow for a longer-term testing period without concern over QoS issues with data and voice sharing the same network. During this phase, quality of voice and call routing will be heavily monitored. Two solutions have been proposed for voice backup if any issues arise. First, a spare card, or a new card if a spare is not available, can be used with the current tie lines to reroute voice traffic, or the calls can be routed to the PSTN. VoIP Corporation will route calls to the PSTN if necessary. This option is in line with the overall strategy of moving away from expensive leased lines. The other solution could require purchasing new equipment for the PABX that will not be utilized if the test is successful.

The current site is given a five-digit extension that coincides with the assigned DIDs for that site. The DIDs are groups of telephone numbers that the telephone company will point to a voice circuit or voice circuits. For the Atlanta office, the phone company will send all numbers matching 404-874-*xxxx* to the

Atlanta voice circuit. So, if a call is placed to 404-874-1234, the telephone company sends the call to the Atlanta PABX, which forwards the call to extension 41234. If a call is placed to 212-726-5678, the call is routed to the New York PABX and forwarded to extension 65678. These same extensions will be used in the deployment of VoIP (see Figure 8.6).

Figure 8.5 The First Stage of VoIP Tie-Line Replacement

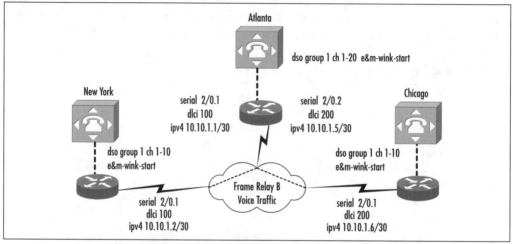

Figure 8.6 Five-Digit Extensions for Each Site

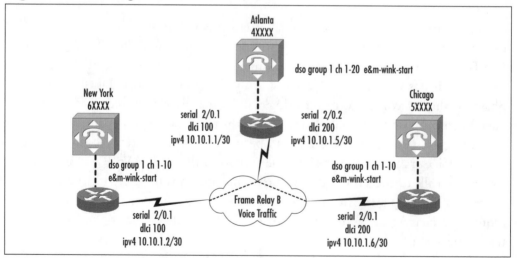

We now place this information into a dial plan spreadsheet (see Table 8.6). This information is then ported in the router configurations. At this point we have a visual diagram of the proposed network and a table format that will ease the task of configuration.

Table 8.6 Our Dial Plan Spreadsheet

Router	Dial Peer	Type	Destination Pattern	Target
Atlanta	40000	POTS	4....	Port1/0:1
	50000	VoIP	5....	10.10.1.6
	60000	VoIP	6....	10.10.1.2
Chicago	40000	VoIP	4....	10.10.1.5
	50000	POTS	5....	Port1/0:1
NYC	40000	VoIP	4....	10.10.1.1
	60000	POTS	6....	Port1/0:1

Configuring a Basic Tie-Line Replacement with VoIP

We now take the design drawings and a table to help complete the router configurations. Care should be taken to ensure that you do not mistype any of the dial plans. Simply mistyping a destination pattern can quickly have traffic routed to the wrong location. Once you have configured both sides of any dial plan, go back over the configurations to ensure that both sides have the correct destination. Figure 8.7 depicts the logical flow for call routing.

Figure 8.7 Logical Flow for Call Routing

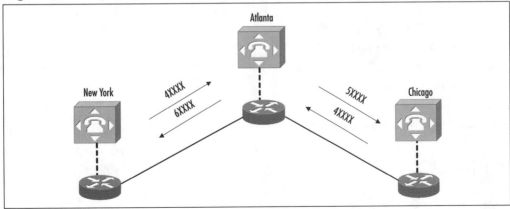

Configuration Details for the Basic Tie-Line Replacement

The VoIP Corporation will use the network diagram and Table 8.6 as the basis for its router configurations. The Atlanta router is configured with a Frame Relay link to Chicago and one to New York, and both Chicago and New York have one Frame Relay link to Atlanta.

Atlanta Router

```
interface Serial2/0.1 point-to-point
 description frame-relay to New York
 ip address 10.10.1.1 255.255.255.252
 no ip directed-broadcast
 no ip route-cache
 frame-relay interface-dlci 100
!
interface Serial2/0.2 point-to-point
 description frame-relay to Chicago
 ip address 10.10.1.5 255.255.255.252
 no ip directed-broadcast
 no ip route-cache
 frame-relay interface-dlci 200
```

New York Router

```
interface Serial2/0.1 point-to-point
 description frame-relay to Atlanta
 ip address 10.10.1.2 255.255.255.252
 no ip directed-broadcast
 no ip route-cache
 frame-relay interface-dlci 100
```

Chicago Router

```
interface Serial2/0.1 point-to-point
 description frame-relay to Atlanta
```

```
ip address 10.10.1.6 255.255.255.252
no ip directed-broadcast
no ip route-cache
frame-relay interface-dlci 200
```

The connections to the PABX are created under the *controller T1* interfaces. For Atlanta, the PABX is connected to port 1/0. The trunk uses ESF framing and B8ZS line coding, which we determined during information gathering. The *ds0-group* command allows us to group individual DS0s to create trunk groups, which can have different signaling types. You can divide the DS0s into separate groups or group all the DS0s into one group.

Atlanta Router

```
controller T1 1/0
  description connection the Atlanta PABX
  framing esf
  linecode b8zs
  ds0-group 1 timeslots 1-20 type e&m-wink-start
```

The *ds0-group* command creates a *voice port*. You can then create dial peers that point to these voice ports. Doing so directs voice traffic to the ds0-group for termination. The Atlanta site is using timeslots 1 through 20 of the T1 in port 1/0 grouped into *ds0-group 1* with E&M wink-start as the signaling type. *voice-port 1/0:1* is automatically created when *ds0-group 1* is defined.

Atlanta Router

```
controller T1 1/0
  description connection the Atlanta PABX
  framing esf
  linecode b8zs
  ds0-group 1 timeslots 1-20 type e&m-wink-start
!
voice-port 1/0:1
```

A dial peer is now created to direct traffic to the destination voice port. The command *dial-peer voice <dial-peer name> type* creates a dial peer type of either VoIP or POTS. The POTS type is used here to indicate that regular voice calls will depart voice-port 1/0:1. The command *destination pattern of 4....* matches any five-digit destination pattern that begins with a 4. The periods (.) are simply holding places that can be any number. The *no digit-strip* command keeps the 4 from being stripped off the destination pattern. The command *prefix 4* could also be used here but would allow the 4 to first be stripped and then replaced. The *prefix* command is more commonly used for digit manipulation, and the *no digit-strip* command is more commonly used when you need to pass all digits. Both *prefix* and *no digit-strip* can be used interchangeably, but the *no digit-strip* command also reduces processing time. The command *port 1/0:1* directs voice traffic with destination pattern 4.... to voice port 1/0:1 without stripping any digits.

Atlanta Router

```
controller T1 1/0
 description connection the Atlanta PABX
 framing esf
 linecode b8zs
 ds0-group 1 timeslots 1-20 type e&m-wink-start
!
voice-port 1/0:1
!
dial-peer voice 40000 pots
 description Atlanta PABX
 destination-pattern 4....
 no digit-strip
 port 1/0:1
```

A dial peer configured with the VoIP type assigns a target IP address of the router that can terminate the call. Chicago forwards any calls with a destination pattern of 4.... to 10.10.1.5, the Atlanta router. The Atlanta router forwards the call to *port 1/0:1,* as previously. This process is repeated on each router for the dial peer.

Chicago Router

```
dial-peer voice 40000 voip
 description forward to Atlanta
 destination-pattern 4....
 session target ipv4:10.10.1.5
```

Notice in the configurations that follows, Chicago and New York do not have dial peers between them. Chicago and New York only have tie-line connections to the Atlanta headquarters. So few calls are placed between sales offices such as New York to Chicago that these calls are currently connected via the PSTN. The dial peers reflect the current network and phone configuration. If in time VoIP Corporation decides that it would be cost effective to route calls between New York and Chicago over the VoIP network, two options are available. The easiest way would be to send a call from Chicago with a destination of New York first to Atlanta and allow the Atlanta router to forward the call to New York. This solution is simple but will use excess bandwidth from the Atlanta Frame Relay circuit. The second option is to provision a PVC between New York and Chicago. This is the best option and could also provide an alternate path for voice and data in the event of a failure.

The router configurations follow.

Atlanta Router Configuration

```
<<Contains Only Relevant Information for Clarity>>
version 12.2
no service pad
service timestamps debug datetime msec localtime show-timezone
service timestamps log datetime msec localtime show-timezone
service password-encryption
!
hostname Atlanta
!
logging buffered 16384 debugging
enable secret 5 $1$rjjd$ULzQ51g5vQTSlXwLElrPz.
!
clock timezone EST -5
voice-card 2
!
ip subnet-zero
no ip source-route
!
no ip domain-lookup
!
```

```
no ip bootp server
!
controller T1 1/0
 description connection the Atlanta PABX
 framing esf
 linecode b8zs
 ds0-group 1 timeslots 1-20 type e&m-wink-start
!
interface Loopback0
 ip address 10.100.1.1 255.255.255.255
!
interface FastEthernet0/0
 ip address 10.1.1.1 255.255.255.0
 speed 100
 full-duplex
 shutdown
!
interface Serial2/0
 description New frame-relay cloud
 no ip address
 encapsulation frame-relay
!
interface Serial2/0.1 point-to-point
 description frame-relay to New York
 ip address 10.10.1.1 255.255.255.252
 no ip directed-broadcast
 no ip route-cache
 frame-relay interface-dlci 100
!
interface Serial2/0.2 point-to-point
 description frame-relay to Chicago
 ip address 10.10.1.5 255.255.255.252
 no ip directed-broadcast
 no ip route-cache
 frame-relay interface-dlci 200
!
router eigrp 96
```

```
 network 10.0.0.0
 no auto-summary
 no eigrp log-neighbor-changes
!
ip classless
no ip http server
!
voice-port 1/0:1
!
dial-peer voice 50000 voip
 description forward to Chicago
 destination-pattern 5....
 session target ipv4:10.10.1.6
!
dial-peer voice 60000 voip
 description forward to New York
 destination-pattern 6....
 session target ipv4:10.10.1.2
!
dial-peer voice 40000 pots
 description Atlanta PABX
 destination-pattern 4....
 no digit-strip
 port 1/0:1
!
line con 0
line aux 0
line vty 0 4
 exec-timeout 0 0
 password 7 0559100A2F585B1B1C
 login
!
ntp server 10.1.1.2
!
end
```

Chicago Router Configuration

```
hostname Chicago
!
controller T1 1/0
 description connection to the Chicago PABX
 framing esf
 linecode b8zs
 ds0-group 1 timeslots 1-10 type e&m-wink-start
!
interface Loopback0
 ip address 10.100.1.5 255.255.255.255
!
interface FastEthernet0/0
 ip address 10.50.1.1 255.255.255.0
 speed 100
 full-duplex
 shutdown
!
interface Serial2/0
 description New frame-relay cloud
 no ip address
 encapsulation frame-relay
!
interface Serial2/0.1 point-to-point
 description frame-relay to Atlanta
 ip address 10.10.1.6 255.255.255.252
 no ip directed-broadcast
 no ip route-cache
 frame-relay interface-dlci 200
!
router eigrp 96
 network 10.0.0.0
 no auto-summary
 no eigrp log-neighbor-changes
!
ip classless
```

```
no ip http server
!
voice-port 1/0:1
!
dial-peer voice 40000 voip
 description forward to Atlanta
 destination-pattern 4....
 session target ipv4:10.10.1.5
!
dial-peer voice 50000 pots
 description Chicago PABX
 destination-pattern 5....
 no digit-strip
 port 1/0:1
!
line con 0
line aux 0
line vty 0 4
 exec-timeout 0 0
 password 7 0559100EXZ585B1B1C
 login
!
ntp server 10.1.1.2
!
end
```

New York Router Configuration

```
hostname NewYork
!
controller T1 1/0
 description connection to the New York PABX
 framing esf
 linecode b8zs
 ds0-group 1 timeslots 1-10 type e&m-wink-start
!
interface Loopback0
```

```
 ip address 10.100.1.6 255.255.255.255
!
interface FastEthernet0/0
 ip address 10.60.1.1 255.255.255.0
 speed 100
 full-duplex
 shutdown
!
interface Serial2/0
 description New frame-relay cloud
 no ip address
 encapsulation frame-relay
!
interface Serial2/0.1 point-to-point
 description frame-relay to Atlanta
 ip address 10.10.1.2 255.255.255.252
 no ip directed-broadcast
 no ip route-cache
 frame-relay interface-dlci 100
!
router eigrp 96
 network 10.0.0.0
 no auto-summary
 no eigrp log-neighbor-changes
!
ip classless
no ip http server
!
voice-port 1/0:1
!
dial-peer voice 40000 voip
 description forward to Atlanta
 destination-pattern 4....
 session target ipv4:10.10.1.1
!
dial-peer voice 60000 pots
 description New York PABX
```

```
destination-pattern 6....
 no digit-strip
port 1/0:1
!
line con 0
line aux 0
line vty 0 4
 exec-timeout 0 0
 password 7 0559100EXZ585A2A1C
 login
!
ntp server 10.1.1.2
!
end
```

Notice that the LAN segment is shut down in configuration. These interfaces will be enabled once the VoIP trial has been completed and the data and voice networks are to be combined.

You should now be able to send VoIP calls across the network. If the calls fail, make sure that the T1 is active by using the *show controller t1* command. You should see *T1 1/0 is up* in the output. If you don't, you could see either *Receiver has loss of frame* or *Receiver has loss of signal*. If you have loss of frame, ensure that the frame type is set correctly on both the router and the PABX. If you have loss of signal, check your cabling. Remember, you must use a T1 crossover cable between the PABX and the router. If the T1 is up, use *show voice port 1/0:1* to ensure the that *Type of VoicePort* is E&M, *Operation State* is dormant, and *Administrative State* is up. Once you have determined the T1 is up and active, you can troubleshoot the dial plan using the command *Show dialplan number xxxx*. The output will provide you with *destination-pattern = "40000"* and *session-target = 'ipv4:10.101.1'*. Numerous *show* and *debug* commands can help you troubleshoot connection or voice quality issues. Remember to first look for the obvious—whether the Frame Relay circuit is down or the PABX trunk is down on one side or the other. Then, if the problem is not resolved, use the more complex *debug* commands to find call-routing issues or even faulty DSPs. Use caution when using any *debug* command; they are CPU intensive and can cause highly utilized routers to reboot.

Configuring Advanced Trunking Scenarios

In this section we configure some of the advanced trunking options. We look at two special cases: the connection trunk and private-line automatic ringdown, or PLAR. In the VoIP tie-line replacement design, voice traffic must cross three different legs while crossing the network: PABX to gateway, gateway to gateway, and gateway to PABX. Although the call is traditional voice from PABX to gateway and gateway to PABX, it is VoIP when going from gateway to gateway. A connection trunk keeps a permanent connection between gateways. This wastes bandwidth when it's not in use, but it guarantees that bandwidth is always available.

You have probably used a PLAR phone many times without realizing it. These are phones that ring an extension as soon as you pick them up. Many organizations use PLAR lines to limit phone use to one extension. One example is a security phone for after-hours entry into a building. The front security desk is closed, and the door is locked. When you pick up the security phone, usually located next to the locked door, it rings the security-monitoring room for assistance. The phone does not allow you to dial any other number. We detail configurations for a PLAR and a connection trunk in the following sections.

Advanced Trunking Options Overview

We should discuss a couple of advanced trunking scenarios that where not covered in the initial design. These are the connection trunk and PLAR configurations. The *connection trunk* is a permanent connection between two PABXs. This trunk in effect takes call control away form the router and puts it back in the control of the PABX. In normal call processing, once the router goes off-hook toward the originating PABX, the PABX sees the call as started. If for some reason the router cannot complete the call, the call cannot be rerouted. A connection trunk is always up, so the far-end PABX can signal whether a problem exists and the call needs to be rerouted. A common implementation across a connection trunk is a *hoot-n-holler service*, which is similar to a two-way paging system across a telephone circuit. Instead of the phone ringing on the far end, you literally "hoot-n-holler" to get the attention of the called party. This service is often used in brokerage firms where seconds are money.

PLAR is similar to a connection truck in that both have statically configured endpoints. However, the PLAR is a switch connection, so no bandwidth is used when the phone is on-hook. When a phone is taken off-hook, the call is automatically connected and the remote phone begins to ring. This type of service is often called a *hot line* or *bat phone*. You will find these phones deployed in kiosks all across airports; they give you instant connections to hotels, car rentals, and dining.

Configuring Advanced Trunking Options: Case Studies

VoIP Corporation is impressed with the VoIP trial and wants to test some of the advanced trunking features offered in the Cisco IOS. The Chicago site does not have a receptionist, and often no one is in the office. When the Chicago office is empty, calls that come into the site are automatically forwarded to Atlanta. This solution has worked well but does not address the issue of people stopping by the Chicago office and finding no one there to greet them. To address this problem, VoIP Corporation wants to install a PLAR phone outside the office door that will automatically call the Atlanta receptionist. A NM-1V module and a VIC-2FXS card had to be purchased to provide a termination point for the new phone. On the Atlanta router, a new *ds0-group* is added to controller T1 1/0; *ds0-group 2 timeslots 21 type fxo-loop-start*. This group provides the destination for the PLAR line to be deployed in Chicago. This command created *voice-port 1/0:2*. Dial peer 40005 directs calls with a destination-pattern of 40005 to *voice-port 1/0:2*, the Atlanta receptionist. Dial peer 50005 directs calls with a destination-pattern of 50005 to 10.10.1.6, the Chicago router. The *dtmf-relay h245-alphanumeric* command transmits DTMF out of band or outside the VoIP compression. High-compression codecs such as G.729 are written to compress voice traffic and do not work well with DTMF. Even though we are creating a PLAR and will not need to dial a phone number, if the receptionist is away we still want the user to be able to go through the phone menus.

Atlanta Router Configuration

```
hostname Atlanta
!
controller T1 1/0
 description connection the Atlanta PABX
 framing esf
 linecode b8zs
 ds0-group 1 timeslots 1-20 type e&m-wink-start
```

```
 ds0-group 2 timeslots 21 type fxo-loop-start
!
voice-port 1/0:1
!
voice-port 1/0:2
!
dial-peer voice 40005 pots
 description direct line  Atlanta receptionist
 destination-pattern 40005
 port 1/0:2
!
dial-peer voice 50005 voip
 destination-pattern 50005
 dtmf-relay h245-alphanumeric
 session target ipv4:10.10.1.6
```

On the Chicago router, an NM-1V module and a VIC-2FXS card have been added to the router. The addition of the FXS card creates *voice-port 3/1/0*. Under *voice-port 3/1/0,* the command *connection plar 40005* starts a call to extension 40005 any time the voice port goes off-hook. This is a Chicago "hot line" phone that automatically calls the receptionist's extension (extension 40005) when the phone is picked up. *dial-peer voice 40005 voip* directs the call to the session target 10.10.1.5, the Atlanta router. On the Atlanta router, *dial-peer voice 40005 pots* sends the call to *voice-port 1/0:2*; timeslot 21 on T1 1/0. *dial-peer voice 50005 pots* allows calls to be placed to the hotline phone from Atlanta.

Chicago Router Configuration

```
hostname Chicago
!
voice-port 3/1/0
 connection plar 40005
!
dial-peer voice 50005 pots
 description hotline phone
 destination-pattern 50005
 port 3/1/0
!
```

```
dial-peer voice 40005 voip
 destination-pattern 40005
 dtmf-relay h245-alphanumeric
 session target ipv4:10.10.1.5
```

In an effort to evaluate the pros and cons of a connection trunk, VoIP Corporation has chosen to deploy a trunk between New York and Atlanta. The company is deploying connection trunks in anticipation of dropped calls once the entire company is moved over to VoIP for tie lines. The Atlanta router is given a third DS0 group. The *ds0-group 3 timeslots 22 type e&m-wink-start* command creates *voice-port 1/0:3*. The *connection trunk 60010* command makes voice port 1/0:3 the master side of the connection trunk with a destination pattern of 60010. The *dial-peer voice 60010 voip* command directs calls with *destination-pattern 60010* to 10.10.1.2; the New York router and *dial-peer voice 40010 pots* sends traffic with *destination-pattern 40010* to *voice-port 1/0:3*.

Atlanta Router Configuration

```
hostname Atlanta
!
controller T1 1/0
 description connection the Atlanta PABX
 framing esf
 linecode b8zs
 ds0-group 1 timeslots 1-20 type e&m-wink-start
 ds0-group 2 timeslots 21 type fxo-loop-start
 ds0-group 3 timeslots 22 type e&m-wink-start
!
voice-port 1/0:1
!
voice-port 1/0:2
!
voice-port 1/0:3
 connection trunk 60010
!
dial-peer voice 40010 pots
 destination-pattern 40010
 port 1/0:3
```

```
!
dial-peer voice 60010 voip
 destination-pattern 60010
 dtmf-relay h245-alphanumeric
 session target ipv4:10.10.1.2
```

The New York router is given a second DS0-group. The *ds0-group 2 timeslots 11 type e&m-wink-start* command creates *voice-port 1/0:2*. The *connection trunk 40010* command with the qualifier *answer-mode* makes *voice-port 1/0:2* the slave side of the connection trunk with a destination pattern of 60010. The slave side never tries to initiate a trunk connection but waits for the far side to begin the connection. The *dial-peer voice 40010 pots* command directs calls with *destination-pattern 40010* to 10.10.1.1; the Atlanta router and *dial-peer voice 60010 pots* sends traffic with *destination-pattern 60010* to *voice-port 1/0:2*. Once both sides have been configured for the connection trunk, a permanent VoIP call will be connected between the two routers. Note that you must perform a shutdown/no shutdown to initiate this process after the configurations are complete.

New York Router Configuration

```
controller T1 1/0
 description connection the New PABX
 framing esf
 linecode b8zs
 ds0-group 1 timeslots 1-10 type e&m-wink-start
 ds0-group 2 timeslots 11 type e&m-wink-start
!
voice-port 1/0:1
!
voice-port 1/0:2
 connection trunk 40010 answer-mode
!
dial-peer voice 60010 pots
 destination-pattern 60010
 port 1/0:2
!
dial-peer voice 40010 voip
 destination-pattern 40010
```

```
dtmf-relay h245-alphanumeric
session target ipv4:10.10.1.1
```

Integrating Voice and Data

Since the popularization of the Internet and IP, the integration of voice and data has been a hot topic. VoIP has arrived and is now being deployed in large enterprise networks. What is the big push to integrate? Where will revenue be recovered? Let's take a look at these questions.

The Rationale for Integrating Voice and Data Networks

Many companies today are looking for ways to stretch their budget dollars. By integrating voice and data, companies are looking to decrease capital and support costs over the long term. These goals include:

- Reduce infrastructure expenses by integrating to a single network.

- Consolidate telephony and network support teams.

- Simplify moves, adds, and changes for telephone systems.

- Offer enhanced services to increase productivity.

- Consolidate network monitoring tools and telephone monitoring tools.

Some companies are seeing a return on the original investment in VoIP equipment in little over a year, but time can be extended by penalties associated with early lease termination on circuits or on PABX equipment.

Integrating Voice and Data: Case Studies

The VoIP Corporation is delighted with the VoIP trial and is now ready to move into the final stage of voice and data integration. The company's managers have to make a choice between a complete or a partial integration. When the LAN connection is moved from the current router to the new router, the Frame Relay circuit can also be moved to the new router. This setup creates a partially integrated network where the voice and data share a router but traverse the WAN via separate Frame Relay circuits. This solution gives greater bandwidth over the WAN and protects voice traffic from the bursty data traffic, but it does not take advantage of the cost savings of dropping the old Frame Relay service (see Figure 8.8).

Figure 8.8 A Partially Integrated Voice and Data Network

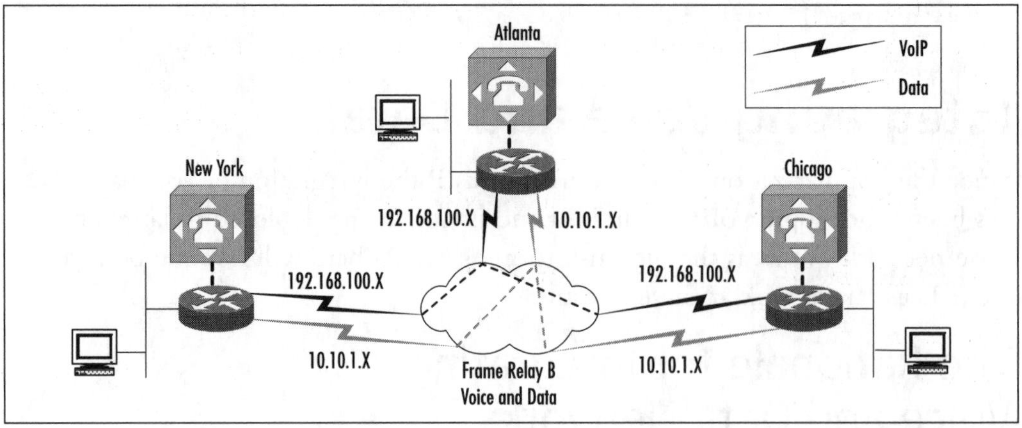

This partially integrated solution is implemented using policy-based routing based on destination networks. Any traffic headed to a 10.10.0.0 network will be sent across the new Frame Relay network, and all other traffic will be taken across the old Frame Relay network. This goal is accomplished by adding the following commands to the Atlanta router. These commands should be applied to each router, making the appropriate changes:

```
access-list 112 permit ip any 10.10.1.2 0.0.255.255
!access-list 112 is for VoIP traffic to New York
!
access-list 115 permit ip any 10.10.1.5 0.0.255.255
!access-list 115 is for VoIP traffic to Chicago
!
route-map New-York permit 10
 match ip address 112
 set ip next-hop 10.10.1.2
!
route-map Chicago permit 20
 match ip address 115
 set ip next-hop 10.10.1.5
!
interface Serial2/0.1
 ip policy route-map New-York
!
interface Serial2/0.2
 ip policy route-map Chicago
```

An access list is created for traffic destined for New York, and a list is created for traffic going to Chicago. *Route-map New-York* matches traffic to *access-list 112* and sets the next hop to 10.10.1.2, the New York router. *Route-map Chicago* matches traffic to *access-list 115* and sets the next hop to 10.10.1.5, the Chicago router. The route maps are then applied to the outgoing interface: *route-map New York* to *serial2/0.1* and *route-map Chicago* to *serial2/0.2*. These changes can be seen in the following Atlanta router configuration.

Atlanta Router Configuration

```
<<Contains Only Relevant Information for Clarity>>
hostname Atlanta
!
interface Loopback0
 ip address 10.100.1.1 255.255.255.255
!
interface FastEthernet0/0
 ip address 10.1.1.1 255.255.255.0
 speed 100
 full-duplex
!
interface Serial2/0
 description New frame-relay cloud
 no ip address
 encapsulation frame-relay
!
interface Serial2/0.1 point-to-point
 description new frame-relay to New York
 ip address 10.10.1.1 255.255.255.252
 no ip directed-broadcast
 no ip route-cache
 ip policy route-map New-York
 frame-relay interface-dlci 100
!
interface Serial2/0.2 point-to-point
 description new frame-relay to Chicago
 ip address 10.10.1.5 255.255.255.252
```

```
 no ip directed-broadcast
 no ip route-cache
 ip policy route-map Chicago
 frame-relay interface-dlci 200
!
interface Serial2/1
 description old frame-relay cloud
 no ip address
 encapsulation frame-relay
!
interface Serial2/0.1 point-to-point
 description old frame-relay to New York
 ip address 192.168.100.1 255.255.255.252
 no ip directed-broadcast
 no ip route-cache
 frame-relay interface-dlci 300
!
interface Serial2/0.2 point-to-point
 description old frame-relay to Chicago
 ip address 192.168.100.5 255.255.255.252
 no ip directed-broadcast
 no ip route-cache
 frame-relay interface-dlci 400
!
router eigrp 96
 network 10.0.0.0
 network 192.0.0.0
 no auto-summary
 no eigrp log-neighbor-changes
!
ip classless
no ip http server
!
voice-port 1/0:1
!
dial-peer voice 50000 voip
 description forward to Chicago
```

```
  destination-pattern 5....
  session target ipv4:10.10.1.6
!
dial-peer voice 60000 voip
  description forward to New York
  destination-pattern 6....
  session target ipv4:10.10.1.2
!
dial-peer voice 40000 pots
  description Atlanta PABX
  destination-pattern 4....
  no digit-strip
  port 1/0:1
!
access-list 112 permit ip any 10.10.1.2 0.0.255.255
access-list 115 permit ip any 10.10.1.5 0.0.255.255
!
route-map New-York permit 10
  match ip address 112
  set ip next-hop 10.10.1.2
!
route-map Chicago permit 20
  match ip address 115
  set ip next-hop 10.10.1.5
!
end
```

The alternate method involves migrating the data traffic over to the new Frame Relay WAN. The actual change itself involves moving the LAN connection at each site from the old 2600 router to the new 3600 router. No new LAN connections are needed. The Fast Ethernet port on each router needs to be turned up. At this point, both data and VoIP traffic will be across the same router and the same WAN circuits (see Figure 8.9). The following are the complete configurations, including the PLAR configurations and the connection trunk configuration. The VoIP Corporation case study continues in Chapters 9 and 10 with an increasingly complex VoIP deployment.

Figure 8.9 A Fully Integrated Voice and Data Network

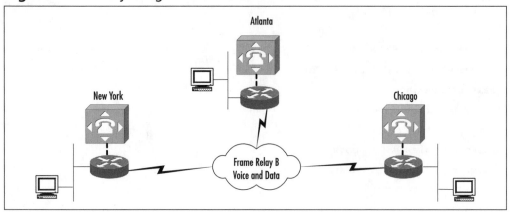

Atlanta Router Configuration

```
<<Contains Only Relevant Information for Clarity>>
version 12.2
no service pad
service timestamps debug datetime msec localtime show-timezone
service timestamps log datetime msec localtime show-timezone
service password-encryption
!
hostname Atlanta
!
logging buffered 16384 debugging
enable secret 5 $1$rjjd$ULzQ51g5vQTSlXwLElrPz.
!
clock timezone EST -5
voice-card 2
!
ip subnet-zero
no ip source-route
!
no ip domain-lookup
!
no ip bootp server
!
controller T1 1/0
```

```
 description connection the Atlanta PABX
 framing esf
 linecode b8zs
 ds0-group 1 timeslots 1-20 type e&m-wink-start
ds0-group 2 timeslots 21 type fxo-loop-start
ds0-group 3 timeslots 22 type e&m-wink-start
 !
interface Loopback0
 ip address 10.100.1.1 255.255.255.255
 !
interface FastEthernet0/0
 ip address 10.1.1.1 255.255.255.0
 speed 100
 full-duplex
 shutdown
 !
interface Serial2/0
 description New frame-relay cloud
 no ip address
 encapsulation frame-relay
 !
interface Serial2/0.1 point-to-point
 description frame-relay to New York
 ip address 10.10.1.1 255.255.255.252
 no ip directed-broadcast
 no ip route-cache
 frame-relay interface-dlci 100
 !
interface Serial2/0.2 point-to-point
 description frame-relay to Chicago
 ip address 10.10.1.5 255.255.255.252
 no ip directed-broadcast
 no ip route-cache
 frame-relay interface-dlci 200
 !
router eigrp 96
 network 10.0.0.0
```

```
 no auto-summary
 no eigrp log-neighbor-changes
!
ip classless
no ip http server
!
voice-port 1/0:1
!
voice-port 1/0:2
!
voice-port 1/0:3
 connection trunk 60010
!
dial-peer voice 50000 voip
 description forward to Chicago
 destination-pattern 5....
 session target ipv4:10.10.1.6
!
dial-peer voice 50005 voip
 destination-pattern 50005
 dtmf-relay h245-alphanumeric
 session target ipv4:10.10.1.6
!
dial-peer voice 60000 voip
 description forward to New York
 destination-pattern 6....
 session target ipv4:10.10.1.2
!
dial-peer voice 60010 voip
 destination-pattern 60010
 dtmf-relay h245-alphanumeric
 session target ipv4:10.10.1.2
!
dial-peer voice 40000 pots
 description Atlanta PABX
 destination-pattern 4....
 no digit-strip
```

```
 port 1/0:1
!
dial-peer voice 40005 pots
 description direct line  Atlanta receptionist
 destination-pattern 40005
 port 1/0:2
!
dial-peer voice 40010 pots
 destination-pattern 40010
 port 1/0:3
!
line con 0
line aux 0
line vty 0 4
 exec-timeout 0 0
 password 7 0559100A2F585B1B1C
 login
!
ntp server 10.1.1.2
!
end
```

Chicago Router Configuration

```
hostname Chicago
!
controller T1 1/0
 description connection to the Chicago PABX
 framing esf
 linecode b8zs
 ds0-group 1 timeslots 1-10 type e&m-wink-start
!
interface Loopback0
 ip address 10.100.1.5 255.255.255.255
!
interface FastEthernet0/0
 ip address 10.50.1.1 255.255.255.0
```

```
 speed 100
 full-duplex
 shutdown
!
interface Serial2/0
 description New frame-relay cloud
 no ip address
 encapsulation frame-relay
!
interface Serial2/0.1 point-to-point
 description frame-relay to Atlanta
 ip address 10.10.1.6 255.255.255.252
 no ip directed-broadcast
 no ip route-cache
 frame-relay interface-dlci 200
!
router eigrp 96
 network 10.0.0.0
 no auto-summary
 no eigrp log-neighbor-changes
!
ip classless
no ip http server
!
voice-port 1/0:1
!
voice-port 3/1/0
 connection plar 40005
!
dial-peer voice 40000 voip
 description forward to Atlanta
 destination-pattern 4....
 session target ipv4:10.10.1.5
!
dial-peer voice 40005 voip
 destination-pattern 40005
 dtmf-relay h245-alphanumeric
```

```
 session target ipv4:10.10.1.5
!
dial-peer voice 50000 pots
 description Chicago PABX
 destination-pattern 5....
 no digit-strip
 port 1/0:1
!
dial-peer voice 50005 pots
 description hotline phone
 destination-pattern 50005
 port 3/1/0
!
line con 0
line aux 0
line vty 0 4
 exec-timeout 0 0
 password 7 0559100EXZ585B1B1C
 login
!
ntp server 10.1.1.2
!
end
```

New York Router Configuration

```
hostname NewYork
!
controller T1 1/0
 description connection to the New York PABX
 framing esf
 linecode b8zs
 ds0-group 1 timeslots 1-10 type e&m-wink-start
 ds0-group 2 timeslots 11 type e&m-wink-start
!
interface Loopback0
 ip address 10.100.1.6 255.255.255.255
```

```
!
interface FastEthernet0/0
 ip address 10.60.1.1 255.255.255.0
 speed 100
 full-duplex
 shutdown
!
interface Serial2/0
 description New frame-relay cloud
 no ip address
 encapsulation frame-relay
!
interface Serial2/0.1 point-to-point
 description frame-relay to Atlanta
 ip address 10.10.1.2 255.255.255.252
 no ip directed-broadcast
 no ip route-cache
 frame-relay interface-dlci 100
!
router eigrp 96
 network 10.0.0.0
 no auto-summary
 no eigrp log-neighbor-changes
!
ip classless
no ip http server
!
voice-port 1/0:1
!
voice-port 1/0:2
 connection trunk 40010 answer-mode
!
dial-peer voice 40000 voip
 description forward to Atlanta
 destination-pattern 4....
 session target ipv4:10.10.1.1
!
```

```
dial-peer voice 60000 pots
 description New York PABX
 destination-pattern 6....
  no digit-strip
 port 1/0:1
!
dial-peer voice 60010 pots
 destination-pattern 60010
 port 1/0:2
!
dial-peer voice 40010 voip
 destination-pattern 40010
 dtmf-relay h245-alphanumeric
 session target ipv4:10.10.1.1
!
line con 0
line aux 0
line vty 0 4
 exec-timeout 0 0
 password 7 0559100EXZ585A2A1C
 login
!
ntp server 10.1.1.2
!
end
```

Verifying and Testing the Solution

In this section we discuss some of the tasks associated with testing and verifying an integrated voice and data solution. We detail some common troubleshooting methods using the case study network configuration, including tie-line replacement, advanced trunking, and voice and data integration. This section introduces some of the complexities of troubleshooting a VoIP solution.

Testing and Verification Methodology

As we merge voice and data networks, many new layers are added to the testing and verification process. In the a large-scale deployment, you must test not only network routing but also call routing in the routers and in Call Manager. A complete test plan must be designed and deployed to ensure that each IP phone can place calls and retrieve messages. You have to ensure that voice has a high priority so it will not experience latency on the network and that data traffic also has a priority that will allow it to flow, even in the heaviest voice traffic. You might have to work with PABXs or key systems to ensure that they are working properly with the VoIP equipment.

Configuring & Implementing…

Acceptance Testing and Rollback Procedures

During the implementation phase, it becomes imperative that acceptance testing and rollback procedures must be defined. All implementation plans must include acceptance testing once the design has been implemented and rollback procedures to quickly return the network to its previous state. With the integration of voice and data, testing and rollback procedures are required for both. These procedures often include testing from the affected users and, as in our case study, assistance from an external party. To ensure success, a drop-dead time should be established. This is the time of day that, once reached without the design being completely deployed, the rollback procedure must begin. After a rollback has been performed, acceptance testing must be performed to ensure that the status quo has been achieved.

Testing the Deployed Solutions

In the following section we revisit various configurations from the case study, including testing tie-line replacement, testing advanced trunking, and testing voice and data integration. We look at some common problems during deployment and the troubleshooting steps necessary to correct those problems. We also look at some common errors that occur during deployment and some *debug* commands that can help resolve them.

Testing Tie-Line Replacement

Here are some problems and solutions you might encounter when you're testing tie-line replacement.

Problem 1

After all the routers have been configured and installed and the PABX has been configured and connected to the router, we cannot make calls to New York, but we can to Chicago.

Solution 1

First, remember that a VoIP call is a three-part call. It involves the PABX-to-router, the router-to-router, and router-to-PABX segments. In this case, we are confident that the trunk is up between the router and PABX in Atlanta because the traffic that is working to Chicago crosses the same trunk. We first check the T1 between the PABX in New York and the router to ensure that the circuit is up. We issue the *show controller t1 1/0* command on the New York router. We could find that the T1 is shut down. To rectify that situation, type the following command at the New York router prompt:

```
NewYork> config t
NewYork> controller t1 1/0
NewYork> no shutdown
```

Now issue the *show controller t1* command again. You should see *T1 1/0 is up* in the output. If you don't, you could see either *Receiver has loss of frame* or *Receiver has loss of signal*. If you have loss of frame, ensure that the frame type is set correctly on both the router and the PABX. If you have loss of signal, check your cabling. Remember, you must use a T1 crossover cable between the PABX and the router.

Problem 2

Calls from Atlanta to Chicago are not completing, but calls from Chicago to Atlanta are going through.

Solution 2

First, we know that network connectivity exists between the two routers, and we know that the PABX connections are up if some calls are completing. We should now troubleshoot the dial plan. At the Atlanta router prompt, we issue the following command: *show dialplan number 50000*. We receive the following output: *destination-pattern = "4...."* and *session-target="ipv4:10.10.1.6,"* which is correct. We now issue the same command on the Chicago router with the following results: *destination-pattern = "4..."* and *session-target=" port 1/0:1"*.

The destination pattern is missing one period (.), which causes the call to be dropped. We insert the period, and now calls are flowing in both directions.

Testing Advanced Trunking

Here are some problems and solutions you could encounter when testing advanced trunking.

Problem 1

The VoIP tie-line replacement is deployed between Atlanta and New York. Calls that traverse the connection trunk are not completing, but all other VoIP tie-line calls are completing.

Solution 1

First, we know that there is end-to-end connectivity between the routers, because some calls are being completed. Our next step is to check the state of the voice ports by issuing the following command: *show voice port 1/0:3*. On the Atlanta router, we see the following: the trunk *Administrative State is UP; Connection Mode is trunk,* and *Connection Number is 60010.* On the New York router, we see the following: the trunk *Administrative State is DOWN; Connection Mode is trunk,* and *Connection Number is 40010.* On the New York router, we complete the following commands:

```
NewYork> voice-port 1/0:2
NewYork>shutdown
NewYork>no shutdown
```

Now on the New York router, we see the following: the trunk *Administrative State is UP; Connection Mode is trunk,* and *Connection Number is 40010.* Calls are now processing across the connection trunk.

Problem 2

Calls crossing the auto ringdown PLAR phone between Atlanta and Chicago are completing with no problems. However, if a call is not answered and goes to the voicemail menu, the DTMF is not recognized.

Solution 2

First, we know that there is end-to-end connectivity between the routers and PABXs, because calls are being completed. We check the configurations for DTMF on both routers to ensure that DTMF is not being passed through with the VoIP traffic. We discover that the Atlanta dial peer is configured correctly, but the Chicago side is missing the following command *dtmf-relay h245-alphanumeric.* With the command in place, the DTMF drives the menu with no problems.

Testing Voice and Data Integration

Here are some problems and solutions you could encounter when testing voice and data integration.

Problem 1

The test for a partially integrated voice and data solution went well, but when the old Frame Relay network was pulled, the data traffic quit flowing.

Solution 1

We first try to ping both routers, to no avail. Next we source a ping from the WAN interface to see if we can bypass any routing issues. We use the extended *ping* command at the router prompt. (You must be in Privileged mode to use this command.) We leave all fields as the defaults except destination and origination. From the Atlanta router, we ping 10.10.1.2 (the New York router) from the 10.10.1.1 interface, with no dropped pings. We check the configuration, and the routers still have the policy routing statements applied. We remove the statements and we are now routing both voice and data.

Problem 2

The VoIP trial has been running smoothly for the past week. On Monday morning, people can still make voice calls, but they cannot pass data.

Solution 2

We first try to ping both routers, to no avail. Next we source a ping from the WAN interface to see if we can bypass any routing issues. We use the extended ping command at the router prompt. (You must be in Privileged mode to use this command.) We leave all fields as the default except destination and origination. From the Atlanta router, we ping 10.10.1.2 (the New York router) from the 10.10.1.1 interface, with no successful pings. We have someone at the New York site check the router because we cannot access it. It turns out that the router has lost power and the voice calls are actually going across the PSTN. Once power is restored to the router, no more issues are experienced.

Summary

In this chapter we traveled from collecting information through the design process to configuring the routers and briefly touched on verifying and testing. The VoIP Corporation has turned to a VoIP solution to replace the tie lines between remote sites and headquarters. Through the discovery process, we determined that another project is running in conjunction with the VoIP trial. VoIP Corporation used the router and new Frame Relay cloud to produce a test bed for VoIP. After compiling the information phase and confirming the results, we followed a step-by-step design process. Major network elements were identified and labeled. Diagrams were drawn to detail the data and voice networks. This information was compiled in a dial plan spreadsheet. This information served as a blueprint for building the router configurations.

VoIP Corporation was satisfied with the VoIP trial and moved forward to test some advanced trunking scenarios. These include a PLAR connection from Chicago and a connection truck going to New York. After growing confidence in both VoIP and the staff's ability to support it, the corporation integrated voice and data abandoning the original Frame Relay network and routers. This case study chronicles the company's first steps toward a converged network. This chapter only touched on the beginning of convergence. Subsequent chapters go into much greater detail regarding a truly converged network.

Solutions Fast Track

Collecting the Information

☑ Before beginning to gather information, define your goals and objectives so that you can focus your fact-finding efforts.

☑ Use a checklist to ensure that important information has not been overlooked. Checklists and questionnaires are very good ways to gather information from your peers.

☑ Gather the information, compile it, and then revisit your audience to ensure that you are both "on the same page."

Designing a Basic Tie-Line Replacement with VoIP

☑ Create a diagram depicting the current voice and data network, including PABXs, switches, and routers.

☑ Create a diagram of the proposed design. Include as much detail as possible without cluttering the diagram. Try to include IP addressing, physical port assignments, and circuit types. The design should be a robust, scalable network.

☑ Add number extensions and destination addresses to the diagram.

☑ Create a dial plan spreadsheet from the information you have collected. This tool should give you all the information you need to configure the routers.

Configuring Basic Tie-Line Replacement with VoIP

☑ Use the diagrams and the spreadsheet from the design phase of our case study as a template to walk you through configuring the router.

☑ Always take time to double-check your configuration against that on the far end of your dial plan. It takes just a simple mistyped extension to begin sending all VoIP traffic to New York.

☑ Once you have developed a template for the VoIP deployment, configurations can be produced faster and with better accuracy.

Configuring Advanced Trunking Scenarios

☑ PLAR offers switched VoIP calls without dialing. Once the phone is picked up, the connection is made and the phone on the far end rings.

☑ Connection trunking creates a permanent connection between two PABXs. This allows call-routing decisions to be made by the PABX, not by the router.

☑ Both connection trunking and PLAR support supplemental services such as hookflash. This will give end users the ability to use advanced features from the PABX, such as call waiting and call conferencing.

Integrating Voice and Data

☑ A partially integrated network allows data and voice traffic to share the same router but traverse the WAN network on diverse paths.

☑ In fully integrated networks, both data and voice traffic traverse the network using the same WAN link.

☑ A fully integrated network offers the fastest ROI, but in the case of one link going down in a partially integrated network, the routers could be configured to temporarily combine traffic until the primary link recovers.

Verifying and Testing the Solution

☑ The best way to test a voice call is to place the call. You will quickly identify call-routing issues or voice quality issues. Use *show voice port* and *show dialplan number* to check for proper configuration.

☑ Special consideration should be taken when you're troubleshooting PLAR connections. These connections take the dialing process away from the end user. If terminating numbers are incorrect, call routing or the PABX is misconfigured.

☑ To test integrated voice and data, ensure that you have end-to-end connectivity with several data applications. You should try doing several large file transfers and placing calls to test call quality.

Frequently Asked Questions

The following Frequently Asked Questions, answered by the authors of this book, are designed to both measure your understanding of the concepts presented in this chapter and to assist you with real-life implementation of these concepts. To have your questions about this chapter answered by the author, browse to **www.syngress.com/solutions** and click on the **"Ask the Author"** form.

Q: Which codec should I use when I deploy a VoIP solution?

A: Each implementation is different. Sometimes equipment that is currently deployed dictates the codec. Often the hardware itself narrows your options. You have to determine the business drivers and solutions that most closely meet those criteria. Essentially, better voice quality uses greater bandwidth, and lower voice quality uses less bandwidth.

Q: Why use VoIP?

A: VoIP brings new possibilities to converged networks. Not only can you save on operational services and capital expenditures—you can also provide unified messaging and personal assistants to your employees.

Q: What type of connection should I use to connect to my PABX?

A: It depends on the PABX you have and on the port(s) you have available, both on the PABX and on the router. Cisco supports many types of telephony signaling, both digital and analog. You should refer to www.cisco.com for detailed information on your specific PABX.

Q: Does anybody actually use hoot-n-holler circuits?

A: Hoot-n-holler circuits are still popular in certain distinct areas. By far the most prominent users are stockbrokers. This technology allows a broker to call the floor to sell or buy without actually having to get someone to answer the phone. Railroads and gas-line companies also use these circuits to complement their handheld radios. Gas lines and railroads traverse desolate places that lack cell towers or pay phones. Radio receivers are set up in these remote locations and attached to hoot-n-holler circuits to complete the radio transmission.

Q: So I have deployed VoIP as a tie-line replacement and I have been impressed with the quality of the calls and the ease of making changes. Now what?

A: You have now accepted VoIP as a viable voice solution. Now you should start considering some of the benefits a total VoIP solution can provide. Some of those advantages are:

- Reduction in support staff by combining voice and data into one network
- Reduction in the expense and time required for moves, adds, and changes on the voice network
- Offering enhanced telephony services such as unified messaging, click to dial, and follow-me/find-me

Intra- and Interoffice VoIP Scenarios

Solutions in this chapter:

- Creating a Basic Intraoffice Dial Plan

- Designing a Single-Router VoIP Network

- Configuring a Single-Router VoIP Network

- Merging the PBX and VoIP Networks

- Configuring a Multirouter Intraoffice VoIP Network

- Configuring VoIP for Interoffice Voice Communication

- Tuning the VoIP Network

- Applying QoS to the VoIP Network

☑ Summary

☑ Solutions Fast Track

☑ Frequently Asked Questions

Introduction

Designing and implementing an integrated voice and data system should follow the same procedures, independent of the scope of the installation. This chapter introduces the process to be followed by first presenting best-practices design methodology. This process begins by determining the requirements for a given customer, designing a dial plan, determining the network components that will be deployed, reviewing the design, and implementing the design.

We start with a simple single voice-enabled router design and build on our deployment in successive steps. We do this by presenting how to incorporate legacy PBX equipment into our design, because this is the most likely scenario that you will encounter in the real world. We build on the deployment by adding multiple sites to our design and present QoS tuning parameters we will find useful to assure voice quality within our network.

Creating a Basic Intraoffice Dial Plan

This chapter demonstrates how to design and implement a simple single-office dial plan with only a few phones and then extend it across the enterprise. The goals of a dial plan will always be the same, but customer requirements will vary, as will the final design and subsequent deployment. Therefore, the process of dial plan design always begins by collecting the customer data (requirements), sketching out an initial dial plan, and reviewing it with the customer prior to implementation. It is by this process of design and review that we gain customer acceptance and avoid undesired results during deployment. We also demonstrate how digit manipulation can be configured for use within the dial plan.

What Is a Dial Plan?

A *dial plan* is a set of rules that govern how numerical prefixes and extensions, when dialed, will reach the final destination for a voice system. A dial plan should be logical in that the numbers being dialed can be used to identify a particular location. Additionally, a dial plan should account for multiple routes to a final destination in the event of equipment failure or an incorrectly dialed number. The plan should define how local, long distance, emergency, and other special access numbers will be handled. Finally, a dial plan should be scalable so that company growth and the addition of new sites will not affect the ease with which users place calls. A dial plan determines which calls will stay within the company intranet (on-net calls) and which will be sent out to the PSTN (off-net calls) via gateway equipment.

This chapter outlines the components of dial plan architecture, which include dialed numbers (DNs), route patterns, route lists, route groups, and route filters and how the use of these components enables ease of use and simplifies administration of the voice system. A well-designed dial plan increases system reliability and provides cost savings through least-cost routing. A well-designed dial plan is scalable. It permits the addition of new sites into the dial plan without disrupting existing dial plan architecture. Users should be unaware of the path a call takes (on-net or off-net), but the dial plan does provide call admission control (CAC)—that is, control of who is allowed access and when this access is allowed. CAC is most commonly used to restrict employee long distance access and to track usage for various classes of service.

Probably the most common example of a dial plan in America is the North American Numbering Plan (NANP). NANP is a hierarchical plan that consists of country codes, area codes, local exchanges, and subscriber numbers. This approach simplifies the call-routing decisions that carrier switches must make in that they will direct call setup by examining just the first few digits before making a routing decision and passing the call off to switches nearer the call destination.

Collecting the Information

Many variables must be taken into consideration when beginning the process of designing a VoIP network. We focus first on details that must be documented to begin designing a simple dial plan. We begin this discussion with the information necessary for a single-site dial plan. Keep in mind that the goals of the dial plan remain the same regardless of whether you are building a 200-phone network or 10,000-phone enterprise system.

Begin by interviewing the customer to determine how the present dial plan is implemented. Find out how satisfied the customer is with the features and benefits that are currently incorporated into the circuit-switched voice network, and gain an understanding of the type of equipment that is installed. A detailed inventory of hardware and software is necessary to determine compatibility should the new packet-switched voice system need to be integrated with legacy equipment. It is necessary to understand how users are separated by the features they are allowed to access. This is known as *class of service* and is not to be confused with the OSI Layer 2 prioritization technique. Once you have gathered all relevant information and understand and have documented the requirements, the design process can begin.

Scenario 1

The VoIP Corporation has decided to begin building its corporate voice system. However, the company's senior VPs have decided that a slow investment in this technology will best suit their corporate policies. They will demand design documents and proof of concept to be shown along the way. The IT department has concluded that a small voice network, using existing analog phones connected to a router, will best allow for corporate buy-in to VoIP technology. The IT staff has settled on the idea of four analog phones connected to a voice-enabled router; at first these phones will communicate only with each other. Future plans for the pilot implementation include a connection to the company's internal PBX for external calls. A diagram of the initial pilot is shown in Figure 9.1.

Figure 9.1 Analog Phone Connections to Router

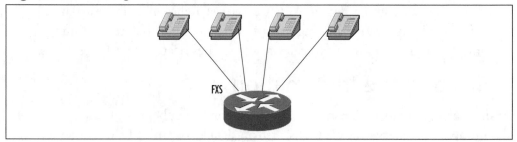

Determining the Requirements

The first step to be undertaken is identifying the dial numbers that the office currently employs for internal use. How does the outside world connect to the employees of the VoIP Corporation? That is, do outside callers dial a single number that connects to a receptionist (attendant) prior to being connected to a company representative, or do outside callers dial directly to the desk of the employee via direct inward dial (DID)? Some corporations use both.

The VoIP Corporation has purchased DID numbers from its carrier; these numbers provides for phone numbers from 777-7200 to 777–7599. Currently, the company uses only 777-7200 through 777-7499. Each of the three branch locations has been assigned one of three extension ranges:

- **Site A** 7200–7299

- **Site B** 7300–7399
- **Site C** 7400–7499

These assignments leave an available pool of phone numbers from 7500 through 7599. These are the phone extension numbers that we will use to begin designing the VoIP Corporation integrated network.

Employees from any of the company's three existing locations may use four-digit dialing to connect to anyone else within the company by dialing the employee's four-digit extension. To dial an outside line, users must dial a 9 followed by the E.164 telephone number. Long distance calling is not currently restricted.

Once we have determined the company requirements and understand what features the company employees are accustomed to, we can begin the process of designing a dial plan that will ease the migration process and be viable in the final converged voice and data system.

Designing the Dial Plan

Dial plan requirements vary from company to company, but from an architectural standpoint, we can break the dial plan into two general categories: calls that will stay internal to a company's infrastructure (on-net) and calls that will need to be sent out over the PSTN (off-net). Calls that would ordinarily be routed on-net will sometimes be re-routed off-net if there is a lack of resources available to connect that call internally. Remember, it is the goal of the dial plan to make these routing decisions as easily as possible with a minimum amount of configuration overhead. See Figure 9.2 for a call flow example.

Figure 9.2 Route Determination

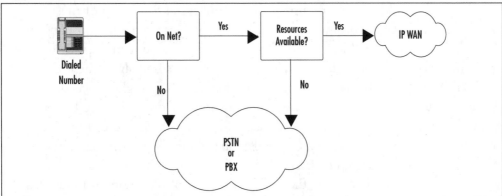

For our initial pilot, we do not have many call route decisions to make. The router will examine the dialed digits from the analog phone that is connected to an FXS port and then forward the call to the appropriate voice port/dial peer combination with which the dialed extension is associated. But this route-decision process is the same one that we will use as we add greater functionality to our voice pilot later in the chapter.

Designing a Single-Router VoIP Network

So far, we have determined what the IT staff of the VoIP Corporation would like to get from its initial pilot as well as information regarding how the existing telephone system functions and the services offered to users. We now use that information to begin designing a solution by selecting the hardware platform that will best suit our needs.

Choosing the Hardware

When choosing the platform that fits our initial design model, it is best to start by making a list of interfaces and CPU power that will be needed to connect the equipment in the design. We know that we need a hardware platform that provides four connections to attach the analog phones, and we also want a single Ethernet connection. Simply put, our requirements are:

- A low-end, voice-enabled router chassis
- Four FXS ports for analog phone connection
- An Ethernet port for Telnet access and future integration

Keep in mind that the equipment that is purchased for this pilot must be integrated into our final solution. We can begin our search for the proper hardware by contacting our local Cisco sales engineer or account manager. By explaining what you have determined during your needs analysis, these Cisco staff will be able to give you several options for how you might proceed.

If you would like to explore your options on your own, visit the Cisco Connection Online (CCO) at www.cisco.com. From there you can browse all telephony products by category. Our needs analysis findings point us toward voice gateway products. Once there, you can select data sheets for particular gateway devices and determine the best fit in terms of requirement functionality, future integration usefulness, and, of course, cost.

The Ethernet connection will be useful as a point of entry should we want to Telnet to the router for configuration or for IOS upgrade purposes. The ports that the analog phones will attach to need to supply dial tone to the phones when they go off-hook. This differs from IP phones for which the dial tone is stored internally to the phone as a WAV file and is played when the IP phone goes off-hook. The port adapter that provides dial tone is called a *foreign exchange station (FXS) port*. FXS ports come on a variety of adapters with differing port density. Our initial design calls for four ports of FXS functionality and at least one Ethernet port. This can be achieved by first installing an NM-2W1E network module into a router chassis. This piece will provide us with the Ethernet port that we need as well as open slots for a pair of dual-port FXS VWIC adapters.

For our purposes, we will select a 2600 series router, which, along with option cards, will provide us the functionality we need now and in the future. Our equipment list looks like this:

- One Cisco 2610
- Two dual-port FXS VICs
- One network module
- One on-board Ethernet interface
- Four analog telephones

We need to purchase these components to complete the hardware design shown previously in Figure 9.1.

Creating the Design Plan

We have now defined the pilot requirements from a functionality and hardware standpoint. We know what the VoIP Corporation wants to get from its pilot and the hardware needed to accomplish the task. Next we put the pieces together to create a functional configuration and test it prior to deployment.

In our initial design, we need to account for how calls will be handled through the FXS ports to which our analog phones will be connected. Due to our design's simplicity, we need to design only for POTS dial peers. Table 9.1 illustrates the type of checklist that shows how the task outlined in Figure 9.2 can be accomplished.

Table 9.1 The Initial Four-Phone Dial Plan

Dial Peer Tag	Destination Pattern	Type	Voice Port	Session Target
7501	7777501	POTS	1/0/0	FXS
7502	7777502	POTS	1/0/0	FXS
7503	7777503	POTS	1/1/0	FXS
7504	7777504	POTS	1/1/1	FXS

Note that we used a dial peer tag that corresponds to the destination pattern—that is, dial peer 7501 maps to extension number 7501. This mapping might not always be possible, but in this case, it clarifies which extensions are associated with separate dial peers. We have begun the process of mapping our dial plan numbers to physical voice ports. We have also begun the process of reserving the 75xx extension range with our pilot voice network. As shown in the sample dial plan, when input digits are in the 75xx range, the router will look in its dial peer statements to identify the physical port connection that should ring.

Configuring a Single-Router VoIP Network

In this section we continue our methodology by reviewing our information and design before setting out to configure our single-router implementation. From our initial design, we can see that we will set up a Cisco 2610 to function as a legacy PBX would in regard to call processing and switching. Let's review our design and then continue to configure this router.

Reviewing the Design

As stated previously, prior to deployment, network best practices dictate that the design must be reviewed to assure that the implementation's will be met. This includes detailing the tasks involved with the deployment, how long the deployment will take, and what risks, if any, might impact normal business operations. There should always be a test plan, cooperatively created with the customer's IT staff, that defines the successful deployment criteria. Do not forget to check for compatibility problems between interfaces and IOS versions as well as hardware compatibility issues that could affect subsequent integration with existing legacy voice equipment. These steps must always be observed, regardless of the size and scope of the deployment.

For our VoIP Corporation pilot, we have collected the necessary information, performed our technical customer interviews, chosen the best hardware platform, and created our initial dial plan. Let's review the case that can be made to the senior VPs to present our proof of concept. First we present our detailed diagram, shown in Figure 9.3.

Figure 9.3 Cisco 2610 Rear Panel Connections

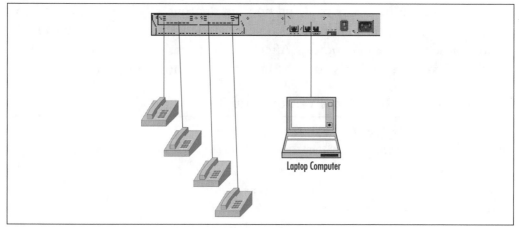

The voice-enabled router outfitted with four FXS ports will simply act the way a public telephone switch would if the phones were connected to the PSTN. As detailed in our dial plan, we assign the prefix 777 to all phones and an extension number from 7501 through 7504. The FXS ports are numbered by slot/subunit/port. The network module (NM) occupies Slot 1. The dual-port FXS cards each occupy one of the two subunit slots, 0 and 1, and each FXS card has two ports, 0 and 1. So, for example, 1/1/0 denotes Slot 1/Subunit 1/Port 0, and so forth.

To begin with, we attach our PC to the console port in the usual manner. Doing so allows us to view the router after bootup, configure the router, and save and view the configuration when we are done. Currently, we have no pressing need to configure the Ethernet port, but we will assign an IP address for future use.

Let's review our objectives for this initial pilot. We want to demonstrate the functionality of four analog phones connected to a single router and begin dial plan and voice system deployment, with an eye to expansion. This means that our router might need to be redeployed when our voice system expands.

Configuring the Router: Step by Step

Assemble the hardware as shown in Figure 9.3. Remember to wear an antistatic wrist strap any time you handle components. Make sure that components fit firmly in place. Never force a card or network module into place if it does not seem to fit. When the module and cards are properly installed, connect the PC to the console port using the cables and adapters that shipped with your router. You can then connect the power cord and boot up the router. It is important to have a hyperterminal session running so that you can view system messages during the power-on self-test (POST) process. After the router has completed the bootup, type **show version** and view output similar to that shown in Figure 9.4.

Figure 9.4 Cisco 2610 Show Version Output

```
Cisco Internetwork Operating System Software
IOS (tm) C2600 Software (C2600-IS-M), Version 11.3(6)T,   RELEASE
    SOFTWARE (fc1)
Copyright (c) 1986-1998 by cisco Systems, Inc.
Compiled Tue 06-Oct-98 18:53 by ccai
Image text-base: 0x80008084, data-base: 0x80823A4C
ROM: System Bootstrap, Version 11.3(2)XA3, PLATFORM SPECIFIC RELEASE
    SOFTWARE (fc1)
Router1 uptime is 6 minutes
System restarted by power-on
System image file is "flash:c2600-~1.bin", booted via flash

cisco 2610 (MPC860) processor (revision 0x202) with 16384K/4096K bytes of
    memory.
Processor board ID JAB023502EE (1302456116)
M860 processor: part number 0, mask 49
Bridging software.
X.25 software, Version 3.0.0.
1 Ethernet/IEEE 802.3 interface(s)
4 Voice FXS interface(s)
32K bytes of non-volatile configuration memory.
8192K bytes of processor board System flash (Read/Write)

Configuration register is 0x2102
```

As shown in the output, the router recognizes the installed hardware and soft-ware. We are now ready to begin configuring the router for our use. We face two configuration issues concerning how we will make these analog phones func-tional. First, we must concern ourselves with the physical operation of the voice ports. That is, what type of signaling will be used between the router and the phones? The second issue is to configure the logical dial peers and associate them to the physical voice ports. Do the following:

1. Enter Global Configuration mode:

    ```
    router1#configure terminal
    ```

2. From the configuration prompt, enter the following:

    ```
    router1(config)#voice-port 1/0/0
    ```

3. Configure a port description. This step is optional:

    ```
    router1(config-voiceport)#description  << This voice port is FXS >>
    ```

4. Configure the type of signaling required:

    ```
    router1(config-voiceport)#signal loop-start
    ```

5. Enable the port:

    ```
    router1(config-voiceport)#no shutdown
    ```

6. Repeat these commands for voice ports 1/0/1, 1/1/0, and 1/1/1. More voice port commands are available, but these are all we need for now. To view other commands, type:

    ```
    router1(config-voiceport)#?
    ```

    or:

    ```
    router1(config-voiceport)#exit  \\ to return to global configuration
                                           mode.
    ```

7. Next, configure our dial peer statements and associate them with the router voice ports. To do this, we must enter dial peer configuration mode. The command-line convention for this task is:

    ```
    router1(config)#dial-peer voice tag {voip|pots}
    ```

where the *tag* is a number between 1 and 2147483647. In our dial plan, we designed these tags to coincide with the extension number. This is not a requirement but can be useful when viewing dial peers or troubleshooting. The {*voip*|*pots*} portion of the command specifies the method of voice-related encapsulation. So our configuration statements will look like this:

```
router1(config)#dial-peer voice 7501 pots
```

8. This brings us to the dial peer configuration prompt. Now enter the destination pattern (phone number):

```
router1(config-dial-peer)#destination-pattern 7777501
router1(config-dial-peer)#port 1/0/0
```

9. We have now associated a DN with a physical voice port. Repeat these commands for the other three dial peers:

```
router1(config)#dial-peer voice 7502 pots
router1(config-dial-peer)#destination-pattern 7777502
router1(config-dial-peer)#port 1/0/1


router1(config)#dial-peer voice 7503 pots
router1(config-dial-peer)#destination-pattern 7777503
router1(config-dial-peer)#port 1/1/0


router1(config)#dial-peer voice 7504 pots
router1(config-dial-peer)#destination-pattern 7777504
route1r(config-dial-peer)#port 1/1/1
```

Our abbreviated configuration now looks like this:

```
dial-peer voice 7501 pots
 destination-pattern +7777501
 port 1/0/0
!
dial-peer voice 7502 pots
 destination-pattern +7777502
 port 1/0/1
!
dial-peer voice 7503 pots
```

```
      destination-pattern +7777503

      port 1/1/0

   !

   dial-peer voice 7504 pots

      destination-pattern +777504

      port 1/1/1

   !

   voice-port 1/0/0

      description << This voice port is FXS >>

   !

   voice-port 1/0/1

      description << This voice port is FXS >>

   !

   voice-port 1/1/0

      description << This voice port is FXS >>

   !

   voice-port 1/1/1

      description << This voice port is FXS >>
```

10. Use **Ctrl + z** to exit Configuration mode, and save the configuration by entering:

    copy running-config startup-config

We have now successfully configured our voice ports, defined our dial peers, and associated the dial numbers with the physical FXS ports to which our phones will connect. Using standard RJ-11 telephone patch cables, we can now connect our analog phones to the router ports and begin testing.

Testing and Verification

Now that we have all the components connected and configured, we can begin to test our pilot voice network for functionality. The first test is to pick up each telephone receiver one by one and listen for the presence of a dial tone. Once that task is performed and deemed successful, we can pick up the phone that is connected to voice port 1/0/0, dial **777-7502**, and listen for ringing. Once the phone at extension 7502 goes off-hook, you can have a conversation over these telephones. This completed call consists of two call legs. That is, each of the segments from phone to router constitutes a single call leg. After this call test is finished, try dialing the other configured handset numbers to make sure that all ports are functioning correctly. Additionally, you may view the success or failure of a call through the *show dial-peer* command, as shown here:

```
Router#show dial-peer voice 7501

        VoiceEncapPeer7501
        tag = 7501, destination-pattern = `+7777502',
        answer-address = `',
        group = 100, Admin state is up, Operation state is up
        type = pots, prefix = `',
        session-target = `', voice-port = 1/0/0
        Connect Time = 64084, Charged Units = 0
        Successful Calls = 1, Failed Calls = 0
        Accepted Calls = 1, Refused Calls = 0
        Last Setup Time = 62379441
```

Merging the PBX and VoIP Networks

It is most likely that a corporation will need to gradually adapt to a VoIP network rather than perform a "forklift" upgrade. It is simply not practical for a company to instantly change the way it is accustomed to doing business. In this section, we present a way to simply merge of our single-router pilot to the existing corporate PBX. This is the method by which a migration can take place at a pace that is comfortable to a particular corporation.

Designing PBX Interconnect Trunks

Up to now, we have not had to design for call destinations that reside on networks other than our pilot router. In fact, we have not yet actually deployed VoIP in the proper sense, because we are only sending calls from voice port to voice port. In this and subsequent sections of this chapter, we begin building on our simple voice system to add functionality. Let's start with exploring design and deployment options aimed at merging the IP voice system with legacy equipment.

Scenario 2

The senior VPs of the VoIP Corporation are pleased with the quick acquisition, design detail, and successful testing of our voice pilot. They have now given the IT staff the task of expanding on the original design to include connectivity to

the VoIP Corporation existing phone system. This goal requires the same infor-
mation-collecting, design, and review methodology that we followed in the original pilot. To keep the costs of this pilot as low as possible, the VPs want to use
the same router deployed in the first pilot to demonstrate connectivity to the
company legacy PBX. The logical diagram for our next step is presented in
Figure 9.5.

Figure 9.5 Router1-to-Legacy-PBX Connection

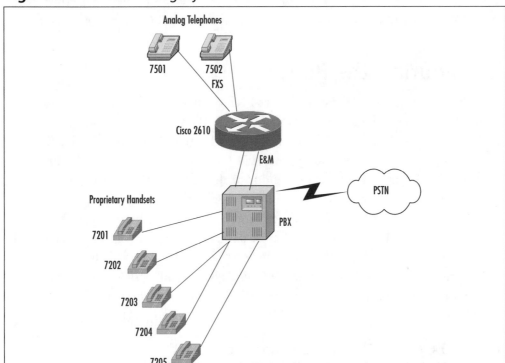

In the previous steps we demonstrated how the Cisco 2610 router platform
performs with limited functionality as a traditional PBX. We want to build on the
previous design to merge our pilot voice system and connect to the VoIP
Corporation legacy PBX. We have several options for connecting a voice-enabled
router platform to an existing PBX. These choices fall into two categories: analog
trunks or digital trunks. Examples of analog trunks include FXO and E&M.
Examples of digital trunks include ISDN primary and multiflex T1. For now, let's
use the existing PBX connections as our gateway to the PBX.

When we're deciding on which trunks can be used, it is best to consult with
the PBX vendor whose equipment you want to connect to. The PBX vendor

representative will be able to provide some guidance in regard to tie-line port availability (if any), trunk card options, and, of course, additional programming of the PBX to accept calls to and from our pilot voice system. The major difference in trunk interfaces is that analog trunks only support a single DS0 (called a *tie-line*) on each interface, whereas a digital ISDN or T1 interface may support up to 24 DS0s for larger call volume. For our proof of concept, we will remove one of our dual-port FXS cards from the Cisco 2610 and replace it with a dual-port E&M card (VIC-2E/M). This change allows us to have simultaneous conversations from our pilot analog phones to other company extensions and/or PSTN destinations.

Configuring the Router

Prior to removing one of the dual-port FXS cards and replacing it with a dual-port E&M tie-line card, power down the 2610. Remove the second FXS card and replace it with the E&M module. The hardware connections on the E&M card are RJ-45 receptacles. These ports will be connected to an E&M trunk port on the PBX. Work with the PBX vendor to determine the correct operation (Types I, II, III, or V), two-wire or four-wire operation, signaling, and pinouts. This step is critical to the successful call setup negotiation between the router and the PBX. This is, in fact, one of the most demanding aspects of configuring VoIP. In our setup, we will reuse the voice ports 1/1/0 and 1/1/1 for our E&M tie-line connection to the PBX. Figure 9.6 displays the router *show version* output of our router, with two FXS ports and two E&M ports after powerup and successful POST.

Figure 9.6 Cisco 2610 Show Version Output

```
Cisco Internetwork Operating System Software
IOS (tm) C2600 Software (C2600-IS-M), Version 11.3(6)T,   RELEASE
    SOFTWARE (fc1)
Copyright (c) 1986-1998 by cisco Systems, Inc.
Compiled Tue 06-Oct-98 18:53 by ccai
Image text-base: 0x80008084, data-base: 0x80823A4C


ROM: System Bootstrap, Version 11.3(2)XA3, PLATFORM SPECIFIC RELEASE
    SOFTWARE (fc1)


Router1 uptime is 4 minutes
```

Continued

Figure 9.6 Continued

```
System restarted by power-on
System image file is "flash:c2600-~1.bin", booted via flash
cisco 2610 (MPC860) processor (revision 0x202) with 18432K/6144K bytes of
    memory.
Processor board ID JAB0237018E (4109491334)
M860 processor: part number 0, mask 32
Bridging software.
X.25 software, Version 3.0.0.
1 Ethernet/IEEE 802.3 interface(s)
2 Voice FXS interface(s)
2 Voice E & M interface(s)
32K bytes of non-volatile configuration memory.
8192K bytes of processor board System flash (Read/Write)


Configuration register is 0x2102
```

As shown in the output, the router recognizes that the installed hardware has changed, as indicated by two FXS ports and two E&M ports. We are now ready to begin configuring the router for connectivity to the PBX. The convention used for the CLI is essentially the same, but we need to configure a couple of different parameters for the new E&M tie lines. Remember, E&M voice port values must match those specified by the particular PBX device to which the port is connected. You must work with a qualified PBX technician in order to achieve this goal. The required parameter commands in voice port configuration mode include:

- Dial type using the *dial-type* command

- Signal type using the *signal* command

- Call progress tone using the *cptone* command

- Operation using the *operation* command

- Type using the *type* command

- Impedance using the *impedance* command

Optionally, we may include:

- Connection mode using the *connection plar* command

- Music-threshold using the *music-threshold* command

- Description using the *description* command

- Comfort tone (if VAD is activated) using the *comfort-noise* command

The following configuration steps detail how we will configure our E&M ports for connectivity to our PBX. Note that E&M configuration from deployment to deployment and depends on the PBX to which you're connecting:

1. From Global Configuration mode, enter:

   ```
   router1(config)#voice-port 1/1/0
   ```

2. This will take you to the voice port configuration prompt. Type in a port description. This is an optional step, but it is good practice to always configure a description for your ports:

   ```
   router1(config-voiceport)#description   << This voice port is E&M >>
   ```

3. Select the dial type:

   ```
   router1(config-voiceport)#dial-type dtmf
   ```

4. Select the type of signaling:

   ```
   router1(config-voiceport)#signal wink-start
   ```

5. Configure the call progress tone:

   ```
   router1(config-voiceport)#cptone northamerica
   ```

6. Select type of operation:

   ```
   router1config-voiceport)#type 2
   ```

7. Configure the appropriate cabling scheme:

   ```
   router1(config-voiceport)#operation 4-wire
   ```

8. Configure the correct impedance. This value will be supplied by the PBX vendor:

   ```
   router1(config-voiceport)#impedance 600r
   ```

9. Enable the port:

   ```
   router1(config-voiceport)#no shutdown
   ```

10. After entering these parameters for one port, write the configuration to memory and view the configuration. Both E&M ports should now have the same settings. Now we must alter our original dial peer statements to accommodate our new E&M interfaces. To do this, we must enter Dial Peer Configuration mode. The command-line convention for this command is:

```
router1(config)#dial-peer voice 110 pots
```

11. This brings us to the Dial Peer Configuration prompt. Now enter the destination pattern (phone number):

```
router1(config-dial-peer)#destination-pattern 77772..
```

12. Then associate this destination with a voice port:

```
router1(config-dial-peer)#port 1/1/0
```

13. Repeat for another tie-line:

```
router1(config)#dial-peer voice 111 pots
router1(config-dial-peer)#destination-pattern 77772..
router1(config-dial-peer)#port 1/1/0
```

These steps give us two tie-lines for calls placed from our analog phones to extensions on the other side of the PBX. Again, you have to work with the PBX vendor to plan how digits will be presented to and from the router. In our example, we are sending all seven digits (the complete DN) to the PBX for processing. This is only one way that this task might be accomplished. Our partial configuration now looks like this:

```
dial-peer voice 7501 pots
 destination-pattern +7777501
 port 1/0/0
!
dial-peer voice 7502 pots
 destination-pattern +7777502
 port 1/0/1

dial-peer voice 110 pots
 destination-pattern +77772..
 port 1/1/0
```

```
!
dial-peer voice 111 pots
 destination-pattern +77772..
 port 1/1/0
!
voice-port 1/0/0
 description            << This voice port is FXS >>
!
voice-port 1/0/1
 description            << This voice port is FXS >>
!
voice-port 1/1/0
 description            << This Voice Port is E&M >>
 dial-type dtmf
 signal wink-start
 operation 4-wire
 type 2
!
voice-port 1/1/1
 description            << This Voice Port is E&M >>
 dial-type dtmf
 signal wink-start
 operation 4-wire
 type 2
```

With this part of the configuration complete, we have configured two call-route options for our pilot router. If digits in the 777-7501-2 range are dialed, the router will look to itself for a corresponding dial peer. If it receives dialed digits in the 777-72*xx* range, it will pass the digits off to the PBX via E&M analog tie line for call completion. We can now test our router-to-PBX telephone connectivity.

Testing and Verification

Testing the successful call to from our pilot phones to the existing proprietary handsets will provide the proof of concept that the senior VPs requested at the outset of Scenario 2. Furthermore, we can view the configuration and operational status using the *show voice port* command. Sample output follows:

```
router1# show voice port 1/1/1


  recEive And transMit 1/1/1 Slot is 1, Sub-unit is 1, Port is 1
  Type of VoicePort is E&M
  Operation State is DORMANT
  Administrative State is UP
  The Last Interface Down Failure Cause is Administrative Shutdown
  Description is This port is E/M
  Noise Regeneration is enabled
  Non Linear Processing is enabled
  Music On Hold Threshold is Set to -38 dBm
  In Gain is Set to 0 dB
  Out Attenuation is Set to 0 dB
  Echo Cancellation is enabled
  Echo Cancel Coverage is set to 16 ms
  Connection Mode is normal
  Connection Number is not set
  Initial Time Out is set to 10 s
  Interdigit Time Out is set to 10 s


Analog Info Follows:
  Region Tone is set for US
  Currently processing Voice
  Maintenance Mode Set to None (not in mtc mode)
  Number of signaling protocol errors are 0
  Impedance is set to 600r Ohm


  Voice card specific Info Follows:
  Signal Type is wink-start
  Operation Type is 4-wire
  E&M Type is 2
  Dial Type is dtmf
  In Seizure is inactive
  Out Seizure is inactive
  Digit Duration Timing is set to 100 ms
  InterDigit Duration Timing is set to 100 ms
  Pulse Rate Timing is set to 10 pulses/second
```

```
InterDigit Pulse Duration Timing is set to 500 ms

Clear Wait Duration Timing is set to 400 ms

Wink Wait Duration Timing is set to 200 ms

Wink Duration Timing is set to 200 ms

Delay Start Timing is set to 300 ms

Delay Duration Timing is set to 2000 ms

Dial Pulse Min. Delay is set to 140 ms
```

Configuring a Multirouter Intraoffice VoIP Network

The previous sections took us through the design and deployment basics of a small-scale voice system pilot. But we have not actually encapsulated voice packets into IP datagrams, compressed the packets, and transmitted them to another voice-enabled router decompression to play out. We have only used standard POTS dial peers to keep our pilot system calls local or send them to the existing PBX for call processing there. This and subsequent sections introduce ways to configure VoIP peers, first over a LAN connection and then over a point-to-point WAN connection.

Extending the Dial Plan

Prior to the purchase of any additional equipment, we must continue with the methodology that has brought us this far. This means defining our requirements, performing a design review, and documenting the information that is relevant to our pilot voice system expansion. Because our initial dial plan accounted for scalability, we can incorporate our original dial plan into something that makes sense for the entire office (see Table 9.2).

Table 9.2 E&M Modified Dial Plan for Router1

Dial Peer Tag	Destination Pattern	Type	Voice Port	Session Target
7501	7777501	POTS	1/0/0	FXS
7502	7777502	POTS	1/0/0	FXS
110	77772xx	POTS	1/1/0	E&M
111	77772xx	POTS	1/1/1	E&M

> **NOTE**
>
> This dial plan is being implemented within the switches and routers that will make up our pilot voice network. This might more commonly be accomplished via Cisco Call Manager servers, but that is beyond the scope of this chapter. For dial plan implementation via Cisco Call Manager, see the Syngress publication *Configuring Cisco AVVID* (ISBN: 1-928994-14-8).

Let's continue to expand our dial plan to include a second router within our first VoIP Corporation location and then extend the design to include a WAN connected location. Our original dial plan design included three sites; this third site will be added using the identical strategy that we used to add the second site. First, let's expand our voice system and show how we might accomplish this goal using a second router. We will keep using the extensions within the 75*xx* range that we began reserving on Router1. We'll set up Router 2 in the same manner as the first. We will keep the total number of phones small to simplify our examples, but this design is quite scalable.

Extending the Design

As depicted in Figure 9.7, we have extended our design to include a second voice-enabled router platform. For our pilot, we should be able to purchase a second Cisco 2610 and NM-2V. We will be able to reuse the dual-port FXS card that we removed from Router1 to make room for the PBX-to-E&M connection. This will give us two analog ports on the second router to which we can connect phones and demonstrate VoIP to the senior VPs. As previously stated, we have chosen these router platforms to keep our pilot both simple and low cost. We could have easily deployed multilayer switches populated with the same type of VICs as those that we installed in the 2610s. This would, in fact, have provided greater scalability in terms of the number of analog phones as well as prepare the VoIP Corporation for the eventual migration to IP phones, but remember that our original pilot was dictated to be as low-cost as possible. When the pilot implementation goes into production, the existing pilot equipment may be used in other voice network capacities. Note that this equipment, whether routers or multiplayer switches, will eventually need to transport network traffic from servers and end stations. We need to start thinking about classification and marking our voice traffic for prioritization. While demonstrating that we can complete calls from one phone to another, we must also assure the voice quality will be what users are accustomed to. We explore some of these options later in this chapter.

Figure 9.7 Router2 Added to Design

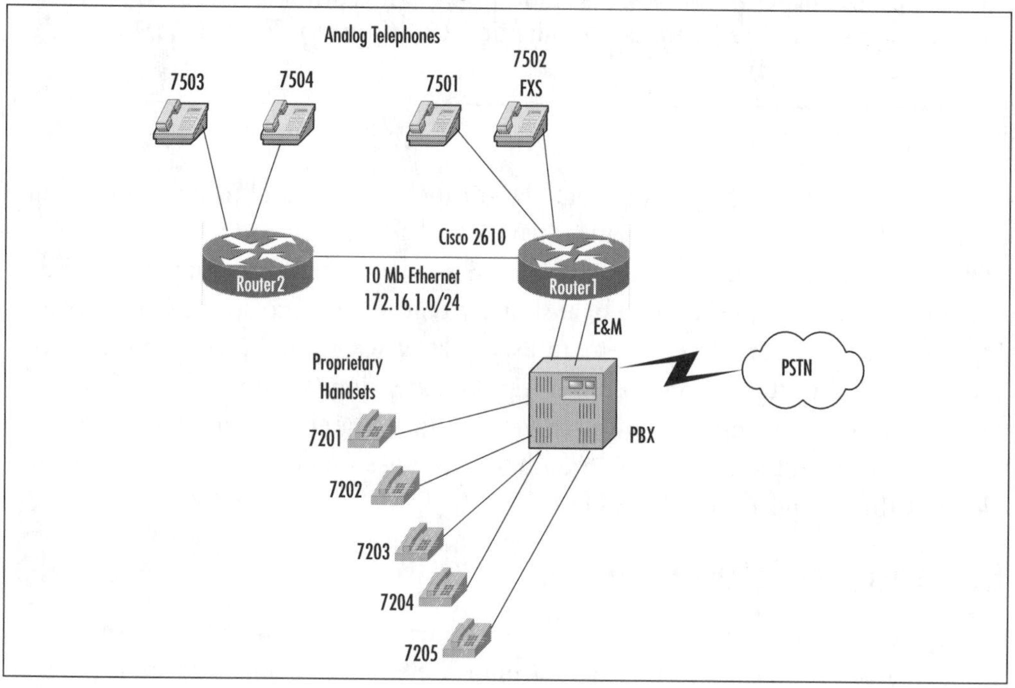

Configuring the Routers

We'll assemble Router2 as described earlier in this chapter. Remember to follow proper antistatic procedures to avoid component damage. The FXS ports will also be configured in the same manner as Router1, although we will review the FXS configuration here. Additionally, we will configure our Ethernet ports on each router for IP connectivity. Finally, we will create VoIP dial peers for communication between the two Cisco 2610 router platforms. Let's start with the configuration of Router1's Ethernet port and VoIP dial peer statement:

1. From the router prompt, enter Configuration mode. From the Global Configuration prompt, enter:

```
router1(config)#interface E0 \ To enter interface configuration mode
```

2. Add the IP address for this interface:

```
router1(config-if)#ip address 172.16.1.1 255.255.255.0
```

3. Enable interface ethernet 0:

```
router1(config-if)#no shutdown
```

4. Exit interface configuration mode:

```
router1(config-if)#exit
router1(config)#
```

5. Next, we configure our VoIP dial peer statements and associate them with the destination IP address of Router2. To do this, we must enter Dial Peer Configuration mode. The command-line convention for this command is:

```
router1(config)#dial-peer voice tag {voip|pots}
```

   where the *tag* is a number between 1 and 2147483647. In our dial plan, we designed these tags to coincide with the destination pattern. Since this is a VoIP peer, we arbitrarily select numbers (200/201) and assign them to a VoIP dial peer. The command looks like this:

```
router1(config)#dial-peer voice 7503 voip
router1(config-dial-peer)#destination-pattern +7777503
router1(config-dial-peer)#session target ipv4:172.16.1.2
router1(config-dial-peer)#exit
router1(config)#
```

6. We will create a second dial peer for the second extension on Router2:

```
router1(config)#dial-peer voice 7504 voip
router1(config-dial-peer)#destination-pattern +7777504
router1(config-dial-peer)#session target ipv4:172.16.1.2
router1(config-dial-peer)#exit
router1(config)#
```

7. Use **Ctrl + z** to exit Configuration mode, and save the configuration by entering:

```
copy running-config startup-config
```

8. Next we turn our attention to the configuration of the necessary commands to configure Router2. After the hardware is installed and powered up, we first assign an IP address to the Ethernet interface:

    ```
    router2(config-if)#ip address 172.16.1.2 255.255.255.0
    ```

9. Enable interface Ethernet 0:

    ```
    router2(config-if)#no shutdown
    ```

10. Exit Interface Configuration mode:

    ```
    router2(config-if)#exit
    router2(config)#
    ```

11. Next we configure and enable our FXS ports:

    ```
    router2(config)#voice-port 1/0/0
    ```

12. Type in a port description:

    ```
    router2(config-voiceport)#description  << This voice port is FXS >>
    ```

13. Type in the type of signaling:

    ```
    router2(config-voiceport)#signal loop-start
    ```

14. Enable the voice port:

    ```
    router2(config-voiceport)#no shutdown
    ```

15. Repeat these commands for voice port 1/0/1.

    ```
    router2(config-voiceport)#exit   \\ to return to global configuration
                                                     mode.
    ```

16. Connect a crossover Ethernet cable to the respective Ethernet ports of each router and assure connectivity. Now we will configure the POTS dial peer statements for Router2:

    ```
    router2(config)#dial-peer voice 7503 pots
    router2(config-dial-peer)#destination-pattern 7777503
    router2config-dial-peer)#port 1/0/0

    router2(config)#dial-peer voice 7504 pots
    router2(config-dial-peer)#destination-pattern 7777504
    ```

```
router2(config-dial-peer)#port 1/0/1
router2(config-if)#exit
router2(config)#
```

17. Finally, we need to configure our VoIP dial peers for Router2:

```
router2(config)#dial-peer voice 7501 voip
router2(config-dial-peer)#destination-pattern +7777501
router2(config-dial-peer)#session target ipv4:172.16.1.1
router2(config-dial-peer)#exit
router2(config)#
```

We will create a second dial peer for the second extension on Router1:

```
router2(config)#dial-peer voice 7502 voip
router2(config-dial-peer)#destination-pattern +7777502
router2(config-dial-peer)#session target ipv4:172.16.1.1
router2(config-dial-peer)#exit
router2(config)#
```

```
router2(config)#dial-peer voice 7200 voip
router2(config-dial-peer)#destination-pattern +77772..
router2(config-dial-peer)#session target ipv4:172.16.1.1
router2(config-dial-peer)#exit
router2(config)#
```

18. Use **Ctrl + z** to exit Configuration mode, and save the configuration by entering:

```
copy running-config startup-config
```

Testing and Verification

As you begin the test procedure, refer to Figure 9.7 for the topology used for this test case. Place a call from the digital phone connected to the PBX to an extension number connected to Router2 and record the results. Verify that the call goes through and that a full-duplex speech path exists between the phones. Repeat this procedure for a call in the other direction (from analog phone to PBX phone).

The abbreviated configurations of both routers now look like this:

Router1

```
!
hostname Router1
!
memory-size iomem 20
!
dial-peer voice 7501 pots
 destination-pattern +7777501
 port 1/0/0
!
dial-peer voice 7502 pots
 destination-pattern +7777502
 port 1/0/1
!
dial-peer voice 110 pots
 destination-pattern +77772..
 port 1/1/0
!
dial-peer voice 111 pots
 destination-pattern +77772..
 port 1/1/0
!
dial-peer voice 7503 voip
 destination-pattern +7777503
 session target ipv4:172.16.1.2
!
dial-peer voice 7504 voip
 destination-pattern +7777504
 session target ipv4:172.16.1.2
!
voice-port 1/0/0
 description         << This voice port is FXS >>
!
voice-port 1/0/1
```

```
 description         << This voice port is FXS >>
!
voice-port 1/1/0
 description         << This Voice Port is E&M >>
 dial-type dtmf
 signal wink-start
 operation 4-wire
 type 2
!
voice-port 1/1/1
 description         << This Voice Port is E&M >>
 dial-type dtmf
 signal wink-start
 operation 4-wire
 type 2
!
interface Ethernet0/0
 ip address 172.16.1.1 255.255.255.0
!
!
line con 0
line aux 0
!
line vty 0 4
!
```

Router2

```
!
hostname Router2
!
memory-size iomem 20
!
dial-peer voice 7503 pots
 destination-pattern +7777503
 port 1/0/0
```

```
!
dial-peer voice 7504 pots
 destination-pattern +7777504
 port 1/0/1
!
dial-peer voice 7501 voip
 destination-pattern +7777501
 session target ipv4:172.16.1.1
!
dial-peer voice 7502 voip
 destination-pattern +7777502
 session target ipv4:172.16.1.1
!
dial-peer voice 7200 voip
 destination-pattern +77772..
 session target ipv4:172.16.1.1
!
voice-port 1/0/0
 description          << This voice port is FXS >>
!
voice-port 1/0/1
 description          << This voice port is FXS >>
!
interface Ethernet0/0
 ip address 172.16.1.2 255.255.255.0
!
!
line con 0
line aux 0
!
line vty 0 4
```

Configuring VoIP for Interoffice Voice Communication

In this section, we extend our expanded pilot implementation to include a remote site of the VoIP Corporation. We extend our dial plan and network infrastructure to test voice calls over this point-to-point WAN link. In the preceding section, we configured VoIP communication between two routers connected to the same IP segment. In this section, we need to add a routing protocol because voice routers Router2 and Router3 will not be directly connected. We also configure number expansion to allow for four-digit dialing between the two sites. Let's begin by reviewing our existing dial plan and then extending the dial plan to include the new router.

Extending the Dial Plan Again

Best practices dictate that we must plan and document changes prior to implementation. This practice serves several purposes. For one, it helps us conceptualize how the dial plan will map out across the enterprise and eliminate any errors prior to configuration. It also helps us in the troubleshooting process or to back out of any changes that are made to the configuration of routers or switches, should the changes have an unexpected or negative impact on our voice system.

Tables 9.3, 9.4, and 9.5 show how we have configured our dial plan so far as well as the dial plan extension for Router3.

Table 9.3 Modified Dial Plan for Router1

Dial Peer Tag	Destination Pattern	Type	Voice Port	Session Target
7501	7777501	POTS	1/0/0	FXS
7502	7777502	POTS	1/0/1	FXS
110	77772xx	POTS	1/1/0	E&M
111	77772xx	POTS	1/1/1	E&M
7503	7777503	VoIP	N/A	172.16.1.2
7504	7777504	VoIP	N/A	172.16.1.2
7301	7777301	VoIP	N/A	172.16.3.3
7302	7777302	VoIP	N/A	172.16.3.3

Table 9.4 Modified Dial Plan for Router2

Dial Peer Tag	Destination Pattern	Type	Voice Port	Session Target
7503	7777503	POTS	1/0/0	FXS
7504	7777504	POTS	1/0/1	FXS
7501	7777501	VoIP	N/A	172.16.1.1
7502	7777502	VoIP	N/A	172.16.1.1
7200	77772xx	VoIP	N/A	172.16.1.1
7301	7777301	VoIP	N/A	172.16.3.3
7302	7777302	VoIP	N/A	172.16.3.3

Table 9.5 Dial Plan for Router3

Dial Peer Tag	Destination Pattern	Type	Voice Port	Session Target
7301	7777301	POTS	1/0/0	FXS
7302	7777302	POTS	1/0/1	FXS
7501	7777501	VoIP	N/A	172.16.3.1
7502	7777502	VoIP	N/A	172.16.3.1
7200	77772xx	VoIP	N/A	172.16.3.1
7503	7777503	VoIP	N/A	172.16.1.2
7504	7777504	VoIP	N/A	172.16.1.2

Extending the Design

In Figure 9.8, the connection to Router3 has been added via a 256Kbps leased-line facility. This will be plenty of bandwidth for our pilot, but it should be stressed that when we're combining voice and data onto the same link, we must carefully consider bandwidth requirements prior to deployment. Depending on which codec is implemented between remote sites, bandwidth requirements can vary considerably. The rule of thumb when provisioning WAN bandwidth is that the combined utilization for data and voice traffic should not exceed 75 percent of the total available bandwidth. Therefore, it is always a good idea to know the data traffic trends for a particular link prior to the addition of voice traffic. This can be done with one of the many protocol analyzer or SNMP-based tools that are available. From the standpoint of voice traffic utilization, each uncompressed G.711 voice stream consumes approximately 80Kbps of bandwidth. With just two phones present at the remote site, we know that we will never consume more than 160Kbps of the 256Kbps of available bandwidth. In the section, "Tuning the VoIP Network" later in this chapter, we explore how we can use utilize our bandwidth more efficiently.

Figure 9.8 Router3 (Remote Site) Added to Design

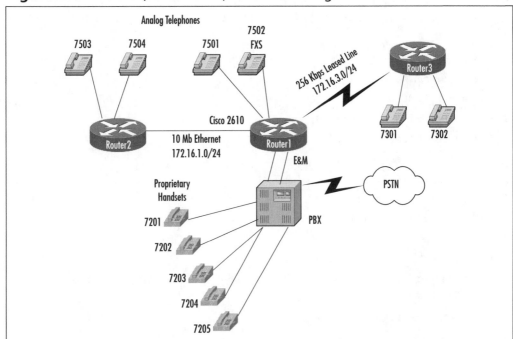

Configuring the Routers

For Router3, let's deploy one more of the Cisco 2610 platforms that we have used already. We will populate it with a dual-port FXS module, but we also need a T1 WIC CSU for both Router3 and Router1. Power down Router1 and install the WIC. Reapply power and type the *show version* command to make sure that the card is recognized by the system:

```
Cisco Internetwork Operating System Software
IOS (tm) C2600 Software (C2600-IS-M), Version 11.3(4)T1,  RELEASE
    SOFTWARE (fc1)
Copyright (c) 1986-1998 by cisco Systems, Inc.
```

```
Compiled Wed 01-Jul-98 11:50 by phanguye
Image text-base: 0x80008084, data-base: 0x808214FC


ROM: System Bootstrap, Version 11.3(2)XA3, PLATFORM SPECIFIC RELEASE
    SOFTWARE (fc1)


Router1 uptime is 1 minute
System restarted by power-on
System image file is "flash:c2600-is-mz.113-4.T1", booted via flash


cisco 2610 (MPC860) processor (revision 0x202) with 18432K/6144K bytes
    of memory.
Processor board ID JAB0237018E (4109491334)
M860 processor: part number 0, mask 32
Bridging software.
X.25 software, Version 3.0.0.
1 Ethernet/IEEE 802.3 interface(s)
1 Serial network interface(s)
2 Voice FXS interface(s)
2 Voice E & M interface(s)
32K bytes of non-volatile configuration memory.
8192K bytes of processor board System flash (Read/Write)


Configuration register is 0x2102
```

1. From the router prompt, enter Configuration mode. From the Global Configuration prompt, enter:

   ```
   router1(config)#interface serial0 \\ To enter interface configuration
                                                          mode
   ```

2. Configure the IP address for this interface:

   ```
   router1(config-if)#ip address 172.16.3.1 255.255.255.0
   ```

3. Enable interface serial 0:

   ```
   router1(config-if)#no shutdown
   ```

4. Exit Interface Configuration mode:

```
router1(config-if)#exit
router1(config)#
```

5. Now configure EIGRP for our routing protocol:

```
router1(config)#router eigrp 1
router1(config-router)#network 172.16.1.0
router1(config-router)#network 172.16.3.0
router1(config-router)#no auto-summary
router1(config-router)#exit
router1(config)#
```

6. While were here, let's configure our VoIP dial peers for Router3:

```
router1(config)#dial-peer voice 7301 voip
router1(config-dial-peer)#destination-pattern +7777301
router1(config-dial-peer)#session target ipv4:172.16.3.3
router1(config-dial-peer)#exit
router1(config)#
```

7. Add the second dial peer:

```
router1(config)#dial-peer voice 7302 voip
router1(config-dial-peer)#destination-pattern +7777302
router1(config-dial-peer)#session target ipv4:172.16.3.3
router1(config-dial-peer)#exit
router1(config)#
```

8. Use **Ctrl + z** to exit Configuration mode, and save the configuration by entering:

```
copy running-config startup-config
```

9. Configure EIGRP for Router2:

```
router2(config)#router eigrp 1
router2(config-router)#network 172.16.1.0
router2(config-router)#exit
router2(config)#
```

10. Again, while were here, let's configure our VoIP dial peers for Router3:

```
router2(config)#dial-peer voice 7301 voip
```

```
router2(config-dial-peer)#destination-pattern +7777301
router2(config-dial-peer)#session target ipv4:172.16.3.3
router2(config-dial-peer)#exit
router2(config)#
```

11. Add the second dial peer:

```
router2(config)#dial-peer voice 7302 voip
router2(config-dial-peer)#destination-pattern +7777302
router2(config-dial-peer)#session target ipv4:172.16.3.3
router2(config-dial-peer)#exit
router2(config)#
```

Clearly, without EIGRP (or some other routing protocol), Router2 calls would never reach Router3 due to the fact that they would not be able to find the session target.

12. Use **Ctrl + z** to exit Configuration mode, and save the configuration by entering:

copy running-config startup-config

Now let's turn our attention to Router3:

```
router3(config)#interface s0 \\ To enter interface configuration mode
```

13. Add the IP address for this interface:

```
router3(config-if)#ip address 172.16.3.3 255.255.255.0
```

14. Enable interface serial 0:

```
router3(config-if)#no shutdown
```

15. Exit Interface Configuration mode:

```
router3(config-if)#exit
router3(config)#
```

16. Next we configure and enable our FXS ports:

```
router3(config)#voice-port 1/0/0
```

17. Type in a port description (optional):

```
router3(config-voiceport)#description  << This voice port is FXS >>
```

18. Type in the type of signaling:

```
router3(config-voiceport)#signal loop-start
```

19. Enable the voice port:

```
router3(config-voiceport)#no shutdown
```

20. Repeat these commands for voice port 1/0/1:

```
router3(config-voiceport)#exit   \\ to return to global configuration
                                     mode.
```

21. Configure our POTS dial peers:

```
router3(config)#dial-peer voice 7301 pots
router3(config-dial-peer)#destination-pattern 7777301
router3config-dial-peer)#port 1/0/0

router3(config)# dial-peer voice 7302 pots
router3(config-dial-peer)#destination-pattern 7777302
router3(config-dial-peer)#port 1/0/1
router3(config-if)#exit
router3(config)#
```

22. Configure VoIP dial peers from Router3 to Router1:

```
router3(config)#dial-peer voice 7501 voip
router3(config-dial-peer)#destination-pattern +7777501
router3(config-dial-peer)#session target ipv4:172.16.3.1
router3(config-dial-peer)#exit
router3(config)#
```

23. Create a second dial peer for the second extension on Router1:

```
router3(config)#dial-peer voice 7502 voip
router3(config-dial-peer)#destination-pattern +7777502
router3(config-dial-peer)#session target ipv4:172.16.3.1
router3(config-dial-peer)#exit
router3(config)#
```

24. Configure a dial peer for PBX-bound calls on Router1:

```
router3(config)#dial-peer voice 7200 voip
```

```
router3(config-dial-peer)#destination-pattern +77772..
router3(config-dial-peer)#session target ipv4:172.16.3.1
router3(config-dial-peer)#exit
router3(config)#
```

25. Configure dial peer statements from Router3 to Router2:

```
router3(config)#dial-peer voice 7503 voip
router3(config-dial-peer)#destination-pattern +7777503
router3(config-dial-peer)#session target ipv4:172.16.1.2
router3(config-dial-peer)#exit
router3(config)#
```

26. Create a second dial peer for the second extension on Router2:

```
router3(config)#dial-peer voice 7504 voip
router3(config-dial-peer)#destination-pattern +7777504
router3(config-dial-peer)#session target ipv4:172.16.1.2
router3(config-dial-peer)#exit
router3(config)#
```

27. Finally, add our EIGRP statements:

```
router3(config)#router eigrp 1
router3(config-router)#network 172.16.3.0
router3(config-router)#exit
router3(config)#
```

28. Use **Ctrl + z** to exit Configuration mode, and save the configuration by entering:

```
copy running-config startup-config
```

The last topic we cover here is how to configure number expansion and how we can utilize this feature to implement four-digit dialing between sites. The goal here is to eliminate the need to dial the entire E.164 telephone number by obviating the need to dial the prefix 777. The following is an example of how we can configure this setup.

From the Global Configuration prompt of any or all of the Cisco 2610 routers (Router1 is shown), enter:

```
router1(config)#num-exp 7 +7777
router1(config)#exit
```

Save the configuration. In the command-line configuration you just saw, we are telling the router that when the single number 7 is dialed first, it should expand that single digit into the string 7777. For example, imagine that a test caller picks up one of the phones that is connected to Router1 and wants to place a call to a user at the remote site of Router3. The caller dials 7302. The router interprets the leading 7 of that dialed extension, expands it to 7777, and adds the 302 to the expanded string, the end result being the same (to the router) as if the entire 777-7302 had been dialed—and the call succeeds.

Tuning the VoIP Network

The pilot voice system has been operational now for several months. The senior VPs have been pleased with the success of bringing this technology into the company and the technical skill-building rewards that their IT staff has gained from it. Now that the leased line is in place, the company has expanded its e-mail system to include users from both sites. In addition, servers at the main site are now being utilized by users at the remote site. However, use of the leased-line link has risen to the point that during the busy hours of the day, the voice quality suffers over the voice and data converged link. The senior VPs do not want to spend more money for additional bandwidth unless it's absolutely necessary. In this section, we discuss various Cisco IOS features that can alleviate some of the issues that are deteriorating voice quality within our pilot voice network.

Tuning the Design

Depending on how a corporation does its business, there could be situations in which the only solution to converged traffic congestion is to increase bandwidth. Usually, however, corporation executives want some level of documentation as to why the available resources are not enough. The VoIP Corporation executives have given the IT staff the task of making the most out of the resources that have already been purchased. How can we achieve this goal? Let's discuss a few options.

As stated previously, a single uncompressed pulse-code-modulated (PCM) G.711 phone call consumes as much as 80Kbps of bandwidth. By selecting a more efficient codec, we can reduce this number by as much as two-thirds. The G.729a codec (CS-ACELP) can bring this number down to approximately 26Kbps. We will use more processor (CPU) cycles by using this codec, but the tradeoff is worth it when we consider low-bandwidth WAN links.

Another Cisco IOS method of bandwidth conservation is called *voice activity detection (VAD)*. This feature provides the nontransmittal of silence. That is, if no one is speaking during a call at a particular moment, bandwidth usage is reduced over the WAN link. The tradeoff with this feature is slight (5–10ms) audio clipping at the beginning of speech. Both these mechanisms can be useful in lowering the voice bandwidth usage and requirements. They can both be configured in dial peer Configuration mode as shown here:

```
router3(config)#dial-peer voice 7200 voip
router3(config-dial-peer)#destination-pattern +77772..
router3(config-dial-peer)#session target ipv4:172.16.3.1
router3(config-dial-peer)#codec g729r8
router3(config-dial-peer)#vad
router3(config-dial-peer)#exit
router3(config)# voice-port 1/0/0
router3(config-voiceport)# echo-cancel enable
router3(config-voiceport)# echo-cancel coverage 16
router3(config-voiceport)# ctrl-z
router3# copy running-config startup-config
router3#
```

Keep in mind that these commands apply only to VoIP dial peers. If codec values for the VoIP peers of a connection do not match, the call will fail. So, in this case, Router1's VoIP dial peer statement also needs to be modified.

The last three lines are not efficiency mechanism commands but rather call quality commands that will help in the event of impedance mismatches and the resulting echo. Echo cancellation values are [16, 24, 32] milliseconds.

Another mechanism to save WAN link bandwidth is RTP compression (cRTP). Within a voice stream, each transmitted packet has RTP, UDP, and IP headers associated with it. The header portion of RTP is considerably large. The minimal 12 bytes of the RTP header, combined with 20 bytes of IP header (IPH) and 8 bytes of UDP header, create a 40-byte IP/UDP/RTP header. For compressed-payload audio applications, the RTP packet typically has a 20-byte to 160-byte payload. Given the size of the IP/UDP/RTP header combinations, it is inefficient to send the IP/UDP/RTP header without compressing it. When we compress these headers, the associated overhead for RTP, UDP, and IP can be reduced to anywhere from 2 to 5 bytes. This can be done from Interface Configuration mode (the transmitting or receiving interface), as shown here:

```
router3(config)#interface serial 0 \\ To enter interface configuration mode
router3(config-if)# ip address 172.16.3.3 255.255.255.0
router3(config-if)#ip rtp-header-compression
router3(config-if)#no shutdown
```

These commands are useful in terms of link efficiency, so when they're used, they can improve voice quality over a slightly congested WAN link. Let's quickly look at a few other voice quality improvements that we can make to our pilot voice system prior to the next section, "Applying QoS to the VoIP Network," where we look into overall strategies for assuring acceptable voice quality.

The single worst enemy of voice quality is the overall delay between the time that a speaker speaks into a phone to the time that a listener hears it. If this time is too long (>200ms), the two parties will begin to speak over one another when a reply does not return to the speaker in an acceptable timeframe. This phenomenon is known as the *satellite effect* because satellite telephone conversations are notorious for long delay. Jitter—variable delay between packets in the same voice stream—also has a negative impact on voice quality. To help improve these situations within our pilot voice system, let's add fair queuing to our output serial interfaces:

```
router3(config)# interface serial 0 \\ To enter interface configuration mode
router3(config-if)# fair-queue
router3(config-if)#end
```

Testing and Verification

We should now be able to test our calls again. Remember to test in both directions and document results. It is important to have a test record in the event that a problem is reported; that way, it might be possible to trace the problem to a recent configuration change. If echo is encountered, we could extend our cancellation coverage. If echo persists, look into impedance mismatches between the interfaces between the calls that are being degraded.

Our final pilot configurations follow:

Router1

```
hostname Router1
!
memory-size iomem 20
```

```
!
dial-peer voice 100 pots
 destination-pattern +7777501
 port 1/0/0
!
dial-peer voice 7502 pots
 destination-pattern +7777502
 port 1/0/1
!
dial-peer voice 110 pots
 destination-pattern +77772..
 port 1/1/0
!
dial-peer voice 111 pots
 destination-pattern +77772..
 port 1/1/0
!
dial-peer voice 7503 voip
 destination-pattern +7777503
 session target ipv4:172.16.1.2
 vad
 codec g729r8
!
dial-peer voice 7504 voip
 destination-pattern +7777504
 session target ipv4:172.16.1.2
 vad
 codec g729r8
!
dial-peer voice 7301 voip
 destination-pattern +7777301
 session target ipv4:172.16.3.1
 vad
 codec g729r8
!
dial-peer voice 7302 voip
 destination-pattern +7777302
```

```
 session target ipv4:172.16.3.1
 vad
 codec g729r8
!
num-exp 7 +7777...
!
voice-port 1/0/0
 description          << This voice port is FXS >>
 echo-cancel coverage 16
 echo-cancel enable
!
voice-port 1/0/1
 description          << This voice port is FXS >>
 echo-cancel coverage 16
 echo-cancel enable
!
voice-port 1/1/0
 description          << This Voice Port is E&M >>
 dial-type dtmf
 signal wink-start
 operation 4-wire
 type 2
 echo-cancel coverage 16
 echo-cancel enable
!
voice-port 1/1/1
 description          << This Voice Port is E&M >>
 dial-type dtmf
 signal wink-start
 operation 4-wire
 type 2
 echo-cancel coverage 16
 echo-cancel enable
!
interface Ethernet0/0
 ip address 172.16.1.1 255.255.255.0
 !
```

```
interface Serial0/0
 ip address 172.16.3.1 255.255.255.0
 no ip mroute-cache
 fair-queue
 ip rtp-header-compression
!
router eigrp 1
  network 172.16.1.0
  network 172.16.3.0
  no auto-summary
!
line con 0
line aux 0
!
line vty 0 4
```

Router2

```
hostname Router2
!
memory-size iomem 20
!
dial-peer voice 7503 pots
 destination-pattern +7777503
 port 1/0/0
!
dial-peer voice 7504 pots
 destination-pattern +7777504
 port 1/0/1
!
dial-peer voice 7501 voip
 destination-pattern +7777501
 session target ipv4:172.16.1.1
!
dial-peer voice 7502 voip
 destination-pattern +7777502
```

```
    session target ipv4:172.16.1.1
!
dial-peer voice 7200 voip
 destination-pattern +77772..
 session target ipv4:172.16.1.1
!
dial-peer voice 7301 voip
 destination-pattern +7777301
 session target ipv4:172.16.3.1
 vad
 codec g729r8
!
dial-peer voice 7302 voip
 destination-pattern +7777302
 session target ipv4:172.16.3.1
 vad
 codec g729r8
!
num-exp 7 +7777...
!
voice-port 1/0/0
 description          << This voice port is FXS >>
 echo-cancel coverage 16
 echo-cancel enable
!
voice-port 1/0/1
 description          << This voice port is FXS >>
 echo-cancel coverage 16
 echo-cancel enable
!
interface Ethernet0/0
 ip address 172.16.1.2 255.255.255.0
!
router eigrp 1
  network 172.16.1.0
  no auto-summary
!
```

```
line con 0
line aux 0
!
line vty 0 4
```

Router3

```
hostname Router3
!
memory-size iomem 20
!
dial-peer voice 7301 pots
 destination-pattern +7777301
 port 1/0/0
!
dial-peer voice 7302 pots
 destination-pattern +7777302
 port 1/0/1
!
dial-peer voice 7501 voip
 destination-pattern +7777501
 session target ipv4:172.16.3.1
!
dial-peer voice 7502 voip
 destination-pattern +7777502
 session target ipv4:172.16.3.1
!
dial-peer voice 7200 voip
 destination-pattern +77772..
 session target ipv4:172.16.3.1
!
dial-peer voice 7503 voip
 destination-pattern +7777503
 session target ipv4:172.16.1.2
 vad
 codec g729r8
```

```
!
dial-peer voice 7504 voip
 destination-pattern +7777504
 session target ipv4:172.16.1.2
 vad
 codec g729r8
!
num-exp 7 +7777...
!
voice-port 1/0/0
 description         << This voice port is FXS >>
 echo-cancel coverage 16
 echo-cancel enable
!
voice-port 1/0/1
 description         << This voice port is FXS >>
 echo-cancel coverage 16
 echo-cancel enable
!
interface Ethernet0/0
 ip address 172.16.4.3 255.255.255.0
!
interface Serial0/0
 ip address 172.16.3.3 255.255.255.0
 no ip mroute-cache
 fair-queue
 ip rtp-header-compression
!
router eigrp 1
  network 172.16.3.0
  network 172.16.4.0
  no auto-summary
!
line con 0
line aux 0
!
line vty 0 4
```

Applying QoS to the VoIP Network

The VoIP Corporation has successfully implemented VoIP and fine-tuned it. Now the senior VPs would like to include some QoS techniques to finalize the design. We have previously discussed a few of the tuning parameters that can be configured via Cisco CLI; this section focuses more on the design considerations for QoS.

Designing the QoS Solution

What is QoS? QoS is a set of network best-practice guidelines that ensure that our converged voice and data network performs acceptably for all types of network traffic. QoS can be implemented via modular command-line (MQC) IOS constructs or via applications such as CiscoWorks. Voice traffic is not the only type of delay-sensitive traffic. The design engineer must be aware of the applications and protocols that are currently being utilized for a given network as well as any that are planned for the future. A carefully thought out QoS design will ensures that all types of network traffic perform up to user expectations. Cisco QoS features fall into one of the following categories:

- **Link efficiency mechanisms** We configured these for our leased-line WAN link in our voice pilot. Streaming video and voice traffic uses the Real-Time Protocol (RTP). IP, UDP, and RTP packet headers can be compressed via cRTP from approximately 40 bytes down to 5 to 8 bytes. This is critically important for WAN links below 1.544Mbps but is unnecessary for links above T1 speed. In addition, Frame-Relay-Fragmentation (FRF.12) and Cisco Link Fragmentation & Interleaving (LFI) perform fragmenting large data packets, interleaving them with RTP packets and maintaining low delay and jitter for media streams.

- **Classification and marking** Packet classification features allow traffic to be partitioned into multiple priority levels, or classes of service. This allows output interfaces to service priority traffic first and service all packets in a manner defined by the administrator.

- **Congestion avoidance** The most common of these is the Weighted Random Early Detection (WRED) algorithm. Although not effective for UDP traffic congestion, WRED allows TCP traffic to throttle back before buffers are exhausted. This helps avoid tail-drops and global synchronization issues, thereby maximizing network utilization and TCP-based application performance.

- **Congestion management** This includes the various queuing techniques available within the Cisco MQC framework. Often a network interface is congested, and queuing techniques are necessary to ensure that the delay-sensitive applications get the forwarding treatment necessary. Cisco's Low-Latency Queuing (LLQ) provides for such a solution. For other nondelay-sensitive traffic (such as FTP and HTTP), other queuing techniques such as Class-Based Weighted Fair Queuing (CBWFQ) may be used.

- **Traffic conditioning** Traffic entering a network can be conditioned using a policer or shaper. A *policer* simply enforces a rate limit; a *shaper* smoothes the traffic flow to a specified rate using buffers. These mechanisms include Committed Access Rate (CAR), Generic Traffic Shaping (GTS), and Frame-Relay Traffic Shaping (FRTS).

- **Signaling** Cisco IOS supports Class of Service (CoS) at Layer 2 and type of service at Layer 3. Cisco IOS supports Integrated Services (IntServ) as well as the Differentiated Service Code Point (DiffServ).

Configuring the Routers for QoS

Here is another example of how we can utilize QoS within our pilot voice network. In this example, we will configure Resource Reservation Protocol (RSVP) to make sure that we will have enough WAN bandwidth between Router1 and Router3 to ensure voice quality:

```
router3(config)#interface s0
router3(config-if)#ip rsvp-bandwidth 48 24
router3(config-if)#exit
router3(config)#voice port 1/0/0
router3(config-voiceport)#req-qos controlled-load
router3(config-voiceport)#exit
router3#
```

For further reading, check CCO for the document titled *Configuring Quality of Service for Voice*.

Testing and Verification

The ultimate test for VoIP is the quality of the voice between the two endpoints of a call. But what if the voice quality is not acceptable? How might the exact cause(s) be pinpointed? For most voice systems, the administrator will find that a full-featured management application such as CiscoWorks 2000 is a necessity. A decent protocol analysis program that is effective for WAN links will also be extremely valuable.

We stated previously that overall delay is the worst enemy of call quality. This delay can come as the result of an overcongested WAN link or from an inefficiently configured router. Only with the proper tools can the administrator evaluate the variables that make up the enterprise internetwork.

For example, if the WAN links between the call endpoints are low bandwidth, compressed RTP is a good place to start. By reviewing protocol analyzer data, we can determine if the WAN links are being saturated. If they are, it will be necessary to implement prioritization techniques and apply the appropriate queuing mechanism prior to packet transmission over these links. Frame Relay links almost always need some level of traffic shaping and/or policing that conforms to the service-level agreement (SLA) from the WAN provider.

Summary

In this chapter, we explored the methodology of designing and implementing a small-scale VoIP pilot voice system. We based our voice pilot on best-practices methodology. Our projects will always have a higher degree of success when we properly define, plan, evaluate, and review the design prior to implementation, regardless of project size. We began our project definition with information collection and client interviews. From this information we developed a dial plan that is effective now and will remain so in the future. We presented how to make this design scalable so that additional sites could participate in our voice pilot. Configuration of analog voice ports on a single router was the beginning of our voice pilot. Port descriptions and dial peer tags that make our system administration easier were presented. The process of design expansion from a hardware point of view was reviewed, and compatibility issues were raised.

It cannot be emphasized enough how important it is to have available personnel who are proficient at PBX hardware deployment and software programming when the converged system must be integrated with legacy equipment. The personnel who will be responsible for this task must be included in the design team and consulted during the design process. It was also stressed that testing and documenting the results of these bidirectional tests is important to gauge project success as well as serve as a troubleshooting tool. When we expanded our pilot system to include additional routers and sites, these tests were repeated and documentation updated. When the expansion was complete, we configured number expansion to accommodate our client's desire for four-digit dialing.

We also discussed fine-tuning our pilot system. We covered voice port parameters and how to configure them. We reviewed compressed RTP (cRTP) as a method of increasing the efficiency of our voice traffic. We also saw how the use of a low bit rate (LBR) codec such as G.729a could conserve WAN bandwidth. Finally, we looked into the voice quality design process, QoS, and discussed the tools an administrator can use to effectively determine network health and efficiency.

Solutions Fast Track

Creating a Basic Intraoffice Dial Plan

☑ Get to know your clients' network trends as well as business models. This information will greatly improve your chances of integrating a voice network into an existing network and will minimize negative business impact.

☑ Review the existing dial plan and determine if there is dial space available for the voice pilot. If there's not, an entirely new dial plan might need to be created.

☑ Gather information. Before the design stage, learn how the current telephony system functions and what features users have come to expect.

Designing a Single-Router VoIP Network

☑ Design the dial plan. Keep scalability in mind. Review this information with the client to obtain customer approval.

☑ Explore hardware options. Cost, compatibility, and the ability to redeploy pilot hardware acquisitions will demonstrate cost awareness to the client.

☑ Review your design and deployment plan prior to purchasing any equipment. Create a success criteria document with client.

Configuring a Single-Router VoIP Network

☑ Follow a step-by-step approach. Test and evaluate.

☑ Dial peer tags that will help describe call endpoints.

☑ Use documentation to provide success criteria for deployments.

Merging the PBX and VoIP Networks

☑ It is essential to have PBX personnel to assist in the design phase as well as to perform programming changes during deployment.

☑ Depending on the number of phones and the business model, scale the tie-line trunks to accommodate busy-hour usage.

☑ Review successful pilot deployment with key client decision makers. Discuss next steps and the key features and benefits that will best suit this company. Remember, no two companies will require identical solutions.

Configuring a Multirouter Intraoffice VoIP Network

☑ Review design and operational procedures.

☑ Be aware of costs. Think ahead to what pieces of the pilot hardware can be reused and where.

☑ Extend the dial plan.

Configuring VoIP for Interoffice Voice Communication

☑ Consider expansion issues. Gather information and requirements for the new site(s).

☑ Determine the routing protocol necessary for indirectly connected routers. This will ensure that the endpoints will be able to locate one another. Check for IP connectivity first (PING) before attempting calls.

☑ Keep the dial plan updated. Test and document results. Is call quality acceptable?

Tuning the VoIP Network

☑ Explore voice port-tuning parameters. Test before and after to determine if the tuning parameter has the desired (or any) effect.

☑ Are WAN links congested? Are router buffers too full or overflowing? Get to know the network baseline and busy-hour trends.

☑ Apply link efficiency mechanisms where needed.

Applying QoS to the VoIP Network

☑ Customers have grown to expect that their telephones will always be available and with a high degree of quality. Deploying QoS can provide this reliability and quality to VoIP.

☑ Review the six QoS categories and determine which are most applicable to the customer internetwork.

☑ Mark packets as close to the network edge as possible.

Frequently Asked Questions

The following Frequently Asked Questions, answered by the authors of this book, are designed to both measure your understanding of the concepts presented in this chapter and to assist you with real-life implementation of these concepts. To have your questions about this chapter answered by the author, browse to **www.syngress.com/solutions** and click on the **"Ask the Author"** form.

Q: How do I begin the process of dial plan design?

A: Check the current dialing plan. Some companies have available dial space or DID numbers that can be incorporated into the new dial plan.

Q: How do I decide what is the best hardware platform?

A: There are several design considerations, including cost, scalability, and compatibility with existing voice and/or data network components. Pilot hardware should have a use in the final production environment.

Q: How do I inventory existing voice equipment?

A: Some corporations have in-house PBX expertise to assist moves, adds, and changes. If so, have these personnel as part of the project team. Some companies use outside vendors for all their voice needs. Contact the appropriate vendor to seek assistance.

Q: How do I measure end-to-end delay?

A: Unfortunately, this is not always easy. A PING from end to end gives some idea, but remember that a PING uses TCP as its transport mechanism. Voice

RTP streams have UDP as the transport, so the network might handle them differently. Furthermore, a PING does not indicate long-term trends and busy-hour performance. Cisco Service Assurance Agent (SAA) is a configurable voice packet-generation mechanism that can help determine real-time packet performance.

Q: How can I review router performance?

A: Many SNMP applications provide this information. CiscoWorks 2000 was mentioned in this chapter, but this is not the only application that will capture this information. Cisco command-line *show* commands give some indication, but depending on network size, these might not be practical.

Q: Where can I find more information on pilot deployments and network QoS?

A: On the Cisco Connection Online (CCO). This resource can be found at www.cisco.com. There is also a pricing tool that will help you find the best fit for your network.

Index

SYNGRESS SOLUTIONS...

Cisco AVVID and IP Telephony Design & Implementation

Many lessons have been learned from the rapid adoption of Cisco's AVVID IP Telephony product line. Companies must cost effectively integrate "old world" technologies with the new, engineer packet transport networks for quality of service, simultaneously bolster traditional telephony and IP skills, and continuously exercise proper risk management. This book will help readers overcome the inherent complexities of IP telephony so that its promise can be fully realized.

ISBN: 1–928994–83–0

Price: $69.95 USA, $108.95 CAN

Building a Cisco Wireless LAN

Wireless LAN (Wi-Fi) technology is significantly more complex than cordless telephony; loss, coverage, and bandwidth requirements are much more stringent and the proliferation of wireless LANs in corporate environments has resulted in interesting security challenges. IEEE 802.11-based products offered by Cisco Systems have quickly become one of the foundational technologies fostering the untethering of data communications. *Building a Cisco Wireless LAN* will bring you up to speed fast with Cisco Wi-Fi technology.

ISBN: 1–928994–58–X

Price: $69.95 USA $108.95 CAN

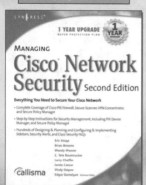

Managing Cisco Network Security, Second Edition

Information security has become an extremely important topic over the past few years. In today's environment the number of touch points between an organization's information assets and the outside world has drastically increased. Millions of customers interact via Web sites, employees and partners connect via Virtual Private Networks, applications are outsourced to Application Service Providers (ASPs) and wireless LANs are regularly deployed. Cisco Systems has placed a high priority on security and offers a wide range of security products. *Managing Cisco Network Security, Second Edition* is important to anyone involved with Cisco networks, as it provides practical information on using a broad spectrum of Cisco's security products.

ISBN: 1–931836–56–6

Price: $59.95 USA, $92.95 CAN

solutions@syngress.com

SYNGRESS®